MW01535874

"The Big Apple"
This is New York City

An anthology of
Wit, Reflections
& Amusements

(signature)

Cliff Strome
Licensed NYC Private
Tour Guide

Cliff Strome

Is a Licensed New York City Guide, recipient of The City of New York Dept. of Consumer Affairs highest rating and has been nominated Best Private NYC Tour Guide by The Association of New York Hotel Concierges (2011 and 2014) and he has been awarded The Certificate of Excellence from TripAdvisor (2013 and 2014) and at the time of this printing Custom & Private New York Tours, Inc. is ranked 6th of all New York City activities listed on TripAdvisor at the time of this printing.

cliff@customandprivate.com
www.customandprivate.com

Cliff Strome
December 2014
382 Central Park West
New York, NY 10025
212-222-1441

3

For Aline
My wife, my candle,
the light of my life.

Table of Slices

Chapter III
Opinions & Perspectives

Chapter IV
"Gotcha Last!"

INTRODUCTION

From the heart and through the eyes drawn from the mind, body and soul of a lifelong New Yorker, one who has always had an active life, relentlessly seeking extraordinary encounters, incessantly expressing eccentric and amusing perspectives, initiating countless humorous situations, obtusely reacting to the antics of others, I have written this anthology defining New York City as never before. Come and take this "tour" of New York City with me. Surely, you'll be amazed, entertained and amused. You are about to experience "The City" up close in the most entertaining and memorable way.

If you love folklore, hilarious situations, everyday life, twists and turns, humor that gets you thinking and laughing at the same time, delve into perspectives on urban life, new spins from the pavement, craziness, seldom known historical factoids, trivia, wisdom, stupidity, anger, off beat opinions and the unusual then this "tour" is yours to enjoy.

Experience "The City" in completely new ways. Slices, a collection of life experiences, opinions and reflections, all peppered with armchair wisdom fascinating trivia, humor and good fun. If you love life, people and New York City be prepared to spend some well-spent time. Enjoy and please don't take everything too seriously.

Tourly yours,

Cliff Strome

Chapter 1
Just for Openers
✿✿✿✿✿✿✿✿✿✿✿✿✿✿✿✿✿✿✿✿✿✿✿✿✿

Dr. Bartha vs. Big Bertha

In this town, buildings are demolished in many ways but there's only one that went down like Dr. Bartha's townhouse. Most often buildings are destroyed legally. Laws and regulations exist, and if a demolition complies, it usually provides safety, does not pollute the air, and prevents gas and water leaks, electrical fires, roof and floor collapses and explosions.

Zoning considerations and housing laws prevent people from losing their homes, limbs, lives, loved or not so loved relatives, significant others, former wives, partners, friends, housekeepers, pets and tenants too.

Some buildings collapse spontaneously as well. Structural failures, due to age, poor maintenance, faulty inspections, inferior construction, poor design and defective planning cause building failures too. Fires claim buildings, usually caused by carelessness, smoking in bed, stupidity, gross carelessness, defective wiring, illegal and unlicensed renovations, kids playing with matches or Bic lighters, Zippos are dinosaurs! And of course, do it yourself types and slop jobs conducted by unlicensed contractors who simply don't know what the hell they're doing take their toll too.

Gas leaks bring down a few now and then, as did Dr. Bartha's. Yes, buildings collapse for a multitude of reasons, but Dr. Bartha's home collapse was truly tragic, stupid and unique and to top it off it also provided a huge benefit for his estranged wife, ka-ching!

Dr. Bartha, a 66-year-old immigrant from Romania entered The United States in 1974 and settled in Queens with his Dutch finance. He also brought memories of a haunting past including a cruel eviction from his home, as a young child, with his family by the ruthless, communist Romanian government. He had witnessed his wealthy father take a beating and thrown into prison by that brutal government. The family had endured extreme poverty and he too had ultimately been imprisoned unjustly as well.

On July 26, 2006 Dr. Nicholas Bartha made good his long-standing promise to his estranged wife, to die in his townhouse located at 34 East 62nd Street. Apparently, in order to prevent her from claiming her half share of their home, as mandated by a divorce judgment he induced a gas explosion and destroyed his beloved townhouse killing himself in the process.

The building had been landmarked and therefore could not be destroyed legally but that did not prevent his illegal prescription to cure his compulsion. Therefore, the good doctor's cure was, to blow it up with him in it!

That was a double demo job. It turned out that he did his estranged wife a hefty favor since the property had greater value without the structure. It was a voluntary, lethal, illegal teardown uptown putting the good doctor inside out and in the process, he forked the property over, with substantially enhanced value, to the one he hated most, his estranged Dutch bride! Jumpin' Doc Barth's is a flash, flash, flash!

In truth, this is a tragic story. The house had been Dr. Bartha's incessant dream but it had turned out to be his worst nightmare. Divorce is very nasty business. The court system and divorce laws in The State of New York are engines for delay resulting in huge costs, fees and injustices, as most New York State divorce litigants well know.

Putting all that aside, another means to demolish buildings is with the big mamma, or as they say, "Big Bertha" steel demolition balls, not to be confused with Dr. Bartha's pair, which he gassed out of existence! Of all the big mamma jobs, "The Midnight Demolition" brought to you by, Mr. Resourceful or Mr. Chutzpah, depending on your point of view, real estate magnate Mr. Harry B. Macklowe!

We all know that "the devil is in the details" as to crossing the line and breaking the rules. Doing so in New York City could result in dire consequences. That's just one reason why lawyers and accountants make big bucks, defending naughty boys and girls. Mr. Macklowe, it seems, knows just how to do that, a real pro, indeed. He's got a big pair of his own too, swingin' in the breeze.

He has had his ups and downs carrying huge debt, highly leveraged, confronting enormous note payments, and he fell into arrears many times. But surely people who operate stratospheric empires, such as he, calculate their risk-benefit ratios, as any good businessperson often does. Those who do so go forward implementing their decisions to build, demolish, or de-construct, at times without permits, often as part of the process. The Midnight Demolition turned out to be, in the end, a brilliant move.

City laws govern demolition of all SRO's single resident occupant housing. Such housing provides refuge for those who live alone having little or no resources or income. The City mandates payments from developers who demolish SRO's and together with the fines mandated by the court to cover violations that deny needed housing for the poor. There was a four-year construction ban on the site that Mr. Macklowe crushed. Ultimately, Mr. Macklowe was ordered to pay the City approximately $5 million for the demolition of four SRO buildings on West 44th Street to "make way" for the construction a new Hotel, The "Millenium" Hilton.

The money he had paid was deposited into the City SRO fund and was used to provide housing for those in need. The City, due to the construction of the hotel, reaps hefty benefits by collecting real estate taxes, room taxes and taxes on all other goods and services provided by the new hotel. The Millenium also adds vibrancy to the immediate area and reduces blight in midtown.

This incident reminds me of a story about an Orthodox Jewish man who paid a visit his rabbi on a Saturday afternoon seeking to obtain permission to shave. He had asked the rabbi if he could shave on that Saturday, ordinarily forbidden, due to his impending participation in a wedding ceremony. He approached the rabbi, who happened to be shaving at the time, and requested permission to shave.

"Absolutely not!" exclaimed the rabbi.

The Orthodox man questioned the rabbi's denial as the rabbi had been shaving that day, a Saturday!

"How come you can shave today, the Sabbath and deny me the same privilege?" inquired the orthodox man.

The Rabbi's retort, "I didn't ask anybody!"

Macklowe was prepared to face the consequences. But, he made sure he had his ducks in a row, sort off. Mr. Macklowe had the good sense not to ask anybody, just like the Rabbi and regardless of the consequences he went forward and got the job done.

As for the City, its laws, rules and regulations governing SRO's, at times fail to make much sense. What was the City's wisdom to discourage Mr. Macklowe's deconstruction of the buildings? The money he paid into the fund rather then letting the buildings stand provided far greater value to the City. The new hotel provided enormous tax revenue as well, directly and indirectly. Paying the City SRO fund and allowing the hotel to rise would have been the best win-win situation for Macklowe, the hotel owners the City and those who depend on SRO's as a means of shelter.

At times, laws and obstructive government regulations disable us from moving events forward and thwart positive objectives. Listen to those who govern us who incessantly chatter and harp on and on about all the good they provide, when in fact, most often, they are running in the wrong direction! In the end, Harry B. Macklowe did us all a big favor!

The most intriguing footnote of the entire episode was created by the manager of the new Hilton built on the site because he had misspelled the word millennium by omitting the second "n". All the signs, invoices, envelopes, print ads, website, stationary, menus, brochures and miscellaneous material had been put in place!

Harry went on to bigger and better projects or should we say taller? He purchased a relatively small piece of land to the west of Park Avenue between 56th and 57th Streets to construct a new mega goliath tower that will rise nearly 1,400 feet!

In order to create the space for this goliath he purchased the Drake Hotel, built in 1926, for $400,000,000, and promptly demolished it. Now that's balls, even bigger then Big Bertha! The Drake Hotel located on Park Avenue at 56th Street, had been an iconic classic and fortunately Macklow's paperwork was all put together with all the T's crossed and I's dotted. You're so New York City Mr. Macklowe! Goody goody!!

On October 21st 432 Park Avenue topped out at 1,379 feet and is now the tallest building in the City exceeding the height of the roof of World Trade Tower I, which is 1368' high, without the 408' pole.

Currently, there are three other behemoths under construction in the West 57th Street that will top Mr. Macklowe's 432 Park Avenue tower. How nice to witness the birth of another "slice" of New York City's spectacular construction hubris!

Who among us has never lost their wallet? I don't hear anyone! We've all misplaced that most precious cargo at least once. Either it's been stolen, misplaced, slipped out of our back pocket, carelessly left behind or just gone missing! No one takes the blame for the loss of their wallet. We all endure the agony when we realize "IT'S GONE, OH SHIT!

When we become aware that our wallet has "split" what is the first thing we mourn? It's our driver's license. Yes! More than our money, credit cards, pictures, health insurance card, 1987 Red Cross beginner swimmer's card, library card or anything else that you've placed beneath your butt and haven't needed for the past fourteen years! When we are separated from our driver's license we turn into ice. It's the driver's license that suddenly drives us all into a spiraling shit storm!

"My wallet, where is it?"

All we think about is our driver's license and the hassle we're going to endure until it's replaced.

We have to appear at the dreaded Department of Motor Vehicles (DMV) or whatever they call it in your state. We trudge though that painful place, infused with lines, document requirements, something that we've forgotten to bring with us, the needed money order, your birth certificate, proof of citizenship, small pox vaccination card, urine sample, statement of no child support, high school diploma, biometric chart and all those Patriot Act requirements, now mandated to "prove" that we and the 85 year old blue haired lady from Boca Raton, with the LV bag, standing in front of we, are not terrorists or illegal aliens. What a thrill! We may even need an eye exam and another road test. I'd rather go to the dentist, the IRS, an accountant or even submit to a colonoscopy! But please, PLEASE not the DMV! On second thought, I'll just pass on the colonoscopy, another big pain in the ass straight up the "Hersey highway."

The unbearable reality of facing the people who "work" at the DMV puts me into a cold sweat. They're incredibly helpful, knowledgeable and eager to provide sincere eye contact, smiles, and a big "glad you're here" dose of attitude! They move the lines as fast as possible and always provide the right information punctuated with blank stares matching their brain. No doubt, even the U. S. Postal Service accepts most of them if they would dare to apply. There are few exceptions folks, let's be fair, few, too few.

Not the DMV, no! My heart rate set a record, my skin, white as a sheet, beads of sweat covered my face and I nearly pass out but couldn't because the place was packed and I could have fallen on the floor if I had.

I planned to go to the DMV the morning after I had become aware of my wallet's departure. I arrived very early that morning with the hope of getting out fast. The only way to clear that place is to yell, "FIRE."

For me, the most convenient DMV in Manhattan is located downtown at Worth Street. It opens at 9 AM therefore; I arrived at 8:30 and was far from the first person in line. I joined in, found my spot and looked back every few minutes and observed that the end of the line disappeared from sight.

Why do people relish the joy of seeing people in line behind them? Isn't it the people who are in front that really matter?

17

I started to "shiver" a double meaning, as in wait and mourn, shiva, for myself over the aggravation·that I was experiencing. It was a clear and sunny January morning. Having not heard the weather report that morning or taken the time to open my window and not getting a sense of the temperature outside. To me, it had "appeared" that the temperature was warm. That was dumb! That's not the way to be weather-wise! How can you determine air temperature by looking out of a window?

I had left my apartment wearing a leather bomber jacket, not quite the best choice for a windy twenty-seven degree day or for flying B-25 Mitchell bomber missions over Tokyo. That decision, the jacket together with my wait in line had created two sources of discomfort for me. The cold and the wait are two of my favorite things, yeah. Such a thrill!

I also needed some amusement, someone to talk with, a newspaper, a cup of hot coffee, something, just anything! As if this was not enough, I had to pee, my eyeballs had turned yellow by now, discomforts number three, four, five and six. Perhaps where was some alcohol still left in my system from the previous night's libation?

Suddenly I began hearing a weird incantation, incredible! It was a song, a lyrical phrase repeated continuously, heard from the distance, at the end of the line. I looked back and saw a thin, young Asian man wearing all the "right stuff" a hat, gloves, scarf and earmuffs. He appeared a bit shabby wearing well worn-out clothes. This guy seemed to be well prepared. I had noticed that one of his hands was clasped holding something. As he walked closer and closer I heard what he had been chanting and I suddenly recognized what he had clasped in his hands.

"Can't go to Motor Vehicle without a pen. Can't go to Motor Vehicle without a pen." He sang this over and over again! The only thing he said that broke the rhythm was, "Cheap pens, one dollar" then he resumed,

"Can't go to Motor Vehicle without a pen."

Okay, I got it. This guy had a gig. This was his "thing." He made "a living" selling pens to those waiting in line at the DMV! Smart guy! I now had one of my six problems solved! Not cold, not coffee, not wait, not pee, not DMV but boredom. I seized the opportunity to have a conversation with this enterprising gent and found out exactly what he was up to hoping to end my dreaded boredom.

As a businessman, I want to know everything about someone else's operation. How much did the pens cost? How long has he been doing this? How many pens does he sell on an average day? Did he have any documents, a resale certificate, business registration, etc.? Was he listed or registered with the NYSE, SEC, DOT, FDA, FEMA, FCC, FAA, ICC,DMW, EPA etc. He was actually a very nice guy and he told me just about everything about his business.

"I come every morning before 'motor vehicle' open. I get here before eight o'clock and bring 100 pens with me. They cost me three cents. I live with my grandmother a few blocks away in Chinatown. She has rent-control apartment and I pay rent and food with this little job. I make ninety seven dollars every day, tax free, not too bad, eh?"

The only thing he wouldn't tell me is where he got the pens. No doubt it was in Chinatown, certainly not

Bergdorf's! A little business, even at this level was a brilliant idea. He was protective of his turf. It was a business. With no overhead, cash sales only, who could blame him? It was shear genius.

He had been doing this pen thing for over three years, he told me. From his perspective he was doing quite well, netting over $25,000 per year, and working an average of only three hours a day. If he was on a payroll, in New York City, unmarried with two dependents, he would have to earn over $45,000 a year gross, file tax returns, have a boss, punch a clock, put in eight hours a day and deal with all the crap that comes with a job, right!

Not so bad. I actually admired the guys, entrepreneurial, creative, resourceful, cheerful and satisfied. Isn't that what we all want for ourselves? He had the benefit of supporting his grandmother and because he was her descendent, living in her rent controlled apartment in Manhattan, no doubt that is where he'll live for the rest of his life, "on the cheap!" That rent-controlled apartment is "grand-mothered" to him. It's a "life estate". What's that worth? Of course one day, down the road, there might be a real estate assemblage and quite possibly he'll receive a pile of cash from the developer and may just become president and CEO of a pen company, eh! This guy had it made! It's very simple: Want less! No struggle, no complications, no fancy lifestyle, no car payments or strangling obligations.

So? Who's the smart one here? That depends on who you are. That's New York City, filled with resourceful people who find a way to survive, one that fits them. There are so many opportunities to make money and put your life together in an uncomplicated way and this guy "wrote the book." One simple incantation, a few hours a day, 100 pens and a pair of earmuffs and you're in business! Until . . .

My license expired sometime the following year. That was bad news because it was time for the mandatory eye exam. I had to "report" back to Worth Street and get on the DMV line again. Fortunately, this time I checked the weather before I had left home and brought something to read. I took a very long leak before I left my apartment, a big plus. I took my place in line and looked for my pen friend, hoping to see him again. This time, I actually had forgotten to bring a pen. I was looking forward to giving him a little business, but it didn't happen. Instead, I spotted someone else. It was big African-American gentleman, football player sized, walking the line, with a swagger blurting out a faint incantation similar to what I had heard in the past. From a distance, as he got closer the melody, the tune and message in a baritone voice became familiar. When I heard the words I knew, "Can't go . . .

Acts of Kindness, a 1,000 a Minute

A ninety plus year old man, a nonagenarian, had entered the B train a day or two prior to December 7th Pearl Harbor Day last year. He sauntered in, tilted, fragile and more than a bit wobbly. Fortunately, he had a cane, an oak stick, a perfect match for the hands and knuckles that revealed his years of work, sweat, toil and pain. His accumulation of years was no secret. Grasping a pole, he gained his balance, as the train accelerated out of the Columbus Circle Station. He remained vertical due to the volume of people, safely sandwiched among them; "sardines" all in a rhythmic vertical sway. It was apparent that this standing package of skin and bones was in great need of a place to sit. No one deserved that more than he. I could only guess what countless sacrifices he had made for family and country in times past.

I got up and surrendered my seat to him without hesitation. Suddenly he was aware that my seat was his and without a moment's hesitation he smiled and slowly parked himself down. He settled in, resting comfortably and well assured that the lurches; starts and stops of the train would not topple his fragile frame.

After he had seated himself I noticed the red baseball type hat that he was wearing. It was adorned with about fifteen metallic military ornaments, the types that are available at Army-Navy Stores. Heroic acts, wounds or service are not needed to obtain them however he, had earned the right, of that I was certain. They were positioned haphazardly on the front of the cap, just below the stitched yellow lettering, "WW II." That was a dead, or should I say live, giveaway that this gent had fought in "The Big

One" or "The Good War" as it has been called. His age and persona seemed to confirm that he was "the real deal."

I had asked him, looking squarely into the depths of his sunken eyes,

"Pacific or Europe?"

"Pacific" was his reply, a barely audible whispered shallow voice.

"Iwo Jima, Midway, Okinawa?" I inquired.

"Bataan!"

Bataan was one of the most brutal and horrific sagas of the war. The cruelty and atrocities inflicted by the Japanese during "The Death March" ensured slim odds of survival, even for the most hardy, tenacious and committed soldiers, our most resolute and indomitable troops.

"I want to thank you for my freedom kind sir. Thank you!"

I told him with a bit lip and most grateful salute.

"And thank you for thanking me." he responded, his voice quivered with emotion.

I detected a tear rolling beneath his moistened right eye. It touched me very deeply. My tear would have to wait for a wipe. I was too touched by him to remove it.

How often people's sacrifices are undetected, unnoticed and unacknowledged? We go about our business, our lives, without a thought that our precious freedom is a gift from those we seldom thank and, of course, from those who are no longer "with us" those whom we cannot thank. We all need to seize opportunities when they arise to express our gratitude to our silent heroes. My acknowledgment made him feel worthy and it gave me a sense of warmth and satisfaction. I was delighted that I was there to give my seat to him. If only I could do that every day. Since then I always keep my eyes open for opportunities to provide my appreciation to heroes such as he.

Ladies and gentlemen, New York City salutes you! Heroes are all around us. War heroes and heroes who do their jobs, who keep this City moving forward, first responders, firemen, nurses, teachers and countless others who embrace their daily tasks enthusiastically, performing their duty and responsibilities without a second thought.

Do not look at people and judge them because they happen to be old, or because their clothing is torn and ill fitted, or those who may seem to be mumbling about a distant memory or appear, to you, to be useless. You never know who is seated next to you on the subway or who is standing beside you as you wait for the walk signal to change on a street corner.

Everyone has something to offer and if you do not know him or her then perhaps you can. Everyone has a story; a victory, struggle, a past and what lies beneath what you see on the streets of New York City has a history, one that we all carry inside, beneath a worn out jacket or ragged and torn pair of shoes that's shrouded in rags.

We are in this together and no matter where we are in life at any particular moment, we all make a contribution. Kindness does grace this City in abundance. Just try, give some. It's a wonderful connector.

I have asked numerous people to do the one-minute test! That is, stand on a corner, with ample pedestrian traffic, open a street map, and count to sixty. I guarantee, GUARANTEE that before you hit sixty you will be approached and offered assistance. Since I have suggested this little experiment to acquaintances and visitors, only once has someone claimed that no one came to their assistance.

In fact, I have tried it myself a number of times and it has never failed. New Yorkers are the kindest people on earth. It must be so! Why? How else could over eight million people live together in such a relatively small place with such a broad diversity of cultures and languages and accomplish so much? We must be co-existing harmoniously. We have to get along. It's a no brainer! I don't think there's another place on earth that can match our record of success! This is truly the melting pot of kindness, an example for the world.

Caucasian boys aid elderly African American women across the street. African American teenage boys assist Caucasian women who are in need of help then carry their baby strollers up the stairs exiting the subway. I've seen several elderly people waiting to "catch" a cab in the rain and a younger person laden down with packages watches the cab that was intended for him speed away without scorn or disappointment. I've seen unsighted people aided across streets by those who come from opposite directions taking their time to provide assistance.

That's New York! It is no longer the metaphor for rude and crude, the rough and tough ill-mannered arrogant, urban, cosmopolitan insensitive bunch. It is the new "heartland." The place to embrace each other and the pot that began melting long before we had ever heard of California, Oregon, Kansas or Colorado! Come and "be a part of it". Come and be as nice as you can be and guess what? You'll know what it is to be a New Yorker. You too can be a part of 1,000 acts of kindness a minute, and that's in a "New York Minute." Want a genuine New York experience? Please be kind!

The Legally Blind Woman

Located on 23rd Street between 6th and 7th Avenue there is a residence for the unsighted, or "legally blind." What's the difference you may ask? Well, that was my question when I had first heard the term, "legally blind."

I had operated the largest One Hour Photo Store in New York City in the 1990's on West 23rd Street known as "Clicks." Those days are long gone, one-hour photo has been a "dinosaur industry" for quite a while. I had noticed, prior to signing my store lease, a huge residence for blind people nearby. Hum! Consequently, I knew that I was opening my photo business in the right place! How could I fail with a huge residence for the blind right down the block?

Seriously, over the years, a ton of business from the "blind" residence flowed in. Amazing! "Legally blind" is not totally blind. "Legally blind" in numerous instances, is blind enough to obtain Federal, State and City assistance but not blind enough not to take pictures and pay for developing and printing. In fact, one of my most talented and prolific customers was a "legally blind" woman who had lived in that residence. She was truly a terrific photographer. She saw things that no one else did, really! On with the story...

One day, as I was approaching the blind residence, I had noticed two young men with their jeans worn at about mid hip level, wearing black head wraps binding their hair, known as "do rags." The pair was standing, leaning against a storefront, each with one foot propped up against the storefront, puffing their cigarettes, and chatting, but not yet noticing the octogenarian, a Caucasian woman about five feet tall tapping a white stick from side to side, obviously unsighted, or rather, "legally blind." They were slacking, smokers, "hanging out" clasping their beer or malt liquor cans in a bag. She, unknowingly, tapped one of them in their shin with her stick, while navigating her way back home.

"Why don't you look where the fuck you're going?" one of them shouted.

"Why don't you go fuck yourself you motherfucker?" she burst forth in "kind."

I had to hold back my laughter, although there was a huge dose of tragedy here. I had to take stock. New York City! That was the best example that day, so far. A tiny elderly woman, unsighted or "legally blind" frail, fragile and impaired woman shouted out in her defense, rose to the occasion, roared expletives who was unable to defend herself physically or take anything back home except her self-respect and dignity and that's big.

She had won the encounter on the sidewalk that afternoon. An elderly legally blind woman stood up against two "gutter urchins", whom she couldn't see and gave them the tongue-lashing they deserved.

Let's give her kudos! She took what they had to throw at her and stood "tall" moving forward with dignity and pride. Wishing her well I, and a number of other pedestrians, applauded her courage and conviction.

As for the others, they are part of New York City's palette. Without them, that New York City moment would not have occurred. The grit and guts evidenced by the unsighted woman evolved over the years due to similar experiences, no doubt

Who knows? Perhaps she had an eye on them all the time, using the moment as an opportunity to shout her anger without fault. How little we know. Could be that she may have been one of my best photography customers? Such is New York City. That wouldn't surprise me. Hum? Nothing here surprises me

"They Better Not!"

This little story is so New York City. It makes a point and it's quite hysterical. That's why I must tell you, here goes:

We are fortunate to have lots and lots of Korean delis in New York City. Koreans do a terrific job of showing the rest of us how to maximize use of every square inch of retail space, operate food stores that are stocked to the teeth, provide fresh and delicious food, hot and cold of every variety imaginable, consistently and abundantly, well presented and reasonably priced. It's amusing that the rest of us seem to be far less able to make this happen. Amazing but true!

The best Korean deli, in my opinion, is located at Fifth Avenue between 18th and 19th Streets in The Flatiron District. They raise the bar. The place is impeccable, organized, clean and fresh, well lite, efficient, friendly and run like a ship. I used to go there for coffee often.

On one occasion I walked in and asked the counter man for a cup of coffee to go,

"Just a little milk, no sugar please."

"Si, jou got it man, no prolen!"

I knew he was Hispanic, duh. They're such friendly, warm and accommodating people, "the salt of the earth."

He prepared my coffee, as I had requested, and gently placed the cup gently on the counter. I reached into my pocket for a dollar; it was a long time ago, a dollar, as I prepared to pay him. He said,

"Jou hab to pay ova der" as he pointed to a little Korean woman seated behind the cash register about twenty feet back toward the rear of the store.

Naturally, I asked him,

"What's the matter? Don't they trust you?"

His reply, *"**They better not!**"*
I roared with laughter, he smiled broadly!
Who among us has the right to condemn this man for making that "honest" hilarious comment? Certainly, it was "tongue and cheek" a humorous quip that had evoked a laugh and a smile creating a brief connection. Should it have been taken seriously? Nah. The world is a place where everyone seeks an edge, an advantage for themselves and their families. This guy was guilty of intentional amusement. He, on stage had seized the opportunity, front and center, and spontaneously created a quip that I've shared with hundreds of people creating waves of laughter. Would he have been a thief if given the chance? You know, "the truest things are said in jest." Do we know if the Koreans who own that place pay 100% of their sales taxes? Take a guess! It's all part of the "food chain." "He who is free of sin . . . "
We, as New Yorkers, know who we are and are unashamed. We work together, Korean and Hispanic, any combination, any permutation. His comment was a microcosm of New York City. We take it with a grain of salt and we laugh with, not at each other and ourselves constantly. Generally, we fully accept who we are and recognize and celebrate the differences among us. That's just one of the things that has enabled us to continue to make New York City such a terrific place.
Sure, there are those who are ready to rip us off and take from us what they can. Be it the most successful attorneys, real estate moguls, window washers or plumbers, the rip-off electronics retailers or your housekeeper, we are all intertwined and struggling to survive in the same tank; sink or swim. We know that

31

this is a "dog eat dog" world and City. But, what makes New York City so special is that a total stranger may be the person who will save your ass and go out of their way to protect you. This is the place where we all play the game, survive and protect our loved ones and fellow citizens. But, more than that, we climb walls, wade through sewers, run miles, jump into rivers, run into building fires, kneel, crawl and cry doing whatever it takes to help our brothers and sisters, black, white, yellow or green.

We are New York City and we are the world. When it comes to caring and helping each other we raise the bar. We are the greatest collection of people in the world; right here, New York City and "der's nutin' you can do 'bout it!

"White brick" has been known to be the low end of "the stick" when it comes to post war residential construction material; a ubiquitous surface for residential buildings built in the 1960's. Visually, it was an expression of low quality construction unlike the quality of pre-war era construction and design. Large rooms, high ceilings, generally characterized a pre-war building; post beau arts ornamentation, real solid walls not the Georgia Pacific 3/8 inch wallboard that an angry five year old can punch a hole through. "White brick" has always been a synonym for cheap crap slap job construction. "Oh, you live in the "white brick" building over there?"

Such phrases cast the notion that you live "in a white brick" because you're unable to afford something better! But, in truth, such buildings are not easily affordable, especially in Manhattan, in these times. There's a large dose of snobbishness in the equation, nothing to be ashamed of. I'd live in a white brick building in a heartbeat if the price and location was a good fit for my needs and pocket.

Okay, enough of that, so here's the story: A twenty story white brick building was constructed on 220 Central Park South back in the early '60's, a very prestigious address and only a few steps away from Columbus Circle, one of the new gold coasts in The City. Presently with The Time-Warner Complex, Trump International Hotel and Condos, formally The Gulf and Western Building, the fabled 15 Central Park West condo designed by Robert A. M. Stern, a spectacular $2 billion edifice, and a totally redone Columbus Circle centerpiece including a high powered spray wash for Mr. Columbus, the first since he adored the circle back in 1892. Bottom line, it's a major centerpiece of the *New* New York!

Related Properties succeeded in emptying out the building, a residential rental structure. None of the occupants had rights to extend their leases therefore; when the last lease expired the building became nearly completely empty. The purpose of clearing out the building was to de-construct it. But, unlike the type of demolition that our dear departed Dr. Bartha brought down upon himself, literally. The difference was that Dr. Bartha didn't plan to kill himself in the process or provide his x-wife a big favor, as the property became worth more without the house. Related had all those white bricks carefully removed one by one and no one got a scratch.

Related's purpose was to de-construct the building, as you may have guessed, and replace it with a high altitude slapping new ultra high world class edifice and market the property to Arab Sheiks, Russian Oligarchs and the slew of billionaire heavy rollers.

Surprisingly, the Related Property boys are far from stupid and they were well aware that there was still one big sized mother of a fly in the ointment.

You see, there was an underground parking garage beneath the building and that garage was leased to another powerful real estate concern by the name of Extell. Therefore, when Related Properties de-constructed 220 Central Park South they left the garage intact because the garage lease, granted to Extell, was still in "full force and effect." That's a big problem because Extell is about as smart as it gets. Extell is not in the parking garage business, they're in real estate, big time. You see, they are the owners of the mega tower marketed as One 57, located at 157

West 57th Street, a 1006 foot tall building, shaped like a waterfall, located directly opposite Carnegie Hall. It's the building whose crane collapsed during hurricane Sandy. That goliath building, nearly completed as of this moment it is currently breaking price records. One of the top floors is allegedly being sold for just a smidge under $100 million.

Quite likely, Extell must have purchased that parking garage lease from the original lessee, which they must have had the right to do, naturally. Obviously, it must have been a deliberate maneuver to hold up Related from de-constructing the building, which Elite figured would likely happen down the road. Like minds think alike therefore, Extell, one jump ahead of Related sleuthed out that parking garage lease and put the kibosh on Related who were apparently asleep at the white brick! No doubt, someone got yelled at for this, big time! Let's get on with the story.

Extell and Related wound up in court, surprise! Extell's position was, since they're their rent for the garage was being paid, complying with the terms and conditions of their lease, keeping the place clean, operating the premises as required then they were conforming and in full compliance of their lease.

Related sued Extell for eviction because, in their opinion, According to the lease at least 50% of the vehicles parked in the garage must be owned or operated by people living in 220 Central Park South. Clearly, Elite was in violation of their lease, so get out! But, Extell defended their position advising the court that it was impossible for them to comply with that condition due to the irrefutable fact that nobody is living in the building simply because there is no building anymore!

35

Related countered by pleading to the court that the lease does not require them to provide a building, although it is certainly implied.

The outcome was, the judge's ruling that both sides must sit down and cut a deal. The court fully understood the reason why Extell purchased the lease and Related should have purchased it themselves if they and their lawyers had their eye on the ball.

The key players and their lawyers cut a deal. Extell was paid $67 million by Related to surrender their lease and paid a $600 fine for some cockeyed violation. They all shook hands, wished each other good luck and went their separate ways.

The real fault lies with the attorney(s) who represented Related and advised their clients to execute the garage lease. Had they inserted either one of the following sentences in the use clause that read the following then there would have been no litigation and surly Elite never would have snagged that lease:

If for any reason or no reason at all the building ceases to exist then the requirement that a percentage of the vehicles parked in the garage is null and void and has absolutely no force and effect.

Or

This lease is not assignable.

"I'm one of the Owners"

Recently, I had the pleasure of providing a tour for four lovely ladies from Florida. Everything was proceeding extremely well, but of course, and we were taking in the sites they had requested. We were enjoying the morning touring New York City, had tons of laughter and were connected with a robust and energized rapport. For me, it was business as usual. For them, they were reveling a real New York City experience, one that they had "bargained for."

As part of the venue we had decided to lunch at Katz Deli and savor those spectacular pastrami sandwiches, the best on earth. One of the current owners used an ancient recipe created his great grandfather who had brought from his homeland, Romania. Katz Deli is the standard by which all other delis in New York City are measured and for many delicious good reasons.

Located on East Houston Street in the venerable Lower Eastside, this landmark has been helping New Yorkers and visitors increase their cholesterol since 1886.

One of the signs, an original is still displayed outside the restaurant reads, "Katz, That's All". According to legend, a phrase used by tour guides as a defense mechanism, that it just might not be true. That sign allegedly resulted from the following conversation between the original Mr. Katz, the founder, and the sign painter who had been summoned to paint the sign.

"So, you vant me to make you a sign?" asked the sign maker.

"Yeah" replied Mr. Katz.

37

"Vat do you want it to say?" asked the sign painter.

"I vant it to say Katz."

"That's all?"

"Yeah"

So there it is, "Katz, That's All"

My chauffeur parked on Ludlow Street, along side the restaurant. We immediately noticed that there was a huge line of hungry freezing patrons waiting to get inside. It was freezing out there! Brrrrr!! My guests were in no mood to stand in line in 26-degree weather even to woof down some of the best pastrami on the planet. As their trusted New York City guide, providing high-end Custom & Private tour experiences, it was my responsibility to go into action and not disappoint.

There was no way I was going to allow these four beauties to bear the burden of standing at the end of what looked like a line that was halfway down to Wall Street in Artic weather and allowing them to shiver their tanned butts off. Not on my watch! I had to have a plan.

The plan: for us to go directly to the front of the line and that is exactly what we did. At that moment, I had no plan other then to get them inside. But how could I?

Together we walked directly up to the front door. I can only imagine what they were thinking.

"How is Cliff going to get us inside?"

"How can he? I can't imagine how this will work?"

So, I reached into my pocket and removed a toothpick, a very powerful weapon. People from other places use guns but experienced New Yorkers use toothpicks. I placed that toothpick between my teeth and just like a switch, bingo; I transformed myself into the suitable persona. Wearing a suit and topcoat, I extended my hand to the uniformed security guard who was standing directly in front of the entrance. His job was to maintain order and prevent "gate crashers" from "cutting" into the line. That was what he was paid to do.

Fortunately, he had seen me there before many times. He had observed me walk in with small groups of people frequently and must have assumed that I was a guide or perhaps a "friend of the house." Who knows? It was not the first time I have given him a few bucks. I've always been warm, friendly and respectful, acknowledging his presence even if only to say "hello" or ask "how you doing man?"

Those are gestures of respect and they're powerful. Most people ignore uniformed people who are positioned to maintain orderly conduct and a sense of fair play.

I approached him with my customary salutation, such as:

"Hey, my man, how you doin'? You lookin' good!"

I handed him a $5 bill, folded several times so that the only part of the bill that was visible was the magenta colored large numeral 5 that appears on a backside corner of a five-dollar bill, have a look! There's one large numeral on a 5, 10 and 20 dollar bill and it is important when tipping a service provider, such as a parking lot attendant, doorman or delivery man so that they can see that you're not giving them a single. When I extended my hand with the bill I looked down, suggesting him to do the same. He saw that it was a "fin" and we shook hands obscuring my "donation" to the onlookers. I gave him a wink and he responded with a smile. Telling him what the bill was for was totally unnecessary.

He promptly opened the door for the four frigid Floridian beauties and allowed them to enter the warmth and pastrami of Katz.

Suddenly, a short statured sixtyish year old woman, standing about fifth in line, no doubt she had been on line for quite some time, bearing her red nose, shivering noticeably. She belted out,

"Hey mister, there's a line here!"

With my toothpick in place I retorted in a demonstrative DeNiro voice, in her face.

"I'm one of the owners."

My eyes drilled right through her. She respected the authority of the toothpick and the "threads" that I carried on my back; a well-pressed suit, scarf and a cashmere topcoat completed the getup. My demeanor dripped with New York City attitude.

By this time my guests had entered Katz and were out of the cold, warmly inside Katz.

As I began to enter, I heard her voice from behind me, with pitched volume, aimed directly at the security guard.

"Is he one of the owners?" she shouted.

"Yeah, he is!"

What is this incident all about? It's about pushing buttons, providing my guests with comfort and fulfilling my value proposition, a New York experience. It's about gaining "an edge" rescuing my guests from the cold. It's about not hurting anyone and providing the security guard with an opportunity to "make a buck."

Is it dishonest, amoral or unfair? Sure, just a little bit, yes. But, since very few do this, it's more about *chutzpah*. It's the kind of New York experience that my guests will take back home and talk about. An opportunity was seized, and made it into a memorable experience and those ladies had gotten into the warmth they craved. They were given what they wanted and that's my mission; one that I embrace with brio.

And, most of all, this spontaneous maneuver, rescuing them was "a game" rewarding me with a moment of power and confirmation that my customers are going to have the best New York experiences possible. Doing what I do brings great pleasure, not only for my guests but also for me, most of all!

"No! You go!"

Driving in Manhattan is laced with numerous insanities. Anyone can who's been here can write a treatise on the subject even if they've never driven a car. Aside from the maddening traffic, the gridlock, lousy drivers, taxi drivers, who happen to think that they own the road along with the pedestrians, messenger cyclists, truck driver, skateboarders and baby carriages and pedestrians, this place is a vast expanse of madness on the pavement.

Do we have a choice? Yes! The solution is really quite simple. First, we enforce the current laws and establish new ones. For example, I see police officers ignoring motorists violating traffic laws while they stand around discussing last night's Yankee game or the high costs of donuts. How often I've seen traffic cops hanging out when Greyhound buses, flatbed trucks laden with steel beams and scores of taxis, limos and plain ol' stupid and inconsiderate motorists inching their way into intersections that will surely place them in the way of vehicles that wait until they clear "the box" the place where traffic will stand still until they are able to move out of the way. It's not the volume of vehicles that causes this; it's the incessant and endless inconsideration, stupidity and immaturity that cause this geometric insanity.

How about taxi drivers who pick up fares without pulling over to the curb and block the street in the process? What about police cars pulling up along side motorists who require their attention and fail to park in front of the motorist who's at issue and keep the lane clear that they're blocking, just for the public good? How about the complete lack of enforcement of the reckless bicycle messengers who act as if they too "own" the road while wreaking havoc and danger for all? Hello? Is anybody home?

Recently I took my Fiat to the dealer to pick up a car cover. My Fiat cabriolet is my toy. I love it! It has a permanent home, underground in a garage across the street from my home for $99 per month, thanks to the marketing genius of Manhattan Fiat, the dealer who lures in hundreds of motivated customers. I picked up the cover at the dealer not wanting my precious toy to be uncovered collecting dust and particles that would threaten it's beautiful Ferrari red sheen.

Upon exiting the Westside Highway at 96th Street I encountered a bit of slow moving traffic piling up on the way to the intersection at West End Avenue, known as a busy intersection with a traffic signal that intensifies the wait. Together with school buses and various construction vehicles added to the traffic mix no one was moving. Suddenly, along side me a car pulled up along side my right and vectored at an angle toward the front of my car in an apparent attempt to get in front of me. I tapped my gas pedal to ensure that this intruder was not going to succeed in encroaching into my place in line.

Glancing at him I noticed he was talking to me but he was unheard. I opened my window and he said that I'd be foolish to allow him to damage my cute little car.

"I'd hate to knock into your little piece of shit car, too." I told him.

"I was ahead of you," he retorted.

"In what dream?" I replied

He laughed. I told him,

"If getting ahead of me is that important to you then go right ahead. I'm really not in such a hurry, go ahead." I insisted.

A few moments later the traffic ahead of us started to move, we were "neck and neck" and he waived me on to proceed first. I did the same for him and as a result we continued to waive each other on and on and on, remaining in place, stopped, and listening to the blearing sound of motorists behind us begging for us to clear the way and get going. We continued to "play our little game" just long enough to avoid the anger from behind to reach catastrophic proportions.

I let him go first, we smiled and waved to each other as we continued on our way.

No cursing, no flipping "the finger" no stupid attitude, just a jocular encounter with a happy ending, except for those behind us, of course!

Chapter II
My Playbook
★★★★★★★★★★★★★★★★★★★★★

1 in 8,300,000

While movin' and shakin' in the singles scene about fifteen years ago I had attended a singles party at Biff's Club on Lexington Avenue in midtown. Don't look for it. It's gone!

The party room was huge, packed, like an overstuffed Bar Mitzvah celebration in a Woody Allan movie in a "classic six" coop on West End Avenue. It was so crowded that in order to take two steps you had to hold and lift your drink over your head to avoid alcoholic collisions. It was so packed that the FDNY had sent inspectors to count heads because the occupancy limits had, no doubt, been exceeded. What a crowd! I wondered. Did they really have to count heads? If the place appeared to be too crowded, then it was, without the fire department counting heads!

"Oh, we had only 699 people not 700 like it said on the sign, your honor. Therefore, we didn't have the right to evacuate the place. If a fire had occurred we would have had an impossible task, Your Honor. We just could not save lives even though the place was legal, occupancy wise! Ah, sometimes head counts are incorrect, but at least we followed the book, your honor.

At the time, my divorce was moving forward, at the speed of a three-legged turtle, thanks to the lawyers and the politicians who enacted the divorce laws in The Empire State, truly a game, a self-serving "engine for delay for the benefit of barristers." I call it raising the "bar."

My time out partying was just one means of distraction and attending them was always amusing and fun whether I "closed the deal" with someone or not. That, for me, was never the most important thing. At Biff's that evening I spotted a very exotic looking woman. I approached her for a closer look. Raising my arm with glass in hand I inched toward her. She had beautiful bronze skin, not an ounce of fat anywhere, shades of beautiful grey and black long hair nicely coiffed, very pretty, lovely shape, wearing a broad smile and a short tight sexy skirt. She was mysterious and exotic, an extraordinary looking "piece of work." She swayed so well to the music enhancing her sexuality and persona. She had me, captured,

"Said the spider to the fly."

I, of course played the role of the fly.

I introduced myself. She was a bit aloof but not impolite. I turned on the charm and we became engaged in conversation, pleasant but guarded. She recoiled, not quite admitting me into her space, not dismissive or impolite. She didn't "blow me off nor did she imply that I should move on.

Her name was Molly, from Trinidad, a descendent of "planters" from India who had been transported to the Caribbean by the British two generations ago. She had been raised on the island and had moved to New York City for a better life. She was employed by New York University as a clerical assistant and was living in Jackson Heights, Queens. After several hours of conversation and dancing I was certain that she had gained an interest in me as well.

At the end of the evening we had agreed to meet at a restaurant the following week even though she would not provide me with her phone number. That was due to the protective shield that she carried, her private and guarded nature. I gave her my phone number, which she had promised to use on the day prior to our dinner date, to either confirm or opt out. I knew she had "issues" and something in her past, most likely, had caused her to distrust and be wary. Ah, "trust issues! I've had a lifetime of experience with that "number"! I gladly accepted the arrangement and had confidence that she was comfortable that I would not invade "her space." I knew my phone would ring as we had agreed. I had no doubt, none whatsoever.

To my chagrin, my phone did not ring the day before our date. I was extremely disappointed, devastated, in fact. How could she have rejected me? I'm a good judge of character. Had I imagined that we shared a fun evening together? We danced, laughed, engaged in continuous interesting conversation and we had clearly taken a hefty interest in each other. There was an abundance of chemistry between us as well, wow! Ah, the singles scene. Shit!

Nevertheless, I showed up at the restaurant, hoping she'd forgotten our arrangement to call me, unlikely but perhaps the best of a bad situation. Or, perhaps she had lost my phone number and she'd show up anyway, just like I did. What did I have to gain by not showing up?

I appeared at the restaurant. I took a shot. So, there I was, a company of one. She never did appear! I was very let down. I thought of Sinatra's best torch songs, "Quarter to three" "Everything Happens to me" and all that. Next stop, I'm the guy in Edward Hopper's "Night Hawks", nursing a lousy coffee at a diner off Lafayette Street in the East Village. It was so depressing for me. I was filled with melancholy and a sick lonely feeling. Self-pity creeps in at moments like that. I'll get over it I kept saying to myself. But you've got to get out there, or nothing good happens. Many inner voices speak to us and that one was the loudest. It's like being a salesman who clings to the mantra; "every 'no' is one closer to a 'yes'!" Yeah yeah yeah.

I had refused to accept the incident as an intentional rejection. It was my belief that Molly had lost my phone number. That was the most plausible explanation I could think of. She must have failed to recall the name of the restaurant where we were supposed meet. She was unaccustomed to such places. I hadn't been rejected but my setback was real. Okay, so I'll get over it. Move on.

But, that's not me. I'm a very tenacious New Yorker. So now what? It was simple, place a classified ad in New York Magazine. Back in those days, before Internet social networking, New York Magazine had a large classified personal section that included a subsection known as "Assortments." It featured miscellaneous categories of small classified ads for people seeking people, specific or generic, birthday wishes, apologies etc. I felt that I had nothing to lose except $20 for the cost of the ad, certainly worth a shot.

Molly! Pretty NYU Triny
Call Cliff you have my #

New York Magazine, a weekly, hit mailboxes every Monday. The cover that particular week had featured "The Best Lawyers!" Great! Going through a divorce I had felt this was the copy I really needed! "Best

Lawyers! Translation is most expensive lawyers. I thumbed through the back of the issue reaching that week's two page "Assortments" classified listings. Scanning the classifieds I found my two-line ad. Sure, fat chance, a city of over 8.3 million people, a two line ad will connect two people who met at a singles party, not in my dreams, not in this City. Honestly, though, I did have hope. This is a dynamic society and strange things do happen. I had omitted my phone number from the ad to stave off crank callers. Naturally, I had hoped Molly would see the ad or someone who she had told our story to would see it and contact her with an idea, perhaps to call New York Magazine and reach out, a stretch for me, sure, a huge stretch! "Hey, you never know!"

I returned to my studio apartment on West 57th Street that Friday at about 6 PM after another workday without a thought of Molly or my advertisement. By this time it was out of my head, a done deal. This was just not going to happen, off my radar screen.

I stepped up to my answering machine, pushed the message button, a routine I had gotten into when I entered my apartment. It was a technical act that took me about a week to master! I'm still at the high end of low tech just like the vast majority of baby boomers. That's what we all did in the early '90's, no cell phones, emails or text messages. We were all tethered to the ol' Radio Shack answering machine and a Motorola pager aka "beeper."

Beep. "Hello Mr. Strome, this is Karen Stein from New York Magazine. Molly does not have your number but, we have hers! If you would like to reach her please get back to me at 212-123-4567."

Whoooha! I couldn't believe it! I knew Molly had been sincere. She didn't "blow me off" after all. Unbelievable! In this City, a two line $20 ad reconnected two people who had met once and knew nothing about each other except the chatter during a casual encounter at a jam packed singles party. What a town? What a place? What a story?

I called Molly immediately and she was delighted to hear from me.

"How could you have lost my number?" I asked her.

She laughed and laughed. I was thrilled and joined her laughter. We roared! That night we met at the restaurant where we had intended to meet the week before. What a night!! We were both blown away! Another New York City story in a town that's really not as big as we had thought. Truly, it was incredible.

Molly and I had dated for about a year. We traveled to Italy, Vermont and the Hamptons. We had lots of fun, and enjoyed so many wonderful occasions together. Then sadly we both felt that going forward into serious territory was not a good idea. We said our goodbyes and lost touch.

Thanks New York Magazine and the luck and good fortune of the New York City mindset. Go for success and don't give up! Never give up. Never!

"Friend of the House"

Do you like to wait "on line" or the "queue" as they say in other parts of the world? Of course you don't. Most New Yorkers desperately maneuver to avoid waiting "on line" or "the que." But, when necessary, most generally do what they have to do. The most common reasons for waiting in line are, the Post Office, Department of Motor Vehicles, Social Security Offices, Unemployment Insurance Facility, voting, airport security, concert tickets, restaurants, Saturday Night Live, sporting events, night club shows, a new Apple product, a free designer "green" bag giveaway at Whole Foods, or eccentric bargain hunters who want to be the first to enter retail stores that "give away merchandise" even at risk of life and limb!

As a New Yorker, I vehemently hate to wait "in line" and I've found a way to avoid it. Don't tell anyone! You'll ruin my secret and you may just find me behind you on a line. Trust me. That's not a good place for either of us if I catch you plying my trade!

Jazz clubs featuring the best performers often have very long lines, usually extending down the block and, at times, around the corner. Many of those "on line" do not have reservations. They simply present themselves with some hope that perhaps those with reservations will not appear or settle for a seat at the bar. Others are content to be admitted just to have a place to stand, as long as they are in ear shod of the music. They're satisfied and the wait therefore is worthwhile to them. Sometimes it's about bragging rights, "I was there!"

I've got a scheme that works quite well for me. I avoid the line completely and find the best seat in the house! Here's how:

For example, on one occasion, I appeared at The Blue Note, a very popular jazz club in Greenwich Village. I was, at that time, with my "future former wife." We showed up without reservations. Tony Bennett was appearing for a one shot make-up performance. His fabulous scratchy voice had been a bit too scratchy, a touch of the flu I suppose, and hence it was the make-up gig.

The line was endless and to make matters worse, the rain was teeming. Most arrived without umbrellas, enhancing their disgust with their waits. Brass stanchions with velvet ropes blocked gatecrashers and a very tall, stocky, grim, well-suited gent guarded the front door, assiduously.

Ah, I love a challenge! I removed a $20 bill from my pocket, folded it in thirds, with the largest number twenty on the bill prominently visible. I pompously unhooked one side of the velvet ropes, disengaged it from the brass pole, extended my right hand with my thumb securely holding the bill, folded down to about one square inch, with the largest numerical "20" visible and I said enthusiastically,

"Hey, great to see you again!"

I looked down at the bill, encouraging him to do the same. He saw it, clasped my right hand, we shook hands firmly with solid eye contact and partial smiles, smirks. I leaned over and whispered in his ear,

"Friend of the house, Joe!"

He got it, the idea and the bill. We're in.

A few shouts and yells, "hey you" were heard up and down the line. "Hey, what's up here?" "Who the hell

are they?" "I'm waiting in this freakin' line for over two hours, I'm getting soaked!"
Even most New Yorkers still don't get it. Amazing!
"Friend of the house!"
My newfound friend shouted back for all to hear as he let us in. Isn't that why he's there? To make money! He's not a cop! He needs the money! Duh! He whispered something to his cohort inside and we were seated front and center. He got a bill too, but not a twenty. Tony was terrific that night. It took a little "scratch," to hear that scratchy voice and it was well worth the money and the trouble.
Do you remember that scene from "Goodfellas" when Ray Liotta escorted Barbara into the Copa Cabana through the kitchen? Well, one evening I took my soon to be second wife aka "my future present wife" to La Mela, a fun, high energy Italian restaurant on Mulberry Street in Little Italy. It was our first date. La Mela is very popular joint with the locals and tourists.
"There's a big line!" Aline exclaimed.
"Don't worry. It's not a problem." I replied.
I was wearing a black shirt, black suit, black leather trench coat, slick gelled hair and, of course, a toothpick in my mouth as well as a $3 Times Square solid white tie, completing the image. Eh?
She was very elegant, nicely "painted" and quite the attractive lady. She was a perfect compliment for the con that was about to unfold. With hands tightly clasped together, we politely bucked the line with the mindset that we were "friends of the house" and strolled in confidently directly to the rear of the restaurant on our way to the chaotic kitchen. Within five seconds all eyes were upon us. Everyone was thinking; who the hell are these people? Hey, you

53

never know! I could have been a "made man" or some capo, a guy they wouldn't want to mess around with and she could have been a movie star! Know what I mean? "Badda bing!"

"Uho's in change 'ere?"

I asked, in a well-pronounced very demonstrative voice, deep and voluminous, as we stood inside the kitchen. Always leave out the h sound in "who's" and "here" or it's a dead giveaway that you're pulling a minor con.

The manager stepped up and smiled. He looked intently into my eyes, curiously, not knowing what to make of this.

"We need a table. You wanta help out the lady or what? Hey *piasan,* great to see you again!"

With an abundance of self-confidence I shook his hand, complimented by a pat on his shoulder and a wide and warm smile. Apparently he knew the drill and he was pleased let me play my game. Besides, he didn't want to take any chances, I guess. I believe he was amused and enjoyed my *sctick.* He admired my chutzpah so; he just went along with it, a real pro.

"It's all taken care of. Good to see you too. Follow me."

With a broad smile he escorted us to an empty table for four, the only table in the "house." As we got seated we noticed that the line had grown much longer. Our waiter gently placed a bottle of red and white wine in front of us. I didn't feel sorry for those folks on line because "Friend of the House" is a rite of passage and if pulling it off is a thing you can do then you've earned the right. This time it didn't cost me a dime, not a freakin' dime! The bill wasn't necessary, "there's honor among men."

Are you a "friend of the house" kind of person? Try it, hey, you never know! Bing!

We left very well pleased with our "friend of the house" experience. We connected, had fun and felt a bit naughty and mischievous. I grabbed a cab and we were on our way to "One if by land, two if by sea" perhaps the most romantic restaurant in "The City."

It had been Aaron Burr's coach house on Barrow Street in The Village. There's no sign in front of the place, so you either know it or you don't. The tuxedoed pianist was playing a torch song on the Knabe ebony baby grand piano. Crackling fires roared in both fireplaces and the familiar bartender was quite busy. Aline and I each grabbed a stool at the bar as I winked at Affie, the bartender, who had recognized my signal as, "Don't reveal that you know me. This is not the revolving doors at Macy's." She played her part.

"How can I help you?"

"Two campaigns please, French!" I requested.

She turned around, poured our drinks and placed them on the bar in front of us. She lifted the twenty-dollar bill that I had placed on the bar, turned around again and faced the cash register. She spun back, faced us, and laid two ten's directly in front of me. I slid one back to her. It was a perfectly choreographed ballet.

"Who are you?" Aline asked me.

"I'm in construction." I replied,

We both laughed our ass off, without spilling a drop of "liquid gold."

Singles "Seen"

Many of you may not find this "Slice" of The Big Apple funny! Why? This is a tale that is somewhat juvenile, serendipitous, whimsical, flamboyant, impulsive, very adolescent and just plain silly. But more importantly, it was all lots of fun. I must admit that I've been debauched a bit during the years I've spent floating through the "singles scene" or singles "seen" in the '90's. It was very worthwhile therapy due to my mid-life crisis, something I had to get out of my system, work it though, explore my "issues", learn life lessons, "sow my oats" and all of that. I was determined to have a blast, work it through and resolve my "issues" an brutally overused word, in the singles scene. "Oh, she has issues! She 'acts out'!" Crappola!

Living, working and playing in Manhattan, the world's biggest and best sandbox for adults on earth makes the vulnerable a little crazy, especially if you have some jingle in your pocket, which I had at the time. I was determined to get "out there" and not risk missing a thing. There are endless opportunities in New York City for those who are crashing through a mid-life crisis. Finding the cure on this 23 square mile island is a no brainer. That's if you've got a good "tool box" and occasional get your "tool" in a nice "box"! Very silly! Childish shit, eh?

There's no need to leave Manhattan because the "B & T" crowd, bridge and tunnel, flock into Manhattan every Thursday, Friday and Saturday night. The "regulars" and the visitors who dared to mix and mingle enter "the culture" that is the New York City singles scene, a mish-mash of "losers" for the most part, with a sprinkle of winners tossed in. They all

56

circulate like a trail mix assortment of nuts, cranberries, "wall-nuts" and raisins.. Don't get me wrong. By "losers" I'm referring to those who appear time and time again at the same bars in the singles party circuit and remain totally clueless as to how to approach, begin or sustain an amusing conversation with a complete stranger. They always leave the place without someone or a coveted phone number or at the very least the recollection of a good time.

There are plenty of books written on the subject and I have not read any of them. There's an art to it, but generally, either you have it or you don't.

It reminds me of the television classic "Wild Kingdom" that depicted various breeds of animals, insects and even plants all equipped with a wide variety of built in apparatus to lure their mates into their liars or "put their lights out" after doing the "nasty" or as they used to say in the single scene, "the big thing." Today the hipsters call it "hooking up."

Singles have studios, lofts, places to live and play, friend's apartments, single use restrooms located in the back of restaurants and hotels, those are great, dark alleyways, the office after business hours, cloak rooms, well positioned trees, limos with darkened windows known as "divisions" or their humble abodes that are stocked to the hilt with liquid and illegal goods. Spiders weave webs trapping their mates. Female spiders literally eat their significant others after the "deal" is done. Flowers emit scents that beckon bees, not that they mate. They do what has to be done to spread the pollen around enabling flowers to propagate. Glad humans don't pollenate that way, but bringing the lady flowers may move you into the batter's "box." Yes folks, the singles scene is The Wild Kingdom!.

"Hey man! Got any pollen on ya?"

And finally, there's the cruelest of the cruel, Venus Flytraps. They glue their prey inside and their horny thorny leaves shut them in as they inject their enzymes emulsifying their captives. There's no sex but they do "hook up" or "clue up." Goo Wee!

That reminds me of a guy who was jamming in the singles scene that cheated on his gal. After foolin' around while he was asleep she Crazy Glued his hand to his "member" and walked out of his apartment. He was rushed to the emergency room and he had to undergo a three-hour surgery to dislodge his fist from his joint. Good lessons don't cum cheap, eh!

Most four legged animals claim and defend their territory and dominance fending off competitors, with growls, claws, quills, stink spray and fangs. Male peacocks spread their colorful feathers attracting their beaus capturing their hearts or whatever else they seek to capture. Why are they called peacocks anyway? Others have been provided by nature with the means to howl, hoot, chirp or scratch their hind legs emitting sounds beckoning their partners.

And then there's us; perfume, makeup, luxurious fast cars, music, expensive watches, coifs, lipstick, nail treatments, money, thigh-highs, pantyhose, high-heels, big muscles, body wash, expensive underwear, exotic trips, tinted contacts, pierced tongues, wigs, wine, restaurants, theatre tickets, tan treatments, booze, lingerie, lace, jewelry as well as illegal substances and that list is too long to provide.

There are the real high-end lures such as Porsches, BMW's, Bentleys, Teslas, beach houses, private media rooms, yachts, hot tubs, ski houses, private jets, furs, swimming pools, helicopters, rubies and diamonds, business cards with MD, PhD, Esq., LLC and CPA, CEO, CFO, COO, CIT, etc. etc. Luxury city condos with outside space abound and toss in the best of all, inheritance, trusts and old money! Upppee! Viva Daddy Warbucks!

The best singles in the scene have other tools of the trade, fast wit, confidence, great appearance, class, good "threads" highend shoes and jewelry all coordinated and fitting well, and lots of effective connectivity. When it's all plied well, over time, that should provide the desired success even without all the material goods mentioned above. There's no substitute for just good old looking good and a balanced, confident persona. The race is on in the singles world. For what, "one never knows, do one." Do the right thing and be smart. Set your goals and you're off and running and running and running.

The first decision that a single "on the prowl" in New York City needs to make is to hit the right places at the right time. The first component of your decision should be to find your places of choice; those that attract the age group that you seek with the right amount of cerebral material. That's a very subjective consideration as single men. For example, if they've got the goods then why not peruse women of virtually all ages? Seventeen is the "legal age" in New York State so be aware that "sixteen will get you twenty-five" as in years in the "clink" "joint" "big house" "lockup" "can" or "up the river" as in Sing-Sing on The Hudson.

A lot of smart guys favor women in their forties. Many sophisticated men in search of fun seek women who have had interesting and amusing life experiences. Mature ladies generally know, or should know, what they're doing. They have "learned the ropes" as they say. Also, women in their forties should, by then, have interesting things to talk about and should have acquired lots of wisdom, life stories and lessons that gentlemen generally find interesting and appealing, if they, the men, keep their mouths shut, sit still and just listen to the ladies. Unlike the "babes" that just popped out of their shells, they provide more opportunities to get engaged in the conversation of life.

Oh, that ubiquitous expression, "the brain is the sexiest organ in the human body" was always on the tip of everyone's tongue back then in the singles scene. There's some truth to it but, in my opinion, it was a worn out phrase like, "he's got issues." The saying about the brain was designed to offer safety to naïve and vulnerable prey who wished to convey the message that sex was not their highest priority on their wish list. Most often that was just pure bullshit. Sex is a big deal when singles meet, after about six months the issue becomes, "their issues."

Some men are attracted to women more mature then forty because with or without "some work" women in their fifties are pretty nifty and even in their early sixties there are quite a few attractive ladies out there; "it's the new forties." I have seen many women in their early sixties that are beautiful, well kept, nicely dressed, equipped with a lifetime of experience and wisdom and typically are among the most interesting ladies in town. They've got a lot to talk about while many young ladies often tend to chat about their jobs, former boyfriends, what they bought recently and their other "stuff." They are generally, not the most interesting ladies at the bar, but there are exceptions. If you find one, hang on to her. That's a double header, no pun intended. Youth, brains, wisdom, compassion, passion, experience and fun spells, "keeper."

Many men and women enjoy intimidating others and are, well, just not real. It's a sure sign of insecurity and there's no shortage of that to go around. Perhaps that's the best reason why there are so many unattached people roaming around plying the trade. So many people are afraid to make decisions and commitments. They don't want to take chances. They don't trust their intuition and are overwhelmed with fear of failure; rejection. They stick and stay in their status quo safety zones! Be careful of accountants, doctors, dentists, pharmacists and those whose clothes reveal that they are cheap. Old watches and shoes are not a sign of lack of money, it's usually a sign of meager spending habits and that spells either poverty or most often c h e a p *putz*! Their mantra is: "I'm not risking my money!" Go ahead, get buried with your money!

Bye folks, life is passing you, "bye"! I've seen that happen time and time again and many of these creatures will be among the richest people in the cemetery because they have nobody to leave it to, give or share when they were above ground either. Well, usually it's left to their nieces and nephews. This is it folks! The cemetery is a singles scene and it happens for the losers, tightwads and stiffs. There is no life after death, but hey maybe there is. But, no one knows for sure right? So, why take chances? Because, if there is no singles scene after this life then those who are waiting for something better will not be disappointed because they'll be dead!

Many single men prefer to play the role of daddy, big daddy or sugar daddy, and seek soft pink pretty women who are "ripe for pickin'" as they'd say. They want to be seen with a "babe" or "trophy" as it props up their egos, which, I suppose, need proppin'!

A lady's age has never been a factor for me. However, in a practical sense, generally up to ten years younger was best because these ladies tend to like the confidence and experience that comes with a man who has gained "an edge" with a few more years of life experience beneath his belt.

But, there are ladies out there who want a younger man, their "trophy" thing. Some love to play big sister, momma "the boss" or all three. I suppose it's a "forbidden fruit" syndrome that turns them on too, including but not limited to a chiseled chest, bulging biceps, "six pack" abs and lots of hair, mainly on their heads. Most of those encounters don't last long, based on what I've seen. The guy gets thrown off balance and the lady ditches the male because he can't keep up with her wants and needs. Lucky him! Get off that trolley buster, see a shrink and get a reality check. "High maintenance" will bring you down fast. If it walks like a duck, well, you know.

After you've selected the places where you want to go, never seem too anxious or desperate, especially if you are. Be confidant and be cool. Then, scan the place for the woman or women you find appealing, not only from a physical or sexy perspective, but check out their body language and facial expressions. Are they smiling? With whom are they talking? What are they talking about? Are they fidgeting, listening, obsessively looking at their watches, intently busy with their .iphones, looking at their mirrors often, texting, unaware of what's going on around them, aloof, etc.? Are they letting the other person(s) talk? Do they go to the bathroom too often especially with their friends for a quickie conference, refreshing their lipstick, makeup and hair? Big trouble, move on or move over! It's "high maintenance" and zero return on investment, hopefully only your time. If you're looking for a quickie, fine. But, you could get hooked and you'll wind up at the end of her line hooked like a fish, forever!

Look for the real ladies, secure and grounded. That's the best advice. Stay away from those gorgeous ladies if they are projecting too much self-interest. It's trouble and not worth it. Focus on what you really want and need in life. Someone who will make you happen and that can only happen if you can make her happy too.

Most inexperienced single men are scared to death to say something, the preverbal "pickup line."

"Haven't we met before?" "Are you from this part of town?" "What perfume are you wearing?"

These noir "lines" right out of the 1930's will either flop or if the lady has a sense of humor and the intro just may be perceived as a joke, and then it could work. My advice, try it if you have nothing else in mind. If you think about it, the "pickup line" is the easiest thing because you have nothing to lose. Get over it and open your mouth. Since you don't even know this woman, why should you care if she "blows you off"? So what? She's not the last person on the island! Move on and say a prayer for the next dude. On second thought, skip the prayer, if he gets in too

63

deep, it's just a little experience for him and that should have a lot of value, unless the putz gets hooked. A ladies reaction to your "pickup line" should tell you a lot about her. Pay attention! That first impression is often quite telling. So, if you don't like her reaction or feel uncomfortable then step on the gas and go. Move around buster! Ya better "shop around"! Ladies who are interested in making you feel off guard with your "pick up" line are jousting, looking to challenge you for one of two reasons. Either they're totally not interested in you and love to make a schmucks out of men or they want to test your confidence, quick wit and skill see if you can stay balanced under pressure.

There are literally thousands of pickup lines for all occasions. For example, here's a shocker,

"I'm looking for the perfect woman. Can you help me?" "I've noticed you across the room and wanted to get a closer look, I'm Cliff, and I'm . . ." or

"I know I've seen you before, perhaps it was in a dream!"

If the lady "blows you off" for any of these openers then say, "nice meeting you" or "bye" or "sorry, must have confused you with someone else" and keep moving! Smile! Never expose any disappointment. Avoid "My name is" just say "I'm _." Don't be a dog or a square.

Other more traditional openers are:

"You have a terrific look" or "I've noticed you. You're very nicely put together!"

Staring is not a good word, it's too predatory. I've noticed you and I'd like to say hi. "Hi!"

"Hi, I'm Cliff. Where are you from?" or "You look so terrific, you must have taken a very long vacation" or "My journey is over. So glad you're here!"

A humorous approach will provide a lot of glues about your candidate. If they find you amusing, intelligent and not the obvious lecher who's after one thing only then you will know, almost immediately. If they make a scornful face at you then remove yourself pronto. "Well, good luck!" and move on. Smile, you must always smile and project confidence. Confidence!

The one you are seeking is relaxed, drinking alcohol, not too much, smiling, listening and attentive.

Don't be miffed if a lady tells you that she's waiting for "someone." That "someone" could be a girlfriend, even prettier then she! I've always replied,

"Oh, what's her name? Maybe I know her!"

That gets a laugh, usually. If her friend turns out to be her boyfriend, then say good-bye to the lady. Don't introduce yourself unless she introduces you to her boyfriend first. If she says, "this is my boyfriend" then you know. If she introduces him as "my friend" then there's a crack, an opening, maybe.

That's good protocol and reflects self-assurance, your secure posture. If the answer is "sure, you can hang here" then she's either grounded and "in good space", and perhaps, not too serious about the guy, she just may be attracted to you and wants to include you in "the game." She could also be using you to "break his balls." Ask what she does and try to get her business card if you can after you believe that she won't consider your request premature or intrusive. Never offer yours, give her your card only if she asks for it. Always.

65

Call her if you wish, but wait a few days or so. Never seem too anxious. Unfortunately, it's a game and never loose sight of that. Be real, deliberate and honest. Let the ladies talk about themselves. Take an interest or stop wasting your time and move on.

The best thing you can say to a lady who you are attempting to get interested in you is simply, "Tell me more!" Let them talk. We have two ears and one mouth that we can shut. What does that tell you? "Tell me more." Ask questions, be sincerely interested and then they will, should, take an interest in you too. If they do not reciprocate then, most likely, they're too self-involved and or not interested in you. Move on.

There's no shortage of watering holes in this town and running from one to another can be a challenge, especially if you are the type that is intent not to leave any of them without some serious elbow bending.

It's not necessary because within a minute or two you'll know if the place has potential and if it doesn't have the goods then leave. If you can't evaluate a place in a few minutes then try another spot or go home and put a C note in your piggy bank. Back then it was a $50 for piggy.

At that time, I had so much fun. The only way was to "work the prowl" but don't ever overdo the cups too so that others will perceive you as being drunk. Ladies are not attracted to big boozers except the occasional lush and that's a signal of trouble down the road. When you find one of those hard drinking ladies, be careful, you can get crushed and hurt big time. New York City is the fastest lane aside from the Indy 500.

Stealing cocktail glasses is one of the most fun things you can do while floating through the singles scene. Why? While "on the prowl", your mindset should be to think outside the box. Be unorthodox and dismiss much of what you have been told all your life. You're on the hunt and not in pursuit of the conventional introduction from an aunt or parent. Rather, a side of your brain should shift into high gear and speak louder to you then the reams of advice, throughout the years, from your elders who never know how to play the game. What you are looking for, they're clueless most of the time. Too many want to please their parents and in doing so and marrying the preverbal "girl next door" usually is a disastrous choice, ball and chain guys. There are exceptions, let's be fair but, few and far between.

"Go get 'em." "Bring home the bacon." or "My adrenalin, testosterone, serotonin and biological instincts are kickin' in." The same part of your brain tells you, "go ahead, and let's try to get away with something, do something naughty, satisfy the devil in you and getting away with something rev's your engine like a can of STP, in those days the concept fueled mine. Stealing cocktail glasses was the catalyst and provided additional courage and confidence in my abilities and chances for success.

Every time got away with it I was supercharged! Now, let's go for the "real prize." That was my mentality, weird, sounds childish but true. It's brain chemistry; it's power, enhances courage and creates a mechanism to achieve your mission, successfully in a adolescent, silly, unusual and creative, fun kind of way. It's not true of all of us, but above all if it doesn't fit your head then don't do it. Certainly, it's not for the weak and the meek.

The best time to pull off this caper is in the winter, or at least when you are wearing a suit jacket. This was the drill:

If I had decided that the place was "86", time to split, I'd tuck my drink against my side beneath my jacket or coat, press my forearm against the outside of my jacket to steady the glass, never wanting to get myself wet. Once outside, I'd grasp the glass and take a sip. One more glass for the pantry! The trip to that joint paid off, even if the drink and glass were my only company. Besides, glasses can only break. Women can break you. Humpty!

One evening, I was out with a platonic girlfriend and we had agreed to go cocktail glass collecting. Even though we were each on our own hunts for separate relationships, we had made a declaration, a game of it. So, even if we each ended the evening without "pay dirt" we'd have something to show for the time, besides the fun and laughter, glasses!

We must have hit about six bars that night and every time we left with our booty safely tucked beneath my "threads." She knew she was not as good at this as me. Therefore, I had to insert two glasses per trip beneath my coat. She always got one. I never, ever wanted two of the same glasses in my apartment anyway. That would have been tacky. No Crate & Barrel or Bed, Bath and Beyond, Pottery Barn or Macy's for me. No matched set. Each glass was unique, a one of a kind.

Early that evening we stopped at a Duane Reade Drug Store to pick up a couple of shopping bags to carry "the spoils of war." By two o'clock in the morning, both bags were totally filled and so were we, "knocked to the bone!"

We left a bar, a converted firehouse, on west 18th Street at about 3 AM. We sauntered across the street, with both shopping bags in hand, when suddenly I noticed bubble wrap! The trash was due to be picked up later that morning and on top of one of the trashcans was a mountain of bubble wrap, you know, the stuff that has air holes. Who doesn't love to snap and pop those air holes? Then an idea hit my brain. I took the bubble wrap, spread it out on the hood of the nearest car and started to remove the booty, the glasses, and I proceeded to roll 'em up, one by one, and recited some nonsense such as:

"Thank you for shopping with us today! Is there anything else I can do for you? Will that be cash, charge or debit, or 'did' you want to open a store account and save an additional 10% on your purchase? Did you find everything you were looking for today?"

We howled, bent over, fell and crashed on top of the trash, chortling and shrieking in pain bursting from our hysterical laughter. We couldn't stop! I was so glad that we didn't have to pee! It was a damn good thing that we were sober enough to use the bubble wrap wisely to protect our precious cargo. If not, we would have crunched all the air out of the little holes and forgotten about the glasses. That's the fun of bubble wrap; squish, snap, crackle and pop pop pop! Everyone loves that stuff. Screw the gift! Just give me Bubble Wrap! Bubble Wrap! I want bubble wrap! Yes! Yes!

The fun of the singles scene is up to you. Have a great time and don't let the "turkeys" get you down. You have to keep it light and keep yourself focused on your mission. Don't be over anxious. Allow yourself to get a little crazy! After all those years in the "singles business" I claimed the most unusually stocked pantry in the city. In no time at all, I must have had about forty cocktail glasses and they were all different and all mine or, in the least, in my possession. I would have had over a hundred glasses but the attrition caused by leaving the apartment with a glass tucked tightly beneath my jacket or coat filled with libation on my way to another singles place always resulted in another donation for a corner trashcan. Why buy my first drink when I can get a head start for nearly nothing? Besides, I like to recycle, glass, that is.

Today I regret that. I could have opened a cocktail glass store in Nolita, Alphabet City, Tribeca or Atlantic Avenue in Brooklyn and retired by now. But, what the hell? Providing private tours is a wonderful profession, a dream job, and lots more fun than stealing bar glasses! Maybe I've grown up? Nah!

The funniest thing about this was that I couldn't help removing that Sesame Street song from my brain "None of these things (glasses) are quite like the other, none of these glasses are quite the same." The question is this. If Sesame Street were on television when I was a kid perhaps I would have grown up. I guess there's a little kid in all of us. Hope so. Be, confident; be intelligent, engaging, and secure. Listen and shut up and be on a high of confidence. That's it!

Formica Beach on the 47th Floor!

Too much sun, over time, can cause serious health problems. You could become so good looking that your sex life can get out of control and boom; you've got HIV, "the clap" or "crabs" and drink too much, neglect your true purpose or windup alone in a dark box! Too much sun can kill you and someone you love. Nah! New Yorkers know all that too but that hasn't resulted in a slew of tar or Formica beaches from closing! Sunshine in New York City is a hit and miss event and getting your share is challenging. Even on the brightest days a walk in Manhattan can be sunless if you want it to be. With the grid street layout, that runs generally north-south, 29 degrees off true north, for up and downtown travel and southeast or north-west for crosstown, one can usually find one side of the street that's shaded and the other side that's blanketed with sunshine. Many of the sunny sides have no sun due to the shadows cast by tall buildings. Smart New Yorkers zigzag through the streets in order to accommodate their preferences, sun or no sun.

There are those among us who know where to go to get "serious" sun and we certainly do soak up the "bennies" aka beneficial sunrays. What a myth that was, an expression from the 1970's when silver foil reflectors were big sellers. Some folks who were low on money tore up corrugated boxes and covered them with tin foil. Here are a few interesting examples of urban sun sources.

First, there's tar beach. You won't find a beach in Manhattan, except at a playground in Central Park or Tribeca. Tar beach is simply a piece of tar that you claim for yourself on the roof of your building or a building that's accessible. There are endless acres of tar for the taking. With towel in hand and a chair just settle in and soak up the rays or spread the towel directly on the tar and fry. The only drawback is that most buildings don't provide a pool or a shower for the rinse off and refresh. Numerous ingenious New Yorkers bring Windex bottles filled with cold water and crushed ice to provide the relief they seek when the sweat pours on. I never knew why so many low flying helicopters hovered over Manhattan on hot sunny days. Hum!

Second, there's Central Park, the place to be if you're "stuck" in the City on a hot sunny summer weekend. The Sheep Meadow is the center of the universe on such days and it's best described as a carpet of people all prone, fully greased with oil absorbing huge doses of vitamin D and gamma rays. Looking good New York City but there's a price to pay for everything.

Central Park is also littered with hundreds of huge flattop rocks, outcroppings with sunbathers propped up, facing the sun, some with those dinosaur silver reflectors. Where the hell do they get them? I do hope that the price is stratospheric! Someone ought to tell the mayor! He'll tax them to death. Most sunbathers are equipped with ipods, ipads, iphones, Blackberry's and all the rest, towels, and chairs of all kinds; portable children's size, large wooden models with colorful stripped cloth and the $5.99 specials, the 1970's vintage woven plastic slats and aluminum frame chairs, light as a feather. Those who sit in the shade on park benches and focus on the triangular "watch "cloths that adorn the brave and bold "fems" sweet spots. Nah, nah, nah!!

Third, are the riverside spots and harbor hangouts. The East River and The Hudson provide numerous popular sunbathing sites along the "greenway." Concrete piers jut out into The Hudson and a swath of blankets cover that valuable grass turf and abundant sun and shade bountifully covering Battery Park too. The East River really needs a lot of attention because the big money has been spent on the Westside shoreline. Why? Because that's where the money is and money is power. I really feel sorry for those Eastsiders, their river spots are sorely hurting and have been terribly neglected by the City. Not fair!

The outer boroughs have their favorite sun spots too with promenades such as Coney Island, Prospect Park, boardwalks and hundreds of acres of grass, The Brooklyn Bridge Park, an incredibly spectacular park, still under construction and thousands of acres of other parks and backyards also provide access to lots of sun in the City without snarls of traffic that the Hampton crowd endures "heel toe, heel toe" in their $120,000 Porsches and other various chariots that shout, "Look at me!!" Ridiculous! Oh, am I dating myself? $120K could that be the cheapest Porsche on the planet?

Orchard Beach in The Bronx isn't that bad. Far Rockaway and Brighton Beach are great choices too via subway and bus or by any means necessary. But you can't beat tar beach for the convenience, if you hate travel, traffic and travail.

A number of years ago I had rented an apartment on the 47th floor at 322 West 57th Street. It was a corner apartment facing southeast, great for light and tons of sun. I was not inclined to trek up to Tar Beach because sunning in my own apartment, impossible for most, had tremendous advantages such as; access to food, liquid refreshments, a landline phone, shower, music of choice, air-conditioning, a king sized bed, privacy or the option not to have privacy, nice company close at hand which can be grand.

The rent will kill you or a quick slip down to the tar on the street if you nod out will. It's the fastest way to get all your bills paid in full. If you roll out "all debts are paid." That'll solve anyone's rent problem. That's why I never put the greasy suntan lotion on my back, slip and slide and down I'd go! But, it would have been an opened box with such a great tan it would have been a waste to close it.

My 47th floor living room was surrounded with huge windows, approximately three feet off the floor and extending up to the ceiling provided tons of sun. I had a built-in Formica cabinet installed against the bottom edge of the windows. It was about two and one-half feet wide and ran the length of the entire windowed walls of the room. That was my beach! Formica beach was just another New York City invention, such an innovation. Ah, New York City!

"Cliff, you what? Are you out of your mind? You could have fallen asleep and rolled out of the window you putz!" I have it down to a science, never doubting my sanity. "Thanks for your concern. How's my tan?" That had been my retort time and again.

"Been to the Hamptons, Cliff?"

"Sure."

I had done this many times, gotten great tans, lots of rest, but I had decided instead to do the environmentally smart thing by not burning a drop of gas to get my tan at Formica beach. It would not have been possible for me to take the plunge because the windows were only about three feet wide and the separators would have prevented the fall, I do believe. I always remained aware and awake; never for a moment did I perceive that I was in any danger except possibly acquiring too much sun or being attacked by a stray Red-tailed Hawk!

Quite likely I was not the only resident who was "taking sun" that way. New Yorkers live their lives in ways that are unheard of compared to residents of other locales. But, they'll shrug you off as if New York City claims to have invented everything. That's just part of the fun of living here. Some of us are well . . . different! Actually, we're all different, that's just one of the things I love about New York City! No two people are nearly the same, and that includes those who get tan, and snag cocktail glasses too. They're all different and wrapped up in their own realities.

A Tree Doesn't Grow in Central Park

Central Park is the most amazing place. I love it! New Yorkers have so much adoration for that park even though they don't know much about it. I'm there all the time, on my own, walking my dog, strolling with my wife Aline or hosting my tour guests. Perhaps it is the most gorgeous piece of ground designed, built and created by man in any urban environment on earth.

Enormous amounts of effort and money, public and private are needed to maintain the park. Millions of dollars have been donated to sustain and improve the park through events, fund-raisers, plaques adorning the benches at a cost of $5,000 each and hundreds who donate their time, toil and sweat volunteering to plant, clean, weed, rake and sweep the park. Truly, it is a community effort. Countless numbers of people have made this 19th century masterpiece the most magnificent centerpiece of New York City.

In 2013 John Paulson, a hedge fund manager with fond childhood memories donated $100,000,000 to The Central Park Conservancy. The Central Park Conservancy, a quasi-pubic agency pays 85% of the cost to maintain the park whose budget is $45.8 million annually. I too have fond memories of the park as a child however I have delayed making a donation of similar proportions. ☺

The Central Park Conservancy oversees the replacement of trees, bushes, shrubs, flowers, repairs damage from storms, re-paves paths, changes bulbs in the standing lamps, supervises the building and repair of playgrounds, repairs walls, maintains the police stables located at the 86th Street transverse, plants and cuts the grass, restores ball fields and maintains monuments, and on and on.

Recently, I had noticed a replacement Weeping Willow tree that had been planted along the shoreline of "The Pool" a small lake in the park at 100th Street near Central Park West. The little weeper was not doing well. Actually, it was dying. These trees replace aging Weeping Willow trees that no doubt had been planted well over 100 years ago and have few years of remaining life. It's impressive, the foresight to plant those trees alongside the aging ones. The park is an ongoing process, one of constant renewal. As a result park goers continue to enjoy mature, and beautiful trees and will for many years to come, extraordinary and gorgeous specimens!

Surely, that replacement Weeping Willow was diseased and in need of urgent attention or the end was surely near. I wrote a letter to the Director of The Central Park Conservancy mentioning what I had noticed, hoping for an answer, but not terribly optimistic that I would receive one. How could I reasonably expect an answer from a large quasi-public organization in a City this size? A letter about one tree in a park that has about 24,000 trees would surely go unanswered.

To my astonishment, three days after I had mailed that letter I received a phone call from the Director of Operations of The Central Park Conservancy acknowledging my letter and he told me,

"We're keeping our eye on that tree." Amazing!

The following week I passed by to take a look at "my tree" and noticed that it had been replaced! I was thrilled and gratified to say the least. There are still some people who do care and appreciate being notified by concerned citizens.

Now I know, through evidence that the park truly doesn't exist by itself. It's a labor of love and devotion that makes us so fortunate. Down to the detail of one little tree it's nice to know that there are people who "have their eye on it." Yes, "A Tree Grows in Brooklyn" and in Central Park too.

"I Got Interests on Both Sides"

That was the "welcome" I had received from the other end of the phone back in 1982 while working at my store located on the northeast corner of Lexington Avenue and 43rd Street.

What a location! The corner of 43rd Street and "Lex"! You couldn't get a better location than that! It's directly across the street from the Lexington Avenue entrance to Grand Central Terminal, the Graybar Building, once the largest office building in the world, and the Chrysler Building, located directly across the street to the south. It wasn't actually a store, per se, but a concession in a Drug Store known as TJ Brothers Drug named for two Jewish brothers. I, together with my partner, operated a sixteen-foot long film developing, film and passport photo counter in the front of the drug store. We opened the concession known as Films R Us in 1977.

We had a bona fide ten-year sub-lease with the owners of the Drug Store. It was a very profitable little business. It was fun to operate, marketed very aggressively, spearheaded with "flyers" handed out on the street. Our low pricing and promotional offers aimed directly at our high priced competitor's customers to direct them our door drove them nuts. We attracted herds of customers through our doors seeking bargain pricing who recognized the value of our services. Our competitors "sued" for peace and we created a way to live together, sort of. They stopped "bashing" us as a "Johnny come lately" labeling us as poor quality hacks and we in turn stopped "shouting" about their high prices. It was great fun! We never gave up featuring crushing prices while making huge piles of cash for quite a few wonderful years. Cheap rent, 90% cash and no accounts receivable is a dream business. Very few used credit cards; we didn't want to take them. There weren't any electronic mechanisms to verify the veracity of credit cards in those days. Accepting credit cards was very chancy. Do you recall when retailers would receive tissue paper booklets with the current list of fraudulent credit card account numbers printed in 2-point type? They were totally useless, a device designed to cover "their asses" the credit card companies.

I recall, at that time, the price of silver, a primary ingredient found in film emulsion, had soared in price. The Hunt family, oil barons, from Texas attempted to "corner" the silver market and drove the price of silver through the roof. Consequently we began purchasing huge quantities of film and we warehoused cases of film in my garage, virtually eliminating space for my car. We sat back and waited for the price of film to climb further and further and then we sold it at a penny above cost, the newer higher current cost. As the price of film rose again we played the same game, over and over again. It provided us with impressive profits and substantial savings for our customers. That strategy drove our business sky-high because our customers had more film on hand then ever before and it stimulated the most profitable segment of our business, film developing and printing. At times we had more customers at our little sixteen-foot counter then the rest of the entire drug store, which was about twenty-five times the size of our little concession. We projected ourselves as doing our customers a favor and our customers were very impressed with out generosity; we felt so sorry for them, sure. It would be like a gas station giving gas away at a 40% discount compared to all their competition. Our customers loved us and we loved that!

My partner, the salt of the earth, but a bit of an obsessive "bean counter" know every conceivable business statistic. He crunched them every way from "here to eternity." He just loved knowing how many crunch, crunch, crunch we sold last year on the same month! Passport photos sold for the corresponding week during the prior year were compared with the current year. What were we going to do with that information? Have another shrimp at Palm Restaurant, our Friday afternoon ritual, yeah, pass the hot sauce! Nice guy, very hard worker. I used to buy him Crunch candy bars. He loved chocolate, but he never got the connection.

****

"Cliff, on line two Tony, he's on hold for you!"

I didn't know anyone named Tony, but I picked up the call anyway. I had a strange feeling that this was the call that I had been waiting for; the opportunity to cash in on a real estate assemblage.

"Hi, this is Cliff."

"I want to talk to you about your film store."

"Who's this?"

"Tony"

"Who sent you?" was my response to this uninvited mystery caller.

"I got interests on both sides!"

He replied in a deep confident and serious tone, peppered with that Bensonhurst, Brooklyn accent. There was no mistake. I was thinking fish now, not shrimp, as I was going to be a pu-pu platter at the bottom of The East River on top of a pair of concrete shoes me, literally feeding the fish. I always hated salt water, oysh! It reminds me of Epson Salts, bad for your blood pressure too, but only while you're alive. Concrete shoes, fuggetaboutit! I was still wearing Weejuns or Clark Wallabies back then. Where's the best deal for cement shoes anyway? Could it be Bergdorf, Saks, Jimmy Choo or Prada, eh? Nah! Try Vinnie's, Butch the Hat or Tony the Rat if you're looking for a pair of concrete shoes, eh?

"So where do we go from here? What can I do for you?" I asked with a touch of sarcasm.

"My shoe size is 9E; can you get me a pair, with a loose fit? I just hate tight fitting shoes. I like a bit of room to roam, know what I mean, Tony?" I've got a bunion just behind my big toe on my left foot that's already killing me!"

Sure, I said that! Right?

"I want to meet you at the Bayonne Diner. We gotta talk about your film store. You're gettin' out a dere. I want to see you tomorra' at 1 o'clock and don't come heavy!"

He told me in a very demonstrative manner, very.

Don't come heavy meant unarmed as in "piece" a gun!

"No need to make that request, I never came heavy in my life. Know what I mean?"

Not a doubt, I was confronted by a pro. After wondering what movie I was in, I told him I'd be there. Then I ran to the bathroom, and got there just in time. I did "come heavy" to the bathroom, that is. Left a lot lighter too!

I showed up in Bayonne with my father, a short, portly grey bearded man who wore a tweed cuffley cap with a cheap cigar, Garcia & Vega, in place. He was the picture of a man in his late sixties who could just as well have been seated on the Grand Concourse in The Bronx in the late 1970's schmoozing with little caped first generation ol' guys sharing stories from the old country, the war and their hot secretaries who were, by then, drooling in their bibs and wearing diapers in "old age homes" as they were called back in those days. He looked like Yentel's father a movie featuring Barbra Streisand. He served as my bodyguard, my protector, witness and advisor.

There were two of them as well, Tony and Johnny. Johnny came heavy. It was obvious or he had a huge tumor or half of a dead chicken tucked beneath his suit jacket on the right side beneath his chest. Obviously, he was a lefty. Since I didn't smell chicken and his color was good I figured that he came "packin'" aka "heavy."

I thought of the scene from "The Godfather" when Michael, played by Al Pacino, snagged a gun from the top of a toilet tank that he had used to "whack" the police captain and the Tattaglia capo in the Italian restaurant in The Bronx's Little Italy. So, I fantasized, thinking that they might have suspected that that's where my "piece" was planted but surely, they never gave it a thought. But, then again, that's probably why Johnny ducked into the bathroom right after we entered the diner. Nah, my mind was racing and I have to admit, although I had a lot at stake, I found the experience very amusing and surreal.

It's the "romance" of facing off with the Mafia. "I'm doin' business with the Mafia! I got something they want!" Nah nah nah nah naaaaaaahhhh nahhh!!" Could it be? A "mademan" had confronted me? No worries, I'm Jewish! Murder Incorporated, that was us! That's another thing that bothered me, oy! I was about to offer them some free film, as a gesture but nah; they must have all the film they could steal. Perhaps they might just become a great new supplier for us, eh? The price of silver could provide an opportunity for us to do some business with them, eh?

I decided not to check the bathroom but I did make a necessary visit, second time I ever came, or went, "heavy" due to my fear. Sure beats X-Lax! Mafia brand laxatives, what a great idea to build drug store traffic! "Take Mafia Brand X-Lax, or X-Lex, promoting our location, wherever you go and whenever you go!" Or how about, "Can't come heavy? Let Mafia X-lax take care of it!"

We ordered some coffee and Danishes, toast and other comfort food. As I recall, they ordered, "prostitute spaghetti." That's angel hair or very thin spaghetti that hookers often ordered because it took no time to make enabling them to get back to work and not miss a "trick." This was going to be a short meeting, as there didn't seem to be any smiles, small talk or niceties. This was strictly all about business.

It had been apparent for quite a few months; prior to this "meet" that the block where our concession had been located was experiencing an assemblage by a real estate developer, Olympia & York (The Reichmann Family from Toronto), although we didn't know that at the time. Talking with numerous other retailers on the block I was made aware that they were "surrendering" their leases for payment. No doubt we would be approached with an offer and the notion of being "holdouts" to get us the best possible deal was a wonderful prospect, pure naivety and fiction, as it turned out. My partner and I relished the thought of getting a million dollars or more for our signatures. Our business was good but not that good. But, that didn't matter to the powers that be. The developer couldn't force us into a deal that we wouldn't want to accept or so we thought. It turned out that we were green, young and stupid to believe that. We were giddy and really dense. That was who we were. With age comes wisdom. I never knew that. For openers:

A clause in our sub-lease stated that if any labor dispute, arising as a result of our business activity, such as picketing in front of the store, must be "cured" within three days or our sub-lease would become null and void; "having no force and effect."

During the negotiations to obtain our lease we almost walked out, "grandstanding" as we referred to it due to the insertion of that clause. We knew that this was a deal breaker on the other side and we needed this deal more than they did. Their benefit, aside from the collection of our rent, was that we provided the prospect that our store traffic would be very advantages for their business. That was the lure. Every savvy retailer wants people who pass by their store to see it packed with shoppers. It stimulates others to come in and we did that very well their benefit and ours. If they had an ounce of imagination they could have done it for themselves but they were both vacuous and very lazy.

About two weeks before I received that phone call from Tony my partner and I were approached by one of the "two Jewish brothers" who was seeking to make a deal with us to "surrender" our sublease. We were offered $10,000 and we laughed hysterically, right in his face, at that opening shot! We practically peed in our pants! We knew they couldn't sell their master lease to the landlord before we had surrendered our sub-lease. We felt that we had the upper hand and decided to chide their offer with remarks that we couldn't take them seriously. It was like "Get back to us with a real number and we'll talk." Certainly, that's what they had expected. That's the way the game is played. It was their opening shot. "Let the games begin!"

Subsequently, there was no talk, just "hardball" tactics such as; them taking pictures of our employees standing behind the counter, waiting on customers and ringing up sales. We knew exactly what they were up to. They had the right, as provided under the terms of our sublease; the right to review all of our "books and records" and taking pictures of our employees was legal, an information gathering ploy designed to scare us.

One item that really concerned us was the payroll. A number of our employees had been working "off the books" and they knew that it. That was another Achilles' heel for us, that and the labor disruption clause in the lease.

We were like a pair of stupid kids frolicking in a sandbox filled with shit. We were too giddy and stupid to realize that we were pawns in a real world multi-million dollar scenario orchestrated by a multi-national powerful Canadian family, The Reichmann's. They were the folks who later went on to build Canary Wharf in London and World Financial Center adjacent to The World Trade Center in New York City. At that time, we didn't have a clue. Okay, it's the big league and we were minor league players. We had to find a way to save ourselves.

Naturally, Tony was prepared to cut a deal, keeping his client's interests uppermost in his mind. No doubt he was well aware of our vulnerably. He had a job to do and I knew that we were walking on hot coals. Cement shoes would have been perfect for hot coals, come to think of it! It didn't take long for me to realize who really had the upper hand. Call it "hand over foot" or feet!

Tony had asked me how much I was looking for. I told him that I had expected him to put a number on the table. I came to the "meet" with no number in mind. I thought the right play for him was to "put his cards on the table." I'm here to listen with an opened mind, not an opened head. That was my thinking.

"Come on! You gotta have some kinda numba in your frekkin' brain! Put somethin' on the table and let's get it done, know what I mean, eh? I know that you could have some serious tax and labor problems too kid. You want those government wingtipped assholes creepin' up your ass?"

The threat, the warning, was delivered with my back against the wall. I knew that I couldn't afford to "fold my cards." It was time for me to stand up for our interests and deliver my message to Tony.

"Tony, I'm not an unreasonable guy. You and your people want us out and that's fine. We have absolutely no problem with that. My partner and I have families and we've got mouths to feed. We're young guys and we have five more years left on that lease. We're not walking away without a fair share of the action. Your people need us out and we don't want to stand in your way."

Like he gave a shit!

"We're just looking for a number that works for all of us, a fair deal. We're not pigs. Our accountants and lawyers have told us that we have nothing to worry about. All tax matters can be straightened out with the authorities if need be. My partner and I have been down that road before and we know how to get passed that. We've got great lawyers and accountants and who've proven to us time and time again that they know their business. It doesn't frighten us, not a bit. I'll get back to you after my partner and I talk it over. I'll let you know in a day or two. He agreed, we shook hands we left the diner. No one slipped into the bathroom, the coast was clear. I never expected anything to "go down." I was just fanaticizing, getting it off internally, a bit of self-aggrandizement.

My partner and I discussed the situation and arrived at $500,000 as the right number for several reasons. First, we knew we were dealing with some very unsavory people who were backed up by some of the savviest businessmen on the planet. We had assumed that ultimately they were going to get their way by any means necessary. Responding to them with an inflated and unrealistic opening shot would have been stupid and dangerous. It would only have intensified their frustration and justified their means, in their minds, to cross the line and get tough with us. This was not the time to be wishy washy; that could lead to swishy swashy, as in an underwater grave with a very long-term lease; forever.

Second, we also knew that we could come up against other types with their own greedy self-interests such as our lawyers and accountants. They knew all about how to create fees that would mount quickly, especially, if we got the desired results. That road would be paved with cancelled checks, ours. I didn't know who to fear most, the professionals, the government agencies or the "boys."

And finally, the best way to handle this was simply to make the best deal we could and move on, period. We weren't looking for broken kneecaps or swimming with the fish and the prospect of prison was totally out of the question. Prison was to be avoided at all costs. Knowing that it was a real possibility scared the shit out of us. I was married with two young children and didn't need a new roommate for the next ten years! Not an option.

I called Tony the next day and tossed out the number, $500,000. Not to my surprise his reply was,

"I can't help you."

I told Tony that there was a little wiggle room. He was unimpressed,

"Nah, let's just go our separate ways and let the chips fall where they may, okay kid." Tony told me with a sarcastic chuckle.

He was a real pro. This guy knew his business, the right messenger for the job. Then the shit hit the fan.

The following week, the mailman appeared at our store with a fist full of certified mail. We "heard" from The City of New York Sales Tax Desk Audit Division, The New York State Department of Taxation and Finance, The City of New York Department of Labor and of course the good old Internal Revenue Service. Now that's power! These guys were heavies and they ran this right up to the top. They had the connections to pull the right strings anywhere. Those fuckers created numerous potentially extremely serious problems for us. We were squarely in enemy territory. These auditors must have gotten the word to squeeze us until we folded and made the desired deal. Otherwise they would keep pouring on the pressure until we knuckled under. We knew we were squarely in the middle of a very precarious situation and, at that point equation we just wanted it all to go away.

We've all seen similar scenarios in the movies, on television read about such encounters in novels, biographies and newspapers but now, we were in the spotlight and didn't like it one bit. It's fun to watch and read about, but hey, I was not a big player, just one of thousands of shopkeepers in the big City, practicing my trade. Suddenly when opportunity knocks, we get slammed in the face. I didn't like the script and my partner wasn't too crazy about it either. I realized that behind every building, on every block there's a story, a history, a struggle in this dog eat dog City. There's power and it rears its ugly head and crushes the meek. But, it is the driving force that builds cities, creates empires, and enriches the wise, the creative gutsy troopers and drives the underworld forward reaping big bucks that creates more power.

They defeat the weak, timid, inexperienced, and fearful. It's the human spirit, the connectors with big brass balls against those that lack them. Balls, in such cases, measure every gain or loss when it comes down to jungle justice on the streets. It determines those who stay in the game and those who do not. Rules, what are they? Some play the game and adhere to fair play but we all know the mantra "nice guys finish last." Ain't it the truth! Thanks Leo, another note of wisdom from the Brooklyn Dodgers manager.

90

Certainly, we were not saints either however, even if we had played by the rules the outcome would not have changed by a nickel!

The day that our mailman delivered those certified audit notices I drove up to Nyack Hospital. When I arrived I feigned that I was having chest pains. I was checked into the cardiac care unit where I happened to have a few "friends" who were doctors. I revealed, to them, the real reason why I had arrived and they admitted me. They performed basic non-invasive tests as a matter of "good medical practice." I remained there for several days making the visit seem credible. One of my doctor friends cranked out a letter that I could not participate in any depositions or tax audits for a period of six months. Then my partner stepped in and did a darn good job of handling the accountants and lawyers.

Our opponents did not pursue the "picketing card." Perhaps it wasn't necessary or was too risky; injurious to their client's drug store business during picketing perhaps. Maybe the union didn't want to stick their necks out either and be a party to such action. Who knows?

Our opponents had revealed that they had some very powerful connections with government agencies and we had no way of knowing the consequences for us. We knew that the audits would not be a picnic. Cutting a deal with the agencies would take the pressure off us but no deals were on the table unless we caved in and "cut bait" with the boys. We wondered what their next card would be.

As for the doctor "friends" of mine they knew my family's medical history; heart disease was in the gene pool, high cholesterol, years of smoking on my part and toss in my zany lifestyle added up to a walking time bomb. That was confirmed the following year when I had quadruple bypass surgery to prevent a certain heart attack or death.

One of my doctor "friends" had admitted to me, years later, that he had tried to convince his colleague that further testing would have been the right protocol.

In this instance, I suppose, the etiquette among doctors was, and still is, to let the patient, a friend, die or have a heart attack rather than violate their "hypercritical" oath, the oath among doctors not to put a colleague in an embarrassing or ruinous position! They proved to me that some doctors are strictly heartless mechanics who are in a profession whose priority is to save themselves more then save their patients. I love how many doctors and other over paid professionals, in many and not all cases, pontificate about their success stories. It's all self-serving heroics and self-promotion. The other tales are not part of the legend. Those patients don't speak because they are "sleeping" in cemeteries. I wonder how many doctors have invested money in cemeteries.

A number of months down the road, while in the midst of the audits, we settled for $150,000, the best deal we felt we could get. After all the papers were signed we closed the store and bemoaned the cost of the fees, the taxes and the discontinuance of the income stream. We each wound up with very little because my partner convinced me that we should invest the remaining proceeds in NYSE Savings & Loan Bank stock, which turned out to be a big mistake. Had we not been so greedy and stupid we could have walked away with much more. Good lessons don't come cheap.

What's the moral of the story? Had played it straight it wouldn't have mattered in the end. The opposition had much bigger shoulders then us. They would have resorted to any means necessary to get what they wanted. Of that I have no doubt. They had the picketing card, friends in very high places and quite likely other friends with enormous power and influence as well. In addition, they had access to the store, off hours, and surely they could have created enormous physical damage to our little business by trashing our customer's photos. That would have destroyed our business fast and we knew that they would have done anything to accomplish their objectives, anything!

We had a good run making very good money for five years, without breaking our asses and were weekly fixtures at Palm Restaurant. All in all, it was very worthwhile. The play with the stock market was a stupid risk, "youthful exuberance.

It was a brief encounter with power, revealing to us the way the real world works, how deals are made and how things get done in New York City. Yeah, we played hardball with the big boys and moved on because we were amateurs, novice kids who were forced to step up to the plate in the majors and we crushed.

It's a story of two guys who were pushed on stage, front and looking back on it all we both learned some very good lessons.

It's part of the history of a couple of New Yorkers who had become more so as a result. Hope it happens again because next time I'll have a "dose of brains" to fall back on I'll cover my tracks and keep my nose clean.

Life, in New York City, is a *quid pro quo*. A major New York City real estate assemblage is a once in a lifetime opportunity and we blew it. A fascinating ride, it certainly was. I'll have another ticket, thank you, and I'll joyfully take it wherever it leads me.

Same Face, Different Place!

Quite frequently, I've had casual and unintended encounters, on the sidewalks of New York City, with people whom I've "known" in the past. These experiences never fail to amuse me.

Having a long active life, intertwined with hundreds of people, I've been afforded chance "bumps" with people, in a city this size, quite often. It's weird. Many times I've heard a shout from behind such as, "Hey Cliff! How are you?" More then you can imagine! This isn't Main Street in Podunk, Mississippi! I do enjoy "running into people" from the past because it takes me back. I love seeing people who have vanished from my life and engaging in a conversation with them, catching up with them after many years. The problem is though, at times, its' very troubling for me and here's why:

Recently, while standing on the corner of 96th Street and Amsterdam Avenue, while waiting for the cross light to change and a woman standing along side me suddenly exclaimed "Cliff!" I turned around and racked my brain, having recognized her face I tried to recall, which she was? Where have I seen her before? In the moment, I didn't try to figure it out because I didn't have a clue. I had to initiate my reply not knowing who this lady was and, at the same time, trying to conceal that I just couldn't "place" her. I literally felt as though I was standing naked in the street. I've experienced this many times and what bothers me is that these people and I may have had long and meaningful connections in the past and the notion of me revealing that I hadn't a clue as to who they were and that's always very devastating. Could they have been a former employee, a nurse, a

95

neighbor or a woman at a bank who had cashed my checks or perhaps a former student, a vendor, doorman or a close friend of a friend? I'm not worried that I'm losing my mind. Over a lifetime there are hundreds and hundreds of faces that are catalogued from the past and they fade from memory. More importantly, I want to avoid insulting those whom I encounter. Surely, there's not a person on the planet that can remember all of the connections behind the faces in their life. Right?

I dread these encounters because I don't know what to say, "Ah hi, ah, how are you?"

Usually, I respond by saying, "Same face, different place!" with a broad, warm grin. I go directly to the point. My little phrase makes an admission, that yes, I'm human, and despite my embarrassment, I accept it and please don't be insulted. The fragility and certainly the hope that I have not insulted anyone is my priority. Why go ahead and have a five-minute conversation before admitting that I just don't remember who they are? That would be jolting for us both when I suddenly reveal that after talking with them for a while and pretending to remember them would make a real schmuck out of me by asking their name.

If you do make believe you know who they are then you are putting yourself in a very vulnerable spot. It's risky. I've tried that a number of times, hiding my little secret and before the end of the conversation, it hits me, ah yes, that's Amanda or Steve and suddenly I recall the connection.

It had turned out, that in this particular instance, she had been a former employee of mine. Having employed hundreds of people over a period of approximately thirty years, I let myself off the hook. I was guilty, but I endured no punishment only because she was not offended. New Yorkers are, as a group, very understanding.

Recently, my wife and I were approaching Tom's Diner, of Seinfeld fame, and were about to enter as a couple was emerging from within. The gentleman shouted my name with a smile. I had no idea who this guy was! He looked familiar though. I knew that I, at some point, knew him, but that was all. But, who the hell was he? Very frustrating!

I remarked to him, "Same face, different place!" Again, I confessed right away that I knew the face but just couldn't place him.

"I'm Ira! I'm Susan's partner in the optical business!" Sure, that was somewhat embarrassing for us both however; I had escaped that awkward moment by explaining to him the reason why I had failed to recognize him. Although I had seen and spoken with him many times in the past I always had seen him in his store where I purchase my eyeglasses. He was always well dressed, wearing a tie and never a hat, as he was on this occasion. Ira has no hair, bald as a peach, and that was his most distinguishing feature, and it was totally concealed. What I should have done was introduce my wife to him and then, quite likely, he would have introduced himself to her and as soon as I had heard the name, bingo! Instead, I said,

"Oh, excuse me. This is Aline, my wife. So sorry for not introducing you."

Then, I would have known instantly who Ira was, a duh. Next time, that'll be the script. If you are a New Yorker, keep that in mind. Others may not be as understanding or as forgiving as Ira. He understood completely. He's a super nice guy!

In a city the size of New York City, and smaller ones too I suppose, people create a web of secondary and tertiary relationships; a dry cleaner, a bus driver, a waiter, a street vendor who pours your coffee for three years and you never knew their names; or a subway station clerk, most do not exist anymore, who you had seen daily and never a word had been exchanged between the two of you, except the customary niceties "Have a nice day!" Over time, when you are "connected" by coincidence, or "knew" that person, when they had been a part of your existence, part of your routine, the past fades into a blur and you begin to doubt your ability to remember. As time goes by, your routines change, your platform, tasks, interactions that often result in displacement and you suddenly bump into someone in a different environment, wearing dissimilar clothing, doing something other than what you were used to experiencing with them and you draw a blank! It's difficult to connect and recall who they were way back during years past. Is this normal? I have mentioned this phenomenon to many fellow New Yorkers and they too have "same face, different place" experiences. They never believed that it was such a common occurrence. Trust me, it is!

This is largely an urban experience. It is unlikely that people from small towns often have such encounters. Aren't they supposed to know each other and all of their business affairs such as: what they ate for breakfast, who got a new car and who has been promoted at the local insurance agency? Are urbanites paying a high price for living their lives in big cities like New York City by having these embarrassing encounters and living transient lives filled with "meaningless" relationships? Are we reminded, by this phenomenon, that there is a void in our existence; a transitory streak that we carry that on occasion reminds us that we live life at a pace that is hectic, superficial and transparent? Like most staunch New Yorkers, I do not agree and I wouldn't have it any other way because those tertiary relationships form part of our wonderful matrix of life. The more people whose lives I touch and who touch mine, the more enriched I feel, the more complete, interested and fulfilled my existence becomes. If I had to trade this in for the comfort and familiarity of small town life, I'd be bored and guarded because my fellow citizens could easily invade parts of my life and some of those parts are private. The chatter would violate my personal existence. Living here, in a City where I don't know everything about everyone else and vice versa provides an endless inventory of contacts, opinions, ideas, smart, dumb and amusing people who will touch me and broaden my existence, with minimal invasion of my privacy. That's just a fraction of the excitement of New York City! Tomorrow I may run into someone that I haven't seen in thirty years. I certainly hope so, unless of course, I owe them money!

"Instant Funship"

Throughout the years, living in New York City, I have had innumerable opportunities to experience quality "alone time." Solitude in New York City is unlike anywhere else because there are endless choices to turn unwanted alone moments into spontaneous social occasions. While I was in between both marriages, a period of about six years, I became the preverbal kid in a candy store. My choices were endless and I indulged in the opportunity with gusto.

There were literally hundreds of opportunities to seek "instant funship". I've always enjoyed the company of others, minus the occasional asshole that crops up. Living in the most densely populated environment in the country and not always with a friend at hand I had felt compelled, many times, to leave my midtown apartment and "ply the pavement" in search of a good restaurant, one with an interesting bar scene or other amusing venue seeking some "instant funship".

An interesting bar scene with the potential of "instant funship" is typically one that consists of a few empty seats, numerous people, well dressed seated at the bar, better with some standees too, adding to the level of energy, engaged in interesting conversation and dosed with good humor, hopefully. I'd peer into the place through the window, if possible, or open the door, enter and take a casual inspection and ask myself:

"Is there 'instant funship' here?"

I'd stroll in, look around and determine the best place for me, based on my assessment of the locations of their patrons, their appearances, their grouping arrangements, body language and with a bit of luck

and a dash of experience, I'd make my evaluation, order a drink and gauge the on-going chat-ability of the bartender as well. I'd ask him or her:
"So, what's uppah?" or "So what's shakin'?" Or my favorite, "Uho's in charge "ere?"
Bartender's personalities are of major importance to detect "instant friendship" levels. Often they hold sway over the hype and variety of people frequenting the place. After ten minutes or so, I'd make an effort to attract interactive attention, make a short comment or two, overhear the conversations close by and gather my impressions of those engaged in conversation. Are they smart, interesting, boring and comfortable in their skin? Do I think they would interest me and would I interest them? Were the conversations stale and mundane peppered with phrases, such as "where did you shop today?" or "I can't stand that apartment it's a one bedroom!" and "I'm entitled!" or "My husband is so stupid and lazy. Why isn't he making more money?" and "Who won the hockey game last night?" and, my favorite, "I just traded in my one year old Porsche for a new one!"
What draws me in are discussions that either are somewhat esoteric, amusing, front page or humorous. "Where is this City going? "How is this country going to get out of this mess?" or "What's going on in Washington, they're nuts. They just don't get anything done!" or "Think we'll invade Aglobistan?"
For me, all sports are out; unless I want to make believe that I know what I'm talking about and fool the group is tons of fun. I just keep repeating, "Yeah, that was a fantastic play" or "He could have made that play?" And the most useful, "Yeah, yeah yeah, yup,

yeh, that's right, yeah, yeah, so true, right." Amazing how those schmucks don't "get it."

I continue to evaluate the group. It takes only a couple of seconds. I don't plan my intro, or an opener, a line that would evoke a reaction, or some comment that would dovetail with the ongoing conversation. I just open my mouth and out it comes, easy. Truthfully, it's a momentary burst, a comment, a thought or a question directed toward the crowd or one particular individual. It's my perception as a connector, spontaneity, whatever works. I take my opening shot. What have I got to lose? It's fun. It's a game, so I go for it. I "work" with what I've got in front of me and just dive right in.

Getting good at this has given me a lot of pleasure. I have developed a near perfect record of meeting friendly and connective people who have welcomed me into their chatter and in a "New York minute." I have mastered the art of playing a role, of steering conversations into all sorts of directions connecting and creating lively exchanges. I fully believe that again and again the chatter was all good, fun, light, peppered with laughter and friendly engagement. That's my objective. At times its gotten a little heavy, you know, religion, politics, morality that sort of stuff but, it's always kept on the right side of civility. No barroom brawls, arguments or hard feelings, ever!

Perhaps there's an art to it, no need to glorify it. There are those who have a seed that enables them to just open their mouths and create a connection, "a connector" one who truly likes people and is interested in them. That's me! So what; New York City is a perfect place for an urban extrovert and what's wrong with that? "Don't get me started!"

But, it's not something you'd want to try anywhere, because there are many places that are socially opposed to intruders, those looking to casually break into conversations, join the crowd and get involved in even the most innocuous discussions. I've been "around the block a few times" and trust me; you cannot do this everywhere. New York City is the best place to be if you are an "instant funship" kind of person. People here are ready, willing and able to give you a shot. "What's this guy got to say?" "Okay, just maybe, this guy is interesting and will add to the conversation."

Body language is an important factor too. Avoid being aggressive, sit or stand comfortably, take an interest in the conversation before you jump in, be agreeable, complimentary and listen to what they are talking about. By taking it in you are gathering points and as such they just may begin asking questions; "Do you live here?" "Visiting? Where are you from?" "What's the most fun you've ever had?" "Do you come here often?" What do you do?" But, be careful! Then, after five to ten minutes of engagement, they dig deeper; "Who are you voting for?" Whether the conversation is deep or superficial, you'll know if they'll let you join in. It starts to flow, questions arise, give and take starts to evolve, introductions are made, and you're in the game. Don't challenge anyone and don't put them on the defensive. Avoid jumping into conversations that are personal, relationships, health issues, financial, or heavy personal stuff, problems, "train wrecks" or depressing chatter. Know when to stay away.

If the conversation is light, show a reserved interest, listen with one ear, subtly, and start out by keeping your mouth shut. Wait until eye contact has been made, exchange cheerful expressions, then:

"So you're here on business?" How'd you know that I'm not a New Yorker?" "I didn't, I just guessed it!" "But how'd you know?"

"Ah, that's a good question. Do you really want to know?"

Don't try this in the rural south, Midwest, Miami or Boston. These and other places, most places, will not "let you in" if you don't look like, dress like, speak like and fit in, just like them. In most parts of this country there's a certain "back off" effect and they will turn you right off. Boston, a nice town, can be surprisingly stiff, starchy and closed-minded. The Midwest generally has little or no interest in speaking with New Yorkers. Many of our friends from other parts of the country misperceive us as arrogant, know-it-alls, walking superiority complexes and successful, which, for the most part, many of us are, and that breeds contempt. Miami is the coldest city in the United States. It's a closed society that clings to its own types and that, in part, depends on the language you speak, what you drive and the part of town where you happen to live, among others. Besides, it's actually the northern tip of South America and the southern tip of the United States; two places in one with cultural and ethnic borders all over the place that will never melt!

New York City, being the melting pot, and the cornerstone of liberalism, has made "instant funship" possible. I've been at the other end of the stick and been approached by others who have struck up conversations with me quite often. I'm only one of many. Perhaps I should start an organization and name it NYIFC, New York Instant Funship Club. Wanna become a member? "Sure, let me make you a member!" (Victor Maitlin, Beverly Hills Cop, remember that scene?)

These encounters serve a purpose in a city the size of New York City. Even a New Yorker with family, friends, and business relationships will find themselves in an occasional alone moment and "instant funship" is the perfect cure. I've had countless conversations with strangers, found in good places, all of whom have interesting things to say about their lives, things we have in common and beliefs that we share or do not share. We discuss everything in a civil, harmonious and enjoyable manner, complete strangers opening up to each other and sharing a moment, is all good, interesting and often is intellectually challenging, and most often lots of fun.

"Instant funship" is sharing similar experiences, assessing outcomes and evaluating strategies taken; I woulda, coulda, shoulda, in each instance is shared and expressed. "If I only knew then what I know now!"

Sharing jokes is the top, the most fun. It's like a ping pong game and if two or three are in it together then one joke brings on another and another and so on. You could literally sit for hours and howl the night away. It feeds on itself and once you get started it's non-stop! So much great material is stuck in my head and I've worn it down to a pulp. But, most folks still get a lot of laughs especially from those who haven't heard my material before.

In New York City people willingly express their thoughts, ideas and beliefs. They want to be heard and will shut their mouths to listen, even me! It's truly something special about this town, the engagement, the sense of community, friendship and desire to know what's inside of each others heads and even exploring what's in your own. I love it. I can always venture out and find the right fit, satisfy my quest for "instant funship" like nowhere else on earth. "Hello New York! I'm Cliff. Where are you from? Want some "instant funship"? Glad you're here! Hope you're glad I'm here too."

So . . . you've been living in Tribeca? For how long?"

The 47th St Diamond Dealer, Extraordinaire!

Who among us realistically expects something for nothing? For the most part, life is a *quid pro quo*, and in New York City, nothing could be truer. No one gives away ice in the winter in New York City.

I had a business, a chain of one-hour photo stores and a commercial digital imaging business in Manhattan that I had to shut down in 2003 due to technological changes in the photo industry. Film had become a dinosaur as the world went digital. Aline and I had gotten married in 1999 and we experienced a most generous and welcomed gesture from a lifelong friend of mine, at the time, the business was tanking or "un-developing" fast!

Michael L. Brown, of M L Brown, Inc. a diamond dealer located on 47th Street, for nearly 47 years, came through when I needed a friend. Friends had become scarce as my financial fortunes plunged. Shouldn't that be the other way around? Friends should be there when you need them most but that's just not the way it works.

We all know the saying, "You'll find out who your friends are when you're "broke" or sick." At the time I was none of the above, but I let 'em think what they "thunk" duh. Financially the picture looked very bleak but I wasn't out of gas, yet. For me, the situation was just another opportunity to start over again and enjoy "the climb" certainly, not my first. Michael had expressed his confidence in me by deed not merely with words. Sure, we all know that for him his was a business but this guy is all stars and stripes. He's a big "stand-up guy!"

Our first wedding anniversary was a home run out of the park, or should I say stadium? We had a blast. Just prior to our anniversary I had asked Aline if she would like a "tennis bracelet" as an anniversary gift. Her answer,

"I don't even know what it is!"

A woman of France, Parisian, dripping with class, verve, style, brains and presence, direct from the continent, Euro-style, the envy of American women who try to duplicate but seldom succeed. She didn't even know what a tennis bracelet was! To me, that was class.

I had decided to give her one; a perfect fit for a New City, New York sweet sixteen over indulged child. The bracelet was just the right size for an eager pandered little brat, an offering from parents who would have been so proud that their "generosity" provided their daughter with the largest tennis bracelet received by her peers in their over self-indulged community thus far. It would be a token, a symbol of affluence, success but not good judgment or love. It's all a stupid game and we all knew it, even the girls did too. God forbid your daughter's tennis bracelet was among the smallest. You'd be in deep shit! What a shame.

"Look what we gave Laurie for her sweet sixteen!" Not an appropriate gift for a child but for striving New City parents, and other similar suburban ghettos, it would be perfect!

"Is it bigger than Rachael's and Samantha's!" Lucky little spoiled imp! Just wait till life kicks in!

Well, "my child" Aline, loved it and I was very pleased. A year had passed and my business fortunes continued to falter. The one-hour photo business floundered, and together we were faced with our second wedding anniversary. How difficult and frustrating it would be for me to disappoint her on that occasion. I wouldn't let it happen. She didn't deserve that. My friend, Michael, "on the street" just might be able to rescue me.

Aline had offered me comfort by suggesting that, as for her gift, I should take the tennis bracelet back to Michael to remove the link whose stone had gone missing.

"Don't replace the missing stone, but rather remove the link" she had suggested impishly.

She was never demanding or seeking gifts. She asked for nothing and encouraged me not to shed a dime. I wasn't surprised but touched and frustrated that she had perceived me as unable to provide what I wanted her to have, something appropriate and well deserved, a bracelet bigger then even "Rachael's" of New City, New York and similar places!

I took her "sweet sixteen New City tennis bracelet" back to Michael. He was aware that I had filed Chapter 11 in bankruptcy court on behalf of my business and that I'd been in much better financial shape in the past. He was also confident that I would, before long, get back on my feet.

I told Michael that I had appeared at his store to satisfy Aline's unspoken wishes for our second anniversary. He was reminded that I had purchased a "starter" tennis bracelet for Aline the year before. I removed it from my pocket and told him that she had wanted a link removed, the one that was missing a diamond.

"No! Don't replace the diamond, eliminate the link!"
I had asked him.
Then I went on to say,

"Hey Michael, listen to me. I have a few bucks in my pocket. If I merge this money with the bracelet·can I move this Chevy up to a Buick, meaning something a bit larger?"

He went to his safe and removed a tennis bracelet and placed it on a black velvet pad on the counter in front of me. To me, it had appeared to be a joke. It was huge, not a sweet sixteen piece, but one fit for a pretentious Parisian import or even a Princess.

"Whoooohaaa! Michael! What? Are you kidding? This is a major piece! Don't feel sorry for me. We'll survive and I don't want you to consider me a charity!"

"Cliff, I know what you're going through, been there, done that. I got through it and you will too. When you get back on your feet, just stop by and give me another $2,000. I will never call you or ask you for the money. I know you'll come through."

I left 47th Street with a tennis bracelet that was quite nice! It was large, dazzling and impressive. I couldn't imagine the look on Aline's face when she'd see it! It would definitely blow her away. It would even be a ·hit for the mother my fictitious little drip "Rachael!"

I entered our apartment and got dressed for the evening. Aline was ready to go, painted nicely and scented like a rose bush. She was a doll, a living doll. As we got ready to make our departure I told her,

"Oh sweetie! Here I almost forgot to give you back your bracelet. Hold out your hand and let me pour it into your palm."

Out of the black velvet pouch that she had, a few hours earlier, placed the "starter bracelet" I poured the new bracelet into her open hand.

The look on her face was pure magic. Her eyes widened and her expression was indescribable.

110

"Where did you get that?"

"Michael!"

"Where'd you get the money from?"

"Eh, stop askin' questions. It's your Chapter 11 bracelet, *capisce!*"

It took about three years for me to finally get back on my feet. True to his word, Michael never called me for the money and I stayed away from 10 West 47th Street, as I was too embarrassed to make a cashless appearance. Aline loves the bracelet. Now she knew what a tennis bracelet was, ah "The Americanization of Aline!"

The payback day had arrived. I walked into Michael's store, and he looked the same; tan, tall, big and handsome. I placed the cash on the counter; he looked at me, smiled and whispered in my ear,

"I never had a doubt."

It Takes a Key For a "Village" a duh!

We were all tired, stressed, encapsulated in our own worlds. We were exhausted from the pressures of the day, each of us were enveloped within our inner cocoons. No one was talking and we made no eye contact. The roar of the "C" train transported us uptown. We sped away from the pressures of our day, one collective mass of humanity, another workday in the big City, a herd of humanity longing to open their own front doors and enter the world of "home" where relaxation would be mixed with recollections of the day. We all anticipated slipping away and entering the world of relief, family, relative quiet and peace.

Suddenly, the train came to an abrupt halt without and without warning in between the 81st and 86th Street stations.

"Oh shit! What's going on?" At first it was a non-event for seasoned New York City "strap hangers" only slightly startling and potentially very inconvenient.

"There's a medical emergency in the train ahead of us. We are stopped until the emergency is cleared. The first car of this train has entered the 86th Street station. If you want to exit the train, please walk to the front car and you will be able to enter the station and leave," barked the conductor.

Well, just about everyone, out of good sense, had decided to depart through the 86th Street station. New Yorkers are smart people, most of the time, that's why several hundred people walked forward, from car to car, toward the front car, including me. When I reached the third car I had noticed that it was packed solid. Upon pushing my way up to the front of that car I had realized that the logjam was due to the front door of the third car being locked!

Immediately, I worked my way back, through the crowd to the fifth car where the door conductor, who had made the announcement, could be found.

"Hey sir! The door at the front of the third car is locked!" I told him.

"Okay, let's go." he said.

Conductors have all the keys. That's a given.

Following closely behind the conductor, similar to, what we all do in vehicular traffic behind ambulances or emergency vehicles to beat everyone else, I weaved my way directly behind the conductor and we passed through the mob and entered the third car. He inserted his key into the lock and opened the door. I was the first person through the portal. Those who had been in the first and second cars were long gone. On to the second and out of the first car I entered the station and bolted up the stairs to the street into the open air leaving the chaotic scene behind.

It was a cold blustery December day. I quickly wrapped my scarf around my neck, buttoned up my coat and put on my gloves. It was good to be outside and above the underworld, safely on the sidewalk.

"Hey! Whas uppa witch you? You hadda be the firs' one outta da train, man! Whas so special 'bout you man?" shouted a fellow passenger.

"Good for you guy. You got out, number one and aren't you somethin'?" yelled another schmuck.

Both comments rang through my ears as I was already buttoned up and off to my final destination, home, on foot. The shouts confirmed exactly where I was, New York City!

"Well, thanks folks. Just to let you know, I'm the guy who got the conductor with the key to unlock the door so that we could all get out of there. That's why

we're here and not there! Merry Christmas!" I
shouted.
"Hey, yeah! You too, sorry guy, Merry Christmas to
you too!"
The other guy just walked away and disappeared into
the crowd.

"Going Postal"

"If it fits, it ships." This mantra brought to you by the U.S. Postal Dis-Service promotes its Priority Mail service. But, not all postal employees know that. Or, if they do, some of them just don't "fit." Here's the mind-blowing story:

Recently, I have been using Priority Mail Service to send copies of my books to various clients as an expression of appreciation as well as a means to promote Custom & Private New York Tours, Inc. Priority mail provides an excellent low cost service, far less costly then UPS or Federal Express. The post office provides a standard envelope large enough to hold a book with a fixed rate of $5.60. It is truly a bargain. If the package weights more than 13 ounces then the package must be handled "over the counter" in order for a postal clerk to "verify" that there are no dangerous liquids, radioactive materials, drugs, weapons, blood, alcohol, used "depends", condoms, Q-tips, box cutters, razor blades or hand-grenades enclosed. That must be a Patriot Act requirement with a dose of bureaucratic ass covering abuse of power.

What I don't understand is this: How will such a regulation prevent a terrorist from putting anything they want to in a mailbox? How would that regulation prevent it? That's like a bank putting up a sign that reads, "No guns or robbers, please!" Or a convenience store posting a notice, "Only unarmed robberies permitted!" Duh!

As a result of this regulation, rather then dropping my Priority Mail into mailboxes, I frequently have to stand on long slow moving lines and confront a clerk, to answer the usual questions, wait for them to stamp the envelope with an official stamp indicating that this piece of mail has passed the muster of a postal employee. Only then, does the article ship, maybe.

Normally, I can tolerate the slow moving lines and clerks, some who even do their jobs fairly well although, without a drop of enthusiasm, absent of any gesture of appreciation and below "par for the course" is customary and usual, as usual "service"!

Recently, I went to four post offices, in a single day, to mail five priority envelopes. The first one had lines practically out the door; the second I shall expand on in a bit, the third also had endless lines and the fourth had enabled me to finally get the job done. Let's back up to case number two.

I was so happy when I entered the Columbus Circle branch of the U. S. Postal Dis-Service. There were no lines! Strange. Perhaps people had stopped using that branch for reasons that I was about to find out. So here's the equation: If a branch of the Postal Dis-Service has long lines then the service may be okay and if the lines are short than maybe the service sucks.

The clerk greeted me well enough. I responded in kind. I placed the five Priority Mail envelopes on the counter, all firmly closed, clearly addressed, proper postage affixed and the contents "fit" therefore; "it ships." Good to go! Wrong!

She leaned down, beneath the counter and pulled out an 8 ½ x 11 white sheet of paper covered with an acetate sleeve. The acetate was well worn. Apparently this was not the first time she had snatched it from beneath the counter. It illustrated, in black ink, two Priority Mail envelopes; one was thick, stuffed, but sealed and the other was thin, also sealed. Along side

116

the illustration of the stuffed envelope it read "No" and along side the thin envelope it read "Yes."

"I don't understand. What does this mean?" I asked her.

She starred, void of expression, at me and said nothing. I repeated myself.

"I don't understand. What does this mean?'"

She continued to stare at me, speechless! She seemed to enjoy the power of her silence. This was her routine, her mission. To piss-off customers and get back at them, retribution for her perception of her life as a looser.

"'It if it fits, it ships,'" I said.

"Are you going to answer my question? Or, are you just going to sit there and hold up that sheet?" I said.

By this time I was quite annoyed, an understatement. Then I let her have it.

"You're a waste! You intolerable, despicable and rotten creep! You are here and overpaid to serve customers, not ply your arrogant and nasty stinking attitude. Who the hell do you think you are? I hope that you and the post office become things of the past and you get tossed on the street where you belong!"

Suddenly she shoved herself off her stool ran to the rear of the store, presumably into the back office area. Not knowing whether or not there was a Postal Police Officer back there, not knowing whether she was having an affair with him, not knowing whether or not she was a liar, I decided to make tracks and get the hell out of there in a hurry taking my five priorities with me.

I could imagine her telling a Postal Police Officer that I had threatened her and the assumed officer may have had the authority to cuff me, a show of machismo that would have surely impressed her and paid off dividends for him as well, maybe.

I jumped into my waiting car and told the chauffeur to hit the gas and get us out of there.

Later that afternoon, after our tour, we pulled up at the Roosevelt Station Post Office on Third Avenue and that didn't work either, the lines were huge. The Rockefeller Station Post Office turned out to be the solution.

There were roving customer service postal workers who "worked" the lines at The Rockefeller Station Post Office providing polite assistance to customers who had questions about the services they were seeking. I asked one of them if there was a problem with my Priority envelopes as I showed them to her.

"No, why?" she inquired.

I told her the story and she shook her head in amazement.

I stepped up to the window, received polite and professional service and left the post office, accomplishing what I had tried to do throughout the day. The window clerk even fastened scotch tape upon the envelope seal to further insure "safe passage" to those designated recipients.

The Postal Service is filled with arrogant, angry and useless employees who abuse the public, think they have their jobs due to a birthright. A powerful union throws its weight around and a cushy "cradle to the grave" secure income mindset snarls the post office staff from providing good service.

I never heard an expression; "I'm going UPS!" or "I'm going Federal Express?" No, it's "I'm going postal." I know why and so do you.

Guess what postal "workers." Your golden "umbrella" is broken. That's because you and others just like you have been the best salesmen for Federal Express and UPS. You have driven hoards of people away from, what once was a good and valuable service. Now, it's a horror to go to the post office. You have become likened to the motor vehicle bureau, Social Security Administration, Taxi & Limousine Commission, City of New York Department of Consumer Affairs and all those government bureaucratic agencies that exist to do you a favor, the tax payer, the customer. They're not part of the private sector answering to stockholders and managers who report to higher ups and push hard to increase the bottom line. To you, the takers, the nasty flim-flamers who take your jobs for granted are biding your time and biting the hand that feeds you. Someday that hand will be out of reach and fade into the distant past. You needn't apply for a job at Fed-x or UPS. You're toast!

It is not impossible to turn this around, but it is quite unlikely that it will ever happen. I sincerely hope that the Postal Dis-Service will die and be replaced by a private company; perhaps UPS or Federal Express to take up the slack and hire people who value their jobs, work to increase customer satisfaction, improve service and generate profits for their stock holders. Is that really the American way? Oh yes, not all postal employees deserve this assessment. Quite a few are earning their money and we do salute them.

Congress! What's that? They don't have the balls to close post offices in their districts or states. Way to go. Each representative or Senator cares only about their constituents and the entire country can go down the tubes, and with that attitude it just might.

"Neither snow, nor rain, nor neat, nor gloom of night, stays these couriers from the swift completion of their appointed rounds." Perhaps this would be better:

"Neither kind nor efficient, but rude and crude, without haste with waste, a frown and a pout are more aptly just what they're all about."

I can't wait to see 'em all on line applying for unemployment benefits and food stamps. If they get the benefits then good luck to them waiting for the U.S. Postal Dis-service to deliver their checks.

"Return to sender, address unknown." Serves you right baby!

The Right Prescription at the Wrong Price

Every now and then we all experience unpleasant surprises. It happens! From out of nowhere we may notice a rash, a bulge, a mysterious lump or a discoloration on our bodies. When that happens we all get that nauseous sense of dread knowing that, this time, something is wrong, maybe terribly wrong. Our worst fears "kick in" and we become anguished that this could be something bad, very bad. Oh no, not "The Big C" that's our worst fear.

Recently, I had acquired a "condition" of yellowing toenails and, as always, I ran to a doctor to take care of it right away. Over the years, I've learned that it's best to take care of such things immediately and not push them under the rug.

I made an appointment with a dermatologist to address my newest mysterious, villainous and uninvited invader. She, the doctor, was a "Board Certified Dermatologist" whose practice was located in midtown on West 57th Street.

My first appearance to her impressive office, filled with all the latest issues of Vanity Fair, The Economist and The New Yorker and not the usual 21 Highlights for children, issues dated from the stone age nor the pile of The Dermatologists Review or other periodicals that are of no interest to patients; pabulum for the masses revealing that the office manager, directed by the doctors who run the place are cheap bastards who know nothing about life outside the medical world!

After my examination had been completed she, my current dermatologist, gave me several tubes of topical gel to treat my nail fungus. The medication was known as Xolegel whose active ingredient was

121

ketoconazole, a Gel, 2% containing 2 grams of medication. The doctor wrote a prescription for me for more of the same and her assistant called the local pharmacy to fill the order.

After a few hours I received a phone call from the pharmacist telling me that the prescription would cost me $500!

"What! Are you kidding? Are you sure?" I asked.

"Yep, that's right. That's why I called you. Do you want me to fill it?

"I'll get right back to you. Glad you called before you filled it."

I got on the phone with the doctor and asked her if she was aware of the cost of the prescription. She claimed that she was not, pure 100% bullshit! Then, I asked her if there was anything else that she could suggest to remedy my ailment. She told me that there's another form of the active ingredient that I might want try instead. I asked her what the difference was and she told me the other form of medication was not gel based, rather it was cream based. She informed me that the gel would stick to the effected area much better. That's why she had prescribed that in the first place she told me.

My question to her was: Couldn't I apply the cream based formula on the effected area three times a day instead of twice to provide the same efficacy as the gal. She told me yes, absolutely. She called in the cream based formula to my pharmacy with a request to have them call me before they filled it so that I would be aware of the cost.

Shortly thereafter I received a phone call from my pharmacist who revealed that the cream based prescription was free, paid in full by Medicare, up to

60 grams. The free sample of the gel that my doctor gave me at her office· was 6 grams, a gesture of "kindness."

Here's the "real deal" and I have no doubt that you know what's coming. Apparently, the pharmaceutical company that manufactures the gel, Aqua Pharmaceuticals of West Chester, PA 19380 must be providing those samples to dermatologists encouraging them, for what consideration I do not know, to write prescriptions for their patients. Why? Because it is a business!

But, what kind of business is it? Is it a business that sells a product that is so terrific and superior that the "stupid public" their perspective, should fork over $500 to get their healing miracle. Are they the only game in town? Are they aware that there is an alternative medication in the marketplace that would cost someone who is on Medicare, nothing? Do they care? Is it ethical? Is it legal? Where is our healthcare system that allows this rip-off?

I was very pleased that Medicare does not subsidize such nonsense and I was driven to the free cream based product that probably costs Medicare practically nothing. And, why could, would, should a gel-based product cost $500!

The most vicious and disappointing part of the entire episode is the doctor's deliberate and intentional attempt to "screw" me through her participation in a ripping me scheme! I'm her patient. I'm her customer. She knew that her prescription would remove hundreds of dollars from my pocket and that didn't mean shit to her. She had apparently made her decision due to her benefit, whatever that might be, loyal to the pharmaceutical company rather than her patient. At the very least shouldn't I have been advised of my choices?

The health system in this country is a mess. These kinds of scams, and that's exactly what they are, cost every one of us a ton of money. If you have health insurance these abuses are built into the cost of your insurance premiums. If others who cannot afford insurance, those who pay nothing, their costs increase the cost of your health insurance. It's the drug companies, their marketing practices, your doctors and the pharmacists who all converge to pull your precious dollars out of your pockets, all of our pockets!!

Will "Obamacare" cure the problem? Who knows? Let's give it a shot unless someone has a better idea. In the meantime, let's get off this trolley and face the music, which is, unless we straighten this out, we, as a country, will face the worst fiscal disaster in our history and flush our currency down the toilet. Our cost of health care will crush us.

And for those who say, "I pay for my health insurance and I don't want to pay for anyone else's insurance" consider this: Should we let people die because they cannot afford health insurance? Should we turn our backs on them? What we should do is rein in the people who screw us with enormous fees for what we are entitled to and aspire for us to stay or get healthy. We must find a way for poor people or those who've lost their employee based health insurance to have the means to obtain preventive care. We need to take care of our dollars, others and ourselves and use our advances in medical technology to get this country up to the highest level of excellent medical care for every American efficiently.

The most gruesome and onerous policy has been that this country has turned its back on millions of people who have not been able to obtain health insurance. "Let 'em die." Is that their answer? To me, it seems to be and that's the lie that they have to face.

This is an urgent problem that we, as a country, have turned our backs on. It's time to give another solution a chance unless and until someone has a better way. Currently, this isn't working for "the people" but it sure works well for a dermatologist on west 57th Street.

The Butterfly Cut

Have you ever driven back to "The City" from The Hamptons on a summer Sunday evening? If not, then you're a most fortunate person, perhaps even very secure; one who has learned that impressing others with what you have is a function of showing others that you reveal yourself as an insecure person, a believer that self-indulgence so important to you or perhaps you just can't afford to play the "game" but try like hell.

It's shallow, immature and childish, right? Those who are impressed by your possessions are not worth impressing. Is that your brand? Is that who you are? Is that so important to you? If so, get off that trolley and figure out life. Get a real one!

Perhaps, the longest caravan on earth is the weekend trek to and from New York City to The Hamptons every weekend from Memorial to Labor Day weekend. Most of these die-hard show-offs are renters of expensive homes or condos for the summer fun and sun season; those who slip into their Porsches, Lexus, Mercedes, BMW's and the other very showy brands aka "the exotics." They ply their trek known as the LIE, The Long very long, Island Expressway, or Distressway to exit 70 or perhaps opt for the Northern or Southern State Parkway, "parking lots" a far better term to describe those "motorways" and the experiences that they provide.

You gotta leave Manhattan before 2 PM on Fridays to make the slog in less than three hours; four if your destination is East Hampton and five if it's Montauk. Some smart folks opt for the Jitney or the Long Island Railroad. Some of those at the top 1% of the wealth spectrum take a chopper and have no worries about traffic, just rapid impact, a real downer.

The voyage begins on a Friday, most often, and the reverse journey back to "The City" is typically on Sunday or if you can get away with it, Mondays after 11 AM is a beautiful thing, ouch!

All this schlepping generates the guaranteed argument that usually ends with complaints as to your choice of the route you've taken, recollections about how lousy the weather was, your restaurant choices were big disappointments too and overpriced and the boring conversations with the same people, or person, that you were with the previous weekends will ring in your ears during the work week.

The $100,000 plus car that you are driving will not alleviate the stress. The music, GPS, Bluetooth, wi-fi air-conditioning and leather seating will not help you. When you shut your motor off after a five-hour jaunt back to your Manhattan apartment and grasp a very tall drink to "chill out" then, the euphoric sense of relief you were seeking in The Glorious Hamptons may kick in as a distant blur. At least you were there! It's like going to the gym. You feel great after you've left.

"I went to The Hamptons this weekend!"

Being seen by others who couldn't care less if you were seen or not is the craziest game. It's the "I don't want to miss anything" syndrome. There's the fear and panic that you may be seen in The City on a summer weekend and perceived by others as a "looser." What a bunch of shit that is! The losers are the ones that venture out there and the winners are those who remain in Manhattan. They have Manhattan all to themselves!

Years ago, on a Sunday evening, after a very long and stressful drive back to Manhattan with a "lady friend" who had spent the weekend with me in The Hamptons, we had agreed to enjoy what we had hoped would be a delightful dinner at Smith and Wollensky's, an upscale steak and lobster restaurant on 3rd Avenue in midtown. I've been there a number of times and the venue always had been terrific. The food, service and the standard steakhouse testosterone atmosphere topped off the setting.

We were starving! We hadn't eaten since breakfast and skipped lunch because we didn't want to eat the junk that's sold along the highway, fast food "*crapola*". Since we wanted to get back to "The City" we stopped only for gas and "to go potty" and we just kept moving along at a snail's pace until we pulled up at Smith and Wollensky's.

The restaurant was very busy, as usual. After the customary and usual welcome we were seated, ordered a bottle of red wine and a filet mignon, medium rare and a few sides.

The wine was terrific and together with a warm welcome we fell into a state of relaxation and calm. We patiently awaited the arrival of our main attraction, a delicious steak with the perfect compliments.

Viola, the waiter arrived with our main course however something was wrong, very! The filet had been butterfly cut! Butterfly cut means cutting the steak horizontally, in the kitchen before the meat is broiled. This technique results in a steak that does not have a pink center but rather is medium-to-medium well done. The succulent juices and flavor are lost. That is not what we had ordered and if the chef was going to butterfly cut the steak, then he surely knew that it was impossible to prepare the steak medium rare. In addition, we should have been asked if we had wanted our steak butterfly cut. Even though we were going to share the filet it made no sense for the waiter to ask if we wanted the steak cut. The proper way to share a medium rare filet is to cut the meat in half vertically, after it's broiled.

I told the waiter that this was not what I had ordered and I requested that he bring us the right stuff. He went to get the "manager" and then the shit hit the fan.

"I ordered the filet medium rare and this clearly is not. The steak was butterfly cut in the kitchen and it's overcooked. Please serve what was ordered and take this back!"

She told me that she would not replace the steak and that "is" what we had ordered!

"Look lady! I don't know where you're from or what your policy is but mine is that we get what I ordered. We will wait a reasonable period of time until we get what we ordered. If not, I will stand up and in an extremely loud voice, I shall tell all who are present exactly what you are doing! I'm not kidding! Now, bring me what we ordered!"

How stupid! What would have been the "BFD" to accommodate a customer with a most reasonable request? What would it have cost them? This was not Tony's Diner in the south Bronx! Even if it were, Tony would not have made that stupid mistake and if he had I would have gotten an apology and a rare filet!

Our table became encircled by a number of other staff members who were attempting to calm me down and convince me to accept what they had put in front of us. My lady friend sat quietly and had expressed her amazement with the stupidity of the restaurant manager, who we had learned was on the job for about a week!

We continued to sip our wine and wait. The side dishes never arrived and neither did the steak. After waiting approximately fifteen minutes it had become apparent that the redo would never arrive. Therefore, I made good my threat.

"May I please have your attention? This restaurant did not provide what we had ordered and they refused to replace an over-cooked filet mignon which they had stupidly butterfly cut. I requested that they serve the medium rare order and they refused to rectify their mistake!"

Suddenly, a big guy, who worked for the restaurant grabbed my arm as if he was preparing to throw me out of the restaurant.

"Get your fucking hands off me! I'll have you arrested for assault you stupid fucking gorilla!"

He removed his grip on my arm and told me that he was going to call the cops.

"Call 'em you putz! You're the one they're going to arrest!" I shouted at him.

The room was totally silent. People in the restaurant were whispering about the incident one that certainly did not enhance the reputation of the restaurant.

The manager and her war party departed from the room and were most likely planning their next move. We finished the bottle, stood up and walked out without paying. I left a twenty-dollar bill for the waiter.

The following day I called the restaurant's main office, and I explained the incident to an officer of the

company who was in charge of "customer service."
After I ·had explained the entire incident she
graciously offered to "buy me a drink" the next time I
dined at one of their restaurants.

"That's it?" I replied.

"Well sir, what do you expect?" she said.

"I can see that your management is clueless to say the
least. You can be sure that every person I meet who
has ever been to any of your restaurants or plans to
go will hear about my experience. I have never
experienced anything so incredibly stupid in a fine
New York City restaurant."

Even in New York City stupidity happens. I still, to
this day, nearly fifteen years since that incident
cannot believe it.

Looking for a great steak in New York City, Keen's at
72 West 36th Street. That's the place to go! Bon
appetite! Teddy Roosevelt and Albert Einstein ate
there and they were pretty smart. Yeah!

Outa Sight and Outa Mind

She was one of my best customers, a wheel-chaired woman, legally blind and suffering from multiple sclerosis. Her name, Whinny Wolf and she was dumb like a fox. This fortyish, thin, longhaired woman had a pretty face and a very offbeat sense of humor. Most of all, she was a fantastic photographer, in a sense, seeing more then those with perfect vision. Yes, she was a photographer!

I was always glad to see Whinny as she wheeled into my flagship one-hour photo store on West 23rd Street back in the 1990's. We always laughed when I welcomed her, "See me when your life is on a roll!" I used to tell her that, evoking laughter.

Clicks, the largest one-hour photo store in the City, offered her everything that she had wanted from Black & White one-hour photo services, the only one in the City, to specialty items, posters, tee-shirts, puzzles, laser copies and Photostats. She had become a "regular" always getting the "red carpet" treatment, excessive discounts and the most attentive service on the planet. She was treated like a queen and all my employees knew she was truly a special lady. At times she was a bit of a pain in the ass but who could blame her, poor gal.

When I launched New York City's only one-hour black and white service I had asked her if I could use approximately fifteen of her black and white photos for promotional purposes. She had literally thousands of photographs that she had taken over the years of the streets of "The City." They were stored in her little apartment in the residence for the blind just a block from Clicks. I wanted to create a window display showing her work, photographs depicting people

132

working, playing, talking, walking and just engaging each other in "The City" each consisting of at least one black and one white person in every photograph. She agreed to participate and I was invited to go to her apartment to make my selections.

Together we sorted though mountains of 8 x 10 black and white photographs searching for the best interracial shots that we could find. She unearthed dozens of suitable images and we narrowed them down to about fifteen. I brought them back to Clicks and one of my printers copied and enlarged them. We produced an amusing and effective window display with the headline "New York is a Black & White Town." She was paid $300 for her contribution, the price that she had requested. The new black & white one-hour service was a smashing success and her contribution was a big part of it. We both looked back on the experience as a wonderful joint venture and we continued to enjoy our wonderful relationship.

Whinny continued to have her photographs exhibited all over the City with rave reviews. She saw things that most people never did. She had an incredible creative bend, combined objects in her photographs, expressing her sentiments through her lens and conceived of views and angles that departed from the ordinary. She was truly a genius and spending time with her was always fun and exciting. What an inspiration!

She came into Clicks on one subsequent occasion to ask me for a favor. She wanted me to provide a contribution to help her fund the rental of a helicopter for an hour to photograph The Flatiron Building. She had conceived of a shot from above, approximately 1,000 feet above ground, to be taken from above the front of the building in order to capture the building with both sides. There is virtually no front of the building because it's triangular.

It was brilliant. To our knowledge this had never been done before and I wanted to participate. I offered to pay for the entire project and I told her that I wanted to come along.

We met at Clicks and together with her motorized scooter we took two buses to The Hudson River Heliport. We boarded the 'chopper, a tiny two-seater with a plastic bubble and no doors. (Check out the photo in the center of the book) She sat in the middle next to the pilot and I was belted on the windowless edge of the seat. It was a very tight squeeze and I was practically hanging out of the whirlybird. My seat belt gave me the courage. This is definitely not for everyone!

Liftoff! We literally had a bird's eye view of "The City." With the noise and shakes of the little bird we topped The Empire State Building, The Pan Am Building, The Chrysler, Rockefeller Center and Midtown. We flew over Queens taking in spectacular views of Manhattan. Wow! It was truly phenomenal. Our pilot vectored the 'chopper in the direction of "The Flatiron" and we arrived at the intended spot for the shoot.

One of Whinny's hands was atrophied and although she was able to steady her camera with her right hand she was unable to press the shutter with the left. On her command, I depressed the shutter button for her repeatedly. After her first roll of film had been taken she switched cameras and we completed the roll in her other 35mm SLR. Then I pointed my camera and took several shots and we returned to the heliport.

We got back to Clicks the same way, a long laborious trip. Our film was promptly developed and printed, with much anticipation. To my surprise, she had failed to capture the image that had she pined for, one showing both sides of the building in symmetry. But, I had gotten the shot. She was extremely disappointed that I got the shot and not she. I suspected that she would have been happier if neither of us succeeded. She was exceptionally distraught. I suggested that we share the image and that we agree to an arrangement that would govern the "ownership" of the image.

She emphasized that it was her idea and therefore she had ownership rights. It was a bit shocking, selfish and overly aggressive. Sure, it was her idea but I had captured the image and paid for the 'chopper. She had suggested that we copyright the image in Washington, D. C. and name the image "Flatiron 'chopter 1" and that we further agree that if either of us makes any money through the sale of the image then we would split it down the middle. I agreed. We filled out the application for the copyright; she had all the forms with her! Together with my check for $25, of course, I send the application to Washington, D. C.

Several months thereafter the copyright was received and I called her. I put a copy of it in her hands and we co-owned the image, legally. There was no intention, on my part, to make money off of this, as I was not in business of selling my images. My business was developing and printing my customer's images.

Sometime shortly thereafter, I used the Flatiron image to feature a poster promotion. The promotion offered 20 x 30 inch color posters from your favorite

135

negative, print or transparency at a reduced price. Customers were drawn to the Flatiron image and asked if they could buy a copy. I did not offer the image for sale. It was merely an attention getter and it helped promote my poster service. That was it.

Several weeks after the Flatiron poster had been on display at Clicks I received a letter, at home, from a law firm that was unknown to me. It was located on Madison Avenue and had a very prestigious address. I didn't have a clue what to expect but I smelled trouble. Unsolicited letters from lawyers seldom bring happiness or good news.

In effect, the letter "put me on notice" that I was in violation of a verbal agreement between Whinny Wolf and me, "to wit" that I had used the image to display a service at Clicks, thereby, using it as a "tool, device and/or asset" for "unjust enrichment." Although I was not selling the image, the letter went on, that essentially, I was using the image, "co-owned by the parties" to make money and therefore, I was in violation of our verbal agreement. Whinny was digging for money, pure and simple.

The lawyer's letter put me on further notice that I was liable, under the law, for up to $40,000 in damages. She knew that I had money, at the time, and I was standing squarely on the M word, money.

Several days later I received another envelope in the mail, this time with her home return address on the face of the envelope. My name and address were scrawled on the envelope, in a handwriting that could only have been written by a young child or an adult with motor movement challenges. Within, was her check for $350 reimbursing me for the full cost of the helicopter rental fee.

Apparently, her lawyer had suggested that she reimburse me thereby removing my "consideration" in the project and nullifying any counter claim that I might have perused against her.

That was a cheap ploy engineered by a lawyer designed to mislead her into thinking that would enhance her position, if she decided to take me to court. In the meantime, it's "billable hours" for the lawyer. Knowing what she was attempting to accomplish I ripped the check into pieces. That took care of everything except two matters of significance.

First, this entire episode resulted in the destruction of what had been a mutually beneficial relationship. This had caused me considerable anguish and disappointment.

Second, I banned her from entering my stores ever again.

There is no happy ending here. What amazes me is this:

Many people's intentions are purely money driven, even if they are "artists." Never mind the friendship, the relationship and the benefit that two people bring to the table for each other over a period of many years. It all came down to her trashing all of that to go for the bucks. Basically, she accepted my offer to pay for the entire project, expressed full ownership of the image, attempted to reap a pile of money due to her attorney's action knowing that it would destroy our relationship. She bit the hand that fed her and exposed herself as a fraud.

"Oh, Cliff! Thank you so much for paying for the helicopter, it's so nice of you."

Miss Wolf was definitely a fox!

Apparently, the value of our relationship was not as important to her as it had been to me. For me there was absolutely not one cent of financial gain in the equation. If she honestly had believed that I was violating our agreement then why didn't she just tell me and discuss it? We all know the answer. It wouldn't have created a possibility of the pile of dollars that she had hoped for.

Loss of hope and a sense of self-pity were never part of what I had experienced between November 2006 and February 2007. Aline and I had returned to New York City from a fifteen-month stint in Miami, Florida. I had been advised to flee "The City" and "get out of town" by the bankruptcy attorney that I had hired to put my business, Clicks, through Chapter 11, due to the sudden death of the one-hour photo industry and my acceptance of the reality that attempting to continue the operation was out of the question.

I had been in the one-hour photo business in Manhattan for many years and together with my digital imaging business I was advised that bankruptcy was the best way to put a dying business to rest. Sudden technological changes had altered the way people captured images. Film had become a dinosaur and digital was the new rage. Knowing that "the next big thing" was here, I had prepared myself and was resigned that my photo labs, laden with huge monthly lease payments, enormous rents and various other fixed obligations was facing the "bitter end." A business that I had built over nearly a lifetime, shattered.

All things come to an end. I followed my lawyer's advice and Aline and I packed our bags, "ran" down to Miami hoping to find a way to carve out our lives anew.

Miami was not the solution for the future, but it was part of the solution to dispose of the ruins of the past. My attorney worked his way through the Chapter 11 and finally, according to our plan, he got all of the players lined up. It was a brilliant and fascinating experience for me due to a strategy that my attorney and I formulated that turned the tide. It was a strategy that had the creditors pleading with us to · execute our scenario one that would provide them with significant funds to settle the debt. We took control and prevailed.

Aline and I made all the necessary arrangements to return to New York City and we were ecstatic with the prospect of returning back "home." The only necessary arrangement that was not made was, how we were going to "make it."

We made our new home in a small rental apartment on West 60th Street. Only the rent was large. Aline got a job in retail sales, commission only. I started looking for a business one that we could afford, one that we could operate together and build a future. All the businesses we had found seemed attractive but ultimately they all had a fatal flaw. I was in denial. Why would someone sell a business without a fatal flaw? People lie and omit. Our research proved that time and time again. "I'm selling due to family illness" or "I want to retire" or "I have other obligations or opportunities." It was all bullshit, time after time.

The final straw was the rejection of our application to purchase a gourmet coffee shop off of Fifth Avenue.

Stroke of Luck #1

The Coop Board of the building where the coffee shop had been located had sent us packing. **Our application had been rejected.** For us, purchasing that business was now completely out of the question. We were devastated. We were back in the abyss, terribly frightened and dismayed.

I stopped looking for a business and perused an opportunity to sell mortgages in New Jersey working for a guy who was one hell of a terrific salesman and team builder. Jimmy showed me the ropes and trained me. I made some money with him until he disappointed Aline and me when we had sought his help for a mortgage to purchase a condo in Manhattan. We had our backs to the wall, facing a rejection from the bank and a threat that the seller was prepared to retain our deposit if we had failed to obtain the mortgage. I had tried to reach Jimmy while he had gone fishing in Montana with his son. My calls went unanswered. Apparently, he too didn't give a shit. Our real estate agent put me in touch with another mortgage broker who ultimately succeeded in getting us the mortgage and he saved us from loosing our $81,000 down payment.

We moved into the condo in August of 2006, a delightful little place on Central Park West. It was a terrific location and we were excited about living on the fabled, Central Park West!

The condo purchase had dried up most of our money but fortunately Aline was doing very well in retail sales and I was out there trying to sell mortgages for the mortgage broker, Alan, who had gotten us the mortgage.

Stroke of Luck #2

After approximately six weeks, working for Alan, I showed up at the office one morning and it had been shut down, closed! It took about two weeks before I found out what the hell had happened. Alan surfaced and called me. He had revealed that **his partner was under investigation** for some white-collar crime. It was illegal kickbacks to obtain legal work and, as a result, their license to sell mortgages had been pulled by The State of New York.

I was nowhere. Where do I go from here? The money that was going to be used to purchase a business had been spent on the condo down payment. At least Aline was bringing in nearly enough money to keep us going, that is, until the money that remained would run out.

Stroke of Luck #3

Shortly after my mortgage career came to a sudden end, **Aline broke her foot**. It didn't seem like luck at the time when she had slipped on the crosstown bus on her way home from work. She hobbled home knowing that there was some damage but she did not suspect that it had been a break. While I was out with a friend her call came as she was making her way home on foot. She was devastated, not only because of the injury itself, but because she knew that she wouldn't be able to work and all of our income, at the time, was totally crushed.

This drove her into a terrible state of depression. She became fearful that we would run out of money, default on the mortgage and be out in the street, plunged into poverty. She was a wreck and I didn't know what to do. I needed an idea. Aline found one but I didn't like it one bit.

Stroke of Luck #4

"Why don't you **drive a black car?** Get your chauffeur's license and look for a driving job. You never know what can come from this. At least, you'll bring in some money. Even if it's $100 a day! At the end of every month it will pay some bills. It's better than sitting around the house and doing nothing!"

She was right. I had nothing better to do at that time and I couldn't think of a good reason why I shouldn't become a "wheel turner." It would be honest work and provide something for us and give me time to think and clear my head.

The next day I went to The Taxi & Limousine Commission in Long Island City and I began the arduous process of getting my TLC chauffeur's license. The process entailed changing my New York State Department of Motor Vehicle license to Class E, chauffeur, getting a copy of my Social Security card which I hadn't seen in thirty years, taking a safe driving course, urinating in a cup for drug testing, getting fingerprinted, filling out a myriad of forms, paying the fees and finally, within about a month, I received my coveted TLC license.

After a few weeks walking around Long Island City, where nearly all of the black car companies are located, I selected the best company I could find, or so I thought, and I became a black car driver.

My work day began at 4:30 AM six days a week; two subway trains got me to Queens and then a six block walk through the 'hood before sunrise reporting to the company garage or "base" as it was said. I was provided with a Lincoln Town Car or an SUV each day and off I went, a certified "wheel turner." I spent the next ten to twelve hours driving people back and forth to airports, New York hotels, meetings and waiting for the next "job." I parked in Manhattan and waited endlessly for the next job to drive into the persistent insane traffic, running into airport terminals, holding signs bearing my client's name, schlepping luggage in and out of car trunks and at day's end I returned to the base and then the six block walk, two subway trains back home and $100 to $125 richer, including tips. Whoopee! This was my "bill of fare" for four long, tiring, cold and frustrating months. One icy morning in January 2007 I was assigned to meet four people at 6 AM at a midtown hotel with their luggage and transfer them to Newark Airport. The vehicle was overloaded with luggage and the weight was far too much for a Lincoln Town car to handle. There was even one large suitcase wedged to my right blocking my view of the front seat passenger and my sightline to my right.

My passengers had told me that they had requested a van. Knowing that the dispatcher had willfully decided to assign the job to me, which, as a result, put us all in danger. It was apparent that this "best" company didn't give a shit about my safety or the safety of their clients. Again, it was all about the money.

Stroke of Luck #5

While driving down the New Jersey Turnpike the left rear tire blew out and the car suddenly started oscillating. The oscillation continued and intensified. The pavement was wet and icy. Eighteen-wheelers and coach buses were whizzing past us dousing the windshield with bursts of water making it extremely difficult for me to see the road ahead. There was no shoulder off the right side traffic lane. We were on the Eastern Spur is an elevated roadway with no shoulders. Even if there were shoulders it would have been impossible for me to see them due to the luggage wedged to my right. I turned on the safety flashers immediately and gently reduced our speed and within a mile or so **I was able to get the car off the traffic lane onto a patch of grass.** The shredded tire had made it extremely difficult for me to control the vehicle off the pavement. I had five lives in my hands, literally.

I placed a call to a Newark van service and they sent a vehicle that arrived shortly afterward to transfer my passengers and their luggage to Newark airport. These beauties failed to tip me for saving their lives! I wished them a safe trip and bit my lip and called the turnpike road service to change my tire and I headed back to the base.

My employer had refused to reimburse me $35, the cost of the New Jersey Turnpike road service. He told me that I should have changed the tire myself! I replied that at sixty years of age, in a freezing rainstorm, it was not my responsibility to do so and that he should "kiss my ass." I had rescued those passengers due to a situation the dispatcher had created no doubt in accordance with his company's culture or rather lack of it. Incredible!

I never returned to the "base" although I did get my $35 back that day because I had threatened to "blow the whistle" on them regarding their illegal business practices. That company and many others in the limo business in New York City, charge their clients tips that are never given to the chauffeurs. The customers think the tips are forwarded to the chauffeurs and as a result they do not, for the most part, tip. That's a wide spread practice in that industry and the TLC knows it. They're on the business owner's side, not

145

the chauffeur's. I wonder why? Hum. Blowing the whistle would have had the less effect then blowing my nose.

Subsequently, they had deducted the cost of car washes from my paycheck and withheld my security deposit of $250 for their Motorola hand-held radiophone for six weeks. When I had made my departure I had returned their radiophone. Bastards!

Stroke of Luck #6

I found another company and they were slightly better. Again, **I had a near death experience.** On one occasion I had met my customers on East 61st Street. While putting their luggage into the trunk of the car I was struck in the back of the head and my ankle by a couple of steel beams that fell as a sidewalk scaffold was being dismantled. I was thrown, face down, onto the street. Fortunately, I was okay although my ankle became very swollen and I was in a lot of pain as I drove this Eastside elderly couple to JFK.

They knew exactly what had happened to me and they didn't give a shit. Tip? Zero! I sued the scaffold company and got a few bucks and I turned out to be okay.

I continued to drive for company number two until I had decided that it was time to move on. Move on to what? I didn't have a clue. This driving thing was going nowhere but twice it had almost taken me straight to my grave. Had that happened I wondered if they would have provided the limos for my funeral *pro bono.*

"Friday is going to be my last day." I told Aline.

"This is not going anywhere. I've got to look for something else."

I knew that I'd find something because I've always found opportunities and with a positive attitude. I knew that this time would be different and much more challenging. There was no money left for us to buy a business. My industry, the photofinishing business, had morphed into oblivion, yeah, yeah, yeah. Everyone tells you that you'll be fine. But until it is, it's all words, just words. It was a long and lonely road and the end was nowhere in sight.

Aline agreed that moving on was a good idea. She was extremely supportive. Her advice and wisdom were good and valuable. All the demons and fears were still nested in our guts. We were reaching a "zero sum game" meaning money near zero. An uncertain future lay ahead of us without prospects in view.

Friday, my last day driving, was a day away. I felt that the entire experience was a nearly a complete waste. Perhaps if I had spent the time looking for other options I'd have found something worthwhile. At least Aline was back to work and I would become available once again to pursue other opportunities.

Stroke of Luck #7

The night before my last day of driving, I received a call from the dispatcher. He offered me a "job" for a mother and child, a ten-year-old boy named Matthew. My job was to provide a three-hour tour of Manhattan, something that I had never done before.

I was very excited about it. I knew the City quite well and viewed it through the mind of a ten year old who was about to tour New York City for the first time. I searched for ideas and sites to visit that would be of interest to him. My enthusiasm was building and I was looking forward to this experience enthusiastically, **my last driving job was a tour. Little did I know?**

We met at The Double Tree in Times Square at 10 AM. I found them waiting for me in front of the hotel and we all greeted with smiles and anticipation. I remember as if it were yesterday. Matthew gladly accepted my offer to sit in the front seat. He was "bright eyed and bushy tailed" full of energy and enthusiasm. His mother was seated behind him and it was apparent that she was excited for him too. It was all good.

The tour extended to eight hours! We all had a lot of fun, went for a ride on the subway, I drove them through Central Park, visited Grand Central Terminal and Dylan's Candy Bar and much more. Matt's mother bought him a toy at F.A.O. Schwarz and I clearly remember him showing me the toy. He told me that he was going to sell it when he grew up because by then it would be worth a lot of money. I remarked, "no, don't sell it. Keep it as a memento of this wonderful day that your mother provided for you."

I wish I had the same toy today as a reminder for me of what turned out to be my first tour.

Stroke of Luck #8

The following evening Aline and I had dinner with my son David and his wife, Melissa. I told them about the tour that I conducted the day before and how much fun it had been for me.

He remarked:

148

"Dad, don't you get it?"

"Don't I get what?"

"Get your sightseeing license, create a brand, build a website, dig in and learn the City as if you built it yourself, design brochures, visit hotels and run with the ball!"

The following morning, with application papers and documents in hand, I went down to the City of New York Department of Consumer Affairs and applied for my Sightseeing Guide license. As part of the application process there is a 150 question test that I hadn't even been aware of. The clerk told me that I would need to study because it was difficult. I took it anyway and succeeded to score so well that I earned a star along side my name on the New York City website, www.nyc.gov. I walked out of 42 Broadway with a new sense of hope and resolve that I was finally going to go into business again. Custom & Private New York Tours, Inc. was about to be born.

If our application to purchase a gourmet coffee shop had been approved, if Aline hadn't broken her foot, if Aline had not suggested that I drive, if I didn't steer out of a possible fatal accident, if the scaffold killed or injured me, if my last driving "job" had not been for a tour, the only tour driving "job" after a grueling four months and if David hadn't put the opportunity on the table then I would not have found this wonderful way out of my career troubles.

What's the moral of the story?

As Woody Allan has said, "95% of life is showing up."

Get out there, try something, look for opportunities, listen to others with an open mind, don't feel sorry for yourself, never give up, be high-spirited, find new ways to apply your talent, experience and abilities and give it all you've got.

Aline and I operate this tour business together. She too has acquired her sightseeing license and provides tours in French and English. Unlike many others in life, for us it's not "all about the money." It's about a passion, a love of New York City and a fervent desire to provide the most enjoyable and memorable tour experiences we can for our guests. No, it's not a job. It's a joy not only for us but, for all the licensed guides who work with us.

In seven years we have, together with our "partners" who speak over fourteen languages, provided over 2,000 private tours, one at a time, each special and uniquely targeting the wishes of our clients.

Oh yes, and finally, you do need a little luck in life, but, you must get out there. When you find your bliss give it your heart, body, soul and sweat. Life! It's the best tour I'll ever have.

Life On a Roll(s)

"If I had a Rolls Royce, I'd never get it washed. I'd ride around attracting lots of attention because everybody would be so amused by the sight of a filthy grubby Rolls Royce dripping with mud and bird splatter. They would think that I must be so incredibly rich because I didn't give a shit if that six figure beauty was rotting from acid rain and *schmutz!*"

At the age of thirteen I understood and appreciated my father's Rolls Royce fantasy as stated above. To me it was classic dad. My father's statement was so typical of him. He, my mentor, looked at life in so many obtuse ways, always drawing attention to himself through words, amusing stories, obtuse behavior, cleaver ways to solve problems, wit and deeds but never his stuff.

He was not a materialistic guy, not a "clothes horse" never wore a watch or any jewelry at all. He had a collection of vintage shirts and slacks from the mid-forties and he wore them to death. He was not a "show-off guy" nor was he cheap. All of the cars he bought had the least amount of chrome, the smallest hubcaps with black tires even when whitewalls were in vogue. His Buicks came with three portholes, not four and never with that optional two-tone paint job. He never owned a Roadmaster or Oldsmobile 98 or even a Super 88 or Pontiac Bonneville. For him, it was Catalina, bottom of the line or a Dynamic 88 Olds, ugly, flat vinyl seats, no soft cushion seating for us. Leather seats were out of the question. His choice was always manual roll up windows and an AM radio without push button pre-set stations forcing us to dial to the number or near it to hit our favorite stations. His wheels always came with a heater because that was "standard equipment." I do believe, at the time, he just couldn't afford better but, if he wanted it, he'd have found a way.

During my "middle ages" the years I spent in between my two marriages, I drove Saab convertibles. It was the perfect car for me, sporty, somewhat impressive but not a "screamer" as in "look at me" and topless. Those Saabs were perfect for a single guy passing through a "midlife crisis."

On a Sunday morning, back in the mid-nineties I was flipping through The Sunday New York Times auto classified ads and spotted a used Rolls-Royce Corniche II convertible. It was "triple" black, four years old with merely 11,000 miles and offered by the original owner. The ad featured the car as *concours*, as in pristine condition.

It was gorgeous beyond belief. There she stood on the showroom of Manhattan Motorcars on 11th Avenue. She was a gleaming masterpiece of classic English design, workmanship and elegance. The leather was mint, like butter and the wood, burled walnut, highly polished and impeccably matched and seamed. The carpets were plush, soft and thick. Truly, it was a chariot of perfection, fit for a King, Sheik, Sultan, Squire, *mensch* or just a guy looking for fun and frolic. This car was built to love. It came with two steering wheels; the standard factory ebony and a Nardi wooden racing wheel with the Rolls Royce emblem embossed on the center of the wheel. One wheel, of course, was stored in the trunk. You didn't think that both wheels were in play at the same time, eh?

The salesman offered me the opportunity for a test drive. Seated behind the wheel of the black beauty and floating up 10th Avenue gave me a sense of exuberance, euphoria and complete satisfaction. Although she drove somewhat like a 1955 Buick Roadmaster, I knew that she had to be mine. I fell in love. Crazy! Isn't it?

All those voices, from the past, were in my head chiming in and speaking to me:

"What do you need it for?" "Go for it!" "Think of the fun you'll have!" "You've earned it." "You deserve it!" "You only live once!" "You can always get rid of it!"

By the end of the week we were one, a couple. I drove her home into the underground garage at 322 West 57th Street, my home. She was assigned a spot in the back of the garage, never to be moved by an attendant. She wore her black cape from head to toe and was parked along side my Saab. I knew we were destined to have a brief and purposeful life together until I got this bit of flamboyancy out of my midlife adolescent system.

The owner of a major catering hall located on the north shore of Long Island was her previous keeper. He drove a short distance to work and kept her parked directly in front of his catering hall to impress passers by luring them as clients. I never had any intention of doing the same in front of one of my one-hour photo stores adorned with a yellow sign; "Every roll supports my Rolls." That would not have been good. It wouldn't have been smart! Eh?

The first order of business was to get vanity plates, custom license plates providing an expression, a catchy phrase to attract even more attention and generate more fun. After racking my brain I finally came up with an idea: I applied for and received: 4GTABTIT (Fuggetaboutit) I received lots of waives, high 5's, smiles, laughter, toots and honks! It was fun, just tons of fun.

The next step was to pick up a jar of Grey Poupon mustard, a needed *accouterment* for the glove compartment. I had so much fun blithely holding up the jar with my nose pointed up high in site of adjacent drivers with others aboard and watching them howl at my gesture and my comment,

"Grey Poupon?"

That was fun, time and again. Surely, you recall that commercial.

Then the *coup!* The Rolls needed a purpose. She was just not going to wait in the garage with the black veil upon her. She needed a life and I found a purpose for her.

I hired a chauffeur to drive me around on weekend evenings to watering holes, restaurants and clubs throughout Manhattan. Places such as, Windows of the World, The King Cole Bar, The Peninsula, Decade, One if by Land two if by Sea, Gotham Bar & Grill, Union Square Café, The Rainbow Room, Tribeca Bar & Grill, Keen's Steakhouse, etc. etc. The gig always started the same way.

My chauffeur brought my filled my thermos with Absolut vodka, Grey Goose hadn't been invented yet. Plenty of plastic drinking glasses, napkins, a few mixers, ice and some snack foods were on board too. My chauffeur, nicely coiffed and "clean cut" wore a black suit, black tie, white shirt and white cotton gloves, smartly capped with the standard chauffeur hat complimented his first class appearance. Upon his arrival at the garage he removed the cover from the black beauty, dusted her off with a microfiber duster, applied the vacuum to the plush carpets added a bit of floral spray, not too much, providing the proper fragrance and we were off.

On one particular occasion, I had connected with a high school sweetheart, a woman that I had not seen nor heard from for over thirty years. Apparently she had gotten married, quite young, to an "older man" who was in his late twenties at that time. She had told me, that way back then, that a more mature man who had embarked on a successful business career lured her. Back then, after college, I was headed to Harlem to teach at a public junior high school. I suppose that that I was not a terribly impressive choice for a pretty young lady who was seeking a man who could provide a comfortable lifestyle.

I located this lost love from my high school days during a brief visit to Florida. A bartender, who I had met, in Florida, had told me that she earned extra money by locating people for her customers, upon request. I offered her an opportunity to find her, strictly out of curiosity, my intention at the time. I provided her with all the information that I could about this woman and promised to send her fee to her, $300, if she was able to get me my lost love's phone number and some updated relevant facts about what was going on in her life at the present time. The next day I arrived back in New York City and as I was placing my suitcase on the floor, in my apartment, when my phone rang. It was she, the bartender detective, and she provided the phone number and some other information and I sent her a check, *pronto!*

For nearly a year I carried the phone number in my wallet. At singles bars I frequently showed it to women. I asked them what they thought I should do. I got every possible answer under the sun such as: "Don't dial pain." "This is what she has been waiting for." "Move on." "What have you got to loose?" Several days before my fiftieth birthday, I dialed her number and left her a message.

"Hi this is Cliff Strome and I'm looking for -- -- and want to make some investments. I've come into an inheritance." She had become a stockbroker after she graduated from college and I assumed that she was still plying the trade. I left my phone number and had hoped to hear from her.

A few days later my phone rang, I answered and recognized her voice immediately. I had just turned fifty, and I told her that I had just turned fifty. I continued by suggesting that perhaps I was now finally old enough for us to spend some time together. We laughed. Apparently, she had remembered why she had ended our relationship many years before. That was a very telling sign of interest. We agreed to meet at the Lexington Avenue entrance of Grand Central Terminal within the coming week and "take it from there."

The black beauty was parked directly in front of the terminal, lookin' good! I was standing outside wearing a gorgeous suit, rather sharp and leaning against the Rolls grill, legs crossed holding a martini in broad daylight. Suddenly she appeared, wearing a nicely fitted dark blue business suit, a briefcase in hand and adorned with long flowing hair and smooth well-tanned skin. When our eyes met we brandished broad smiles.

"When did this happen? A boy, the last time I saw you. And now, you're a handsome and impressive looking man!"

"You're 31 years, four months three days and fifteen minutes late." I scolded her.

"Is that your car?"

"Yes, Alex will open the door for you."

It was a magical moment. One substantially amplified by the car, not a doubt. It complimented the moment. Truthfully, the Rolls wasn't necessary but it was the cherry on the cake together with a long stem rose. I have to admit that made the moment so much more fun for me. It was a scene out of a Richard Gere movie. It was the *raison d'etre* for buying the car, fun and excitement.

The evening was wonderful, fun, reminiscent, filled with engaging and magical conversation and romance. We continued to see each other for nearly a year until we went our separate ways.

****

Turning the page, the best Rolls-Royce moment occurred in connection with my stepfather Lou. Lou a 73 year old successful man with a great rap, looked like an older version of Humphrey Bogart, had told me that he had to rent a car because his current auto lease was about to expire and he had to wait about a month for his new car lease to kick in.

"Take the Rolls Lou! You'll have a blast!"

"I can't do that Cliff. Are you nuts?"

"Lou! Take it! You've done so much for mom all these years. I want you have it. Take it! Enjoy!"

Several days later we met at a diner on West 57th Street, across the street from where the Rolls was "stabled." We had lunch with his son and my mother.

He was excited like "a kid in a candy store" anticipating the month ahead driving that car around and pulling his *shticks*. (A *shtick or shticks* is a Yiddish word for jokes, one-lines or gags that amuse, trick or entertain. Most noted for those were entertainers and comedians such as Woody Allan, Henny Youngman, Jack Benny and George Burns.

Lou was able to afford such a car even new but he never went for it. He had purchased, over the years, more Cadillac's then anyone I knew, including a turquoise '57 coupe de ville way back then. He loved the "flash" but a Rolls was way over the top to suit his way of thinking.

Before we left the diner to pickup the car I gave him a Rolls Royce letter opener, a Rolls Royce book and a Rolls Royce key fob.

After lunch, I drove the Rolls out of the garage and we met on the sidewalk. He climbed in, seating himself in the driver's seat. He noticed the gold metal plaque that I had ordered and placed on the glove box.

This Rolls Royce crafted for

Louis G. Rosenstock

Lou was "in heaven!" He drove off, no doubt, floating on air, sheer bliss. I was a thrilled as he, so pleased that I was able to do this for him.

The next time we saw each other he bombarded me with stories *shticks* that had taken place since he had gotten behind the wheel of the Rolls. He told me about his first trip to a gas station.

"Hey, where'd you get that buster?" asked a gas jockey.

"I won it in Vegas. Some asshole tried to sucker me into a bet and I drove away with his wheels. Nice, eh? A putz!"

On another occasion a parking jockey at a snazzy restaurant asked Lou.

"What'd you pay for that chariot?"

"Nothin'! Some creep tried to "crush" me. Son of a bitch! I chased him down the alley and he begged me to take the car instead of whacking him. I threw him a break, lucky bastard."

In a shopping mall a couple of fifteen-year-old boys asked him what he paid for the Rolls.

"Quarter of a mill. I got three of 'em."

There were more encounters but honestly, I just can't remember them all.

I was amused by how this toy was fulfilling the mission, fun! You just gotta love it!

My chauffeur and I were "hitting" the bar scene on Friday nights. He'd wait for me in the Rolls as I rambled through the scene. I met quite a few ladies and left with a number of interesting and impressive looking woman lured by my rap and the prospect of having fun riding around town in style.

One particular evening stands out. A very classy lady in her early forties, seated next to me at The King Cole Bar at The St. Regis and she had accepted my offer to buy her a drink. We became engaged in a fun and interesting conversation but, honestly who remembers? She was a great looking woman that I remember, very well dressed, smart, funny and looking to have a "joy ride".

"Ya wana barfly with me in my chauffeured Rolls Royce? It's parked outside."

She accepted my offer and we spent the entire evening going from place to place, drinking, laughing and just having a terrific time, just like "the rich and famous". People looked at us as we exited the car like we were some famous couple or royalty. Sorry paparazzi, no cigar.

We agreed to see each other the following weekend. We met at her apartment on the Upper Eastside. I was flattered that she had invited me in, that's always a sign of trust and interest. We had a drink, some chitchat and left for a *redux* in the black chariot.

We climbed in and my chauffeur drove us down to Windows of the World, atop The World Trade Center. What a view, what a place, "the top of the world!"

We drank, laughed, danced and enjoying each other and left at about 3 AM. There was a long taxi line and all eyes were upon us as we got into the car. I recall that as she got in her mini skirt got much more mini, about twenty pairs of eyeballs were drawn to her inner thighs.

We were "smashed" but she was alert enough to notice that the steering wheel seemed different to her then the one that she had seen that past weekend.

"Hey Cliff, I remember that you had a black steering wheel. What's up with this wooden wheel? Did you replace it?"

"No my dear, last week we were in the other Rolls!"

We each laughed our asses off!

The Rolls and I parted company after nearly a year. I played it out and it was time to put it behind me. I had my fun and I got it out of my system. The black beauty found a new home. I sold it to an NBA player and it seemed like a better fit. I do hope that they're both happy. He paid a bit more then I did and certainly he could afford it a lot more then me. Hopefully, he's having as much fun as I did.

At times we do silly, flamboyant, spontaneous and extravagant things. So what? Isn't that part of the journey? Have fun, enjoy and love the ride, life!

What a Main Break for You!

Working on Saturdays always has been a pleasure. Saturdays are more relaxing and less stressful then weekdays. Weekdays are fast paced, chaotic and much more traumatic. Operating five stores in Manhattan brings on an intensity that demands patience, spontaneous decisions, and frequent unexpected demands that often screw up a day, one day at a time.

Working on Saturdays is an escape from family trips to the mall, babysitting, cleaning the garage or doing what "needs" to be done around the house. You know, "Honey do this, honey do that."

The fast paced one-hour photo business in New York City, like most other businesses, is filled with unreasonable demands, employee whining and complaining, customers who just can not seem to be satisfied, accounts that don't pay as promised, landlords imposing unreasonable demands, tax auditors hounding, frightening and bleeding you, competitors launching attacks seeking to thwart your marketing strategies, unexpected deliveries that arrive at the worst possible time, equipment that fails to preform, inventory "shrinkage" and numerous other unanticipated events that creep up, in your face, threatening to put a halt to your fragile operation and your sanity. Then, there's the totally unexpected, the unthinkable.

According to a local reporter:

"On January 6, 1990 a water main burst under Fifth Avenue between 18th and 19th Street, spewing water with a force that gouged a block-long crater and wrought havoc among several production companies in the vicinity. At press time, it appeared

the production companies that had sustained the most significant damage were Rawi Sherman, at 8 West 19th Street, Spots Films Services, at 156 Fifth Avenue, and HIS, at 7 West 18th street.
The burst destroyed a brick sewer and flooded the basements of numerous buildings, knocking out gas, electricity and telephone service in neighboring buildings.
'It was a monster break.'"

While driving down the Westside Highway that morning I had overheard a news report on the radio that I just couldn't quite make out. There was something about a water main break in the City but I didn't hear it well. Did the announcer say Fifth Avenue or Sixth Avenue?

At the time, I had a terrific store located at 134 Fifth Avenue between 18th and 19th Street. The announcer had identified the location of the event, clearly between 18th and 19th streets. I was anxiously waiting for a replay of the story to clarify on which avenue the break had occurred. I knew that if it had occurred on Fifth Avenue then this was not going to be a typical Saturday, duh. The winter season was upon me. About a week after Christmas and New Years day, business takes a dive and cash flow slows down to a trickle. I wondered: Was it better that disasters occur at the slowest time of the year or the best time of the year, the summer? I decided that it sucked either way. Money in this business is made in the summer but the winters were tenuous and bills had to be paid. Either way, it would be a most unwelcomed event.

When I arrived at the parking lot on 23rd Street between Fifth and Sixth Avenue I had just passed Sixth Avenue and I haven't seen any commotion. As I got out of my car I saw fire trucks and police cars up ahead at Fifth Avenue. Therefore, I expected the worst. I race-walked in the direction of the emergency vehicles. My heart was pounding. When I got there my worst fears were confirmed.

When I reached Fifth Avenue I saw a calamitous scene with a maze of roadblocks, emergency responders, police and fire vehicles and water was gushing all over the street, pouring into sewers, flashing lights, crowds gathering, a number of news vans and a chaotic scene was unfolding before my eyes.

As I walked down Fifth Avenue from 23rd Street the insanity worsened. The height of the water kept rising and the force of the stream was increasing. A torrent of white caps likened to the rapids of The Colorado River was raging down Fifth Avenue. A cop at 21st Street stopped me to prevent me from entering the disaster zone. The area was cordoned off as an emergency zone and no one was permitted to enter the restricted area.

This was big. In fact, it was the most catastrophic water main break in the City's history, on New York City's premier boulevard, Fifth Avenue.

My store had been a gold mine. With only six hard working employees this little store provided substantial profit and succeeded in building a large following of loyal customers. That little store had become a cash cow providing enormous benefit for my business and lifestyle. Furthermore, it was easy to operate. There were no major stresses, glitches, disappointments or difficulties. The team was blue ribbon, honest, efficient and dependable. They loved their jobs. The store was void of aggravation and trouble. It was a seamless delight.

Now, this utopia had been slammed and stopped dead in its tracks. Only the rent and equipment payments survived. I was determined that the team would remain intact. I paid their salaries in full until I was able to reopen the store, many months later. I rotated them with employees who worked in my other stores by forcing them to take their vacations and finding "busy" work for an overstaffed crew during the slowest months of the year. I was determined not to loose any of them. They were the "glue" that kept this store going and I ensured that they would survive. I was committed and determined to bear the cost, no doubt a very good investment.

On the following Monday, I was able to visit the store. My equipment was intact because they were installed on platforms above the floor and the level of the water. The sidewalk had collapsed, the pedestrian traffic was zero, the hole in the street was likened to a crater and the electrical system, water service, vital components of the film processing business, and the telephone service in the building had been knocked out completely. Neighboring buildings were dark as well. Other stores were slammed shut and no doubt huge sums of money had been lost and some businesses were going to fail, no doubt.

Business interruption insurance was a joke. In order to collect, a business owner had to prove their losses by producing tax returns that demonstrated irrefutable evidence that money that had been made would not be duplicated due to the event. But what if the profits of the current year were due to be greater then any prior years based on trends? That was unprotected, uninsured due to the terms of business interruption insurance. A business owner had to "show" the profits on their corporate tax returns to reap the benefits of their insurance policies. It's called "the fine print" or "read between the lines" but seldom do inexperienced and naïve business owners read the fine print. That's the "hook" as insurance company lawyers well know. In addition, many policies are written to screw the business owner. For example, if a catastrophic event originated externally, outside the business premises, then there were, most often exclusions. Exclusion means, "You get no money." I was determined that I would not be a victim of "The City", insurance companies or myself. I had to find a way.

Shop owners began chatting amongst themselves, trying to find out what others were going to do to handle their problems and losses. Most of them bantered about suing the City. I had no intention of doing so. That's a long and costly road and leads down the wrong path. Those who have had no experience with litigation are unaware of the costs and all the crap that comes with the process of litigation. It's an "engine for delay." Most people are naïve regarding the process. It's a Pandora's box and often backfires. Fighting city hall is fraught with unknowns. They have weapons and strategies at their disposal such as tax audits and building violations inspectors and much deeper pockets, to name a few. Retailers come under very close scrutiny due to the nature of their business, cash. I avoided that trolley like the plague. No thanks buster!

I decided to take the high road, "P.R." public relations. A bright creative woman, who I had met at The Dale

Carnegie Center of Excellence, had established a pubic relations firm and I told her about the water main break. She offered me a program in lieu of the legal route that others had been discussing. I was impressed and we agreed to implement a plan. She did a terrific job featuring my Fifth Avenue store on page one of the City Section of The Daily News, "The Real Victim of The Water Main Break." She clinched appearances for me on television and radio evoking sympathy and interest from the public including many of my suppliers and customers. I often ran into people who expressed their regrets and concern for me, many who had learned about the disaster through the media. Customers asked me when and if I was going to re-open Pro-Print One Hour Photo due to their sincere and most appreciated concern. Support and loyalty ran thick and deep. It was very overwhelming and heart warming.

JD Camera Shop, located across the street on the next block had remained open during the entire crisis. The water main break never affected them adversely however they did take advantage of the situation by aggressively promoting their business by putting a "Kodak Color Watch System" stanchion with Bill Cosby's life size likeness standing on the sidewalk featuring film processing and film at "drop dead prices." You may remember Kodak's ad campaign, "We have The Color Watch System." It was pure wingtip upstate New York marketing bullshit, smoke and mirrors. I didn't hate JD Camera Shop's owner for it. He took advantage of an opportunity and hey, it's a business! I planned my strategy to take care of my business down the road and "fix his ass" big time!

Street repairs crept along slowly. The work to be done was huge. A 48" water main needed to be replaced, electrical connections had to be repaired by Con Edison and the City had to replace all of the collapsed sidewalks. Building owners were responsible for repairing their electrical systems and businesses had to replace their damaged inventory and destroyed mechanical systems that were beneath the water level. The damage was huge and the cost was colossal.

Our mayor, David Dinkins was never present, didn't bother to show up once as a gesture of support. There was no expression of interest or sympathy. There were no ideas, no loans, no proposals, no nothing! He was absentia, 100%. Dear ol' "Do Something, Dave!" a nickname coined by the tabloids.

After over five long months the sidewalk had finally been replaced. The electricity was restored at my location and the time to reopen was approaching. The street was still closed due to the construction process. I was anxious to pounce and get back into action.

Opening our doors with a splash, with "full steam ahead" enthusiasm and ideas that my staff and I enacted as if we were at war; a war to reacquire our business and more taking away from our competitors. I was determined to crush my competitor across the street but it was nothing personal, just business. He had his "day in the sun" and now it was my turn to crush him. When the time came I was ready. This too is going to be big.

First, I hired four very attractive young ladies, models, to pass out flyers promoting the reopening of Pro-Print One Hour Photo. They were clad in tank tops and short shorts with roller skates. They skated

168

up and down the local sidewalks handing out flyers offering free film and Fifth Avenue Candy Bars just for walking into the store. My supplier, Agfa Corporation, provided me with thousands of rolls of film, free! I bought thousands of Fifth Avenue candy bars from a friend who sold them to me at his wholesale price, 18 cents a piece. At the time they sold for 50 cents, retail. I hired a number of men who were equipped with stencils that were made at a local print shop. Those guys spray-painted police stanchions with red water based paint, "Pro-Print One Hour Photo is Open." They sprayed buildings, sidewalks, store windows, subway entrances, and anything they could find that would alert the public that we were back in action. Since I used water based paint the "damage" easily vanished after the first rainfall or a few swipes with a wet cloth. The cops who visited me knew that I was the "perp" behind the stenciling but they only requested that I cease and desist, nothing more. They were actually very sympathetic. I gave them some candy and film and subsequently they became, "hang arounds". It sort of reminded me of the scene in Goodfellas when the cops took a few cartons of Lucky's and Pall Mall cigarettes from the young Ray Liotta right off the truck!

I named the promotion "What a Main Break for You!" It "blew" the doors off the store. People came in droves. They felt sorry for us, loved the free film and candy and they were happy to support a local business. No donations, no sacrifices, just show up, support us and get some booty in the process. That's a no brainer. Everyone loves free stuff.

A year after the rupture the street was still a mess. I received a call from the TV station were I had appeared nearly a year earlier requesting a follow up interview. They edited most of my interview because I had expressed anger with the City, most of all with Mayor Dinkins. How could it be? A city with such resources had allowed a major commercial district to be disrupted for an entire year. A year! Incredible!

We thrived. The team was back in action. The trade magazines and newspapers printed stories about this event, "Making Lemonade out of Lemons in The Big Apple" a story about my fight to get back my business and keep my employees on the payroll. JD Camera Shop closed their doors for good. They packed their bags and took an early retirement to Florida. Their mistake was sitting back and not reacting to my promotion. They should have gone on the offensive rather then gloating about their success that the water main break handed them, just in the moment.

In sum, when life hands you lemons, make lemonade. In New York City, as elsewhere, don't crawl into the corner and cry, "mommy." Put on your boots, grab a handful of guts, be positive and seize the lessons that your experience provides with determination and fervor. Create, fight and run with the ball. Run, run, run and don't look back. Be strong and push back the demons that haunt you and the fears that can destroy you. Play ball and play it hard.

That's the New York City that I love. Looking back, I'm glad there was a "water main break" on Fifth Avenue that cold January morning. As a result, somehow I do feel sorry for those retailers over on Sixth Avenue because they'll never know the joy that lemons can bring and you won't see me in court guys! "Next, can I help you?

170

Chapter III
Opinions & Perspectives

✿✿✿✿✿✿✿✿✿✿✿✿✿✿✿✿✿✿✿✿✿✿✿✿✿✿✿✿✿✿✿✿✿✿✿

"If You Can Make It Here, You'll 'Make It' Anywhere"

Well, that's quite a statement! Do you agree with the lyric cited above from the song made popular by Frank Sinatra, New York New York?

Here's the quandary:

What does "making it" mean? The answer is subjective, no doubt. "Making it" is something for some and something else for others. I have often considered that lyric a bit puzzling; meaning, if this is perhaps the most competitive City on earth, boasting the smartest, most imaginative and resourceful people found in abundance then why are they so confident that if they can make it here then they can make it anywhere? I don't think so and it really doesn't make sense.

Intense competition certainly cannot ensure success for all. Competition, by definition confirms that some do and some don't "make it." Even if you did "make it" here then why would you, according to the lyric, be able to make it "anywhere"? Most places are void of good opportunities and therefore making it there, wherever that may be, is much more difficult or even impossible than making it in New York City. "Making it" is a relative destination.

It's hard to make it where there's more competition like New York City and it's also difficult to make it in most others places because they do not provide opportunities to "make it" at all. "I'll make it anywhere" is a lyric that sounds good especially when ol' blue eyes sings. Some are pretty good at making it in New York City and others are good at making it in Little Falls, Iowa.

It seems that making it is about people's expectations of themselves, being satisfied and complete, their self-image, feeling comfortable in their own skin. And even for those who are at the "top of the heap" as the song goes; with an abundance of talent, energy, effort, imagination and ambition etc. then their chances of making it are diminished by herds of competitors swirling around them, trying to elbow them out of the game. Its "dog eat dog" from start to finish.

"You can make it here, you'll make it anywhere" perhaps if your standards are low. Anywhere means everywhere and if you have lofty goals you can scratch off most places. Where else would you spell success as in New York City that provides opportunities for all level of success? In other places, by comparison, there is no place that provides opportunities in virtually every field of endeavor that compares with New York City? It's the big fish in the little pond syndrome. You have to decide which one you are, a little fish or a big fish or somewhere in between.

So, you've decided to come to New York City, settle in, ply your trade, pursue your ambitions and hope to become successful at what you do. You've tried and tried elsewhere such as Ohio, Florida, Michigan or Oregon, wherever. You write, act, sing, draw and sell widgets or what-cha-ma-call-its. You take a shot, come to New York City and point yourself in a direction and shoot for the stars, your stars. You set goals, explore opportunities again and again with fervor and determination knowing that there are more possibilities here than anywhere else. What separates the winners from the losers, from those who stay and those who pack their bags and split?

Successful New Yorkers are those who come with a steel mind and determination to make it here no matter what. They believe in themselves with a burning intensity. They know that the opportunities here are greater than anywhere else and that drives their passion, energy, resolve, optimism and confidence. They harness their determination; talent, experience, commitment and tenacity to propel their success. They are open minded, determined to learn, listen, experience, and break their ass to make it to the top. They roll up their sleeves, dig into the grit of the City and broaden their perspectives and maintain their focus. They yearn to learn the ropes; the rules of the road by taking in all they hear, see and glean. They will acquire a treasure trove of experience built on other's successes and failures. Many toss out the old textbooks that their college professors had encouraged them to study. They re-write the book, their own. They're here to blaze trails as millions of New Yorkers have done before them. They seek to find better ways, not to do the same "ol' same ol.'" It's the proverbial, "build a better mouse trap and the world will beat a path to your door."

Because the stakes are so high in New York City, the cost of rents, the breakneck pace of life, the casting call that has your knees clacking, the insecurities that dwell deep inside you, the self-doubt, fear of failure, and all those demons that speak to you, inside your head destabilize you and your mission and that can thwart your goals.

It's commitment and persistence that keeps you going against all the odds. Many voices in our heads drive conflicts within us; demons elevate our fears of failure, shame, loneliness and despair. There are days when those demons are shouting at you and on other days you barely hear them, drowned out by the mantras of the enthusiastic and encouraging voices that too dwell within you confirming your true destiny, success. Who are those voices? Which voices define you? You must follow your path until you discover whether your destiny is success or failure, however you define it. It's compelling; it's the mirror in front of your face. Who and what are you?

However, for those who succeed, there is also another voice that lurks within. It's the one that says, it's okay; you're equipped with all you need to "make it" here, and why not? That's up to you. That voice harnesses your relentless commitment to succeed at what you are meant to do, your destiny, your calling! How many "foreigners" have arrived at our shores and launched themselves, their careers and their lives and have soared into the stratosphere? How many have come with pennies in their pockets and a dream in their hearts? For those who have made it here it is the ability to merge their drive, humility, eagerness, brains, fortitude and positivity with the magic carpet, the endless canvas of opportunity that is New York City. For those who doubt that, in 2010 over 3,000,000 New York City residents were born in foreign countries, more than ever before! Some will make it, most will not, and that's their subjective definition of "making it." What's yours?

If you shy away from the challenges of succeeding in New York City because you perceive that the competition is just too great then why not ply your trade in Oklahoma City, Wichita, Santa Fe, Orlando or Ashville? Certainly, the competition there is not nearly as intense as it is in New York City and if you're elsewhere and success provides you with the means to pay your bills, live a nice lifestyle, then you've succeeded, correct? Only you will know and that is rooting in your assessment of yourself. And if you do succeed, wherever you choose, then your success is not less significant because no one has the right to judge your success, except you? Many can make it in small towns that can't make it in New York City. Many who can make it in New York City don't have a clue how to make it in small town America. It's truly a matter of where you fit in, where you're comfortable and what works for you, your personality and your persona. The notion that "if you could make it here, you'd make it anywhere" is purely a myth, a lyric!

If you can make it here, you can make it anywhere, as long as there's enough left over for you "there" and that's a challenge that is perhaps greater then making it in New York City. There's much less booty in a small pond. But, with a full breast of energy and enthusiasm, you're sure to find what you're looking for here, more so than elsewhere. If you make it here it's because you have tooled yourself to take advantage of this great City and have merged the best you have with the wealth and breath of the City and what it has and can offer you.

To paraphrase John Steinbeck: Only New York City has a heartbeat that may grab you and if you find something you love and passionately pursue then you will become a part of that heartbeat and if you're fortunate you'll never let go. Never let go!

Have you ever considered going to a cemetery to take a walk, relax, enjoy nature and immerse yourself even if it's a cemetery in a beautiful man made landscaped environment? Have you ever considered taking the time to visit a cemetery without searching for the monument of a departed relative, friend or to seek out a famous person's resting place?

Perhaps, you if you had lived in a filthy, crowded and stench ridden urban environment rife with diseases, filth and squalor lacking a decent park with gorgeous trees, walking paths, bodies of water and the sound of chirping birds?

Sentiments, such as these, gave rise to the "rural" or "garden cemetery movement" in France and England in the early 19th century. Its purpose was to enhance the experience of cemetery visits, for the living, of course! The result was, to provide a respite for those seeking an escape from urban environments, to come and enjoy solace and peace by "inhaling" these splendid places before the creation of landscaped parks. Shortly thereafter, this movement reached The United States in New York City, a place called Central Park.

"Inspired by romantic perceptions of nature, art, national identity and the undermining of the melancholy themes of death" such cemeteries were generally placed on the outskirts of large cities such as Boston, Cincinnati and New York City on high ground with excellent views of the cities. Naturally, the views were intended to provide a pleasing panorama for the visitors, to enhance the experience that put that place, the cemetery, a specific gravesite in unison with the city making it a part of city life and inspiring a spiritual experience.

Views are not intended for the departed, but strangely many plots are purchased for that reason, huh! It's an old put-on that the departed have great views and people pay extra for such raised plots, as every plot salesmen well knows.

American landscape design, pioneered by Andrew Jackson Downing, Calvert Vaux, Frederick Law Olmsted and Jacob Wrey Mould integrated their skills creating spacious and tranquil grounds where the combination of nature, their esthetic visions and the artful hand and mind of man would result in lush and well-planned places of beauty and art. They created cemeteries, essentially park like grounds, providing an escape from the dirty, crowded and stench filled air of urban environments, a bucolic and natural setting that "spoke" of life and laid the departed to rest in an organic and peaceful place of beauty.

The pallets that these men created were environments with an abundance of hilly wooded places, vast open areas of thinned out trees, void of plants amidst broad vistas and varieties of natural looking bodies of water all co-existing harmoniously as if they were made by nature. Many plots were adjacent to magnificently carved bodies of water providing nearby benches for reflection and a connection with nature granting solace and repose. These settings stimulated a sense of appreciation for nature and the continuity of life and death as a return to nature, an extension of existence, the next phase of eternity.

Leonard Bernstein is "resting" atop Battle Hill, the highest point in Brooklyn, over 200 feet above sea level in Greenwood Cemetery overlooking Manhattan. Trees planted beside a stone bench inscribed with his sir name, shade his monument. It is a spectacular site, a final place, evoking communion with the living, nature and eternal beauty.

A walk through Greenwood Cemetery, the resting place for over 600,000 people, many who were the "movers and shakers" of New York City for over one-hundred and fifty years is extremely inspiring. If you imagine this 478 acre landscaped ground, established in 1838, without the monuments, you cannot help but perceive that you are strolling through the most magnificent park on earth. Truly, it is a perfect extension of the glorious and creative lives of those who "reside" there.

After a two-hour leisurely walk through Greenwood, I did not leave with a gloomy sense of sadness but rather a peaceful and serene sensation of calm. This place provides the best possible opportunity for visitors and for those seeking consolation and the belief that existence itself is an endless journey. Surely, this cemetery and others are more for the living then the departed.

Among some of the most notable residents at Greenwood are: Henry Ward Beecher, preacher and brother of Harriet Beecher Stowe, DeWitt Clinton former Mayor, Governor of New York, inspiration for the Erie Canal and the 1811 Street Grid in Manhattan, Horace Greeley, poet, publisher and advocate of Central Park, Samuel F. B. Morse, the genius behind the first Atlantic cable, Margaret Sanger, birth control pioneer and Lewis Comfort Tiffany, artist and of course the infamous Mayor William M. Tweed and many more. You'll also see stones bearing numerous names of Brooklyn streets that are familiar to many of us, a sure giveaway that they were important without us knowing why; Remsen, Joralemon, Montaque, Boerum, Henry and Hicks, street names found in Brooklyn. It's interesting to write the names of those that appear on the largest monuments on the highest ground and "Google them." You'd be surprised to "meet" whom you have visited!

Many of the monuments are quite impressive and original. Pyramids, sarcophagi of various sizes with incredible ornamentation are found everywhere. The names, dates and sentiments are a tour through New York's past. Richard Upjohn, architect of Trinity Church and Grace Church in Brooklyn Heights, designed the highly ornamental brownstone "gate" at the 5th Avenue entrance. That alone is truly worth the trip. Go there, you'll be glad you did, but don't stay too long, please! Just a visit! Interestingly, before the construction of Central Park many Manhattanites crossed the East River by boat and walked up steep hills in Sunset Park to Greenwood Cemetery to enjoy a day in the "park" a cemetery and precursor of perhaps the greatest park on earth and you know where that is!

One final note: The most popular tourist attraction in America throughout most of the 19th century was Niagara Falls. The second most popular tourist attraction was Greenwood Cemetery!

Watching people enjoying the park, walking hand in hand, sitting and reading a newspaper under a tree gazing at joggers taking another lap around the reservoir or observing adults showing off their ice skating skills at one of the park's two rinks, at times, annoys me. I dislike observing those who amble through the park to escape the City, enjoying a few precious moments of solace.

And what really irks me is observing young parents with a child tightly secured to a bicycle handlebar basket or rear seat peddling through the park, gliding along a footpath or meandering through the North Woods.

It reminds me of Mel Brooks' comment in the comedy sketch, "The Two Thousand Year Old Man" when asked something like, "What do you think of man's conquest of space and sending a man to the Moon?" His reply, "That was good!" Yeah Mel, Central Park is good too.

Central Park was our moon shot 150 years ago and most of those who enjoy the park haven't got a clue as to how it came to be! They take it for granted, never knowing that it was the first park to do what it does and provides. It is, together with the Brooklyn Bridge and St. Patrick's Cathedral, one of the three foremost monumental technological achievements of New York City in the 19th century. It is the culmination of the ideas and efforts of so many who had pushed for the concept, persuaded the City to pay for it, to purchase the land, through an act of eminent domain, and plan the world's first public landscaped park built for all, not just the wealthy and advantaged as was customary in Europe, but created a park in an entirely new and spectacular way.

The Central Park, as it was first called, is still a primary destination for visitors to New York City boasting over 40 million people visitors annually. I am truly bothered by the vast majority of those who meander around and enjoy the beautiful variety of trees, expansive lawns, secluded forests, spectacular bridges, gorgeous man made bodies of water and landscapes that envelop the park who do so without any interest as to how it all came to be.

Seriously though, in truth, I do take pride and pleasure watching people enjoying Central Park, but what puzzles me is that the vast majority of those who know nothing nor are they interested in learning anything about how the park was built, yes built; the why, how, when and at what cost. What did it take to create this first ever-landscaped urban park, paid for with public money, to be used by all of the people? It baffles me! "This park was designed and built by the hand of man!"

In the early 19th century "The Garden Cemetery" movement had taken hold enabling visitors to pay their respects to their forbearers in a bucolic and natural environment while experiencing spiritual solace, appreciation of life engaging in deep reflection, enjoying nature's beauty and observing visual natural evidence that death is a continuum, a component of living, it's nature's way.

The concept of landscaped parks grew out of this movement and provided the means to escape from the stresses of urban life during the dawn of the industrial revolution. It continues to provide people a much needed respite from the pressures of life in crowded, noisy, stinking, filthy and dangerous urban environments such as New York City had been.

Forward thinking leaders of New York City, such as William Cullen Bryant, Horace Greeley, Mayor Fernando Wood and Andrew Jackson Downing, America's leading landscape architect all clamored for such a park. By the mid 19th century the idea took hold and through an act of eminent domain passed by the state legislature in Albany 700 acres were set aside for "The Central Park," from 59th Street to 106th Street. Due to the extreme rock formations at 106th Street it had been decided to extend the park up to 110th Street thereby increasing the park size to 843 acres.

The Park Commissioner held a contest to design "The Central Park". Thirty-two entries were submitted and Fredrick Law Olmstead, an American park supervisor together with Calvert Vaux, a UK architect won the $2,000 prize and the right to supervise the construction of their design known as The Greensward Plan. They hired 20,000 men who worked ten-hour days for the princely sum of $1 per day over a period of fourteen years to construct the park. More explosives were used then in The Battle of Gettysburg, the largest battle on the North American continent, soon to be. They hauled tens of thousands of tons of soil barged across The Hudson River from New Jersey. They evicted between 800 to 1600 inhabitants from a place known as Seneca Village in the west 80's section of the park, planted 230,000 trees, bushes and scrubs, installed over 100 miles of water pipes beneath the surface to provide for water transfer and drainage between all of the man made bodies of water. They moved millions of tons of soil altering the topography, conceived and created four vehicular sublevel transverse roadways to avoid vehicular disturbances to park goers and eliminate the possibility of chaotic traffic snarls at both ends of the park. Enormous quantities of stone were cut and utilized to build walls, bridges, tunnels and support embankments. They laid six million bricks, designed and built equestrian, pedestrian and carriage paths generally non-intersecting, built 37 bridges and tunnels, all unique.

A distinctive and varied lush natural environment was created, one never before conceived ensconced with a six-mile stonewall built around the entire perimeter of the park wrapping up this masterpiece as though it were a gift to all the entered which, in fact, it was and still is.

At that time, the park was too far north for most residents of Manhattan to enjoy as most folks lived below 14th Street. However, the visionaries got it right, because they knew that the City was growing north and, in time, it would be the ideal spot to be located, in the center of the expanding City.

They created names of the entrances to the park glorifying humankind, such as Ladies' Gate, Boys' Gate, Engineer's Gate, Scholar's Gate, Artist's Gate, etc., in opposition to numbered streets mandated in 1811 named "The Grid Plan" that had laid out the street system and was rapidly becoming a reality.

The technology applied to the transport water underground was visionary, feeding various man-made bodies of water and providing necessary drainage in the park, a man-made labyrinth of underground pipes that was years ahead of its time. The topography was carved out with slopes dug below the level of adjacent roadways providing greater peace and quiet for park visitors, while those who enjoyed the brilliance of it all deceptively never noticed that the mind and hand of man had created it all!

Perhaps that's the brilliance of the park, to fool the eye, *trompe l'oeil*. The designers deliberately did not want those who enjoy the park to notice that it is a man made creation, and not to be noticed as such.

In effect, therefore, I should be pleased when I see people enjoying the park those without a care and completely clueless as to how it all came to be! That's the genius of the designers, the ultimate confirmation that their design was a decisive success; a man made park that appears to be nature's creation and as a result, the ultimate deception.

At a cost of over $5,000,000 for the land, at a time when The United States government paid slightly more for the entire state of Alaska, one has to reflect that the commitment to provide this great City with a park equal in size to the two smallest countries on earth, Monaco and The Vatican combined, was quite a remarkable and unprecedented achievement. It was, up until that time, the greatest investment made by this City for its people, a statement that we as a city were exceeding the efforts of other great cities of the world. It was another declaration that New York City was committed to be the primate City of the world.

To those who lament the value of the property, the 843 acres that is Central Park, if those acres were instead developed into luxury housing of the best construction and design would have instead provided an impressive and enormous real estate tax grab, ought to take note that had the park never existed the increased value of the surrounding properties, due to the existence of the park itself, is of far greater value than would have been had all of the park's acreage been "developed" by real estate barons. Tax-wise the City has come out way ahead due to the park's existence and the total estimated income that the park provides with all the activities, attractions, donations and employment, its contribution to the City's coffers exceeds one billion dollars. In fact, the City government contributes merely 15% of the total cost of the maintenance the park. Philanthropists as well as numerous meager donations provided by wealthiest and most generous of us fund the overwhelming majority of the cost to operate the park.

Enjoy Central Park! The more you learn about this unique and incredible park the more you will take pleasure and gain an enhanced sense of appreciation. It is truly the 19th century American Artistic Masterpiece, a natural, organic piece of art that truly spells America, glorifying its valleys, rivers, streams and mountains. The designers have replicated nature, the Hudson River Valley, right here in the center of Manhattan, in the most magnificent, impressive and beneficial way.

We, as a young country, had no other palette to project our visual imagination. Unlike Europe we had no history of tapestry, furniture, mosaics, architecture, oil paintings, sculpture, costumes or jewelry. Nature was our palette and Olmstead and Vaux, together with Jacob Wrey Mould, created the park at a cost of $7,000,000 plus the cost of the land.

As you walk through Central Park imagine as though you are passing by each scenic landscape, opening your eyes observing the varied and magnificent sites, likened to freshly painted landscapes unfolding before your eyes. Imagine as though you are walking through an art gallery and carving portraits in your mind's eye. That was the designers stated intent, to take you on a tour, as if you were strolling through a museum inviting you to savor every pictorial wonder unfolding before your eyes, masterpieces, in three dimension made with real material and formed to appear natural but made and designed by the hand of man. That is the magic and art of Central Park. You are participating and experiencing an interactive journey through an 843 acre canvas of art created by mankind, a journey into the mind, heart and soul of the imagination of man.

Enjoy it even more, now that you know the history and purpose of this beautiful place. Perhaps now, you know that you didn't know anything about Central Park! Experience the park, perhaps the most beautiful man made place on the face of the earth, in the middle of "The Island at the center of the world."

With approximately 5.5 million paid "rides" on an average weekday, the New York City subway, the fourth busiest on earth and by far the world's largest, together with the largest hybrid electric bus fleet in the country saves The United States half of all the energy that's saved in The United States due to all the nation's mass transit systems.

Ours is the only subway system on earth that was built with express tracks from the "get go." Our subways do not have multiple fare schemes for distance traveled, at least not yet and it is also the only subway and bus fleet that runs entirely on a 24/7 basis. We are truly "The City that Never Sleeps!"

The genius of building the subways in New York City with express tracks from the very beginning is one of the most significant and innovative ideas that have enabled this City to grow and thrive. Imagine if we didn't have express tracks! We never would have been able to handle such vast numbers of people and transport them so rapidly. The volume would overwhelm the system and the limits would have impeded the growth of the City. Travel time to and from Manhattan from the outer boroughs would have doubled. Far-flung neighborhoods would not have become so dense and the sluggish inefficiency of local trains would have overwhelmed the subway system. We would have had impressive skylines in outer borough neighborhoods closer to Manhattan with more open spaces further out if our subway system were unable to handle to load with the efficiency of express tracks. The subways would not have penetrated those further away places because it would have been impractical to extend the subways to such far-flung places to collect small numbers of people, a fiscally loosing proposition. Certainly, the underlying story as to where tracks were laid was all about alliances between the bureaucratic subway decision makers and the titans of real estate. One could write a history of such deals and relationships that ultimately determined where stations were to be built based on who owned what properties and who know whom; such affirmation and evidence must exist.

Express tracks have provided the opportunity for outlying real estate values to soar enabling residents to enjoy quicker access to their jobs from places of greater distances from Manhattan thus making their lives more enjoyable, increasing their work and leisure time immeasurably.

"Honey, I'm home!"

"So soon, you should have taken the local, and whose lipstick is on your collar?"

Express tracks make it possible to leave home later and get home earlier and that makes it possible to argue with your spouse longer then those who ride the local rails to and fro! Could it be that express tracks have resulted in larger sized families and higher divorce rates? More time with your spouse may have spun your life and marriage one way or the other, a larger family or a broken marriage! Maybe both, eh? Express tracks! Save money, have a smaller family and spend more time in the subway and less time at home! Funny? Sure, but, no doubt it's true!

When you enter the subway you venture into a completely different world. Rich in its own cultural mores and codes of conduct written by The MTA (Metropolitan Transit Authority) and those codes authored, but not written, literally, by the ridership or "straphangers" as riders were known years ago whose rulebook governs "street smart" behavior on the rails below ground.

Just about everyone who rides the subway has a love hate relationship with the system. It gets you where you want to go inexpensively, safely and quickly but, it's noisy, often crowded, with long waits, especially at off hours and weekends, in sum, it's a challenge, but tolerable and acceptable.

The love argument goes like this:

It is by far the fastest way to get around the City. It's statistically the safest way to travel compared with taxis, driving, biking taking a bus or walking. It is reasonably dependable, more then any other means. Without it, this City simply could not exist! Even though Manhattan has more vehicles entering and leaving daily than any other city in The United States, we rely on our subways to transport the overwhelming majority of people who travel in and out. There simply is no other way.

Those who travel in opposite directions of the voluminous flow enjoy many benefits: space, comfort and seating, less noise and a little peace. It was the subways, initially the L's (elevated trains) that enabled people to increase the distances between home and work, expanding the city and making it possible for people to live in larger homes abandoning their tiny tenement dwellings, making room for newcomers, the next wave of immigrants who enjoyed more space, the ultimate luxury in New York City. Subways are the arteries of the city, its lifeline, cheap, fast, safe and air-conditioned. Kill it and the City will die!

The hate argument goes like this:

It's unfit for humans, there's too much trash, dirt, bottles, newspapers and many people are filthy. There are not enough people on staff to keep the system clean, it's "disgusting"!

Recently, I picked up a newspaper off a seat and thought the news that I had read two weeks ago had reoccurred, that's how old the paper was! The trains are extremely noisy; the express trains roar through stations compelling many to stick their fingers in their ears. You could go deaf! The trains are, at times, far too crowded and the wait is often much too long. Many people are often literally unable to squeeze in or they just refuse to try and they extend their waits, I do at times. Most often I simply wait for the next train because they're usually nearly empty and that's well worth the wait.

The worst thing about the subway is the crowd during rush hour. We are at times packed, crushed up against people who are in your face, pushing, leaning against each other, and all the unpleasant smells and shouts of those among us who are arrogant, selfish and inconsiderate. Backpackers swing around forgetting or not caring that their packs are crashing into others. It doesn't have to be that way, does it? At least we don't have "pushers" people hired by the transit system in Tokyo who push and jam people into trains to maximize the load! I can't imagine that happening in New York City. That would be the most dangerous job on the planet, even as nice as New Yorkers happen to be!

The MTA's code of conduct is something that we all could have written in five minutes; no spitting, littering or radios! Radios? That's a timely notice!

191

People listen to their music via iphone, ipads and with earphones. Radios? Don't hold the doors, step back when a train is entering the station, etc. etc. The unwritten rules are far subtler. Why do people spit? Some do so every twenty seconds or so. What does that accomplish? I guess it makes them feel tough, just like those who wear their pants down to their mid thighs. To me, both make them look stupid. Perhaps they are!

People tend to sit or stand at the greatest distance possible between each other. You'll never see two strangers take adjacent seats if there are numerous empty seats available throughout the car. Providing the greatest distance between each other is rule one. If you put yourself next to someone and had the option to sit with space around you then you'd get a look that would kill. Everyone cherishes his or her own space, especially in the subway.

Many riders peer into the windows of a train as it enters the station looking for unsavory riders in each car as the train slows down enabling them to seek avoidance from crying babies, boisterous inconsiderate children or cars filled with herds school children who perform acrobatics on the steel bars and poles, and those who appear to be scary, threatening, hostile, insane and unpredictable. Something should be done. They're in your face and they're a loud heard of pains in the ass!

"Strap hangers" generally opt to enter an adjacent car if they so desire, eying a sleeper, a person with an abundance of black plastic bags, a cart or evidence of "persons of interest" who are not mainstream. I never enter an empty car because I believe they are less safe. Eyeballs reduce crime so you should "hang" where there are the most people are to be found.

Riders generally do not move to the center of cars, the space that is the greatest distance from the three or four sets of exit doors, depending on the subway line that you are riding. This results in more overcrowding near the doors; more jamming and squeezing then necessary. People tend to be lazy and hate to do what they should. It's like an ant colony crawling all over a lump of sugar. Stand back, you'll get your turn.

Conductors frequently make announcements during rush hour; most riders comply with their requests, albeit unenthusiastically. What's in it for them? Space! Many push to leave the train blocked by those seeking entry fearing that the doors will shut in their faces and leave them standing on the platform. It is customary to let people leave the train before allowing those who seek entry. But, that doesn't include everybody. How dumb! Let's all get in and then let the others out. Duh!

"Stand clear of the closing doors," announced prior to the closing of the doors by the conductor or the electronic PA system on the newer trains. Some riders cram an arm inside and hold the doors for a friend very aggressively. Or, they force doors open to gain entry. This is dangerous stuff and it will never end! But it could, if the City wanted it to! Just hire some plainclothes enforcers and issue summonses en mass. Isn't that a primary cause and effect of society? It's the failure to provide reasonable and deliberate enforcement and if that doesn't work then get nasty. Don't we know enough about reducing crime? Why are we so tolerant and accepting of unacceptable behavior? Let's get with the program. We have demonstrated, as a City, that we've done that better than any other city. It's called pushing for "voluntary compliance." What's the problem?

We have more than our share of obesity in New York City and I could swear that the seats keep getting smaller. Manhattan is the thinnest county in the United States, not thin geographically but rather demographically; average body weight. Often people who are seated on a bench seat are suddenly joined, literally joined, by an overweight rider who consumes a seat and a half! I have even seen some consume two seats, entirely! That reminds me of a lyric from a Michael Feinstein song, "Let's all _join_ the ladies and make one big lady." We should try that!

As for me, I quickly rise from my seat if a real super sized "hefty bag" parks her butt next, or on top of mine! I choose to stand for the duration of my trip if I fail to find another entire seat. I glue my eyes on them and "drill" holes through them with my fixed glare. Many others remain seated and endure the big squeeze. Perhaps the MTA will create a surcharge for seat and a-half-riders as some airlines have done. Forget the calorie counts that require posting in chain restaurants to thwart huge caloric in-takers and the attempt to ban supersized sugared drinks. The people who need that information the most, read those caloric counts the least. The MTA should consider a surcharge for those who are "weight challenged." What a shame. I really feel sorry for those people and hope they can get the help they need, namely from themselves.

Seriously, this is an enormous problem and needs immediate attention not just for fellow strap hangers but for those challenged by excessive weight most of all. Perhaps we should be standing on a scale as we swipe our cards and if your weight exceeds x then an additional swipe would be required to gain entry, or an extra half a swipe, a surcharge. For many, that'd be a good thing, longer, healthier lives and more seating for others. In fact, there is an MTA law that states, those who inconvenience other riders, and that includes occupying more than one seat must rise and provide fellow riders the benefit of both seats. I do believe however, that some folks are so huge that standing for their entire ride may be a grueling physical challenge and may be life threatening as they could fall on top of someone and crush them to death! Recently, I took the annual vintage subway ride sponsored by the MTA. The train that I rode was a model that had been in use during the 1930's-1950's, equipped with wicker seats, tungsten light bulbs, porcelain handles and void of air conditioning. The print ads featured cigarettes, the ones that most doctors preferred. Brands such as Lucky's, Camel, Raleigh and good old Chesterfield, all non-filtered cigs were featured. That really took me back, way back. What made the biggest impression on me was the size of those seats. Most people today would not have had adequate space and todays large Marge's wouldn't have the space for half their butts. Tiny seats that seemed so normal back then today look like seating for fifth graders, but not all of today's fifth graders by any means could fit in those seats!

Many stations are now equipped with elevators and escalators and far too often many are out of service. They were paid for at great expense, just about a billion dollars or so according to what I've read. So fix 'em or get that money back. No can do? Bet there's inadequate language in the purchase orders and agreements that the MTA signed with the contractors, giving them the right to foot drag or play dead. If not, who's minding the store? I'll bet all the elevators and escalators in Bloomberg's are working just fine. It's amazing! If the MTA were a private company competing in "the real world" then the elevators and escalators would be working under threat of well-written contracts that include penalties crafted by attorneys who knew a thing or two about contract law. No competition or stockholders equals unreliable elevators and escalators. MTA, the proof is in the pudding! Overall for $2.50 per ride you are doing a fine job ("Brownie") but there's a lot of room for improvement, and that doesn't include another "annual" increase above $2.50 in the very near future. The best way to prove that you are "giving away the shop" is to launch some of your union employees who sector and watch what happens. They'll die of starvation. It's about votes? Yeah! Perhaps, anyone who has anything do to with keeping their mouth shut or supporting those increases won't get my vote. How about yours? When lines for applicants seeking MTA jobs approaches zero, then you know you're offering the right deal. This is not Walmart! We don't want to see people squashed lining up for a toy or electronic gizmo for half price. We want enough qualified people to run the system and earn a fair wage, not a balloon giveaway or a handout. Some of those who work for the MTA cannot make an announcement that is understandable. Some are walking around in a haze, or daze. Others are taking up space. If this was run like a business and we straightened out the unions, enforced the Taylor Law that forbids public employees to strike, ala Regan's strategy that busted the FAA air traffic controllers union, then we'd be able to create a system that is the envy of the world. What are we afraid of? Another strike? Let the National Guard run the subways or cut their pay for every day they decide to hold this City hostage. Hallelujah! How about releasing all those in prison for non-violent small size marijuana busts and offer them jobs to run the subways, eh? That is a real money saver!

Isn't it amusing that the MTA has implemented an audio system that advises us when we should expect specific trains to arrive at the station?

"Ladies and gentlemen, there is a Brooklyn bound train arriving on the local track." Or, "There is a Queens bound train two stations away."

How often I have stood on the platform and waited for the "arriving" train that confirms with that improper announcement. At times, I've entered the station and seen the Brooklyn bound local pull out of the station while the announcement is blearing that it's one station away! Soon it will be, but moving away from the station, not toward it. I've heard two announcements simultaneously canceling each other out! Try that in the real world folks. It would be beneficial if the announcement cited which local train the announcement is referring to: The C and the B trains both travel to Brooklyn or uptown! Let us know which of the two is coming. What would be the big deal? Ah! It's twenty-five year old technology. Oy, come on folks. Wake up. It exists! Do you?

The customary and usual unwritten code, for escalators, is to stand to the right and allow walkers to walk up, or down, on the left. Many riders prefer to walk up escalators rather than wait and stand on a step. Unfortunately, many stand on the left and pretend that they don't hear you from behind, "Excuse me please!" They block you from moving and take pride in the acquisition of this little piece of temporary real estate. They know very well that people may be behind those who would like to save a bit of time and get a little exercise and walk up the escalator but they continue to just stand still. They're angry people. This too will never go away. This creates more anger and frustration on both sides. Some people love to express their anger in public places especially in the subways an excellent place to push those buttons. Get up, grow up and get over it you childish creeps! Stand right and pass left, got it? Hey MTA, why not post signs, such as: Please stand right and walk left with an illustration that anyone will understand. They probably figured out that no one would read or understand them. I don't agree.

Those who wait for trains on the platforms generally are gathered at the center of the platforms and will therefore enter a mid-range car. There are ten cars per train. The obvious result is that the center cars are the most crowded and the end cars are sparse, by comparison. People want to be in the center of the platform in off hours, there's safety in numbers. During rush hour it makes little sense. More sophisticated riders opt for the first and last three cars putting themselves at their desired station upon their arrival. Our subway trains are 644 feet long. That's longer than two football fields! Doesn't it make sense to enter a less crowded car and enable your diaphragm; the one nature gave you, not your doctor, to do its job?

Backpacks are another major challenge for subway riders. Imagine being in a crowded subway train with a person who is standing next to you who decides to take an about-face! Whissssh! You just got smacked with a 180 degree "about face" with a 20-pound backpack across your face as they are 9 inches taller then you. It has literally become a part of human anatomy without consciousness. People forget that they are wearing them! This new marvel of modern life is a terrific convenience for many however; they should be sold with instructions, you think? Nah, people wouldn't follow them anyway, not in the subway. Will they ever go away? Time will tell! Keep them off the subways and let the back-packers head for the hills; like "take a hike" up a mountain! They're new, backpacks on subways. Let's add shovels, picks, ropes and portable gas stoves too! It's like people have become turtles or camels. They've grown storage space on their backs! Front packs would be better; at least "frontpackers" would see what's going on in front of them. Yes, front-packs! It is inevitable that someday they'll be prohibited no doubt by Homeland Security. With all the time, effort and money spent to ensure subway safety, backpacks are the Achilles heel in the equation. One backpack can .. . I don't want to go there! Homeland Security will outlaw them one day but guns, that'll be okay, second amendment, you know. You'll never know when an American Indian or a grizzly will break into your apartment. Hey! What happened to the American Militia?

In truth the book publishers haven't learned yet how to make money with e-books. That way kids and grownups alike will have all their books stored in ipad devices, nooks, etc. and that should diminish the loads substantially. When it comes down to it, isn't it all about money? Where is Chuck Schumer, a do nothing Senator who knows how to get on the side of the mindless not controversial issues. Have you heard what he said about railroad safety? He's in favor of it? Have you heard what he said about abolishing luggage surcharges for heavy carryon luggage at airports? He wants to eliminate it? Have you heard what he said about Putin's last provocation? No! Why? He said nothing! Too controversial Chucky boy? How about those suitcases and duffle bags on the A train out to JFK? I shutter at the thought what could be inside them too. One day we may just find out, oy!

At times entering a subway station and passing through the turnstile can be like a medieval jousting match. Often some people, about to swipe their metro cards, are faced suddenly with someone coming from the opposite direction racing toward them seeking to exit the station. You wait, they crunch through and you attempt to swipe again and perhaps this time you get in. It's most discourteous of course, but it is outrageous when you are about to pay for your ride and someone, knowing that, blithely exiting pushes the turnstile in the opposite direction that you need to save your fare. Wouldn't it make sense for them to wait a moment for you to enter? What train do they have to catch? The Twentieth Century Limited? I guess we're all in a hurry and "my time is more valuable than yours." It just doesn't mean a rat's ass to me" is that kind of logic. Those people are truly exceptional. We still can learn a thing or two from Parisians whose subway system provides separate places to enter and exit. Huh huh huh, *Viva la France*! Rubber rimmed wheels too on subway trains in Lyon, nice and quiet!

Recently, I see people jumping over the turnstiles to avoid paying their fare. That's something that I haven't seen in years! Some pull the mechanical barrier bar toward them half way and create enough space for them to squeeze their thighs through. Others duck beneath the barrier to gain entry and others jump over the barrier bar and some are so tall they just step over it. Lately, I've seen two teens, normally thin get though together and pay one fare. If they can be that smart then why can't they get past Algebra 1a? We can do a better job of reducing this. If you see this happen, be smart and keep your mouth shut. They all should be arrested every single one of them, without exception, including adults and the elderly too. If we let them all get away with it then you can expect rising crime rates and that's the real problem folks!

Recently, I did react when I saw a tall woman, about thirty-five years old, well dressed, step over the turnstile and proceed to walk downstairs to catch a downtown local. I shouted,

"Officer, she's gone to the downtown level."

I walked quickly, a safe distance behind her and as I got to the lower level and I saw her talking hurriedly weaving through the crowd.

I shouted. "Right here officer, that's her!"

She quickened her pace and darted out of the station from the other end and disappeared. There was no officer; I wanted her to think twice about doing that again.

As a citizen of this great City I want to do all I can to thwart those who forage off this community. These "gate-crashers" are vermin the losers that threaten our lives, feed off us and must to be punished for their offensive behavior.

In the late afternoon, herds of homeward bound school children flock into the subway. In New York City many adolescent students travel long distances to attend school. Voluminous numbers of students take the subway at the same time and depending on which subway line you happen to be riding, you are likely to encounter flocks of students who are loud, obscene and very annoying. There should be a code of conduct taught in school and at home. Roving patrols of trained personnel should be enforcing those codes and confiscate offenders metro cards or issue summonses to their parents who ultimately are responsible for their children's misconduct. Teachers who are on their way home at the same time should be required and given the authority to address this problem as part of their jobs. They're the professionals who are trained to control children. Most of us work an eight-hour day. Why shouldn't they too? Could it be the union and politically intimidated politicians prevent this from happening? Or, perhaps they make it up by staying up nights correcting exams and students homework. Oh yes, sure.

Just about the most annoying thing is arriving on an express train into a station as the local train across the platform, the train you need to board to complete your trip, is stopped with the doors open. As soon as the express train stops, and its doors open, the local's doors close and pulls out of the station with hundreds of people who have just emerged from the express left standing on the platform and forced to wait for the next local.

The conductors who do this use those opportunities to express their anger and control and as a result they detain thousands of straphangers. It's a "power for power" thing. They are paid very well for what they do but that is not part of the job description. With all the benefits they receive to perform their jobs they must cut out that mistreatment. Such *chutzpah!* Who's monitoring that?

And if not, why not? If we're doing such a great job monitoring terrorism then why not this! To me, this is a form of terrorism. It's real and occurs thousands of times daily! Does the MTA have a system that monitors the amount of time commuters wait and if so do they attempt to fine tune performance to reduce waiting time? Do they tabulate the average waiting time for "straphangers"? Are there goals set as targets that they seek to achieve? Why can't and why won't the MTA use a little imagination, authority and concern, union or no union? Just shut up and take care of it? I'm going *subway* about this! (Not postal this time.)

And finally, on a "good note" the vast majority of riders and MTA employees are polite, respectful and considerate. It doesn't take more than a few to make a safe, inexpensive and fast ride an unpleasant experience.

There simply are better ways to move the volume of people faster, cheaper and more pleasantly.

203

It's the huge numbers of people that make the subway exciting, as long as it doesn't get too cozy. The glass is half "full" because looking at everyone, wondering what they're thinking, each encapsulated within their own consciousness, daily lives, connected in time and space, vastly different, from so many cultures speaking so many languages, different dress and attire, all coming together, in the moment, enriching each other's experience as we "fly" beneath the ground, under the streets of the greatest City on earth. This will always be a thrill for me. I must admit that I like it I really do. There's a certain sense of connectivity, being alive in The City and traveling with the herd. Not everyone gets it. Do you?

You don't agree? Ok! Leave New York City, go to Miami for one year and when you return you'll yearn for the sound of the subways, "Stand clear of the closing doors." It will be the best sound you've ever heard. If you do not agree then look for an apartment in Homestead, Florida or Main Street in Podunk, Iowa and die of boredom. Well, it's not that bad out there is it? For the true New Yorker, we'd rather live in 780 square feet of space then give up our beloved City. Wouldn't you?

Of the two choices, love and hate of the subway, I'm among those who love it, despite the hate side of the equation does creep under my skin a bit now and then. The benefits far outweigh the inconveniences. What matters most is your attitude, which is true of most imperfect things that we all experience in life. It's not a perfect world and providing 5.5 million rides on an average weekday is a very tall order, especially for a government agency. Taken with a grain of salt, a ride on the subway in New York City is not a bad thing! Try it sometime. You just may find yourself on the love side of the equation.

You'll get to where you are going faster, cheaper and safer then any other way to transport yourself in The City of New York. You can't beat it with a stick and hold this thought: How much gasoline would the "straphangers" burn if they drove like the rest of the country, polluting the atmosphere, wasting time, sending money to The Middle East, and becoming fatter? Ride on New York City! Ride on and please "Stand clear of the closing doors!"

The United Boroughs of New York City

Kingdom of New York City, Capital City, The Estates of New York, The New York City Union, The Federation of New York City, or perhaps New York City, LLC, are just a few names I'd like to suggest to replace "The City of New York" if it were transformed into an independent country, or at least, a state. Gotham, The Big Apple, The Empire City, Global City and The United Boroughs of New York too aren't too bad either.

"Let me be perfectly clear." Who said that before? I intend no treasonous act against The United States of America nor do I intend to encourage the next Civil War nor am I advocating the succession of this City from the glorious and well-managed State of New York whose motto is Excelsior, translation, "We're outa money!" Maybe a dose of Putin may help to set things right, eh? You know that we, New York City is getting the short end of the stick.

Consider these: We're more akin to Europe than the heartland in innumerable ways and we're not politically in synch with most of the nation. We send much more tax money to Washington and Albany then we get back in return, a lot more.

We are the most diverse society in the country, and the world too, the nation's center of culture and commerce, producing over 6% of the gross domestic product (GDP) of the United States consisting of less than 3% of the country's population. We go to the beat of a different drum and possess a unique perspective that defines us as much more liberal, accepting, non-judgmental, less dogmatic, more embracing or all cultures, religions and diverse ethnic origins much more so than the rest of the country.

Our values and perspectives differ from most of the rest of the country; gun toting, "stand your ground" prejudices, racism, anti-abortion, anti-gay marriage, voting rights suppression laws such as maneuvers to restrict voters with or without photo ID, anti-universal healthcare, mores and roots that define many Americans who reside in the rest of the country. Numerous other examples abound but there are still some areas where exceptions exist, however they're few and far between.

The advantages for New York City would be enormous if we were a separate state, a city-state such as Monaco or Vatican City. Fiscally we'd be a lot richer by billions annually. We might step up like China, Japan and India and lend money to the United States, hum, but would we? We would probably opt out; we're too smart for that trap with our country's fiscal problems and Washington, D.C.'s dysfunction and reduced credit rating. Confidence in Washington has gone "south" Deep South and we're not to blame.

Banks would invest in our New York City dollars by the ton but we'd change the name of our money to Gotham's. "How much is it? Five Gotham's! I like that. Can you lend me 10,000 Gotham's (G10, 000) please? "Hey buddy, can you spare me a Gotham?"

Our surplus would be spent to educate, house and provide healthcare for our own citizens. We'd rebuild our infrastructure faster and better then what is now possible. For example, the Second Avenue Subway would have been a reality fifty years ago and built with express tracks too! We'd provide more recreational space for our people, even rid ourselves of bedbugs, renovate our subways, perhaps some ceiling painting is overdue, extend subway lines further and stimulate dramatic growth in Red Hook, Riverdale and other far flung places such as we're doing in Midtown West. It seems as if we're pawns of the real estate interests more then anything else. We'd computerize the entire subway system reducing costs further, improving service and reduce fares. Perhaps we'll find a way to eliminate fares, reducing traffic dramatically. Taxi the top 3% to subsidize mass transit so that more hard working people will flock to New York City, LLC and stimulate even more growth and prosperity for all hard working citizens.

The "West-way" idea that died in the early 1980's would become the next Brooklyn Bridge type project, a tunnel highway on the Westside like it was supposed to be, but they didn't have the money! Or, build a new Highline from the length of 59th Street down to Battery Park with buildings straddling the trestle all the way down to Battery Park. That too would elevate the property values in all those neighborhoods east of the highway and provide greater access to the Hudson River and the adjacent park. Do the math. Put the value on all that cement covered real estate from 57th Street down to Battery Place and build that road beneath the surface or the trestle above it. Access to the water, greenway and the value of that real estate would exceed trillions. Let's lease some tunnel boring equipment from the Germans or Indians and create wealth that's just sitting there. It'll happen. It's just a matter of time if only we can beat down the saps that eat off our backs with their do nothing government jobs. That's what New York City can do and not Washington, D.C. the guys who are going to force us to spend millions to redo all our street signs because they're not capital letters or they're not the right fonts. You didn't hear about that one? Lunatics!

How about all the chatter about the very necessary additional Hudson River train tunnel? What are we waiting for? Pay now or pay later. Mr. Christie, you seem like a smart guy but put your nose, girth, teats and guts into it! Hey, let's regret that we built the Garden State Parkway, Pulaski Skyway, NJ Turnpike, Meadowlands, PATH train tunnels and all that! Okay, let's disable New Jerseyites from getting to work in New York City and let them work in Paterson, Newark and Camden. No new tunnel, no new jobs for New Jersey residents in New York City. It's as simple as that! Screw them or get on with it already!

This guy is too busy playing "payback time." The nerve of closing three vitally important lanes on the world's busiest vehicular bridge because Ft. Lee's Democratic Mayor refused to support the Humpty Dumpty governor! The real crux of the problem was probably Christie's hearing problem, meaning, he was told to close "the frig" but he though he was told to close "the bridge"! After all the investigations are complete, wouldn't at least three have been enough? We'll have the definitive answer. It will be I predict that this will stop this fat boy in his tracks, before Halley's comet returns and lay him down in the crap heap of history.

Presently, our public transit system is the least subsidized, based on percentage of government money for fare subsidies of any major city in The United States! Why? Isn't ours the most vital? Doesn't ours save the most energy? Doesn't ours provide the most benefit for the environment? Wake up New York State and Washington, D. C. If our subways didn't have express tracks, like most other cities, then New York City could not possibly have grown as large as it has. People would not have the time or the patience to spend twice the time getting to and from work from The Bronx, Brooklyn and Queens. Thought the City was crowded now? Huh?

We'd streamline our government and all its agencies creating greater efficiency and providing more benefits for our citizens by rewarding some or discarding others, just like the real world of B U S I N E S S usually does! We could be doing more of that right now!

We'd build another airport; replace that rat hole, Penn Station that finally after over a decade seems to be showing signs of life. Senator Daniel P. Moynihan was so right. Find a way. We'd invest in those neighborhoods that need help, especially those that exist alongside the express lines that run into Manhattan, a natural catalyst to stimulate private sector participation and enterprise, and encourage neighborhoods to become nourished by public and private sector investment and creative participation though incentives and the obvious rewards of good governance and entrepreneurial efforts and imagination. No one does that better then New York City. Look at The Highline, Jane's Carousel, Battery Park City, Lincoln Center, The Hudson River Park, The Roosevelt Island Tram, re-zoning Soho, 125th Street and countless other projects and ideas that have been put to work. Look at Harlem!!

The prisons would be upgraded, not only with better facilities but also with a better trained and supervised staff who currently seem to be breaking records by breaking bones and cracking heads, of inmates. Have you looked at all of the statistics? They're shameful! We need to provide job training, effective psychological rehabilitation and return many of those inmates back into society as productive citizens. The City has unlimited and important work to get done. We should hire the down trodden and put them to work. Prison guards would be compensated based on results meaning; if the return rate of inmates to prison declined then bonuses should be paid. That makes sense because the net saving of keeping people out of prison is huge in human development and treasure.

New York City would spend some of the surplus dollars to fund additional research for our colleges and universities, finding new cures for diseases, discovering new medicines, leading the world in stem cell research, diabetes breakthroughs, AIDS treatment and in the creation new revenue streams improving the quality of life not only for ourselves but for the world as well. New York City would become one of the smallest countries in the world with an impact that rivals the largest. In fact, we do now, even with all the obstacles that limit greater success due to the snags placed upon us by Washington, D.C. and Albany.

I'd love to see public paid promotions on the internet, social media and mobile apps that promote new technologies, medications, medical devices and treatments that save lives while enriching our resources for spurning further breakthroughs in all areas of science and technology. The profits would be plowed back into additional research. We'd lead the world, not only in innovative ideas but also in inventions and discoveries that provide impressive quality of life advances. Since the most valuable real estate in New York City is the sky, we have all the space we need. New technologies are making it possible to achieve greater heights in construction. Just have a look a what's going on in the 57th Street corridor in Manhattan. That's just the beginning; another phase of skyscraper technology is underway. Some find it obscene and others applaud such hubris. In fact, New York City would import dirt, subject to the "blessings" of the federal government, to expand its limits. Better yet, screw the federal government and get the dirt from Canada, after they thaw it out! We know what to do with landfill, and we're darn good at it! Seventeen percent of Manhattan is landfill and brother, that's a pocket full of change, huh! Why not add another 17%? We'd import more dirt from everywhere just like our Jersey dirt deal to build Central Park. Jersey's got tons of dirt and there's nothing wrong with Connecticut or Pennsylvania's soil either.

Don't leave out the arts, performing, visual and music. We'd be the cultural Mecca of the world, perhaps we already are. The dough would roll in and this City would be enriched beyond belief.

We would not need an army or Department of Defense. Our police department would suffice and do a far better job than our Homeland Security Officials or our CIA, NSA or FBI did on 911, right? Did you hear that they didn't talk to each other or exchange information that may have, just may have prevented the 911 attacks? Did you know that Bush 43 failed to take a look at the Daily Security Assessment Report that highlighted the intelligence that terrorists were planning to attack The United States with planes? Did you know that Iraq had nothing to do with 911? Sure you do! What a shame. Regime change, uh, duh! Whose regime change, theirs or ours? Based on what's going on in the Middle East we would have been much better off with Saddam Hussein at the helm in Iraq. All that blood and treasure gone and for what?

We share information. We are a lot smarter and more in touch then the folks down on the Potomac. Some should be in the Potomac not on it. Hey Bush was chopping wood! There ya go! I hear it's cold in Afghanistan.

They have proven they cannot protect us. Now, I just love how they took credit for "keeping us safe since 911" because there have not been any successful terrorist attacks since then. Ah, who was minding the store on 911? Hum? How much of our money was used for our defense? Do you recall that on 911 our Air Command or whatever name is used to describe our air defenses (SAC, NORAD?) sent two, TWO fighter planes out over the Atlantic Ocean! What was that about? How much planning and dollars went into that scenario? Where were they going, Iceland, Nova Scotia The Canary Islands or the Azores? No, was it Greenland!

Our importance, New York City, to the entire world would entitle us protection by The United States of America and in the most effective possible way, just like on 911! Oh please! What were those people thinking about? You know, the ones who take the credit for keeping us safe? Safe! September 11th was the biggest attack on the soil of The United States, ever! Safe? That made Pearl Harbor seem like a picnic!

213

We certainly spent, or borrowed, a lot of money, got little or nothing back. Hey, that's the American way! But, they loved keeping us scared, many of the folks along the Potomac. I wonder what those costs were. It's the Stanley Kubrick nightmare, the Dr. Strangelove scenario come alive, Act I. "Good job Brownie!" New Orleans didn't have to be destroyed. It was just another glitch. Sure! Way to go Army Corp of Engineers, yeah! Let's make sandcastles and go play at the beach! What beach! Thanks to global warming all the 1%'ers have the bucks but the beaches are disappearing for us all!

"We save you every day!" That's the good ol' USA! Our economic, cultural, research and development resources would create a consensus that would be unrivaled. The lack of a military force would put us in neutral territory similar to Switzerland and The Vatican. After all, we are the world. We would welcome trade and relationships with the entire world, except; a huh, "The Axis of Terror." We'd remain powerful by sheer force of our wealth, intellect, ideas, culture and the results that we produce and provide. We'd export New York City to the world, they would welcome, need and breath us in, lining our pockets creating a greater oasis of wealth, love and culture that the world has never known. Don't agree? Who knows? "Build a better mouse trap and the world will beat a path to your door."

Our national anthem would be Sinatra's New York, New York; "Start speadin' the news" . . . written by Kander and Ebb, and we wouldn't even have to change the lyrics to accommodate the new name! "I

214

want to be a part of it, New York, New York!" Yes, a touch of nostalgia.

Sure, we'd havé to establish our own post office, and that would be great fun! We'd have post offices that would be user friendly, fast and efficient. They would be privately owned, franchised, people would rush to buy shares of stock and performance would be enhanced because it would be run like a business, not by those slowpokes, who are doing us a favor when we wait and wait. "Step up, step up, step up" No more grumpy, rude and slow counter people. "Can" their asses!

They would sell us stamps with pictures of Seinfeld, Jackie Mason, Woody Allan, Calvin O. Butts III, DeWitt Clinton, John Roebling, Stanford White, Cornelius Vanderbilt, John Jacob Astor, A. T. Stewart, R. H. Macy, August Belmont, Mickey Mantle, Willie Mays, Joe DiMaggio, Lady Gaga, Lena Horne, Joe Namath and Leonard Bernstein, Jacob Reis, Marcus Garvey, Langston Hughes, Norman Mailer and Jane Jacobs to name a few.

"Everyday people" such as bus drivers, firemen, nurses, The Doe Fund employees as well as dogs, cats, and Baldo, our honored dog statue in Central Park, would adorn our postage stamps.

Ed Koch would look great on the face of a stamp with the phrase, "How my doin'?" Abe Beame and Fiorello LaGuardia would share a stamp because they were too short to have their own. The lions on the steps of the 42nd Street Library, Patience and Fortitude would be featured on large postage stamps. They would be our symbols of strength as is the Bald Eagle who represents The United States. Hey, maybe pit bulls, rats, bedbugs and raccoons and the all mighty beaver

215

would be best too, nah! We would have Pale Male and Lola, our two departed Red tailed Hawks as our late-mascots.

There'd be a building series; park series, taxicab series and each borough would have their favorite politicians adorned as well. And why not Stanley Friedman, Donald Manes, Meade Esposito, Barnard Kerik and all the rest of those crooked public "servants" would be there for the lickin', on stamps of course! Maybe a Mafia series, the guys who got wacked would be a "real killer" series and, no doubt, the largest series of all! "Collect 'em all! Be the first in your neighborhood to have the entire set!"

Whose pictures would adorn our currency? I suppose Alexander Hamilton would be placed on the twenty, a nice boost from the ten-dollar bill. On the hundred, I believe Jane Jacobs, Fiorello LaGuardia or DeWitt Clinton would be great choices. On the one-dollar bill may I suggest Boss Tweed, Gov. Spitzer, Robert Moses or Typhoid Mary serving as a constant reminder that all paper money is dirty and can harm you? Why have only one person on each $5 or $10 or $20 Gotham bill, have a variety of faces, a set or collection. Why only one?

Oh yes, we'd still have pennies so that a slice of pizza can be offered for 99 cents and for those little copper discs I'd suggest Bernie Madoff featured in low relief behind bars promoting the notion that scamming fellow New Yorkers will nail you in the end, occasionally.

I'd keep Jefferson on the nickel; after all, it was he who brokered the deal with Hamilton to move the nation's capital to Virginia. Great move, Alex! Who wants those uniformed military types and wingtipped crooked politicians, scammers, lobbyists and cronies flooding our streets? We've got enough problems with the Wall Street hardnosed business tycoon types. Steal a loaf of bread and you go to jail, rip off billions from trusting investors and you go to East Hampton and party with Ron, Billy and Rufus the Dufus who are not the "clink" yet!

New York City would pass a traffic congestion plan, such as the one that had been vetoed by Albany's self-serving politicians who feared that their constituents would vote them out of office; those who drive into Manhattan from the outer boroughs. The gall of trading cleaner air, less congestion and a more manageable city so that they can warm a seat in Albany for another two years is incredible.

This time we would succeed in reducing the traffic snarls in midtown Manhattan by getting rid of cars! "THIMK" (ala IBM) It can be done but is isn't done.

Why? It's those weak, stupid and gutless politicians. Who needs cars in Manhattan? The rich! Raise more money for mass transit, clean up the air even more and more, thanks Mike, and put more Pedi-cabs out there to provide rapid transit in Manhattan that would be environmentally beneficial. Don't worry Sheldon Silver, State Senate majority leader in Albany, only people from Staten Island vote for you, most anyway!

We would provide all who wish a Segway at key places, for small change, to get around reducing the number of taxis, which by the way, change their shifts during rush hour when people need them the most. We are the "greenest" major city in The United States, producing the least carbon dioxide per person, "CO_2 footprint", into the atmosphere, but that doesn't mean that we can't get greener! It's a self-liquidating investment folks. Wake up! Fewer cars are a boost to our economy. Consider giving New Yorkers who get rid of their cars a reduced annual metro card fee, or free, based on the amount of miles they had been driving their car. That would help unclog the streets and a portion of the proceeds from the sale of their cars, such as the sales tax, would be devoted to capital improvements for public transit.

Motorized electric bicycles would be provided to all citizens who needed them, at cost, manufactured in New York City, of course, perhaps in our prisons and by those who need jobs. The goal would be to subsidize mass transit from vehicular related fees and taxes enabling us to reduce the transit fare down to $1 or less. Let's give the little people a break. They'll spend the money and put it back into the economy, much of it in the poorest neighborhoods. Trains . . . more trains and soak the car owners to reduce, or eliminate, the subway fare and improve the service driving ever increasing numbers of "strap hangers." "Fare" enough?

Most of all, the greatest city on earth would govern itself. No more "the tail wagging the dog" by the Albany "fat cats." As soon as we get control of our own money, taxing authority, we will be able to focus on our own problems without interference from others who have misguided and self-serving agendas with state and federal interests. We need Albany's approval to change income tax, sales tax, excise taxes, liquor, cigarettes, etc. Hey Albany and Washington! "Lead, follow or get out of the way!"

If we can get the crime rate down by over 75% as other cities scratch their heads, we can do anything!

Back to the Future, City-States, I like that, but please don't send me to Riker's! Ouch!

Take Back a Piece of New York City
In Your Heart

Everyone who comes here for the first time arrives with their own preconceived notions of New York City locked in their heads. No two people have identical templates of New York City locked in their heads.

It's all a composite of external their experiences; media dribble, misinformation shot straight to us from a distance; CSI, Special Victims Unit, The Taking of Pelham 123, Fort Apache, American Gangster, Taxi Driver, our inner selves that misperceive, rearranging the blitz, our fears, and notions of all the fictions that bombard us masking the reality that is the true essence New York City, its past, present and future.

For those who have never been here before, it's a pure abstraction, a kaleidoscope of the indirect, imaginary "experiences" that constantly assault our lives from afar. The New York City they "know" is built upon images, of what they have read, seen on television, heard from strangers, friends and family, filtered by their own values, fictitious expectations and specious fears.

Reruns that never end such as "Sex and the City", noir movies such as "Miracle on 34th Street", "New York", "Goodfellas" "Once Upon a Time in America", "The Gangs of New York", "The French Connection" and countless sources providing the essential backdrop conjuring up distorted views of New York City, the old New York City and the new fiction that newbies buy into by the quart.

We are new and improved unlike any other city has ever been before. The real New York City is unknowable unless you experience it for yourself.

The music of New York City provides "sound images" that ring in our ears and conveys our own New York City that's locked in our heads. Who hasn't seen The Rockettes, The Empire State Building, The Lady in the Harbor, and those ubiquitous street scenes of thousands moving through traffic struggling to reach their destinations from distant places before entering "The Promised Land"?

New York City is the broadest, widest and deepest stage on earth. Those who arrive catalogue all those places, images and characters with great expectation and sought them out putting them all together and struggle to reconcile all those forms of reality in comparison with their imagination and preconceived notions gathered from afar.

It's a matrix, a kaleidoscopic fancy of what they have thought that they would experience when they are here. They fully expect to leave with the same impression they come with, but few rarely do because all images and impressions gathered from afar are tossed aside or compared with the "real deal" seen up close and inhaled through all the senses.

There's romance, nostalgia, mystery and pause. We look at street images from afar; the taxicabs constant and incessant needless stupid honking reveals elements of anger, road rage blended with the backdrop of people shouting at one another. We observe quiet and seemingly lonely souls reading on park benches, children romping in million dollar plus playgrounds, subways roaring passed stations with many who plug an endless variety of devices into their ears cancelling out the sounds of the City while still clinging to the energy of the City as they continue to dwell in its presence, a choice that millions have chosen to make. Commuters run to catch a bus and bicycle messengers dart through traffic competing against themselves to complete their rounds to "make a buck" while putting thousands in harm's way without caring as if they're weaving through a handheld digital game without consequences.

More people, cars, trucks and trains enter Manhattan on a typical weekday, than in any other city in The United States, much more. With only twenty-three square miles of terrain, Manhattan works and plays at a furious pace. This segment of the City, only seven percent of the total land area of the entire City, together with its enormous structural verticality, is the center of energy, creativity and innovation on earth.

Consider this: Where else is so much happening in every field of human endeavor, in such a relatively small place, layered with abundant diversity, all with an abundance of harmony? No doubt, many visitors fail to put that notion out front and they are forced to redefine their misperceptions of New York City in countless new ways. It's more about the volume of everything that overwhelms the tourist and the enormous choices that one has here. It's everything from "A to Z" and more of it than anywhere else. It's the volume of life that engulfs the newbies and many of the rest of us at times. It's a give and take that requires personal management, introspection, reflection, self-searching and meaning. The sum of it all is this: New York City offers more choices and easier access to get to those choices then any other place on earth. That's the *summa magnifica* of New York City, access and choices. (Don't bother looking up the Latin italics. I made it up.)

Most visitors cannot imagine, if a resident moves one block down the street or even to the other side of the same block, their dry cleaner fears that they'll lose their business because every block has a dry cleaner or two and enhanced convenience might be the deciding factor to trash one vendor vs. another.

Take Duane Reade for example; they've got a drug store on practically every third block and they wouldn't be putting them there if they didn't expect to make money. The population density is incredible, of people who live in the neighborhood and those who happen to work, pass by and just happen to be there. If you've got something to sell and know how to sell it then you'll make money here, more than anywhere else.

I just love those who complain that retail rents are too high! People are paying them and like everything in nature not all survive. So, for who are the rents too high? Simple. The rents are too high for the schmucks who rent stores and don't know what they're doing. Finding the highest justifiable rent is the best place to open a store, right? Who wants to be on 10th Avenue, off the beaten path, waiting for trade? But, lately parts of 10th Avenue are not so terrible for retail, hum? It'll only get better and better. Just look up! All those people who live in the sky must come down to earth for a quart of milk or a bottle of shampoo. It's simple, here's the deal; Let's say you open a bar and across the street from two sixty story residential buildings and down the block are three 35 story buildings within four square blocks with approximately 9,000 additional residents. That's like having a "watering hole across the street from a total of 17,500 people! So, what should the rent be? High! But not so high as to make it unlikely that a savvy businessperson can not make enough money to make it worthwhile. That creates the equation that would justify a monthly rent of approximately $60,000 a month or more! That's a real pleasure for a smart operator.

Frequently, I have asked visitors, who are about to take a tour, what their pre-conceived notions of New York City are, especially those who have never been here before. Landlords aren't stupid people.

"We all come to New York City with our own New York City in our heads. What's in your head?" I ask. All that you have seen, heard, read and thought about New York City is locked inside you, right?

How much will *your* New York City change by tour's end?" I ask a few questions and people respond.

"I came here thinking that it would be dirty, mismanaged, rude, crowded and unsafe."

My job is, to provide an entertaining and engaging tour experience, on that enables my guests to view New York City through a different lens and reformulate their pre-conceived notions so that they take back a different and better New York City then the one they came with and that's what a Custom & Private New York tour experience is all about.

New York City is a favorite place for producers to portray urban ghettos, crime, mafia, violence, police corruption, terrorism, disasters and tragedies, King Kong, runaway subway trains, burning skyscrapers, street gangs, schoolyard knife fights, shootouts, car chases beneath "L" subway trains, multiple vehicular collisions, bank heists and chases that result in gun fire and death. These are the "themes" that producers love to film here. It's a business and that's what sells! When tourists see Central Park they comment about crime. Harlem still strikes fear in many and the sound of police sirens creates puffed-up anxiety. Films and many television series filmed and themed in New York City are laced with violence and that is the overwhelming genre of choice.

Sitcoms projecting New York City life in Seinfeld, King of Queens, Will and Grace, Friends, The Jefferson's and the classic All in the Family have the power to dominate the "tube" or the silver screen as the action and violence of the crime dramas, sex themes that are trashy and vacuous always get "top billing." Although there are valuable messages among some of those mentioned above, you too know what they are. Hence, those people that come here carry the image that is projected by "Hollywood" but that's not the one they take home.

Regardless of where my clients want to go, tours are peppered with many themes. Why do so many people continue to come here to visit over and over again? Why do so many people come here to visit or carve out their lives? Do they find what they are looking for? How did New York City succeed in reducing the crime rate so dramatically? Essentially, what have been the thematic forces that have driven this city in the past and what is driving it now? What does the future hold?

What path are we going down now? What's the real quality of public education, the numbers that define the real disparities of wealth, the extent of the problem of the underclass, opportunities, job equality, health care, housing, the transportation infrastructure and more? What are the limits of vertical growth in Manhattan? What will be the future of the enormous building construction boom, will it die or explode and who drives the outcome? In the customary and usual course of life how and why will it come to an end or burst forth in more impressive and imaginative ways?

Innovation, ideas that drive success, a non-judgmental liberal culture, ubiquitous kindness, un-dogmatic thinking pervades, enormous pride in the City, cooperation abounds, hard work, mutual respect, goal driven people from every walk of life and most of all "reaching for the sky" literally and figuratively is what we do and what we're about.

We're forever making it bigger and better and taking bold steps, always reaching for the future and, in many respects, not clinging to the past as, in most instances, our European friends had been doing for decade after decade, century upon century.

Our skyline is the greatest visual symbol of this City. It's our footprint. Our "temples" provide the graphic archive of our past, present and future. If New York City were to stop growing it wouldn't be the same, like a train falling off a track. Meaning; change is part of the present because change is always in our face. Noticing change, a constant, is part of every experience. Change, that's the only thing that stays the same in New York City. The energy and culture demand it. It's who we are. It's our DNA, pure and simple.

When possible, pointing out the who, where, when, why and how of places adds a great deal to people's understanding of what New York City is all about. For example; we can research on our own, the height of the Empire State Building, how long it took to construct, the number of windows and amount of steel needed to support it but, that's not the real story because it fails to deliver the human factor, the drama and the reason for its very existence.

Folks want to know about the forces that came together resulting in the creation of bridges, monumental buildings and other impressive monuments and temples that help define this town. Who decided to build them? Why? What were the driving forces?

We can discover how Wall Street acquired its name and certainly, any guidebook will give you the size of Central Park. In fact, you need not come here to accomplish that. Knowing why Central Park was built, how the idea to build a landscaped park emerged, and what makes it so magnificent? What did it cost and why is it considered a technologically innovative landscaped park unlike any other before? What makes it so special is certainly an enthralling story.

Discovering many of the characters who have played vital roles in shaping this City over the last 400 years is another element that not only provides fodder for rearranging the New York City that's in your head, but it adds drama and excitement seldom found in guidebooks or heard on public bus tours.

No doubt, tourists who visit many large urban centers throughout the world have their preconceived notions redefined after their visits here. New York City is a City that, I have discovered, generally is either loved or hated. Rarely have I meet someone who expressed that they "like" New York City. People express passionate opinions about this City and vocalize their reasons that justify their hardened opinions with demonstrative intensity. In recent times, our City has taken on quite a few more devotees then in the past, that's why there are no "I Like N Y" tee shirts.

Our efforts to clean up our "act" and create a welcoming environment provide more of what people want and less of what they don't then ever before. We have, for good reasons, become the world's number one destination for those seeking just about anything they want to do; shop, see, eat, experience, meet, learn and drink, enjoy!

For those who come here for the first time, or have not been here for over fifteen years, I say:

"Save some room in your hearts because you're going to need a place for New York City. It will dwell deep inside you, right where you tick!"

If you are the kind of person who looks, not just sees, who listens, not just hears, then the heartbeat of New York City will grab you and you'll fall in love with this town. Grasp the greatness of New York City, as the producer of so much that is beautiful and worthy, created by its people and given to the world and then you will acquire an advantage, one that will provide immeasurable pleasure, excitement and experiences during your visit that will remain with you forever.

People who find it difficult to "inhale" the huge volume of people, traffic, noise and energy ought to caste aside those negative emotions and try to absorb the City piece by piece. Don't let it daunt you as if you were standing in front of a spectacular buffet and haven't eaten in two days. Take small bites and move on to the next entrée.

Those who do not welcome the City in their minds and hearts remain encapsulated within themselves.

Perhaps that's a consequence of small town life, monolithic cultures of sameness, a lack of exposure to other cultures and values that tend to, at times, thwart acceptance and trust of those who have different ideas, ideals and customs preventing them from opening their minds and hearts. Many are skeptical and do not accept our values, politics and lifestyles, quite different from their own. In truth this is more common with fellow Americans who hail from the heartland, the south, rural places and the west. Europeans, Asians, Australians, South Americans and Africans tend to embrace New York City more openly and express a wonder and excitement not often seen from numerous American visitors.

What creates this suspicion? Surprisingly, many visitors from The United States actually believe that New Yorkers are less patriotic than our fellow countrymen even though we are "the melting pot" City, every bit a part of the United States. We are as proud as they are to be American. Our contributions to this country are incomparable in nearly every field of human endeavor. Certainly, some of that resentment and contempt is borne out of jealousy and envy of our success and by those who are truly unhappy with their own lot in life. "Success breeds contempt."

Our "free-wheeling" ways produce greater expression, less dogmatism, our population that de-emphasizes religion for most New Yorkers. New York City is the ideal place to live if you are half of a mixed couple whether it's gay or interracial. This troubles others from more conservative and evangelical places. Why? We have the right to live our lives the way we want to just as anyone else! Who you love and who loves you is no one else's business. We do not impose our lifestyles on anyone. Why are many people so harsh and critical of our liberalism and ideals? Far too many truly believe that we are sinners because we have too much fun. Let us go about our lives and we will continue to let you go about yours without judgment, criticism or scorn. This is America and the diversity of our people is part of what has made this country the best on earth from "sea to shining sea."

If you want to see America, don't come to New York City. If you want to see the world, come, bring an open mind and open heart and enjoy!

Welcome!

Eastside, Westside, Bestside?

It's sort of like that universal schoolyard incantation?
"Na-na-na-na-na NAH!" Remember that?
"You live on the Eastside? I enjoy the Westside. That's
where I choose to live. So, what about it?"
How many times have we all heard one version or
another of that ubiquitous flim-flam, that goes back
and forth with residents extolling the benefits,
praises and justifications for choosing to live on one
side of "town" or the other? We are, of course,
referring to the "Upper" of each, not the Lower East
Side, aka LES, and don't bother looking for the lower
Westside, there isn't any and there's no "Middle East"
either in New York City.
Although the distinction is discussed in good humor,
most often, the Upper Eastside has traditionally been
known to be more moneyed, old money derived from
smokestack industries, coal, and steel, shipping,
aluminum, bananas, pineapples, railroads, iron,
copper, etc. People involved in finance, banking,
insurance, the "well-heeled" have settled into the
wealthiest zip codes in the United States such as on
the Upper Eastside, the fabled zip code 10022. I've
had the "joy" of mailing alimony checks to that zip
code for years. Still trying to get it out of my mind,
10022 or is it 10002, eh?
Fifth Avenue, long referred to as the "gold coast"
contains co-op apartments that run into tens of
millions of dollars most with very unreasonable and
demanding coop boards that scrutinize the wealthy in
every way imaginable. In many cases, they require
the buyer to have a net worth many times the selling
price and all if it invested in high-grade "liquid" form

231

such as T-bills, U. S. notes, triple A corporate bonds, etc. No mortgage please either, cash deals only!

East of Fifth Avenue Madison Avenue is the Rodeo Drive of New York City, currently home of upscale global clothing purveyors, art galleries and top-notch accessory stores that sell less for more. The Eastside is a wider terrain then the Westside stretching from Fifth Avenue to East End Avenue, putting many residents further away from Central Park, and their one subway line on Lexington Avenue. What a shame! Their East River Park is a pinch park compared with Riverside Park, wider by far on the Westside that runs nearly the entire length of the Upper Westside, another Olmstead and Vaux masterpiece.

Take a look at Fifth Avenue, a one-Way Street since 1966 and much narrower then Central Park West, which is a wide two way street with subway stations nicely spaced up and down the entire fifty-one block stretch and with far more humanity and canines then you'll see on fabled Fifth Avenue. Sure there are lots of dog walkers, doctor's patients, domestics, building employees, people on their way to and from work and the usual flock of museum goers on Fifth. The neighborhood does not have the energy, bounce, spark, diversity, soul and feel of Central Park West. Frankly, it's a bit stiff. Nice people, I suppose, who pay a lot of taxes, just the right amount, right, in the 13% of taxable income range. Hum! Many of the owners of those opulent co-ops are absentia as in London, The *cote d' azure*, Dubai or The Hamptons.

Did you know that, historically cities tend to settle on the eastside of town first because the westerly direction of the morning commute puts the sun behind and on the trip back home at the end of the workday the sun is behind as well. This has been the case even before the advent of automobiles. Horses hate sun glare too.

"White, bright and polite" a phrase that has characterized the Upper Eastside, tongue and cheek, has much truth. It is far less diverse than the Upper Westside and more inclined to be snobbish, dotted with its brash neighborhood restaurants, boutiques, banks and shops.

A recent article in The New York Times revealed that only two-percent of its residents are Latino and African-American women who are seen lunching in the neighborhood are assumed to be nannies. Bloomingdales, several Ralph Lauren stores with $1,500 alligator belts, art galleries, Dean & DeLuca's, Dylan's Candy Bar, Serendipities and all the rest, have given this neighborhood less of what New York City is really all about; liberal leaning politics and diversity. It seems to have more of the Republican, Tea Party spin with the Fox twirl, Rush Limbaugh hoopla and Bill O'Reilly's spin and that's out of synch with 90% of New York City.

Still, it is a well-liked, not so loved, part of town, not nearly as much as before. New and trendy neighborhoods have emerged and compete with The Upper Eastside for the dollars of the gilded "1%." Still, it is a safe haven for new comers and those whose parents or trusts are footing the bill, for sure. "You're not living on the Westside, it's not safe!" What a myth! The Westside packs the most creative energy, actors, musicians, composers, producers, writers, choreographers, designers, artists and more of those who think outside the box, except when it comes to politics, which is generally liberal and Democratic

Party devotees. There are far more parks and cultural attractions out west. It tends to be younger, I do believe. Broadway bisects the Upper Westside and has it all, wide open and adorned with lush plantings, benches in center medians, more subway lines, red, blue and orange, theatres in abundance, Columbus Circle, The Time Warner Center, Lincoln Center, Julliard School of Music, The Museum of Natural History, The Rose Space Museum, Columbia University, CCNY, The Cathedral of St. John the Divine, Grant's Tomb, Washington's HQ, Alexander Hamilton's home, Pomander Walk, better and less costly food stores and the best Jewish Delis, Zabar's, Citarella, and no shortage of fine dining, more multiplex movie theatres and great housing stock, which is, cost wise, just about parallel with most of the Upper Eastside nowadays. Its diversity, creativity, liberalism and less pretentious feel are its primary distinctions compared with The Upper Eastside.

There's more friendliness and acceptance of every ethnic group. Ever since the construction of Lincoln Center and the gentrification of Lincoln Square, the Westside began to shed its stigma as a less affluent, perilous and hostile environment. Those days are over, unless and until change comes, and in New York City, hey anything can happen but a downward spiral is very unlikely in the foreseeable future.

Truthfully, I am not claiming that one side is better than the other. They're different and depending on who and what you are, either one is a better fit, your choice entirely, unless the rent is paid by someone with a bit of financial control over you. Certainly, many Eastside residents would find the Westside a better fit for them but preconceived notions, advice, fear, listening to their mother or friends who have their own thoughts, at times, push their priorities or a sense of prestige and snobbery upon their dependents, "it's safer" and that may have driven them there, east.

Just because someone lives on either side doesn't mean they fit these commonly believed stereotypes. The Upper Westside is more a bastion of liberal wealth, one of the few left in the country. If that suits you better then "go west young man" or woman.

East End Avenue is a long way from the Lexington subway line. The Second Avenue line now under construction will take a long time to complete! So if you love burgers, banks, bars, candy and tobacco, card shops, drug stores, nail places, Chinese takeout, dry cleaners, hardware stores and baby strollers then east might be best for you.

The west is for the rest. Oh yes, and if you decide to sit down on a bench in the median on Broadway you'll notice a lot of interesting characters to talk to. On Park Ave, you can do the same thing except please keep in mind that the flowers don't talk but some have been known to listen.

Observing people walking, crossing the street, using escalators, climbing stairs, crammed, jammed and rammed in New York City has always been quite amusing to me. By now, I have the "rules of the road" down pat! There are so many tell tale walking traditions and you too can become an expert if you watch, mimic and just give it a shot.

New Yorkers are the world's greatest walkers. We have to be. We have by far, fewer cars than any other American city. In fact, only 22% of Manhattan households have a car.

The streets are flat, traffic is a nightmare and Manhattan is so walk-able and parking is extremely scarce and extremely expensive. Public transportation is incredibly cheap, safe and fast. It's the way to go. Most people in New York City, most notably Manhattanites have no use for a car. It's perceived as an unnecessary expense, a burdensome and nearly useless piece of equipment.

The City, especially Manhattan, was a massive pile of rock, hills and ruts when Henry Hudson arrived, but thanks to the Commissioner's Plan of 1811 that mandated streets and homes to be built on flat ground requiring the removal of all rocks and filling in valleys and the removal of mounds of earth.

"Oh, New York City is such a great walking city! It's flat, and the streets are numbered, parallel and perpendicular. They're so easy to navigate!"

Tourists are not the only ones who don't know why. New Yorkers generally, don't have a clue about the grid plan.

The Grid Plan of 1811 was a major innovative and forward-thinking concept and together with The Erie

Canal as well as the subway system combined added to our growth and success with natural advantages, the Hudson River, Harbors, firm bedrock and diversity enabled this town to expand impressively and so rapidly.

Streets were numbered, according to the plan, enhancing communication among the masses. Those seeking directions were more at ease by accepting a piece of paper from a stranger with a street number written upon it rather than attempting to decipher one of nearly sixty languages spoken here back then. That was vastly easier then attempting to communicate bizarre street names for those seeking to find their way. The street blocks were designed to be extremely short, providing more corners because corners are worth more money providing abundant light, two views and enhanced ventilation in an age prior to electricity and air-conditioning.

This plan resulted in the creation of perhaps the best walking city on earth. All the rocks had to be removed to build homes, schools, hospitals and commercial buildings and, of course, pave the streets. Hence, New York City is the most geologically transformed urban space on earth, right here in Manhattan, "island of many hills."

Observing the rushers, not walkers, appears as though they are skating on their shoes dancing to a waltz gliding and maneuvering through throngs of sidewalk traffic. Perhaps it's rather a ballet of sorts choreographing every step measured in nanoseconds searching for their paths, selecting turf 20 or 30 feet ahead of them is far more amusing and entertaining than formal theatrical dancing. It's a science, a sport; a weave to the left, "no not there, the tandem strolling tourists are blocking the entire width of the sidewalk and perhaps I'll step off the curb and bypass this trudging herd of "large Marge's" uh!

It's almost a contest, with yourself, to be the first one to get to the end of the block, synchronizing your steps, not breaking stride, checking out the street lights to decide whether or not to "do the diagonal" which is to start crossing where the cars are about to reach a red light within a few seconds and judging from the solid don't walk orange signal and if the cross street is vacant then "diagonal it" and make that cross a "double cross", because the shortest distance between two points is a straight line or nearly straight. Northeast corner directly to southwest corner without breaking stride, we do it all the time. We twist our necks peeking at the tourists behind us waiting like good little school children.

"You want us to J-walk? We're forbidden to do so back home!"

Becoming an expert takes a lot of practice so watch the professionals before you dare. Stand against a building wall or take a seat, if available, relax on a double fire hose valve sticking out of a building wall and watch. Why do they call them "Siamese" anyway? I know why, do you?

Many who appear to be in a hurry are rushing for no reason other than to speed. It's in their DNA and it can't be helped! Most speeders on the highway are not in a hurry; speeding is their nature, same as walkers. It must be that New York City heartbeat that fuels their walk.

Who can explain the logic of speed walking on the way to the subway? Because whatever pace you choose to walk the chances of saving time once you get down to the platform has nothing to do with speed walking. Walk slowly and the train may leave the moment you get there or it may just be pulling into the station. Run and then you may wait for the same train that the walkers who got there before you will take. Fly down the steps and you may be in an ambulance and just miss the train that was never intended for you, like an E and not a C train. It's all the law of averages. It's not as though the trains know whose running or walking above them, right? We've all just missed our trains and swore that if we didn't stop to give someone directions, or if we had made the cross light, or didn't stop to buy that coffee or answered the ringing cell phone. Let the cell phone ring and had you not taken the call before you had entered the subway station then you'd have been there when the B train entered the station. Hey New York City! Get off that trolley! We walk fast enough. Don't run, please!

"Get a grip and have some dip!"

It's like waiting to pull the handle on the slot machine and yours is the turn that yields the prize. There's no way to know!

New Yorkers walk quite efficiently, darting, ducking, and dodging, anything and anyone who gets in their way can be fodder and mowed down. New Yorkers step with a cadence, a deliberate, mindful stride that pushes them forward, taking them to their destinations, not only post haste, but with a number of maneuvers that always hasten their arrival to their destinations. Others, generally, don't do, can't do, don't know or just don't care or don't dare! It's in our blood, pure and simple.

New Yorkers are straight walkers. Not doing so, on the sidewalk, is an unwritten law, it's a felony against the public, and so don't get caught! Tourists do not comply. Tourists don't walk straight; they sway along, meander, stop, and look and they stand in small groups blocking our superhighway, the sidewalk.

New Yorkers plan their walks, moment to moment. By calculating, instinctively, where walkers who are ahead of them are going to be in fractions of a second, calculating hundreds of times throughout a two-block walk on their way to their destinations. There's a mini-computer in our heads that provides solutions to these equations, our own built in GPS, stealth and cerebral based laser guided drones in our heads guiding our every move. That's us!

Pedestrians who waver or change their speed are not New Yorkers. They disrupt the rhythm of those around them and thwart others trips, yes trips, by trapping them. Don't they realize that the sidewalks of New York City are superhighways dominated by herds of striders with deliberate intentions moving forward at calculated speeds. It's a gait that should not be disrupted. Tourists, visitors and neophytes plague the cement are the number one pet peeve of our citizenry. Oh, it's so annoying!

"Lead, follow or get out of the way!"

New Yorkers have their own strategies at corners too. Tourists wait for the light to change, even if there are no cars coming, ah duh! New Yorkers step off the curb, look both ways, and cross. They are aware of bicycle messengers and cross if no cars are coming or if they see vehicles moving forward slowly most will attempt to take their chances. They glance at the volume of pedestrian traffic that prevents vehicular movement into the turn, make snap decisions, and decide whether or not to walk. Why wait? Tourists never make that conclusion. That's a decision made for them by the light. It's inexperience and fear. You can't blame them because many are from towns that have one traffic light, maybe two. Poor critters, I suppose that's why they come; to experience the excitement of New York City and watch the traffic lights change. Glad you're here and don't get squashed, please! Last year over 500 pedestrians, in Manhattan, were hospitalized due to bicycle collisions. Please! Look both ways.

And then there's the "STOP"! Frequently tourists see something that catches their attention and poof, they "stop dead" in their tracks! A New York City walker is baffled because they proceed directly into a building or store entrance whereupon a tourist will stop without warning in the center of the sidewalk and confer with their friends, whomever, and ask,

"Is that The Empire State Building?" as they stare at The Chrysler Building.

Then they'll refer to a map, halt and determine if they've arrived. The camera or iphone comes out and a picture is composed of a companion positioned on the other side of the sidewalk expecting all to halt until they compose their photo in the middle of the superhighway. Keep walking New York City because they're not going to waste precious film anymore. The world has gone digital!

Large groups of tourists walk in tandem, side by side, consuming the entire sidewalk, disabling others from moving forward or permitting others to pass them as if they own the sidewalk is the major "pet peeve" of New Yorkers. This is particularly annoying. It's like drivers clinging to the left lane on a highway creeping along at 45 miles per hour blocking motorists from moving forward! It's a blocked artery! They are low-density cholesterol, LDL's with high-density oversized body parts, blocking our sidewalks.

People stand in the middle of crowded sidewalks talking, looking at maps or chatting, oblivious that they're in the middle of a traffic lane! Folks, this is not a cornfield, this is where the greatest volume of pedestrian traffic exists. No soybeans, corn or sorghum grown here on 47th and Broadway. What the hell is sorghum anyway? This is particularly troublesome to New York City walkers because the sidewalks are for walking, not waiting, blocking, talking or standing.

If you have to take a break and re-equip then step aside and find your way, refer to your map, or ask a New Yorker, who'd be delighted to help you. But, just standing in the middle of a crowded sidewalk is not smart; remember it's a sideWALK, not a "sideWAIT" or "sideSTAND"! Thanks a lot guys. Let's hope we all get there before tomorrow!

Make way and be considerate of others. We need to keep moving and that's what this City is all about, moving, moving forward. Get out of the way, be smart and please recognize that you're not in Ohio, or Indiana where the sidewalks are vacant. You can try that in Miami too if you wish, because there's no one out there. They're all in their cars, garages, fast food restaurants, homes, assisted living units or office buildings. We scramble to get where we're going, moving through throngs of people who are competing with us. Despite unintended misplacement, offenders who thwart our greatest asset for mobility, our sidewalks, are most welcome but take a course, Sidewalk 101.

The best place to watch New Yorkers walk is Grand Central Terminal. That huge inside public space where people are always in a hurry, coming from every direction, crisscrossing, gliding through the maze, anticipating where the oncoming walker will be by the time the passage between them and you has been synchronized. It's a ballet. It reminds me of ants or bees in their colonies going about their business without disrupting each other. It all gets done and everyone reaches their destination with precision, no tussles, no tumbles, "no runs, hits or errors." I wonder. Do ants punish their fellow citizens who do not adhere to the rules of the road? Does that irritate those compliant little creatures? Sure it does. Just snatch a piece of sugar from them and you'll know better next time!

The best strategy is to keep moving, be kind, duck and dodge. Keep that peripheral vision radar on and maintain your speed. It's a graceful cadence that enables you to survive so you will catch your train to meet your beau for that end of day embrace or tongue-lashing.

"Where have you been? I was sick with worry about you!"

There's a bit of science to it, not the rocket type. Just get familiar with the drill, we want to keep moving, we have schedules, appointments to keep, jobs to get to and miles to go "before we sleep." Sidewalk space is very limited in some parts of town and your cooperation will be much appreciated, or else! What we really need to do is to trade off some of the streets for pedestrians and that's exactly what we've been

doing. As a friend from a tropical island once told me about New York City,
"Too much people!"
Someone's got to teach this lady how to talk; her walking is pretty good though, as I recall.
After you think you've mastered the "walk" then head out to Park Slope, Brooklyn. Claim a square foot of the sidewalk on Fifth Avenue, out there, and pretend that you're a pinball! The double width baby strollers for twins, the friends of the mother and their apparatus too will challenge you. If you get to the end of the block before sunset then you are a certified New York side-walking expert! Congrats!! Caution! Watch out for those odd shaped modern day baby milk bottles and monster backpacks. You could trip and damage the sidewalk! And last but not least: "Don't step on a crack or you'll break your mother's back." Remember that?

Living in New York City is dwelling in an ever-changing environment and a significant part of that change is how we "tawk." In most places language changes slowly, but not so in New York City. We have a brisk, always changing and forever morphing vernacular. It's new and improved, or at the very least a forever changing lingo that we call "communicating".

Language is an expression, one of change that helps define New York City. Restaurant language is a particularly amusing example of linguistic evolution. We'll get to that in a bit.

The use of foreign worn out expressions and phrases and uncommon syntaxes have been replaced with a new means of expression. New words constantly seep into our lingo. Words are spoken in English, quite often, that carry phrases imported from every speaker's native tongues, such as:

"You need do me that!" "Let me bring you out." "You need not go back ways." "I was standing on my clock an hour." In the order listed above, those phrases in Yiddish mean: "Don't do that to me." "Let me explain." "Don't go behind my back" and "I was kept waiting for an hour."

Expressions that meant one thing years ago acquire new meanings today. Many words or expressions used today on a regular basis were unheard of in the past or had meanings that are no longer valid. Let's start with "diner-speak."

I recall when waiters and waitresses chanted their orders in a language that most people would not comprehend today, for example:

"Burn the British" "Give me a radio, whisky down", "high and dry", "stretch a pair", and on and on. Translation, in order listed is, toasted English muffin, tuna is radio "tune-a", "whiskey" is rye bread as in rye (i.e. Canadian Club) and "down" is toasted. "High and dry" is no butter, stretch a pair is two Cokes, and "stretch," relates to the soda coming out of the soda fountain, or stretching. Many of those phrases are no longer in use. Today we have "deluxe" for burger deluxe and that includes the burger on a bun, French fries, lettuce, a pickle, a slice of raw onion and tomato, which is also known as "the works" and don't forget about that tiny paper cup with one cubic inch of coleslaw which is also used by dentists to hold abrasive cleaning mix, come to think of it! Someone thought of it first and it has become the template of the ubiquitous "burger deluxe."

BLT is an obvious favorite, also the name of a high-end restaurant chain that bears the initials of the founder, Bistro Laurent Tourondel. Don't leave out "hold the" for leave it out, and the forever popular "86" for cancel which was derived from Chumley's, a bar, located at 86 Bedford Street in the West Village when it had been a speakeasy. The owners had an inside arrangement with some of the local police who would call ahead alerting Chumley's (est. 1926 during prohibition) patrons of an impending police raid. The shout "86" would clear the place. It's still the only bar in the City that doesn't have a sign, due to reopen after its renovation is completed and its SLA (State Liquor Authority) re-issues their permits. The lines are forming as of this printing.

I was in an elevator recently with my daughter, who was in her mid-thirties at the time. We were accompanied by a few other baby boomers, folks in the mid-fifties and older. A conversation began and I take the blame for that. I used an old expression in the context of that brief chat, "you're darn tootin.'" My daughter looked at me quizzically, and asked, "What does that mean?"

"You don't know what that means? You've never heard that expression?"

I was astonished that she had never heard it before.

"No!" she exclaimed. The baby boomers on board were all surprised too! That expression vanished from the vernacular and none of us even knew that! For those of you who don't know, it means, you're darn right.

Another phrase that has vanished is "after all is said and done." But this one has been replaced by the ubiquitous, "at the end of the day" a phrase that has been beaten to death by every standup comic, broadcast journalist and suited office worker during as much useless and endless office meetings. I hate that expression almost as much as that stupid expression "phone tag" that worn out phrase describing two people who tirelessly attempt to reach each other and get the usual voice mail, "I'm either on the phone or away from my desk" which is another invention brought to us by linguistic geniuses. I love the "either" in the previous example, as if those are the only two possible explanations for the failure of the owner of the ringing phone to grab it. There are quite a few people who do not answer their phone who are neither on their phone nor are they away from their desks. Many do not have a desk, or are not on the phone either. Maybe the phone isn't being answered because of "caller ID", another term that has entered the lexicon not long ago. Toss in "call waiting" "call forwarding" skype and a "phone card" new words that have joined us too.

What could Mr. Executive and Ms. Secretary be doing besides being "either on the phone or away from their desk"? Just once I'd love to hear the voice mail: "I'm either with my arms wrapped around my secretary or my secretary has joined me for a "dirty" martini."

The most annoying phrases that I can think of are the automated phone digitally driven menu dribble such as: "This call may be monitored for quality assurance or training purposes." My favorite is: "We are experiencing longer than normal wait times. Please be patient and the next available operator will be with you shortly. Your call is very important to us." But, it's not as important as being short-staffed because that saves us money and they don't give a rat's ass if you have to wait. Truth be told, your call is obviously not too important to them.

We all know why this automated system is in play. It's a means to prevent some ill-trained or underpaid live person from irritating the shit out of a customer or client, driven by their budgetary priorities which are more important to them than the caller, you! No doubt it saves the company or institution money but it distances the company from the caller. If given the choice, I'd opt to speak with a live person rather than respond to a machine. How about you?

"Hail a cab" is never used, now it's "grab a taxi" or "get a taxi", the more correct current blurb. Have you ever asked a taxi driver to, "Follow that cab?" That's old noir from those black and white Jimmy Stewart, Edward G. Robinson or Humphrey Bogart movies.

What newsstand vendor shouts? "Extra, extra! Read all about it" Do you ever hear, "Brother can you spare me a dime?" the classic from the Great Depression. Today it is either, "change please" or "can you spare some change?"

There's a panhandler in my 'hood who never heard the word, "change." He asks for a "dollar!" Perhaps he's got an MBA from Harvard. No one would waste his or her time asking for a dime even in these difficult times, you would think? But those folks standing next to folding tables with huge empty water bottles pleading for donations for the homeless ask for pennies! President Obama's mantra has been "change" and that inspired me to suggest to a number of panhandlers to alter or "change" their pitch to "It's time for change" or similar words to that effect. Some have actually applied the idea with good results! I know because they've told me, amazing. It's not what you say or ask for, it's how you ask: Sales or Panhandling 101.

"Twenty-three skidoo" where did that come from? New York City! The Flatiron building located at the intersection of 5th Avenue and Broadway at 23rd Street, a 1902 triangular steel frame wonder that causes wind to cascade and swirl down 23rd Street that lifts ladies dresses up revealing peeks above their ankles or thighs. Way back then ladies dresses touched the pavement and men sat eagerly and patiently waiting on benches across the street in Madison Square Park for those propitious moments. The cops chased them away with the chant,

"Twenty-three skidoo! Get out of here!"

Most people under the age of forty never heard of that expression. Gone from the lexicon, as one generation is doomed to the passage of time.

At the time The Flatiron Building, completed in 1902, was the first place where "Edison Actualities" were viewed in stores through kinescopes featuring New York City street scenes. They filmed horse drawn wagons, omnibuses, pedestrians, dogs and women's dresses rising as swirling wind currents around the Flatiron Building initiated the desired effect. "Actualities", a word no longer in use, has been replaced by the word movies. Could it be that those "actualities" were the first porn flicks? Google, Edison Actualities and you'll see them. Behave yourself!

The most significant change in language is that people simply do not speak, face to face, as much as they had in the past. When was the last time you were in an elevator with no one wearing ear buds or talking on their cell phone or smart phone or emailing someone on a Blackberry or iphone, listening to their ipod, ipad or reading their Kindle or Nook, texting or playing an electronic game, hoping to kill twenty-five terrorists, villains or street hoods before the elevator arrived in the lobby? Yes, Steve Jobs has changed the world!

On many occasions, I've been in an elevator where every person was "connected" to a device including, but not limited to, reviewing their incoming calls on their "cell" using some electronic marvel that did not exist several years ago. Such as "Texting" a new word in today's lingo, checking the weather, making a reservation for dinner or finding the best route to wherever they're driving today or searching a GPS, another set of initials that everyone knows instantly but ten years ago, a duh! "There's an App for that." Five years ago that meant nothing! Today, if you ask someone about the weather, or acknowledge someone with a polite "hello" or "good morning" then you're out of luck!

Oh, and don't forget the kids! They're wearing out their thumbs with electronic "games" by maneuvering robots between the twelfth floor and lobby of my elevator ride or figuring out how to steal cars, "Grand Theft Auto II." And for those who are not electronically inclined there's always Sudoku, KenKen, crossword puzzles and other means to keep their mouths shut too. At least they can be done with paper and a pencil, not just on a handheld device. Now that's progress. "Bridge" anyone?" "What's dat?" Oh yes, there's an app for that.

I have watched New Yorkers crossing the street while emailing on a handheld device while the driver who they should have been consciously attempting to avoid was talking illegally on a cell phone while "running" a red light, and perhaps steering with their knees while texting their daughter trying to find out where she is, that's if she doesn't have a GPS tethered to her necklace while he's trying to balance his cup of hot coffee, black, no doubt, on his crotch! Hope it spills on the family jewels!

Are we moving in the wrong direction? I think so! Take me back to the days of the busy signal, or an unanswered ringing phone. 411, remember that? "What number do you wish please?"

Unfortunately, all those great pranks now live in history. I remember my mother yelling, "Are you fooling around with the phone?"

"No mom, of course not!" as I watched a car with a sign Lincoln Park Pizza pull up in front of Mrs. Cooper's house bearing four large pizzas with anchovies! Why anchovies? Because nobody orders that! At times, after about fifteen minutes after I placed my order, knowing that the anchovies were blistering the pizza in the oven, I'd call the pizza place and tell them to cancel the order. They shouted, "Whadda you mean, eh? Whad I'm a goina do wit four anchovy pizzas?"

I told him,

"Why not use them as hubcaps on your pizza mobile or strap them on your flying saucer, eh!"

What fun! Now gone forever due to caller ID. What a shame. What a crying shame! Amazing that most of us grow up some day.

We have become a disconnected society thanks to our modern day technological revolution. We've morphed into a society mired with devices that have become the centerpiece of our existence. Although they are intended to increase our connectivity they impede it. Personal face-to-face contact as we stand two feet from one another has vanished.

Email me, text me, fax me, tweet me, go to my facebook page, but don't call me! We seem to consider a phone call the closest form of engagement when people about one hundred years ago must have been saying similarly, "I never get to speak with blabla face to face! He just calls me and that's crazy!" People who express a desire to connect through the web on sites such as classmates.com, Facebook, EHarmony, JDate, Christian Mingle, LinkedIn, YouTube, Twitter, Flicker, Instagram, etc. reach out but do not call; no talk, no speak, no see, no close up. It amuses me that I receive countless emails from people requesting that we become contacted on Linked-in, a business relationship site on the Internet. Most of those requests come from people I don't recall ever knowing, meeting, seeing or speaking to. I crush those requests with a click. Self-serving strangers encroach on me without a hint of "how are you?" That's social networking? Please! Go away if you don't have enough sense to ask, "How are you?" Why would they want them to be Linked-in with me? It's transparent! Want me to be your buddy, then give me a call and let's find out why or at least send me an email.

It's all about money because Linked-in is a site created to enhance your "social network" on the Internet creating traction to make Linked-in money. Ka-Ching!

Recently, I received a Linked-in request from the chef concierge of a five star hotel in New York City to be connected with me. I used to stop by many times seeking business for Custom & Private. I left her gifts, brochures and other various items to create a business connection and she never gave me a thing except a phony smile. That's okay. You can't win them all! But, why then does she request that we connect on Linked-in? I responded to her request with a message asking, "why." I never heard from her so, crawl back into your office and get out of my cyberspace baby!

In this electronic world, even in New York City, many people have lost their ability to have a conversation, write a letter, let alone have a postage stamp. What's a postage stamp? Are we raising children who perceive communication as a lesson in typing? Some school districts in this country have discontinued teaching cursive writing! *Unbelievable!*

The film camera has gone the way of the trash heap, so has the movie camera, cassette tape recorder and player, typewriter, and next it will be the spiral bound lined notebook and plain old book, pen, alarm clock, telephone book, etc.

Those who have created these devices may have known all along that this would be the effect on direct person-to-person communication; in fact, they wished it. But, for corporate icons or titans it didn't hurt their bottom lines, bonuses, stock options or perks. I believe that inventors and geeks are out to change the world for the better and indeed they have given us the Internet, the ipod, ipad, the PC, imac, Dell, cell phone, smart phone and the ability to move business and life much more quickly, but we are paying a very high price.

Here's a short list: CNN, CDR, DVR, ATM, RPG, DWI, TSA, NSA, GPS, spam, .com, .net, the web, "goggle that", Metrocard, ip address, browser, "call or click us", tweet, debit card, flat screen, global warming, drones, square, dirty bomb, text me, yahoo, twitter, apple TV, Amazon, Facebook, Ipad, Angie's List, Greg's List, Kindle, Nook, TripAdvisor (I like that one) and on and on. Who knows a 13 year old who won't pay a price to wear out their thumbs instead of their tongue?

"Walkman" was a new thing not all that long ago and WOW! We could listen to our favorite cassette tape in our pockets. That was big, very big. Now, Apple nano touch on a watchband stores over 2,500 songs, digitally and it's there at the touch of a finger, and it doesn't have to be a thumb! That's good, real good but don't talk to me because "I'm in the zone, man!"

Public speaking; those two words put together make me laugh. Hey, one-day technology will replace the laugh, sneeze, smile, belch, fart and yawn. Are the basic communication skills of our next generation up to par with their predecessors? Have they tumbled back into the Stone Age? Are their face-to-face conversational skills falling into the abyss and has confidence in interviews hit rock bottom? Perhaps the class of 2018 will be interviewed via email. I wouldn't be surprised if that's going on right now in an interview "chat room"! Sure, of course it is! College degrees are attainable on the Internet and that's nothing new. That reminds me of the MAD magazine spook years ago, "Brain Surgery self-taught" via U.S. mail. If peers compete against each other, raised in a society with the same "tools" then I suppose it's a level playing field, somewhat lower level, eh?

Whatever happened to "The 3 R's" as in good ol' reading, writing and 'rithmetic? What change would the song "I'm Gonna Sit Right down and Write Myself a Letter" have today? Oh, make that an email or text and thanks very much.com! "I'm Gonna Sit Right Down and text my babe a text." Not good, not good at all!

We use tools invented by geniuses but at what price? Press one for English, press two for Spanish and some day it will be press 6 for Portuguese and 12 for Russian. How are people ever going to learn how to speak their new local language? There's a device that enables you to point it to a sign, with a menu in virtually any language and it will display the translation you wish for on the screen and, if you want. It will provide an audible version of the translation as well. It can also translate words spoken and instantly provide the audible translation to the language of your choice. This is amazing stuff!

If you want to speak to an agent say "agent" or "representative." Does that annoy you? I want to speak to a person right from the get go! What is this world coming to?

"Okay, let's get started. Let me pull up your records. Okay, I see you have an account with us. Is that correct?" Ouch!

We have become a disconnected society immersed in a world of technology that has reared its ugly technology. The myriad of inventions that have come forth, intended to enhance our lives have encapsulated us, even in a City as dense as New York City. With 71,000 people per square mile in Manhattan, the densest county in The United States, is there anyone to talk with? Sure, lots, just get unplugged.

New York City is a place where direct communication will never die because we're so densely packed and it's still growing. I fear that other places with greater distances between people will fall and fail to hold on to the graces and benefits of direct eye contact, body language and the nuances of traditional modes of communication. So much is lost via emails; the emotion, raised eyebrows, frowns, wrinkled foreheads and the intent that language alone fails to convey, as only facial expressions and voice inflections can do. Electronic devices disrupt and distort communication, causing irreparable harm to relationships, lost business deals and opportunities gone by despite the benefits that electronic superhighways strive to provide. It could very well be that we, as a race, will revert back to pen and paper, the busy signal, ask a neighbor what the weather forecast is and we may again ask if we can borrow their newspaper and "brother can your spare me a stamp." Somehow, I just don't get the same "kick" out of an email as receiving a handwritten letter, especially with a lipstick smack on the back doused with a splash of perfume and the initials, S.W.A.K., sealed with a kiss. Mr. Gates, Mr. Dell and Mr. Dorsey, Mr. Ellis, Mr. Jobs will never improve that.

I'll take my chances here in New York City as the best place to ride out those changes and know that I can always find opportunities to communicate the old fashioned way which is: up close and personal. By the way, "Please text me, email me, be my friend on Facebook, tweet me how you are and what's new with you?" But don't call me. I just may not know what to say, or how to say it! Is that my phone ringing?

Starbucks

Most active and energetic New Yorkers crave a few cups of "Joe" throughout the morning and in afternoon hours too as well as late evenings. Granted, it's on the low end of "the speed spectrum" but it provides that extra lift that can be very addicting, the basis of Starbucks. Know what I mean?

I've never understood the "draw" of Starbucks. Sure, it was a new concept, a "coffee emporium" with its endless variety of coffee preparations, cappuccino, espresso, latte, schmatte, tall, which, incidentally, means short or small. Don't you love the genius of marketing the Starbucks way? Add whipped cream, cinnamon sprinkles, sugared caramel syrup, almonds, marshmallows, green mint slime and all of that and you've got a caloric mountain in the palm of your hand all for only $8.99.

Then came the peripherals because the rents are high so that a cup of coffee for about $2.25 and up isn't going to cut the rent. Along comes the high priced sodas, biscotti, health food bars, salads, sandwiches, and music to go, coffee by the pound, mugs, gift cards, books and music DVD's provided for those standing in long lines waiting for their brew to help pay the rent, Starbuck's, no not yours! Imagine. Standing in line, in New York City, for overpriced bitter coffee . . . no sir!

My alienation from Starbucks extends to all the bland American chain stores, such as Dunkin' Donuts, Pappa John's Pizza, McDonald's, The Gap, Subway and The Banana Republic, Duane Reade, now owned by the behemoth middle American Walgreen's, owned by people who know absolutely nothing about New York City and man, it shows. "Your drugstore, your City."

their tagline featured in Duane Reade's display windows. Yeah, it is our City, not yours! They're creations of Middle America, they're imports and void of our local culture, history, politics and way of life. Now present in Manhattan we have a piece of Texas, brought to you by The Southland Corporation, 711!

Recently as I was handed my change and receipt, about a foot long, at a Duane Reade drug store the cashier said to me,

"Have a great day and feel good."

The following day another cashier said,

"Hope you have a nice day and be well."

I asked her if she had been told by store management to say two nice things to each customer when they completed their transaction because it was obvious to me that some out of downer marketing genius put that one down. She replied, "yes." For me it was obvious and insulting. Programing people to be nice is such a plastic and obvious ploy. Trickle down manners from management to a cashier directly to you! They couldn't trust the concept of just asking their cashiers to be nice, smile and pretend to show an interest. It had to be specific; two pleasant things must be said. OMG! Yes sir, sir!

Where are we, in "the mall" or a drive up strip mall in Oklahoma, Missouri or Nebraska? A walk through New York City reveals that we're moving in that direction, in a place that has, or had, its own identity, the melting pot, a multiplicity of cultures, small businesses, a different venue on every block, the characters, soul, personality and an extension of the unique and distinct persona of the owner(s) of those places, of course, with a New York City flair or New York City no flair. But, New York City the "real deal" is a diminishing backdrop! That panache, the personality of New York City is evaporating like a cup of stale coffee. It's called suburbanization. I have a better name for it, Middle America Mall-O- Mania.

When I walk into Starbucks it's always for one of two reasons. Either I need to blow my nose, wipe my eyes, or my forehead in hot humid weather or in cold windy weather.

I enter, grab a few of those industrial strength brown paper napkins, just blow or wipe and leave them there, in the proper receptacle, of course. Walking in to use the restroom is frequently a waste of time. By law, food purveyors whose establishments have seating for twenty or more patrons, in New York City, are required to provide bathrooms for their customers. Ever notice how many places have nineteen seats? Look around! Starbucks consistently has more than twenty however their bathrooms, in my experience, are most often "out of order" more than any other chain operation in the City. Why is that folks? I never heard of one of their coffee machines needing a royal flush, hum? Recently, there was an article in the New York Times that cited Starbuck's "barristers" aka coffee pourers, as deliberately locking bathroom doors and posting "Out of order" signs. Breakin' the law you upstanding down right wrong coffee pourers. Barristers?! Would someone please tell Howard Schultz that barristers are lawyers, OMG! I'll bet the toilets work just find for you! There's an old Japanese saying that "the fish stinks from the head." Step aside Howard; I have to pee!

I dare not enter Starbuck's with my six pound Yorkshire even for a napkin, because I've been told by more than one coffee pourer to leave because dogs are not allowed in food establishments in New York City, even though I'm holding that little canine, it's still not allowed. Okay, so ask me to leave but don't bark at me. Even my pooch doesn't do that! Being nice is a part of New York City's culture.

Jackie Mason had a terrific "routine" about Starbucks in one of his terrific one-man shows on Broadway. He put the nail right on the head. He characterized the high prices, lack of adequate seating, the attitude and the taste of the coffee as plaaahhh; "so vhat's the bargain? Vhat's so terrific? I have to pay $4.95", an exaggeration, but true if you go for the fancy stuff.

"I can get a cup of coffee anywhere for about a $1.50 on the street! And, hey, it's very good coffee! Fancy schmancy!"

The KidfromBrooklyn.com, a website featuring an Italian guy, approximately sixty to sixty-five years old, wearing a white tank top undershirt, aka a "wife beater" and a newsboy cap, has a variety of videos available on his website, and YouTube, just for the clicking, he does a "number" on Starbucks, something to this effect.

"I gotta be nuts ta go ta Starbucks, eh? I go ta Tony's on Atlantic Avenue and get two eggs, toast, bacon, sausage, and coffee wit refills, a large OJ all fa $5.95, an a coffee ta go! Ya can't beat dat wit a stick. If I go ta Starbucks I get a Latte wit notin' else fa $5.95! What am I a freakin' jerk or what, eh? Gi me a freakin' break!"

Hey folks, if you love or even like Starbucks and there must be thousands of you so you must love the taste, service, locations and atmosphere and I'm happy for you. But do you know that you're contributing to ripping the melting pot apart? Every one of the hundreds, yes hundreds, of Starbucks that litter the City deprives us of the opportunity to sit down at Mary's or 64th Street Coffee Stop or Harry's Coffee, all fictitious, never to exist establishments. Or, perhaps the candy stores, private card shops, unique places with New York City flair that could provide and compete just like New York City is intended to do but sadly it's too late for that.

We're not a strip mall or a piece of Middle America! Sure, it's a free country and Starbucks has the money and the power as well as all the connections to invade Manhattan and the outer boroughs with the highest priced coffee, "suburbanizing" the melting pot putting their footprint on our precious soil and robbing New Yorkers of opportunities, choices and the neighborhood look and feel. To me this is a not a good thing!

Drink up New York City but remember the City that you are drinking to may not be there when you smell the coffee! Try the street vendors because for $1.50 you'll get a real New York bargain and help a New Yorker support their family, not stockholders and fat cat landlords.

It has been said that an excellent New York City licensed tour guide is a virtual walking, talking encyclopedia! The last thing that I, as a licensed New York City tour guide, want to say is, "I don't know!" Therefore, even though it's a fun line of "work", I embrace my profession very seriously, with an ever-present sense of humor, and that includes the notion that "if a tour isn't fun then, well, it just isn't a tour."

I must have my content down extremely well; including quips, tales, amusing stories, folklore and interesting personal experiences that make a point and when possible, get my guests laughing or at the very least capture their interest by creating stimulating, engaging and amusing dialogue.

At the outset of every tour I ask my guests to please interrupt me as we go along because if they see something that captures their interest; anything that raises their curiosity then "Please stop me and ask, because after we've passed a site that captures interest, you may be unable to describe it well enough for me to know what you've seen and it's lost!"

Sure, I've read literally piles of books, articles, walked miles and miles, spoken to hundreds of people from all walks of life, visited hundreds of places of interest, strolled into neighborhoods where I have never been feeling like a investigator or even an anthropologist on a mission many times, soaking up all the information I possibly could. Not just the facts and figures, but the folklore too, the stories: it's about who, where, when, why and how. No one said it better than Don Hewitt, the late executive producer of 60 Minutes, remarking on the success of the record breaking news magazine program, "It is all built around one of the first things we ask of our mothers, 'Mommy, tell me the story.'"

For example, people want to see The Empire State Building. Sure, it's incredibly impressive and the story behind it is enthralling. But looking at it doesn't provide information that will fascinate. The travel and guide books typically focus on factual information such as the numbers, when it was built, how many windows did it have, how many tons of steel, how long did it take to construct and so forth, generally omitting "the story" as to who had the idea, what was the motivation, what innovations were created, the triumphs and tragedies that are all entwined within this storied edifice. In other words, it's not just the dry facts but also the legends, the stuff that provides entertainment and captures interest. In fact, you can get basic information anywhere, thus making your visit here more compelling because getting a sense of the history and the drama adds enormous value to your tour experience. People enjoy the drama of the story when told with expression and enthusiasm. It's entertainment and that's what people want.

When I take my guests to see The Empire State Building, they not only see it; they hear the inside scoop that makes it come alive; the characters who actually had the idea to create it, how it happened, where the initial conversations took place and what the components of those discussions were from a personal perspective.

Mr. Rascob needed a titular head, a spokesman, an adored and colorful public figure to represent the building; glorifying it, stimulating public fervor and passion for this spectacular project; the newest symbol of this ambitious metropolis, an accomplishment that would be the envy of the nation and the world.

In this case John Jacob Rascob and Alfred E. Smith were in the men's room of the Lotus Club. Rascob, a Director of General Motors was seething because Walter P. Chrysler was in the process of building The Chrysler Building, soon to be the world's tallest. Smith had just been smitten due to his crushing loss of the presidential election in 1928 and was committed to re-invent himself once again.

So . . . as the story goes, they were standing in the men's room each with their martinis in hand, holding their "nozzles" with the other hand and Rascob asked Smith the question,

"How would you like to be the Director of the world's tallest building?"

With wild abandon Smith exclaimed,

"Where do I sign?"

We, even as New Yorkers, wander around, going about our "business observing the City with blind eyes and rarely take a moment to stop and think or ask ourselves; "Why is that there? What were the motivating forces, challenges, decisions and innovations that provided the means to create such a magnificent structure?" Sure you'd like to know, yes? What was there before? Well, it was the first Waldorf-Astoria!

"How high can you make it so it won't fall down?"

John Jacob Rascob asked, seated in front of William F. Lamb's desk, the leading architect he had chosen to design the world's tallest building, while removing a #2 pencil from Lamb's desk. He stood the pencil on its eraser with the sharpened point face up, and so the well-documented story goes.

The rest, as they say, is history.

This was the age of "can do" of reaching higher, "the age of man and machine." Not only were they reaching for the sky, striving to enhance the ever-surging prominence of New York City but keeping this city on top, the center of ideas, innovation, construction and achievement was their chant. It was truly their calling and our destiny. Constructing a towering structure of this magnitude would insure New York's crown for generations to come. In fact, it was the world's tallest building for forty-three years. That is unlikely to ever happen again. It was to be the culminating symbol of New York City's supremacy and greatness, a visual achievement affirming our technological and forward thinking culture, not to be matched for years to come.

Alfred E. Smith was the symbol of New York City, the son of a poor Irish Lower Eastside immigrant laborer. A son who had climbed to the top of New York State politics, whose life had been described aptly as going from a Brown Derby to a Grey Fedora and finally to a black silk top hat. Indeed, he was the perfect choice to hold the crown that gave all "everyday men" pride in The Empire State Building and moreover the City itself.

For every New Yorker it created an indelible footprint, no matter whom they were, from where they came and what they had, rich or poor. It belonged to all of New York City. It was truly this City's building. Every New Yorker felt that they owned a part of it. Their sweat and toil contributed to the City that had made such things possible. Everyone

266

identified with it as his or her own monument. Truly, it was a prize for us all. It was the embodiment of every New Yorker who loved this City and in many ways it still is and will be well into the future.

New York City is a mystery to nearly all its residents, not only to its visitors. Often when I am with a fellow New Yorker, discussing the City, invariably something comes to my mind that I know that the other guy doesn't. For example, what's the world's only fourteen-lane bridge? How come Staten Island is a part of New York City and not a part of New Jersey? Which one of our tunnels carry more traffic then any other on earth? What percentage of Manhattan is landfill? What is the second tallest building in New York City? What's the shortest street in Manhattan? Why was New York University established? Where's the highest elevation in New York City? What was the original name of Park Avenue? Where is the 9th ward and what is it called today? Where's Extra Place in Manhattan? Wouldn't you love to have this address? One Extra Place, New York, NY. What's the largest building in Manhattan, in terms of total square footage?

The history of the City is unique! A young city, literally built by the world, a world of immigrants who toiled, invented and created completely new technologies, applied original ideas, pioneered new methods and took bold chances enabling this City to grow, prosper and became the capital city of the world.

The next time you take a stroll look around and open your eyes wider than ever before and you will see history everywhere. Each block tells a story, a layered history with a soul. If only the walls could talk, what we would learn. And, if you pause and ask yourself a few questions curiously wondering why that park is there, why is that building still standing, why is that street so wide, when did that happen and why did it, then you will learn to love this City even more because to comprehend it is the bond that will enable you to embrace New York City as your own secret love.

If you lived in London and visited New York City and were asked: Where are you from? You'd say "London." Right? That's a no brainer. If you were asked the same question in London, would you say, London? That's unlikely. Your answer would be Marble Arch, Piccadilly or Barkley Square, or another neighborhood, yours. When we conceive of a city from afar we are not looking at it under a microscope. London is London, and New York City is simply New York City, if from afar. Got it?

The collection of its neighborhoods enables New York City to take on a unique character, the most harmonious and diverse city on earth! Therefore, saying that you're from London or New York City is an answer that lacks precision. It's as if an American were asked, within the United States, where they are from and the answer is "Oh, I'm from The United States" instead of replying Colorado, Maryland or Wisconsin or whichever state the respondent happens to reside. If the reply is a state fine, but it would make more sense if the response were a large city such as Denver or Houston, the state would be assumed, Colorado or Texas in these instances. But, even though New York City is much smaller than any state, in size only, the diversity of its neighborhoods is vast and varied, far more so than any place you can name in any other state, city or county in this country or any other place on earth for that matter.

If New York City were a state, only eleven states would exceed its population. For starters, Queens is the most ethnically diverse county in The United States, The Bronx has the poorest congressional district and Manhattan is the densest and also thinnest, by average body weight, not geographically. Brooklyn is the second most ethnically diverse American county, and Staten Island has the greatest percentage of Italian-Americans of any county in the country. Within each of the five boroughs vastly different neighborhoods exist, each having their own unique character and culture. Not only is New York City the most culturally diverse place on earth, it is a quilt of patches of life that are ever changing, a virtual mosaic of the world, a dynamic state of changing cycles.

When asked the question:

"Hey, where are you from, New York City?"

When that question is asked, in New York City, it generally reveals that the questioner is not a New Yorker.

If asked, "Do you live in Manhattan?" that would have been more New Yorkish but, not a dead giveaway. If I had been asked,

"Do you live in the neighborhood, you seem like a New Yorker? So what part of the City are you from?" Then, I would presume that this person is, most likely, a New Yorker.

In most cases, people I encounter in the City will respond to the question citing their neighborhood name and less frequently their borough.

A borough answer may signal of lack of pride in their own neighborhood. Staten Island is an exception because very few New Yorkers are aware of any neighborhood names in Staten Island. Who lives in Brooklyn Heights, undoubtedly Brooklyn's most historic and beautiful neighborhood and responds with the answer, "Brooklyn"? Who lives in Manhattan and answers the question, "Manhattan?" Those who live in Tribeca, Soho, The Upper Eastside, Upper Westside, West Village or Sutton Place, etc. respond with their neighborhood name. However, those who live in Inwood, Harlem, Washington Heights, Hamilton Heights or El Barrio may be more likely to respond, "Manhattan." But that depends, of course, on who asked the question and who answered it. I've never taken a poll but I have found there's truth to those who respond with either their borough or neighborhood name, which ever evokes the most pride due to ego, a sense of shame, self-image or satisfaction; whatever?

Many who have been raised and still live in their old neighborhoods, tend to have a greater sense of satisfaction with their neighborhood. Their roots are there, their friends, the corner grocer and all that. They have become part of the landscape and carry a strong and entrenched comfort zone, truly their home. They know their way around like the back of their hand, it's their turf, their "'hood."

But, for many new residents, who have settled there in lieu of a neighborhood of their choice, normally due to their financial constraints, there is often a sense of humiliation or disappointment discouraging them from making their neighborhood name an admission, "I'm from Mott Haven!" That's the poorest neighborhood in The Bronx, the first to bear the name, "The South Bronx" so, the new real estate name, SoBro, anointed by real estate developers, nice try but there's a long way to go before that one latches on.

Times are changing, always in New York City. Many neighborhoods that have in the past been defined by crime and grit are now filled with condos, Starbucks, banks and nationally known chain stores revealing confidence by corporate managers who have determined that such investment choices are now profitable, even in neighborhoods that were long overlooked. Isolated neighborhoods no longer carry the stigma that they have endured for many years. Many of the residents of Alphabet City and Harlem as well as parts of Brooklyn and The Bronx are filled with an abundance of pride and so it is with Bed-Sty, Greenpoint, Bushwick, Woodside and Washington Heights. We, a forever-changing City continue to welcome newcomers most who must settle for much less than what they would have hoped. As we look back we have evidence that this is nothing new and it's getting more out of reach and more difficult for those with only a little jingle in their pockets to lay down tracks even in some of the worst shrinking neighborhoods in The Big Apple.

The Lower Eastside, "LES" is casting out a new and more vibrant set of choices. Just look up and open your eyes and you'll see a trendy new "watering holes" boutiques, high-rise condos and hotels. The East Village is a voluntary choice for many, those who still cling to weirdness and counter-cultural mores. It's a great location and there's a lot more going on there now, good stuff, choices, attractions, safer and filled with more diversity, movers and shakers as well. There are a booming variety of restaurant choices; an assortment of private shops, tons of fabulous vintage clothing establishments. Look around and you'll agree that the list of so-called "bad" neighborhoods keeps shrinking.

"Where are you from?"

That's a question that every New Yorker should be proud to answer! "Nah, I'm not from New York City, I'm from ... "

President "O'Bama"

Chicken pot pies deep, filled with an abundance of large succulent chunks of fresh white meat, luscious carrots, potatoes and peas bathed in a fat creamy laden white sauce, ensconced in a crusty shell and piping hot were prepared and served at Kennedy's Pub at 357 West 57th Street in Manhattan. Trust me!

Sometime during the summer of 2008, after the Democratic Party "cleaned house" paving the way for Barack Hussein Obama to acquire the presidential nomination, the chatter at Kennedy's Pub had shifted to the two would-be candidates, Obama and McCain.

John McCain has been around for a long time, served his country in Vietnam, was a prisoner of war and a long time U.S. Senator. On the other hand, Barack Obama was not only a newcomer, much younger and far less experienced moreover, he was an exceptionally well-educated man, a spectacular speaker, smart, steady and charismatic, if you liked his politics. Oh, and he happens to be African-American, as if you didn't know.

Stepping into Kennedy's, an Irish Pub, duh, one had to realize that McCain would be the likely favorite, a man of Irish descent. I knew that speaking with the regulars, whom I virtually didn't know, had signaled caution for me to keep my mouth shut, at least that's what I had intended to do until . . .

It's amusing why some folks vote for a specific presidential candidate, not terribly esoteric without an ounce of thought. My father told me back in 1960 that he was voting for JFK because Jackie was better looking then Pat Nixon! Some people cast their votes against a candidate simply because they don't look presidential or because they didn't like their stance on one minor issue or another rather then vote for the candidate who would be best for the country as a whole, one whose position on the major issues makes the most sense, not for one specific sector or region but for the nation as a whole.

Some people I know discarded the notion of voting for Mitt Romney because he walked like a faggot. He did! But, we had a great president, FDR, who couldn't walk at all! Hey, let's vote for the man whose wife has the biggest breasts or a really nice ass, eh Joe! People are so incredibly stupid! It's mind boggling!

Seated several seats from me at the bar were two men nursing their third midday scotches discussing the upcoming election. Judging from their accents, it was no mystery to me that they were of Irish descent. Both gentlemen were well dressed and speaking loud enough for me to get the gist of their conversation. With a few scotches under their breaths, the volume added to their voices could have easily filled MSG. (not from NYC?, it's Madison Square Garden, not mono sodium ...)

I parked myself, silently, a few bar stools away from those guys and waited patiently for my sinful luscious lunch. I reaffirmed my refrain to keep my mouth shut in matters of presidential politics. This was absolutely not the place to put in my two "pence." I had to mind my P's and Q's as they say. Just Shut up!!

"Nah, not a chance! How could you expect me to vote for a man with that name, Obama! I simply can't imagine that, President Obama! The name doesn't even sound American. I couldn't get used to that on a bet unless, of course, there was an apostrophe after the O, O'Bama, yuk, yuk. And when you throw in that guy's middle name, Hussein, that takes the cake lad.

275

The thought of a black man in the White House, with the name Barack Hussein Obama is just too much for me. I'd rather see a women or even a Jew in the oval office. God help us all! God save America!"

Wow! My thoughts were; what is America to him? Wasn't America supposed to be the country where everyone has the opportunity to be whatever they want to be, regardless of race, religion, gender, sexual preference or national origin? Isn't this the land of immigrants and more than any other place in America, New York City, truly the "the melting pot" the bastion of tolerance?

We all know the Irish had a rough time gaining respect and admiration here for generations after they finally acquired a decent wage, good jobs, dignified housing and adequate healthcare. Most ethnic and racial groups looked down upon the Irish. Many didn't even consider them Caucasian years ago not that Caucasians are any better then anyone else, of course. Because the masses didn't put them in their rightful place, due to prejudicial misconceptions their struggle here was enormous. They, more than any other national group, have built our parks, subways, staffed the fire and police departments and have had a powerful and beneficent presence in City government, education and the building trades for years and years. Their contributions to this city have been huge.

However, the more I listened to their tirade of prejudicial trash at Kennedy's Pub, meandering meaningless tripe, the more irritated I became. Despite my own best advice I simply could not hold back any longer.

"I've been listening to your conversation and I'd like to offer you guys my thoughts. May I, gentlemen?"

"Yeah, what you got, pal?"

I began a little timidly however, knowing that I was at Kennedy's, although a very safe place, I had felt somewhat ill at ease, as I knew how many scotches were brewing in their bulging bellies! I was well prepared to accept the insults and abuse that I felt were about to be hurled at me, at least that's what I had thought. I did not expect any punches or assaults. The reaction to what I was about to say would be more about the manner in which it was said, not the message itself.

"Gentlemen, I've been overhearing your conversation and I, an American, the son of an immigrant can imagine, President Running Bull or Little Bear in the Oval Office. Sure, why not?"

"What's your name?" one of them had asked me.

"O'Bama! You know like O'Brian or O'Leary, with that apostrophe?"

"Sure, that's funny!" one of them commented.

"It's Strome, that's my name."

"What kind of name is Strome?"

"American" I replied.

"I'm only saying that to make a point. Sure we've had presidents whose names sounded very presidential such as Buchanan, Grant, two Johnsons, two Adams and two Bushes, two Roosevelt's and a Harrison, Coolidge and Hoover. And, gentlemen, I ask you, with such terrific names; a number of them didn't accomplish much that was productive or impressive, right? We've had Presidents with names from all over the world but none from America. There's been no Broken Arrow or Brave Warrior, right? My point is that the name is unimportant. Isn't it the man or woman that matter? It's not about where their ancestors are from. We all know that a president has to be born in The United States, the Constitution requires it, and on that note John McCain was born in Panama, not The United States!

Therefore, if either of the two candidates are constitutionally disqualified for the office isn't it Mr. McCain, a great American, so I've been told. Isn't that candidate unqualified even though he has served this country with courage, sacrifice and honor, not constitutionally qualified for office in The White House? Not!

Furthermore, Mr. McCain is an Irish descendent, born from immigrants like us all, including Barack Obama! I do hope that people will vote for the person they believe will be the best president, doing what you believe is best for the country, not their cronies or back slapping buddies who are looking for favors or opportunities to fatten their wallets and build "Bridges to Nowhere." For me, Obama is likened to Lincoln, who was perhaps our greatest president, born poor, self-educated and from the back woods. He certainly was far from the best-looking president we've had. Do looks count too?

Would you vote for a guy named Schwartz, Feingold or Cohen? Or how about Sanchez, Diaz or Garcia, what about Molotov, Singh, Chow or Yang? If you wouldn't and you do want a president whose name you can pronounce, spell and recognize as sounding presidential then you, in the truest sense, are not acting, as Americans ought to act by making your best decision that you feel is right for the country."

I was too young to vote for John Kennedy, an American of Irish descent, but I would have because he rallied this country when we needed a leader who made us feel good about ourselves and provided an uplift for a new generation to whom "the torch is passed." Additionally, even back then, I didn't care for Mr. Nixon. What kind of name is Nixon anyway?

I will vote for Mr. Obama, because he makes sense to me. He is smart and cares about the vast majority of people who have built this country with their hands, those who have struggled to provide the foundation for the wealthy, a byproduct of sweat, hard work and good old-fashioned American optimism, hard work and imagination and that includes the Irish people. How many have struggled to get an education, health care and housing, a chance to advance themselves, their children and their children's children? If I believed that Mr. McCain would do a better job then I'd vote for him. Many Americans, immigrants, except for the few who are indigenous, have cast aside their preconceived notions that a person can be judged by their name.

And as for his middle name, Hussein, I have no doubt that the man is of the Christian faith and although I am not, it does not matter. Religious beliefs have no place in government, the constitution "guarantees" it, "separation of church and state", and for those who are fearful because a person has religious believes that do not match their own, well, they too are behaving un-American.

Why would I care if Mr. Kennedy were Catholic, as long as his religious beliefs, whatever they may be, did not clash with the business of governing? And even if Barack Obama was a Muslim, which he is not, doesn't he have the right to hold his religious beliefs and practice them as long as he doesn't violate his oath of office? We are not at war with a religion, it's a minority, terrorists who happen to have "hijacked" a religion and are using it as a calling card to enlist millions of their "brothers" to their cause, a Jihad. What's in a name, gentlemen?

I believe that if Barack Obama had the choice of voting for president, he'd cast his ballot for the person who had the goods, in his opinion, without knowing their name! I would. So, ask yourselves. Why aren't you too?

Gentleman, have a good day."

They gave me a look that could kill. I figured that it was time to leave even though I should have stayed to hear their response. Eh, but what for? Politics is one topic that never invokes change, especially during an afternoon, for them, of hammering down scotches. Time to move out and on!

Walking out I reflected on the encounter. The poet Langston Hughes, an African-American Harlem resident wrote a poem, "America." It's about the American ideal, its precepts and principles that were laid down on paper in The Declaration of Independence. The Constitution and The Bill of Rights espouse high standards of equality in virtually every walk of life, with some disgraceful exceptions, such as slavery, no right to vote for women, nothing about gay rights or Jim Crow Laws and injustice everywhere.

Hughes' proposition was that our founding father's words laid down on paper were all conjectural and that the litmus test had failed. How do you legislate the elimination of prejudice, hatred and notions that others, who do not pray at your church, or have different skin color than you or possess cultural backgrounds that differ from your own are not your equals?

How thankful we all should be that America is a diverse nation of immigrants simply because every group has made so many significant contributions, countless achievements in every field of endeavor. Who among us can name one ethnic, religious or national group of people who have not made substantial contributions to this City and country?

To me, I find it particularly irksome hearing conversations of hate and ignorance, especially in New York City. Isn't this the place where the "melting pot" experiment has been an overwhelming success? Sure, we've had the despicable draft riots, and other incidents that have ignited the fury of specific groups when they felt disenfranchised. Perhaps they were.

It isn't a perfect system but, the bar chatter was an example of what's wrong here and everywhere. The cure is information, education of our glorious history, taught with truth and without the ever self-righteous historical figures that we deify as though our past is overflowing with omnipotent and exalted heroes, "my country right or wrong", "manifest destiny" that "God is on our side" and "God Bless America" and rhetoric fueling a blind eye that America is always right. It isn't. Do our countrymen actually believe that God has favorite countries? How about states and counties too?

If those two Irish gents knew who Mr. Obama is, what his struggle entailed, how hard he worked, how he succeeded against seemingly insurmountable odds, how he could have accepted any job offered to him for big bucks but rather he took a $10,000 a year job in Chicago's Southside as a community organizer, struggled to help the needy to uplift themselves, their lives and families and build a better future for their children and this country then maybe, just maybe, they would have acquired a balanced and constructive perspective one void of racism and ignorance.

I have no doubt that President Obama knows the struggle the Irish have endured. The potato famine in the 1840's drove a major portion of the Irish people to the United States, a down trodden people who struggled with back, brawn and brain to carve out better lives. They have succeeded against the odds to live the American Dream and have done quite well.

Let those who talk hatred, close their minds and hearts to the achievements of others and take a look at them.

When they face the mirror those two Irishmen, may very well see the face of a man who became our first African-American president. If so, he'll be looking back at them with an opened mind and heart. No Irishman here, a new president, just another red blooded American presented to us all in living black and white, literally! He's our choice, this time, fair and square. There was no photo-ID required from the poor and elderly to vote. No butterfly ballots that shifted the election of 2000 and no shortage of voting machines at Democratic college campuses in Ohio as in 2004. That's a nice change, eh? Hey, our president is biologically half black and half white! It's not a black and white issue. If we don't like him then it should be strictly about politics and policy. Truly, it's about not liking ourselves, a little bold, but hey, that's what it is.

Photographs

1. Outa Sight and Outa Mind re: "Slice" on page 132
2. Life on a Rolls re: "Slice" on page 151
3. What a Main Break for You! "Slice" on page 162
4. What's So Great About Central Park? "Slice" on page 206
5. Hangin' Out and in the "Clink" "Slice" on page 337
6. Graffiti Now and Then "Slice" on page 364
7. Beggars, Panhandlers and the Homeless "Slice" on page 401
8. Tonight Giz, a Love Story "Slice" on page 432
9. Crime, Way Down and "How"? "Slice" on page 488
10. Our signature photo: Central Park, The Gapstow Bridge

Chapter IV
"Gotcha Last!"
****
6'5" vs. 5'6"

It was bad enough that the check for $1,846.00 had bounced a second time from a man who stood very tall, 6'5". I didn't expect to see that money or him, ever again. I had placed "that bouncer" in my desk drawer as a daily reminder that I should not to be too trusting. It sat in my drawer for over a year until suddenly he made another appearance in my store. It had been as if he had vanished from the planet and suddenly he surfaced.

He used to be a great customer, usually paying in cash. Yes indeed, a very good customer was he, Dave. I was always glad to see him, especially this time.

I had made every attempt I could to find him. Every effort to even the score is a way of life for me. As my father used to say, "Chase 'em down the alley." It was his high-spirited m.o. to get his money that I learned from the old man that drove me. I had sent my two largest and gruesome looking employees to his home, hoping that he'd be there to greet them. He was "scarce" and despite my best efforts he was nowhere. As they say, he was the guy who only showed up for supper.

Alas! Dinosaur Dave suddenly appeared! He walked into my one-hour photo store on West 23rd Street, Clicks One Hour Photo, as if nothing was ever "afoot."

I greeted Dave with raised arms and a pat on the back, lower portion with a big broad devilish smile and a "How great you look! Dave! How the hell are you?

285

"Cliff, you look great too!"

Don't you just love the bullshit especially when there's one obvious purpose behind it? I knew Dave walked into my store for a reason and I was relishing the chatter anticipating knowing what he was after.

After the small talk, I asked Dave how I could help him, with no mention of the bounced check, duh! It turned out that he needed hundreds of color laser copies, of various teddy bears, little stuffed animals, "plush toys" that he had apparently been selling. He sold them, by the hundreds; to corporate accounts with their logos custom imprinted on those fluffy little creatures. He solicited orders from banks, insurance companies, car dealers and real estate brokers and of course, hey, one-hour photo stores too. I'd be the first. Sure, why not? Ha ha ha! This was an opportunity that I couldn't miss. After the customary and usual chitchat I had asked Dave if I could take a peek at his catalogue.

"I'd like to see it." I asked.

"Sure."

He eagerly and unwittingly, handed one over for me to explore. I asked him, with my mascot right beside me, Gizmo, a five-pound Yorkshire terrier, if he could customize a job for me with Gizmo's picture on the stuffed toys together with my company logo.

"No big deal, how many do you need?"

"What do they cost Dave? I would like about 300."

The price was approximately $2,600.00. Perfecto! I made my selection, gave Dave a signed purchase order and anticipated my shipment's arrival due to in about four weeks.

The copies Dave had ordered that afternoon were paid for in full in cash with crisp hundred dollar bills.

286

Discussion of the "bouncer" never came up. What for? Perhaps, he had forgotten all about it. You never know. Some folks drop bad checks all over town and simply loose track of them. Like bears, they leave tracks but they can't retrace everything. Little stuffed teddies leave tracks too but I would just have to be patient and wait a while! Hey, it's fun to wait for the pile that's just about guaranteed especially if you can help someone learn a good lesson. I love teaching. I was a teacher! What a lesson plan for Big Dinosaur Dave. I knew he'd get straight A's.

It was so nice to see him, even if I had to strain my neck a bit, just like the schmucks in the "glass is falling from the sky" story in this book! See Slice "New Yorkers Are Not So Smart."

Four weeks flew by and Dave made his appearance with a helper and together they schlepped in about twenty cartons filled with 300 teddies! The teddies had landed!" Praise Dave!

"Hey Dave, it's great to see you again! Can you guys put them downstairs? Let me show you where I want them." ·

We went down to the warehouse. Dave and his assistant stacked them very neatly. The bears were silent, sleeping in the darkness, waiting for their purposeful debut.

Dave prepared an invoice for me. He was better at that than preparing checks! I went to my office, removed the $1,846.00 rubber check from my desk drawer, still in great condition, stapled to the insufficient funds advices that I had received from the bank with the service fees attached. Hey, banks have to eat too, right!

I kept imagining that Dave was thinking about the $2,600 check that was coming his way. Boy o boy, wow wee, some nice payday for the big guy. Uh huh, nothing doin'!

Little did he know that I had previously attempted to ply a trick that my father had years ago that made a bad check payable. My father had accepted a $500 check that had bounced twice. He went to the bank, asked the teller how much was needed to make the check good. He was advised that $120 would satisfy the deficiency. He removed the necessary cash from his pocket and made the required deposit. Anyone can deposit cash into anyone's account at least back in those days. Today, I'm not that sure with all that Patriot Act shit out there, rules and "regs", eh? The teller certified the check for him, as he had requested, and his loss was reduced from $500 to $120, not too bad. I couldn't have accomplished the same thing with Dave's check because what was needed to make that rubber check good was about $1,700! Not an attractive plan.

I gave Dave back his check and told him,

"Here's your money!"

It took some balls. My big guys surrounded me, just in case I waited for his reaction, with a bit of a grin, and it didn't take too long! I knew that he would be pissed off but I wasn't afraid that he would launch me out the front plate glass window. He was a sweet guy. Not all thieves are total shitheads. He was only a partial high-end shithead, a guy with his head up his ass way above the clouds.

"Hey, that's not fair, this is a $2,600 invoice, and I want the rest of the money, about $750. I only fucked you for about $1800. Come on Cliff!"

At this point he had admitted that the pointed end of the screw was pointed in his direction; that he would be satisfied to accept his bad check as partial payment for the teddy order.

"Dave, the price you charged me, for the teddies, was not your direct cost! You stood to make approximately $750 profit on the transaction as I see it, that's my guess. I believe that your rubber check of $1,846.00 covers it, *capise*! That's why I upped the order to $2,600!"

Yeah, he *capised*.

He left, not too happy, and we shook hands. How could Dave have been such a schmuck? Greed and stupidity are the only reasons I can think of. Perhaps he learned a valuable lesson, I doubt it.

Now, what was I going to do with 300 teddies? All my employees were pleading for one. Christmas was just around the corner. They were all over me my ass with that. "I want a teddy, I want a teddy." So childish!

"What are you going to do with them? What are you going to use them for?" I was asked over and over again. Why are people so needy for a stupid little toy? They could have purchased similar items for $5.99 back in those days. They just had to hammer the boss incessantly! To me, it was amusing that they had such great jobs with me; these well paid hard working adults with such juvenile pea brains.

"I don't know." I knew I'd think of something, a no brainer. I didn't want to sell them. There's no logic to it. I'm not in the toy business. Selling merchandise that has your company logo is so tacky. It diminishes your brand. There was no benefit there, none.

After my teddies spent about two months "sleeping" in the warehouse it was time for them to awaken and make their debut. On a day of lousy weather I told my employees of my plan and we put it into action. The teddies were brought upstairs into the store and with enough Velcro to sink a battleship. We stuck them every place we could find and tacked up all 300 teddies. We adhered Velcro to them and stuck them on top of printing machines, copiers, enlargers, shelves, walls, ceilings, window ledges, racks, etc. etc. All the customers who came in wanted to know how to get one. How much are they? "I need two!" A lot of buzz was afoot! "I WANT ONE!!!"

I had a flyer printed and we inserted one into every shopping bag, package of photos, film, etc. and handed had them out on the street, pasted them on buildings, traffic light poles and offered each and every customer the opportunity to walk out with a free teddy on the day after the Christmas and New Year holiday weekend. All that was required was to drop off one roll of film for processing. Nothing else!

It turned out to be the best day we ever had! We opened the store early and ran our processing equipment all night in order to accommodate all the business.

I do not recall exactly how much business this promotion provided but it did have an enormous impact and it was tons of fun. Most of my customers worked in the neighborhood and for years thereafter they told me,

"I still have my teddy on my desk."

Ah, that's New York City. Taking a bounced check and turning it into an opportunity was a blast. I wish I had one left over for you, teddy bear that is, not a bounced check.

"I'll keep all the bounced checks I can get until I find a way and "chase them down the alley" just like dear ol' dad. Hey, you never know!

This a true tale but, to the vast majority of New Yorkers, such events are remote, off their radar, unheard of and just don't exist. It's like A Tale of Two Cities, one half has no idea what the other half is doing and visa versa.

Once upon a time, I had met a woman who was to become my second wife. Aline, a woman from France. She came to New York City to find adventure, fun, work, romance and opportunities. Together, we found them all! She arrived with a work visa in hand and plied her trade, retail soft goods sales in the fashionable upscale Upper Eastside. It was a commission only job and she did extremely well.

Shortly after our relationship began to bloom she received ominous signals from her employer, who had signed off on her work visa every year and as a result of her employer's misguided instincts, she had decided not to sign Aline's visa when Aline made her last request. For her, it was out of the question.

Aline never had any intention of leaving her job. Because this woman knew that Aline and I were off to the Hamptons every summer weekend in my Mercedes convertible and that had created the notion, in her bosses' little head, that Aline would inevitably toss her job away and live off the income of her new beau, *moi*. Therefore, her boss acted very stupidly and rejected Aline's application for her visa renewal. Incredible! She had reacted foolishly due to her misperception that I was wealthy, which was a reasonable presumption. Rather then retain her most productive salesperson, out of ego, insecurity, pride and stupidity, she let her go. You'd be amazed how often stuff like that happens, incredible. Why didn't she discuss the matter with Aline? Or, in the least do nothing and wait for events to unfold?

Don't you just love when someone rejects opportunities due entirely to a misperception of events creating their own sense of reality. They think circumstances may hurt them but they are the ones who fall on their swords? I love that! "Self-inflicted emotional stupidity" is the best justice. It's like the accused throwing the switch on themselves! ZAP. Better than "Old sparky" the Sing Sing electric chair! You don't have to say a thing! They just self-destruct and spend their lives justifying their lost fortunes because they were the victim; in their own little stupid heads and that doesn't prevent them from continuing to blame the blameless, in this case Aline and me.

Lack of good business judgment resulted in a loss for the boss and an opportunity for Aline. It's a true and amazing fact of life that has repeated itself for Aline and me many times. "You dis'd me!" It's all in their heads, dumb! Thanks, in large part, due to the emotional stupidity of others Aline and I have thrived over the years.

Without the visa-sponsored job, Aline's legal residency in The United States was in jeopardy.

A suitable solution was needed, fast. With trust and confidence in our relationship, we had agreed that the best way to resolve this was to hire an immigration attorney and find another way. The way forward was an investor visa. A $50,000 investment in a new business would provide the necessary visa for her. For the record, Aline is now a citizen of The United States. A real Franco-American Yankee Doodle Dandy! God bless America!

We took the right route; I found a near perfect opportunity to sub-lease a store in the building where we lived on West 57th Street. Gizmos One Hour Photo was born, a terrific little store, another pocket for us and a way to rescue Aline's American legal status.

The store lease was a sublease, meaning, her landlord, owner of a video rental business next door, sold film developing and printing service, as a side add-on for his customers. We insisted that he agree to insert a clause in the lease that would restrict him from selling those services to his customers, a non-compete clause, that was a given, naturally. He agreed, at least that is what he had said and he signed the lease affirming his commitment legally. His reluctance to honor that clause turned out to be his undoing, the next retailer whose stupidity helped to bring him down and, in the process Aline and me a notch higher.

Several years later Aline had an opportunity to move her business to a better location on Lexington Avenue, one that suited her objectives and dovetailed with my deteriorating business situation at that time. By comparison, my business was far larger employing over sixty people. in six location. The one-hour photo industry was in the throes of a near end. Her volume of business on 57th Street had fallen and we found a much better place for her to park her equipment and re-establish her business.

On one occasion I entered the landlord's video store, next door to Gizmo's, to deliver his rent check and I noticed a sign behind his counter featuring photocopy and photographic services. Clearly, this was a major violation of Aline's sublease. I knew I'd crucify him for cheating us. He was taking business away from us, clearly a major breech of our sublease! For me, it was a yes moment, a mechanism to escape from the clutches of the sublease, providing a clean break and escape to relocate the business and get even with a greedy snake.

I got in touch with a friend who happened to be a very large, skinhead Italian guy who also was one of the smartest guys I had ever met. I told him about our dilemma and he agreed to implement the solution for us, one that I had devised.

Putting the plan into play, he walked into the landlord's video store, looked around, pretended to be interested in the terms of their video club membership, which was a customary marketing tool back in those days. He and Aline's landlord became engaged in a conversation regarding the privileges, benefits and cost of video club membership. After the completion of the conversation with the landlord he revealed that he had noticed the sign behind the counter featuring the photo copying service. He placed an order, waited for his order to be completed and then he acquired all the receipts, in detail, and strolled out.

I called my lawyer immediately and he promptly prepared a lawsuit for $100,000 against the landlord. About two days later the landlord was "served" with a "summons and complaint". It was a slam-dunk! Naturally, we didn't provide the evidence we had gathered against him. That would have been dumb. But, he knew, in his heart, that we had the goods. The trap was set.

A day or two later he approached us and attempted to negotiate a settlement. Ultimately, we agreed that we would drop the suit in return for a release from all the obligations under the lease. That enabled Aline to move her equipment to 360 Lexington Avenue, a much more favorable lease opportunity at a far better location. The schmuck landlord on 57th Street was left with an empty store because cheating is not good business. Some just keep denying what they should have learned the first time they tried to screw themself out of a beneficial relationship.

Only one of my most fervent business creditors attempted to prove that Aline's store was actually mine. I do hope that she spent a lot of money trying to prove what she never could prove. It was just another emotional misperception by another ego driven insecure little person who was slithering down the wrong trail and that little trip down ultimately got much worse for her and she slithered down the pole like a greased rat. Aline and I roared when she "folded her tent" again though just not for the last time, yet! We anticipated that and were licking our chops because we rightly predicted where the next SNAFU was coming and it came like a Nor'easter from down there in Dixie.

I guess that creditor once again had thought that I was just not too smart. Dumb da dumb dumb DUMB! Yuk, yuk!

We played it smart and found the sweet spot, planned and implemented a strategy that helped save our asses.

By and "bye" the video store vanished and our photo store at that site became a doggie wash and dry, bones, leaches not leases. Our new location did much better. We moved to Florida for a year or so and Aline ran the business from Miami. It was the easiest money she had ever made!

Ah, New York City is a place where anything is possible. This time someone had wanted to throw my wife out of her film store. That sort of reminded me of Tony,
"I want to talk to you about your film store." Unlike Tony, we had interests on one side, ours! See "slice", "I Got Interests on Both Sides."

Some Dumb Sun

Sun had seemed to be an attractive person; meaning her intelligence, sophistication, background and ability to engage in stimulating and interesting conversations was readily apparent to me. She was a good-looking woman, not a babe or runway model, a bit overweight, mature looking, perhaps you could say middle age, very conversant, extremely smart. As one who had held an advanced degree from a very prestigious university located in The People's Republic of China, she spoke nearly perfect English, very well informed, self-expressed, and socially engaging. Yes, I had assessed her as a very "attractive" person.

In addition, she was energetic and anxious to connect with me as a resource to enhance her fledgling tour business. She was a licensed New York City tour guide with multi-lingual abilities, a potentially valuable resource for me as a guide to hire on a by tour tour basis.

Our first conversation was on the phone. She had called me in response to an ad that I had placed on a guide website. As a result, I invited her for us to meet and discuss business opportunities.

Our conversation was engaging and she seemed to have an excellent background and substantial knowledge of New York City. We each expressed an interest in going forward with our discussion and agreed the meet at a coffee shop on the Upper Westside, not a Starbucks!

Several days later we met. I had coffee and some comfort food; she had tea and some health food. I love eating with weighty people who order health food. No doubt, they are "closet" eaters. If they're eating healthy food regularly then how did they get so plump?

Sun told me quite a bit about her background, her childhood in China, the hardships that she and her family had endured, the scarcity of food, their meager housing, political fears, their struggles to survive and the challenges of creating a productive and secure life in, what was at the time, a third world country.

Sun had inquired about my background and business experience with an ear bent eager to hear how I had, in a relatively short period of time, built a successful private tour business in New York City. She had asked numerous questions such as:

"Where does your business come from? How do you use the Internet as a business tool? Who do you use as a vehicle provider?" I felt that despite her intelligence, it was obvious that she was picking my brain, surely an unfriendly competitor. I was a bit disappointed and insulted because offended my intelligence and it revealed her true mission primary mission. That too revealed that she had not as smart as I had thought.

She was clearly reptilian, blatantly voracious. Apparently, she had not realized that I "got it!" I perceived that she had a "wheel" missing and that had raised my suspicions but it did not eliminate the prospect that she would work for us as a Mandarin speaking licensed guide.

After "the sit-down" and some further evaluation, I decided to give Sun the opportunity to join other tour guides who were part of our repertoire. She was pleased to have succeeded in acquiring this new opportunity, one that might advance her tour-guiding career. I subsequently made the preparations to put her on one of our websites in order for prospective clients to become aware of her and "book" tours with her through our business.

At a New York Guides Association Christmas party Sun meet Aline and enveloped her with attention. Aline remarked that she was smothered with chatter by Sun who was seeking to create a firm and powerful connection, make an impression that she was capable and available for opportunities going forward. Nothing is wrong with that but she was overly dominating and very intrusive. Aline perceived that this woman was unauthentic. Instinctively Aline did not trust her and it turned out, in the end, that she was right.

She cautioned me about this woman. There was something strange about her, she said, and that I should be on guard. I had not sensed that yet, much to my surprise.

A number of weeks had passed and Aline had gone to France to visit her parents in Nice. During her visit, I, being alone, had gotten antsy and decided to seek some company with someone and pursue some interesting conversation. Despite Aline's warning, I called Sun and invited her to meet me for a tea, a drink and a bite to eat at a moderately priced restaurant-bar in midtown one afternoon.

She agreed however she had suggested that we meet at Trump International Condo and Hotel on Central Park West. I immediately rejected that idea, due to the cost. A little bell went off in my head, hum, what's up with that? Trump for a casual meet for chitchat? Duh?

We met at the restaurant where I had suggested and became engaged in some very interesting conversation. We spoke about her life, background, what it was like to live in China as a child, her fears for her family, survival, and her tour business. I spoke about my background, family and how I got into the tour business, and so forth. She had told me that she had a teenage daughter and that her first husband, her daughter's father, was living in China. Currently, she was residing in Brooklyn with her second husband and her daughter and trying to hold her life together and make a successful live here in New York City of her tour business.

I concluded that, quite likely, she had "trashed" her first husband and married the second husband in order to begin the process of obtaining citizenship in The United States for her daughter and herself as well.

We said goodbye with a handshake, she stopped by the ladies room as I left the restaurant on my own.

Aline's stay in Nice was extended. Her parents are very elderly and her presence there provided a great deal of support and benefit for them. I encouraged her to stay; it was the right thing for her to do and at that time of year, the winter, when the tour business in New York City plummets. Her absence was not a burden for me.

I had told Aline, during one of our daily conversations, that I had met Sun for a drink and we had engaged in some small talk. I was quite surprised that Aline had cautioned me not to see her again. Keep it strictly business she had warned me. This was not a jealousy issue. Aline is a very secure woman, very. She also knew that I enjoyed the company of smart ladies and they enjoyed being with me too, so

I've been told. It was not a threat to her just a word of caution for me to be on guard.

Good conversation is not easy to find especially with people who are extremely bright, very well educated, and who come from vastly different places with different cultural backgrounds. Sun provided all of that and we had a very interesting discussion at the restaurant that afternoon.

Contrary to Aline's advice, I called Sun about a week latter and invited her for a *redux*. She accepted and we met a few days thereafter at the same place.

We continued our prior conversation discussing Chinese history, culture, economics, and her life. We talked about my life, struggles, family, politics and current events. After a few hours, I peppered her with stories of my life, some silly, a few off color jokes. I steered clear of vulgar or inappropriate humor that may have been considered such by most ladies, especially those from foreign cultures, that perceived as inappropriate. I was very careful not to cross that line. We left the restaurant and again went our separate ways.

I was comfortable that we'd had another pleasant time, terrific conversation, fascinating and esoteric. There was no interest on my part for any "fun and games" whatsoever. In the first place, I am loyal to my marriage and even if I wasn't, Sun was not physically attractive to me. She carried excessive weight and, for me, that would be a non-starter."

Several days after our second meet at the restaurant-bar I received a very strange email from her quite contrary to all the others that I had received before. Those initial emails from her read, such as:

302

You are the most intelligent tour guide I ever
met in my 8 years career.
How can I get Chinese visitors' information?
*****

Actually, I would like to discuss with you
about the marketing stuff, my new tour
plan, since you are certainly a pioneer
in this business field, and your website,
Etc. What would you like to discuss about?
*****

Let's meet at _____ at _____ Mon
At 3:30, ok, Sun
*****

I made the reservation for Monday 31th's (sic)
Lunch at 3:15 PM at Nougatine Jean Georges
under my name Sun M. It is at Center (sic)
Park West, the 1st floor of Trump.
*****

My emails:

Just to clarify, I am accepting of your email and
know that you're Chinese, and that's not relevant.
I am married and love my wife. My only intent
was to have a business meeting with you, with
the purpose of exploring opportunities. My agenda
is pure and simple.

The emails kicked back and forth with more chatter
from Sun that included very inquisitive and defensive
suspicious posturing. It seemed that she was
attempting to lure me into a trap; to agree to buy her
an expensive lunch, or go out to her neighborhood
and determine if I had a desire to go out of my way,
perhaps to be near her home and to "come on to her"
while my wife was away. It didn't add up. I saw it as a
devious ploy at the time. I was beginning to access
Aline's admonition as good advice.

303

The final emails tell it all: After the second meeting at the same restaurant, she sent me another email that floored me and confirmed that Aline's instincts were "on the money" in more ways then one. Having a robust sense of humor, during our meeting I tossed out several jokes, some a bit off color but not in bad taste, in my opinion, but maybe just might have been in hers. Nothing in any way intended to create the notion of, let's get out of here. I never invited her to leave the establishment with me nor was it implied.

Here it comes:

> It was disgusting that you talked about sex in the
> meeting. I felt deeply insulted.
> *****
> 1,000 apologies for yesterday. I didn't mean any
> disrespect. Our friendship means a lot to me.
> All I ask for is your friendship and forgiveness.
> *****

That email was evidence that I backed off because her email revealed to me that either culturally or otherwise she was, very unusual, a rogue looking for a "mark" to go after.

Knowing that she had left her marriage, came here, met a man who had at that time, been engaged to be married, and she had chased him despite that, then married him, and brought her daughter here from mainland China, legally, due to the marriage. She had used him as a mechanism to bring her daughter to The United States with legal resident status. The following email from her confirmed that.

> Don't write me anymore. I don't forgive that. I don't want
> to see you or hear from you any more, including the

> marketing meeting, otherwise I don't know what would
> happen when I am very upset. I preserve (sic) the right about
> what to do.

To me, this is evidence of three things: First, that she's nuts. Second, that she consulted a lawyer, or had prior experience in such antics. "I preserve the right about what to do." That came directly from an attorney. She got it wrong because she meant "reserve" but the cat was out of the bag.

What was that about? You'll find out. Third, it was to set a trap. Final email from Sun, here comes the strike!

> Or mail me a $1,000 check by the end of next
> week instead of 1,000 apologies. Then I would
> be able to throw out the fly I was force (sic) to
> swallow down by you.

So, it was all about money, extortion. Her insanity became as plain as the light of day. Boom! What the hell was that about? And the stupidity of asking for money in writing and payment by check! Perhaps her lawyer hadn't finished law school yet?

The prior email that I shouldn't contact her anymore reconfirmed her craziness because after my investigation I was told that if I had called, emailed or contacted her in any way that I could have been confronted with a knock at my front door by a couple of cops at three in the morning arresting me for "aggravated harassment."

That was the reason for that email: "Don't write me anymore . . .!" It was a sequence of events leading me down a path that she had plotted, one that could have ruined my life, my marriage and business.

305

Before Aline came home from France I had consulted with a friend, a NYC Police Officer, an attorney and a doctor, a very close friend filled with a lifetime of wisdom.

The cop suggested that I file a complaint and have her arrested for extortion. To him, it was a black and white case. I had all the evidence needed via emails and truly it was a slam-dunk case of extortion. I turned away from that because it could have become a "can of worms." I had no idea who she knew or of what craziness she was capable. In addition, she could have hired a "legal aid" attorney or a hit man. People lie and they love to take advantage of "the system." I had fit the type, in her head, of what she was hoping for. If you are married to someone with assets, especially if they're not your own, then chaos can ensue that can destroy you. Therefore, my friend may have been a terrific cop, but life experience was not in his arsenal. He didn't know how to look at all the angles.

The lawyer's advice was that the notion that the late night knock at the door by police was a long shot, but not impossible. We agreed that the best thing to do was nothing. I did have the ace of spades; the extortion email and certainly she knew that was her Achilles heal or perhaps she was too stupid to think that I was unaware of that. It was a chance that she had apparently decided to take. Desperate people do desperate things.

The doctor asked me what I planned to do when Aline got home. I decided not to tell her because I had felt that the entire situation would go away. There was no logic to waking up a "sleeping dog", about a "fly that had gotten swallowed" when nothing of significance had actually happened. As it turned out, events unfolded in a most beneficial and interesting way.

The email exchange between Sun and me created a trap due to her last email and, as a result, she had gotten herself tangled in her own web. Nothing, however, had tipped me off about what was about to happen next.

Aline came home from France and got back into her routine. I did not tell her that I had seen Sun the second time. It probably would have disappointed and annoyed her and accomplished nothing. Although I had disregarded Aline's advice not to see Sun again, it was far from a betrayal or unfaithful act.

I wanted to avoid the potential of disappointing her or creating a few lousy evenings between us therefore; I had decided to keep my mouth shut. I had no guilt, but I felt just a bit regretful that I hadn't followed her advice. I was feeling a bit contrite.

Certainly, I had believed that a little space, in such a way, was within bounds. At best it was my decision and again, it turned out that I should have taken her advice.

I never contacted Sun after the extortion email and suspected that the threat would evaporate. Moving forward and pressing charges against her would have accomplished nothing good and it could have resulted in a "shit storm". Sure enough I never heard from her again, but Aline did!

Several days after Aline returned home. She met a friend at a restaurant for a leisurely lunch in Soho several days after her return. While sipping her wine her cellphone rang. It was Sun! Sun had received Aline's business card at the guide's association

Christmas party that we had attended about a month before her lunch with her friend.

When Aline returned home later that afternoon, she had asked me, "Guess who called me while I was having lunch?" I had a strange feeling it was Sun. After Aline told me that it was, I asked her what she wanted. She told me that she told Sun that she'd call her back when she got home later that afternoon. There was no conversation between them due to Aline's wish not to disrupt her lunch engagement with her friend.

I, without hesitation, told Aline that there was an incident and I spelled it out to her in detail. I showed her all the emails between Sun and me.

The only disappointment Aline had was that I didn't accept her advice not to see Sun a second time while she was in France. I agreed that it was a mistake and admitted that I should have heeded her warning.

I had shown Aline *all* the emails including the last two, the $1,000 extortion email and "the stay away and don't communicate with me email" before she got on the phone to return Sun's call. She was shocked!

She agreed to call Sun right away. Sun was no match for her. Aline steered her right down the good old alley, pow! I, with Aline's consent, listened quietly on the other phone during the entire conversation.

"Hi, Sun. This is Aline."

"Oh hi! How are you doing?"

"How can I help you Sun?"

"I just want you to know that your husband took me out for drinks and some food twice while you were away and he spoke to me in a very inappropriate manner, telling me jokes that were not in good taste. I was very insulted and want you to know that we met while you were away in France."

"Didn't my husband offer to meet you and me when I returned from France, the three of us instead of the two of you? You could have met with us both instead if you had felt uncomfortable just meeting him alone? Did he provide you with that choice?"

"Yes he did."

"Sun, let me ask you, what is the purpose of your call?"

"I want you to see *all* the emails that were sent between the two of us."

"Okay, send them, here's my email address ... "

"But, Sun, what is the problem? My husband gets along very well with women. He enjoys having conversations with women and they find him an interesting, amusing and sensitive guy, unlike most men. In fact, he has more girlfriends than I do. You know, it's about interesting people to talk with, nothing more."

"Let me just send you the emails okay?"

Sun sent the emails but somehow omitted the two finals, the extortion and the threat. Hum?

The intentional failure to send those last two emails was an obvious act to mislead and lie, by omission. Aline never responded to Sun, what for?

There are a lot of good lessons here:

First, the tale of the wolf in sheep's clothing. This seemingly normal person, intelligent, interesting, engaging and well-presented articulate person was a sociopathic nut job. She was a person out to destroy a man or at the least make a "buck" for herself in a deceitful and despicable way. But, she miscalculated because she misjudged, thinking that I would be so upset, weak, and guilt ridden and fearful that she would contact my wife and that I would crumble, giving into her demand for $1,000, by check! That was the stupidest and most desperate part of it all! A check!

Second, she could have called the cops and I could have faced criminal charges, enormous legal fees, lost time, stress and a ruptured a marriage if had I been married the someone else, a person who could have blown this bullshit way out of proportion and pushed it into a break up.

Third, if I had pressed charges against her, the worst case scenario could have been a financial calamity, one with the potential of one or some of her "friends", from the other side of the tracks, causing me bodily harm or even death, seriously! This person was a certifiable nut job and potentially capable of anything.

Fourth, even an experienced person can be fooled. The world, and this City are filled with wackos. Be careful and watch out for yourself. People are, I have learned, not always who they appear to be.

Be aware that it's a jungle out there and don't get wooed into a trap. Good luck and follow your instincts. When in doubt, assume the worst and go with your gut. Seek advice and don't fold your tent.

As for my "friend" Sun, how did she make out for all her trouble? Well, she accomplished absolutely nothing good. She tossed away an opportunity to have a beneficial business relationship with us. She exposed herself as the fraud that she is and damaged her reputation.

Finally, I could have taken, a potential deportation route for her and her daughter to be thrown out of the country or landing her in jail. If I had perused that enthusiastically, I believe it very likely would have prevailed. Fortunately for her, I've got better things to do.

I "reserve the right" to do that and she, on the other hand, could conceivably, attempt to convince a judge or jury that I contacted her after her last email simply by lying. Justice is an iffy. There's always a chance that the unexpected will happen. Never count on anything in the criminal justice system. Nothing.

It's a real crazy story that just can't be made up. Be careful out there. Some people are on the streets that are certifiably crazy! Watch it out there, seriously.

The Mis-Guided Russian Guide

Although we have several excellent Russian speaking guides on the "team" I responded to an email from a Russian-speaking guide who was seeking an opportunity to be on our roster. There's no harm acquiring additional qualified guides especially those who have excellent foreign language skills. It's good business to have backup and it costs nothing to recruit excellent licensed guides.

Igor was pleased with my interest in meeting him at The Time-Warner Center at Columbus Circle, for an interview. We made a date, and I requested that he call me, when he arrived, due at 11AM. At 11:13AM I received a text message from him that he was "here." I replied that I too had arrived. My phone rang again at 11:15AM and he told me that he was "here." A duh!

Upon sighting him, as he waved, I didn't know how to recognize him any other way, I walked toward him and we shook hands and I promptly told him,

"I can't use you because you did not follow my instructions and your phone call was late. How I can only assume that you were here on time." I continued. "Sorry but, I cannot depend on you to follow instructions and show up on time. When you called me you were nearly fifteen minutes late and that is totally unacceptable!"

He pleaded with me to give him another chance and babbled about the distance that he had traveled to meet me, having had train trouble and that sort of crap.

I told him that I was not "buying" it and that being prompt is the first axiom in business especially for an interview. He was persistent and tenacious, incessantly begging and pleading with me to reconsider.

My cell phone rang in the midst of all of this. I promptly took the call. It was a hotel concierge asking me if I could be there as soon as possible to provide a tour for their guests. I indicated that I would be there within half an hour.

Igor was still standing about a foot in front of me. I told him that perhaps he had learned a good lesson and I asked him to please "get out of my face!"

He continued to banter, asking me for another chance again and again and begged for my forgiveness relentlessly. I turned and walked away from this *putz*.

I arrived at the hotel and while I was engaged in conversation with the concierges I started to receive text messages from Igor. After I received about the eighth one, I read them all to the concierges. Here they are:

I just want you to know that it's your
loss buddy. You should really reconsider.
You have poorly judged a great tour guide
wrong. Good luck doing business. I.

You probably don't get much business
anyway with your impressive personality.
That's probably why your wife left you
and went to Europe. I.

Wouldn't be surprised if she's cheating
on you and just staying with you for the
money. People like you are funny. I.

Probably got a small dick too, you short piece
of shit. I.

Probably got a small dick too, you short piece

of shit. I.

The above text I received twice

No hard feeling though, but we just can't escape
the truth. Call Me (sic) if you rethink your decision.
I might reconsider given that You (sic) will be nice
to me.

I showed these emails to one of the concierges and
had explained the story to them. One of them
suggested that I reply in the most hysterical way and I
did.

OK you got the job! C

We were practically falling on the floor with laughter
when I hit the send button! Then his text messages
continued!

What? I.

Are you serious? I.

I don't know it could be a trap. You are probably
furious about what I sad (sic) to you. Why would
you about what I sad (sic) to you. Why would
you want to give me the job? I.

Plus, I don't know anything about this job. Why don't
you call me and tell me please. Is it a full time? How
much will I make? What sort of hours? R.

I can't trust you, I think you are a con artist of some
kind. I have tried meeting with you 3 times already.
You first approached me in central Park while I was
Giving a R

314

While I was giving a tour, you told me you were impressed. You were trying to get me to work for you. Then a few months later I contacted you. R

Its been 3 or 4 times. You are a very sketchy man. Really, Buddy, I can't trust you. I should report you to the authorities perhaps, but you know. What I don't want Trouble. R.

Where can I meet you if you say I got the Job? Time Warner Center again? 11 AM, that seems to be the time & place all the time. When I call you you're always in a noisy place. I.

Very suspicious I

Your office address is a home address I

So tell me how can I become part of the team at Custom & Private tours? I

? I

Do I come to Central Park West & 96th St? Is that where your office is? I

I would have to send you my correct resume with the correct name and address through (sic) & information. I

When can I send it? I

What is your email? I

Real on please. I

These text messages were flying in every few minutes while my tour had just begun. It was distracting, annoying and revealed much about this guy. He was vulgar, extremely angry and totally screwed up. He exposed himself as a liar and suspiciously neurotic. I

315

told my guests that I had a "cockroach" in my cellphone and that I wanted to kill it.

"Please excuse me for a moment as I'd like to get rid of it." I shot him the following final text message.

I am putting you on notice that there is no job due to your messages and disrespect and further attempts to contact me will be reported to the police as grounds for malicious harassment. Cliff Strome

Amazing how one experience can provide a benefit for the next. It's just another example of "reading" people and learning how to survive in The Big City.

Juan Comes Back Home

Years ago, I operated a retail photofinishing business that morphed into one-hour photo and commercial digital imaging. With a staff of hardworking New Yorkers from all over the world, the business thrived. Together with those talented and hardworking employees, a terrific business was built and thrived for many years. In the beginning, I employed two hard working people, an Irish woman from Queens and a young Dominican man who had proudly earned his high school diploma, Juan.

Juan was a most likeable guy; enthusiastic, energetic hard working and he always got to work on time. As the business grew and prospered it took on additional employees he became well liked and respected. Always ready, willing and able to pitch-in and lend a hand, Juan was an eager learner as well. He learned a great deal about the production end of the business and eventually he taught others how to print, mix chemicals, maintain the machines and monitor quality control. He took great pride in his work and was happy to "advance" himself, seeking to build a bright future for himself and his family. He appreciated what was provided for him and he was a perfect example of a kid from the ghetto looking to create a better life for himself.

There were others, employed by me, who had advanced and exceeded his growth, income and responsibilities. Although Juan was making a very good salary, with benefits, he built up some "steam", sensing that I was holding him back, due to his ethnicity and country of origin. Others from Puerto Rico, Jamaica, The Dominican Republic, Africa, China and other far away places, who were better educated, with excellent sales and computer skills, training in electronics and management were advancing faster then him. He became resentful and seemingly unhappy. Climbing the ladder of success suddenly became an unattainable goal, in his mind, and consequently his morale and performance faltered. We spoke about that on several occasions and my efforts to uplift him were unsuccessful.

Much to my surprise and dismay he quit without notice. I was terribly disappointed. He wasted no time applying for unemployment insurance benefits and had been denied, as he should have been. Subsequently, I also received notice from the unemployment court to appear at an appeal hearing, at Juan's request. I presented myself in court and much to my amazement he won! Juan lied about the facts and erring on the side of safety, the administrative judge ruled in his favor, something that has happened to me in the past.

For me, it was an arrow through my heart and a possible big dent in my checkbook. Every time an employee collects unemployment benefits the employer's rate increases and with nearly sixty employees that resulted in thousands of dollars of increased payments for my business.

His next strategy, having one win under his belt, was to file a complaint with the EEOC, The Federal Equal Employment Opportunity Commission. That's potentially big trouble for any employer. The law is on the side of the employee, or former employee. This commission was created as part of the 1965 Civil Rights Act. It is designed to protect the employee's interests with callous disregard for the interests of business owners.

The examiners have enormous discretionary power and the prospect of taking an employee to court is very repugnant to employers. Being accused of violating someone's civil rights in front of a jury of proverbial "postal workers" is not a good thing. I am the dressed up suited Caucasian business owner and in their eyes I'm living "large" abusing the poor hardworking minority who are merely getting by and "breaking their asses" by a "fat cat" who's enriched from the sweat off their backs. For me, it was the "system" with scales of justice tipped in the favor of the employee. Clearly, I was on the wrong side of the law.

I had an experience in the past with another former employee who had become pregnant. She had taken advantage of the system and me. She, a "manager" had become very lazy and excessively obese during her pregnancy. She took long lunches, was frequently late for work and complained about everything and nothing. She topped off her lunches with Twinkies, Ring Ding, cream filled snowballs and Devil Dogs. I cautioned her, out of concern, about the consequences of eating such junk while carrying a child but she choose to ignore me. She had the right to eat whatever she wanted. An extremely emotional woman; she built her case, hired a sleazy lawyer and slammed me with an EEOC complaint.

I was compelled to hire an attorney, prepare for a hearing and upon my attorney's advice, after a long arduous process, I paid her $25,000 to avoid facing a jury who my attorney had assured me could award her a six figure settlement or more! Because her child had been born with a mental defect caused by, as I was told by an employee who had a close relationship with her, a difficult birth due to oxygen deprivation, as a result of her excessive weight causing complications. Therefore, she and her child suffered the consequences. I too could have been a victim of her lust for sweets, in court.

Enter Barbara, the nail polishing, obsessive and self-involved "manager" with the over painted face, hair all perfectly in place, high high heels and mirror, always in close reach was an experienced one-hour photo store manager, so I had thought. She had even owned a few of her own stores in the past. Needing a manager desperately I had decided, against my better judgment, to hire her and give her a shot. She "worked" for me for approximately six months or so and I became disappointed with her lack of performance, sloppy work habits, lack of leadership skills, completely void of technical knowledge and lacking an ounce of sales ability. I gathered evidence that she was all about Barbara and the job was just a means for her to pay her bills, nothing more. Inevitably, a separation was in the cards.

Without notice, she, following in Juan's footprints, quit her job. Off she went, to Wall Street. No, not to stake her claim in the lucrative game of finance, but rather, to open a one-hour photo store of her own. It was far from the best location on "the street" because it was east of Water Street and that was a much quieter part of "the street" and a bit "out of the way." The foot traffic was very unimpressive and she was up against some very stiff competition a few short blocks up "the street" where the action was, where the rents were much higher. No doubt she had loans, equipment leases, still a hefty rent, insurance, start up costs, construction, fixtures, inventory, personal

guarantees and all the other expenses and commitments that came with the such an operation. .
Of course, I did my homework and visited the store to see what was going afoot. I checked it out and looked for opportunities that I could extract for my business playing the role of a typical New Yorker. I did find "pay dirt" and licked my chops knowing that I had discovered was going to be "pay dirt."

Juan was working there "off the books" and collecting unemployment insurance benefits at my expense! Wow! It was time to make a plan.

The first thing I did was to send my biggest and strongest employee, Dan, down to her store with a camera. Dan showed up there on a Monday, the busiest day of the week in the one-hour photo business. His mission was to enter the store, casually walk up to Juan and while seated behind a printing machine, whip out a camera and snap a few photos of Juan, hard at work. He also took some shots of "nail polish Barbara" seated at the front of the store. That was all that I needed to put the first phase of my plan into action. "Let the games begin!"

I called a New York State Department of Labor investigator and reported what I had found, Juan, working "off the books" and collecting unemployment benefits. He told me to mail him the photos and he assured me that swift and proper action would be taken. Several weeks passed without hearing from the investigator so, I called him. He was unavailable, always. Getting him on the phone was impossible. I wrote several letters, certified mail, return receipt requested, and to his supervisor as well and to the commissioner. Nada. No one home! I got those little green postcards back from the post office verifying that all letters had been received. That's it, government hard at work.

I called Juan, at the Wall Street store after I gave up with the Department of Labor and I asked him if he would sit down with me for a meeting. He was glad to hear from me and we scheduled the meet. We got together, very cordially, exchanged small talk and then got directly down to business.

He was very contrite and regretful for what he had done to me. We discussed his quick and improper departure from his job, his fabricated reasons, the unemployment insurance ploy, the aid and assistance he had given to Barbara, by accommodating her by working off the books and helping her start her business and last but not least, the EEOC case. He went on to tell me that he didn't like working for her because she was abusive, lazy, didn't know a thing about the business and didn't pay him well. She knew that he was receiving unemployment insurance payments and he had admitted, that his employer was paying him in cash. She was using him as a tool enabling her to bilk the system. She also knew that his unemployment checks were coming out of my pocket and therefore, I too was subsidizing her business. Balls!

Juan expressed his deepest regrets, apologized and wished he had not left his job. He admitted that I had always been good to him and he wanted to come back. He was in tears. I explained the plan to Juan as he eagerly listened to every word.

"Ok Juan, here's the plan. On the day after Memorial Weekend, one of the busiest days of the year in this business, you'll be back on my payroll. You'll start at 8 AM and you're back to work as if nothing ever happened. All's forgiven. You are not to provide any notice to Barbara that you are not showing up for work the day after Memorial Weekend. She'll open her store without you, no printer. That will crush her. Your participation and silence is vital and required or all bets are off. He understood completely and was wearing a broad smirk on his face from ear to ear. Juan was in the game

"I will notify the unemployment agency that you have started working for me and that your unemployment checks will cease. You're back, paid on the books and I want you to contact the EEOC and drop your case."

He was ecstatic and the plan was executed flawlessly.

So, here's the windup: I got a good employee back. Juan learned a lesson, Barbara got what she deserved, Juan got off unemployment insurance and he dropped the EEOC case.

There are people out there who believe that the road to success is paved with gold by feeding off others. It's not the way to go. Play by the rules, work smart and do the right thing! Get even with those who try to succeed by bringing you down. It's called "street justice." Batter up.

The Free Bulgari!

Salesmen come in all shapes and sizes and certain Mr. Chuck White was an oddity in many ways, not just shape and height and balls included. A man who, at the time of this story, was in his late thirties, impeccably dressed, great suits, coats, shined shoes, perfectly fitted, tie and shirt flawlessly matched. Chuck was always groomed to a "T".

He was thin and tall, very tall. He was even taller then Dave, our friend in the prior teddy bear story (6'5" vs. 5'6"). Chuck was perhaps 6'8". He was a "smooth operator", quick talker, so quick that I often had difficulty understanding him. But, I knew why he spoke so fast. It was his way of hoping that he'd slip in a glitch, right through the cracks. His slick talking ways had enabled him to remove big bucks from unsuspecting customers. He created his own trouble, with me that is. Poor Mr. White, as a result of his tactics, I felt that someone had to teach this guy a lesson and it might as well have been me. Here's the story.

Mr. White sold high-end color copiers for a distributor of a Canon Copiers. He was very successful, worked very hard, aggressively and tenaciously, but, at times, his strategy was a bit too "creative" for his own good. His technical skills were well above average and he knew his business inside and out. He knew how equipment would make money for his clients and was very good at driving home those benefits creating a ton of business for him. He knew every "trick in the book" and many that were not "in the book".

At the time, back in the late 1980's through the early 1990's the color copier business was new and booming. Digital copiers and large format bubble-jet color copiers were new technologies and those who had gotten into it and knew how to sell the service had the opportunity to "print money" by targeting their market effectively. My business had been granted a spectacular opportunity to participate, at the inception, as a beta test site for Canon. We were one of seven companies in the United States selected by Canon to test the equipment to help them how to best target the market. Their objective was to define if there was a nitch for the product and find out by could make it "fly."

Business was so hot, the following year after the beta test program, that I had decided to purchase an additional unit and that's where Mr. C. White came in, stage left, not "*right*." I told Mr. C. White that I would provide a purchase order for the copier if he added four "heads" with the delivery of the copier.

A "head" was a $2,500 part that needed replacement from time to time depending on the volume of use. Therefore, I had added $10,000 to the purchase order for four "heads" and told him to deliver them with the copier. The benefit for me was cash preservation. I would not have to pay for those heads every time I needed one, rather they would be financed with the equipment improving my cash flow just a little bit. He agreed, the papers were signed, sealed, but not fully, delivered.

The copier arrived and installed but there was one problem, one "head" was missing, that had been agreed and specified in the lease. Mr. C. White pressured me to sign the "D and A" delivery and acceptance document in order for the leasing company, or bank, to pay him for the copier and to begin collecting monthly payments from me. I told him I would sign it when I received the missing head. He pleaded with me. I relented and signed however; if I do not receive that fourth head before I need it then I will create a lot of unhappiness for him. I warned him that I was not someone to "play" with and that I would not tolerate his bullshit if it should come to that! He assured me that I had nothing to worry about it. "No big deal" he told me. I saw it as an opportunity to trust him and if he didn't come through then I had remedies at my disposal and I was very firm, very.

The best predictor of the future is the past. This was not going to be an exception to the rule. Mr. C. White didn't disappoint prediction. He ignored my phone calls and reminders regarding that absent fourth head, which was paid for in full.

"I got two left."

Then a month or two later,

"It's Cliff, I'm down to my last head, buddy! There's still time."

Then the call that I had hoped not to make happened.

"I'm out of heads."

I gave him a week to show up, call or have the part delivered. He never called and never showed. How stupid!

I ordered the replacement, well in advance, and it came through the normal pipeline. We remained up and running again without skipping a beat. Fortunately, I had ordered it ahead of time, just in case. One has to anticipate all the possible failures to protect their business and provide for their customers because it's so difficult to acquire a terrific reputation and easier to loose it.

Within a week or so I called my attorney and had him draw up a lawsuit, a claim of damages of $100,000. We knew that my costs didn't amount to a fraction of that amount however, if you're going to get even then take out the big guns and push forward. He had been paid in full and I could have been left in the lurch. He didn't give a shit. Had I been unable to obtain the part I needed it could have resulted in enormous harm to my reputation with my customers. Suppliers do run out of parts. Had that happened or if I had failed to order it in advance I could have lost a lot of business and income and damage to my reputation, big time!

I warned him again and again. People's actions must have consequences. He behaved like a child and I was determined not to accept this crap, especially from him.

After several days before Mr. C. White's court imposed deadline to respond to the complaint I had received a phone call from him.

"I want to come to your office and talk to you, "He said.

"What do you want to talk about?" I asked.

"I want it to go away. You know what I mean?" He told me.

"Okay Chuck, stop by."

He appeared at my office several hours after I invited him to my office. He was anxious to get this monkey off his back. It was a stupid and needless incident caused by his failure to follow-up and that should never have happened. Consequences!

All the chairs in my office had been removed, just prior to our meeting. I had asked my assistant to do so to ensure two things. One, this was going to be a very short meeting and two, that his very tall statue did not intimidate me.

He entered my office and looked somewhat puzzled upon noticing the absence of chairs. He removed a sealed envelope from his breast pocket, placed it on my desk and pushed it in my direction.

"What's in the envelope?

"$5,000."

I pushed the envelope back to him, without opening it.

He promptly asked me what would make it go away.

I told him that there's a rather nice gold watch in the window at the Bulgari store on the corner of 57th and 5th and I'd like to see on my wrist. You know what I mean? If you've got some fat plastic with you then let's jump in a cab and that will make it go away. The watch was worth three times more than what was in his white envelope.

We took a cab to Bulgari. It all went away, except the watch, of course! As a gesture, due to my kindheartedness, even for an asshole like him, I suggested that Bulgari ship the watch to my sister's home address in New Jersey saving him 8% on the sales tax. And, oh yes, I paid for the cab.

Canon Fires a Dud!

Back in the 1990's a terrific opportunity emerged for my business. We were invited to participate and blaze a trail to test market a new technology as a beta test site for, a soon to be release, color copier known as the Canon Bubble-jet A-1, the device mentioned in the previous story.

This revolutionary copier produced color copies, "off the glass" 24" x 36" size prints. This had never been done before. "Off the glass", in the copier business means that copies could be produced from originals that are laid upon a glass platform of a copier, not from digital files, something that, at that time, was yet to come.

A beta test site is a marketing program designed to gather information regarding customers' reactions to pricing, quality, uses and acceptance of a device's output in order to create the most effective marketing strategies to introduce a new product in, what is hoped to be, an expanding marketplace.

My flagship store was one of seven sites in the country that were provided with the beta site opportunity. It turned out to be very profitable for us and it opened a lot of doors.

The arrangement was this: Canon provided the copier, ink, paper, parts and service for us for a fee per copy that we produced. We made copies and sold them to our customers at a price, set by Canon, $60 each for full size copies. We split the gross sales revenue with Canon 50/50. That's all we paid, just half of the gross revenue.

The beta test was conducted over a six-month period. We sold more copies than any of the other beta sites.

Our sales exceeded $100,000 and we captured a robust clientele. I enthusiastically looked forward to purchasing a bubble-jet for the business to continue to enjoy and expand the business.

All the beta site test companies were offered a Bubble-jet A-1 at full price, $100,000. I received a call from the Canon sales manager, from Texas, offering me the "opportunity" to purchase the device.

"Are you offering me a new bubble-jet or a used one?" I asked.

"We're offering you the opportunity to purchase the one that you have been using during the beta marketing test period." He replied.

"Now why would I want to pay full price for a used machine?" I inquired.

That arrogance of offering the opportunity to purchase a used machine at full list price reminded me of the scene in Godfather II that took place in Michael Corleone's office at Lake Tahoe with the corrupt senator. He senator tried to bilk Michael out of $250,000 and 5% of the gross receipts to obtain a casino gaming license. The legitimate cost of the license directly from the state of Nevada was merely $5,000.

Remember that?

Michael's reply was classic:

"Senator, you can have my answer now if you like. My offer is this: Nothing. Not even the fee for the gaming license, which I would appreciate if you would put up personally."

I told the Canon representative that I would purchase that used machine at full price less the money that I had already paid Canon during the beta test period.

That just about cut the price in half, a saving for me of about $50,000.

The folks at Canon were scratching their heads for weeks. They wanted it both ways and that was, in my opinion, unreasonable. I called the other beta test companies and asked each and every one of them if they were purchasing their beta test copiers and they all agreed to purchase their bubble-jets at full price. I did not tell them what I had up my sleeve. Doing so would have thwarted my strategy. What amazed me was that the other beta site business operators were the best and brightest in the business and my strategy had not occurred to any of them, not one. Was it because they didn't have the DNA in their veins? I just didn't know!

Several weeks later, as I was pondering my next move, I received a call from the Canon sales manager, the national marketing manager of Canon who was in charge of the bubble jet A-1.

"I have a Bar Mitzvah present for you Cliff!" he said.

"We'll go along with your proposition. I'm sending you all the documents via overnight Federal Express. Just sign the papers and return and keep the lid on this too. If the other beta sites find out about this I'll have a big problem."

I was a bit offended by the "Bar Mitzvah present" comment as if I, because I am Jewish, sniffed out the money with a long nose or was it a compliment because Jewish people have a reputation for being savvy business people? I'll never know what he meant and I don't care. What mattered was the money that Canon tried and failed to get out of my pocket. I call that "burning the candle at both ends."

Our continued use of the bubble-jet had a different arrangement then the beta site program. We paid the leasing company the monthly payments for the BJ-A1 and we received ink, paper, parts and service from Canon for a fixed $12 per copy fee billed by Canon. The bubble-jet had a built in meter that counted the number of copies we produced keeping track of our account to Canon.

We "broke the doors off" and we enjoyed a huge volume of business. We collected $60 per copy, paid the $12 fee and the monthly lease payments and that was like printing money. We were clearing, over $40 per copy! This was unheard of. It provided a net, pretax profit of 66%. We also drew more business for other phases of our business as the increased store traffic as a result complimented other services that we provided. In addition, our reputation soared as a source of cutting edge technology services in the industry.

Interesting, how huge success can cast a new perspective upon the "cash cow" equation and one benefit befalls other unanticipated ones too. At the end of every month I received a statement from Canon for approximately $15,000. When I considered their cost of ink, paper and parts, I felt that it was outrageous. It was a "locked in deal" because there was no other place to purchase those goods and services. The bubble-jet rarely required service; occasionally a new "head" the device that drove the ink to the paper was needed from time to time. That's the item that my friend, Mr. C. White, who had sold me as part of my next bubble-jet lease, was supposed to provide, a set of four and he only had delivered three. Refer to the previous chapter for further .details.

My outlook was that I should have had the right to purchase ink and paper outright for customary and usual pricing, at industry standards. Carving out a new deal would save my company a fortune. If I needed parts or service, I would have much preferred to pay a standard industry rate to keep "the iron" humming.

They balked, squirmed and refused to negotiate. I wrote letters to the top brass and they ignored me. I refused to give up. I decided play hardball and stop paying them altogether. Building leverage was my game plan.

I've always thought that I'd rather be the party that owes money than be the one to whom money is owed. Why? Because I've gotten the benefit and it's the creditor who's at risk, not me. The more I owe the better off I am and the worse it was for Canon. That doesn't seem logical to the ordinary person who has no business experience but, if you think about it, it'll click in!

I continued to have my manager order ink and paper in huge quantities, far beyond our entitlement based on usage. We stockpiled enough supplies to sink a small battle ship! Apparently, Canon never coordinated the count of the copies made with their customer's orders for ink and paper. In other words, we were billed only for the metered clicks, $12 per copy. The shipments of ink and paper continued to be delivered without additional charges that were the deal. We also obtained parts on the black market at very low prices from Canons repairmen, further evidence that Canon didn't have a clue as to proper management and control. Our relationship with Canon's technicians was a big plus for us. Thanks to Canon!

Before anyone at Canon took action against us I had piled up over $160,000 in unpaid bills. Certainly, they were also asleep at the money switch. Another "failure to communicate." Good old "Cool Hand Luke."

Eventually, I received the expected letter from Canon's accounts receivable manager advising me that our account had been suspended, something that I had expected would happen. They finally woke up. "Good morning Canon!" That's exactly what I wanted, because now they had to stop billing me that $12 per copy charge. You can't sue for what you don't bill and you can't bill a suspended account.

In addition to that, what would they be billing us for? We ordered nothing from them after that final statement and the termination of the account was like Canon tying themselves up in knots! With all my advanced planning we were on the fast track riding upon the good old "gravy train". Another $20,000 a month saving for me paid a lot of bills; such as college tuition, trips, dinners, whatever.

Canon sued my company for the money. Naturally, I expected that and I was ready to do battle. My lawyers had been "sharpening their knives" doing their due diligence and gathering all the information we needed. This was going to be fun.

My lawyers, through their research, had learned that a recent court case had been filed in The U.S. Supreme Court and resolved an issue regarding the following: Can a service contract be a "condition" of sale for a device? In other words, if a car, or any other device is purchased, is the buyer required enter into a contract for service of that device? The decision of the court was "no." The case was filed against Eastman Kodak, another stupid goliath that eventually fell on its sword.

I, the David, with the slingshot, countersued Canon for the immediate and permanent discontinuance of the service arrangement on a permanent basis, the condition of sale of the bubble-jet, and the return of all the money that I had paid them up until that time for service. I knew that the money that I had paid them was well spent providing me with a handsome return. However, it was illegal for them to do so because I was forced to do so and that was contrary to the court's decision.

The thrust of the legal justification is also known as "unjust enrichment." We had the briefs and court decision in our hands. The highest court in the land was on our side but would that be a viable defense for non-payment of a service that we had agreed to accept.

I suggested to Canon that having sold hundreds of bubble-jets worldwide it was not credible that any of their customers had arrangements that departed from their "boilerplate" plan. With evidence in my hands, I had gathered, I demonstrated to them that I've mustered media attention time and again in the past with The Wall Street Journal, Daily News, trade magazines, etc. and they were well aware of the damage that such publicity would cause them. Naturally, I knew that their advertising dollars carried a lot of clout, but as an industry leader I knew how to spread the word and my intimidation to pursue a class action suit, would have been a disaster for them. That was another slingshot they just had to duck and dodge.

After numerous meetings with all the lawyers we agreed to a settlement. I paid Canon one half of the money I owed them and they granted me the right to purchase supplies, parts and service at a fair price.

In sum, I simply could not allow Canon to get away with their program for numerous reasons. The effort that I, and my staff, put into creating our bubble-jet success enriched Canon very well. I paid Canon more than any other bubble-jet customer during the beta test site period. They gathered a great deal of useful information from us and that provided them with enormous advantages while formulating their sales and marketing strategies.

In addition, we spent a lot of time and money to obtain that business by developing new customers, not only for ourselves but for Canon as well. We purchased the device, and it was ours alone. They acquiesced only when it was in their best interests. That's how it works. Everyone has to cover his or her ass and that included mine.

The apartment was small, high with large windows. At 640 square feet it was a matchbox compared with my prior home, a five-bedroom center hall colonial that sat on a shady one-acre lot forty minutes north of the City. Even though the studio apartment was tiny, by comparison, in many ways, I had more space then in the idyllic 3,200 square foot suburban mansion.

My new abode, the first of many after my departure from my first marriage, was a magical place. Perched on the 48th floor of The Sheffield, a high-rise midtown luxury rental building, located on 57th Street, I was living a dream. In many ways, I had more space in that little nest then I had in my prior residence, much more.

Apartment 48S had been occupied by a Norwegian cabinetmaker that transformed a cookie cutter studio into a unique and beautiful setting with a personality, a soul. It was the most spectacular studio in a building with over 850 apartments, most of them, studios.

All the doormen, maintenance men and other staffers in the building loved that apartment. It was adorned with pink ash stained cabinets, bookcases, an alcove divider, wooden window moldings, elegant hand painted art, a platform for the dining area with built in planters atop wainscoted wall carpentry, halogen lighting, sconces, faux painting, stained floors, original art painted on the doors and walls and a built in desk, also handmade with beautiful detailing.

The City view from this studio was equally impressive. Facing west it provided magnificent views of The Hudson River and the New York skyline to the west. I never tired observing ships of every type moving up and down the river and sunsets were an ever changing show at day's end. I furnished the apartment with an upright piano, two bar stools, fresh flowers, a leather couch, off-white carpet and glass accessories complimenting it all perfectly.

The final touch was a custom made 80-gallon salt water fish tank installed in the alcove wall divider visible from the bed alcove and the living room. A marine biologist serviced the tank monthly keeping those gorgeous fish happy and swimming. Entering that studio at day's end with the fish tank providing the only illumination created a warm and dramatic welcome. It was the picture of cozy and comfortable luxury, a late 20th century garret in the sky fulfilling all my wishes for a place I could call my home and no one else's.

Windows! The building did not provide a service to clean them nor would they recommend a window cleaning service. I suspected that the cost of insurance and the potential liability was too great. The building was not equipped with a scaffold, at that time, lowered from the roof, with a swinging arm, to allow safety for such brave souls. For me, it was the only flaw in the apartment. With great views it was an impeccable sky-high studio with grimy windows. I had no solution and I stopped looking for one.

Several weeks after I had made my final attempt to find a solution I came upon a man who was walking down 57th Street wearing work clothes, a blue shirt and matching workpants. He was carrying a bucket, a window wiper blade and a few rags slung over his shoulder.

Suddenly he approached me,

"Do you live in the neighborhood?"

"Yes I do. Why?"

"I clean windows and I wana get some business. I need the money, bad. How big is your apartment? How many windows do you have?"

"It's a studio. I have two large combo windows each with smaller windows on each side. I'm also up on the 48th floor. Are you willing to clean them?"

"$20 bucks and we're done, man!"

I accepted his offer and together we entered the building and up we went to my sky studio. Imagine, a guy on the street, someone I didn't know and together we entered my apartment, as if this guy was my brother!

As soon as we entered he asked me if I wanted to "do" a joint and a beer.

At that moment I noticed that he didn't have any safety equipment, no straps, belts or gear to protect him. Amazing!

"No, I don't do weed anymore, thanks very much. But, are you about to get high before you go out on a window ledge? I mean really get high, up here, without any safety straps? Are you for real?"

"Yeah! I do it all the time and haven't fallen yet."

"You're fuckin' nuts man! What if the ledge is slippery, the wind kicks up or you loose your balance, or just slip, or a hawk lands on your head, eh? Did you ever think about that?"

"I'm in complete control man. That's what I do! Why do you think I don't go in planes? I have no control in planes. Hey, I'm not stupid, man!"

"Okay, do it!"

I grabbed my camera and when my new friend was totally out there, although mentally he was "out there" too, holding on, with his hand wrapped around one of those pink ash stained moldings, I took a picture.

I couldn't believe the balls and the stupidity of this guy. What would have been the harm of wearing protective gear? This, blew me away, not him, thank the Lord.

After he got back inside after cleaning the other window we had a few drinks. I was in need of a means to relax and calm down. Drinking, smoking grass and hanging out of a 48-story window! Finally, I can look back on someone who did something stupider than texting while driving!

We exchanged names and phone numbers and said our good-byes with firm fist bumps and hugs of respect and affection. He was quite a dude and a source of a terrific story for quite some time to come.

About four or five months later I received an envelope, in my mailbox bearing my address, hand written with his return address that I had difficulty reading. The handwriting was hard for me to decipher. The only thing I could make out was Riker's Island and NY, NY. Riker's Island is New York City's Alcatraz. I opened the envelope and it was from the "stoned" window guy. He had written that he had been "busted" in Times Square for attempting to purchase "coke" from an undercover cop. He was sentenced to one year in the "clink." The purpose of his letter was a request that I send him some necessary goods such as; underwear, levies, talcum powder, a sweatshirt, shaving cream, disposable razors, deodorant and a few other wants and needs. So, I went on a shopping trip, purchased what he had requested and put the stuff together with a note and I sent it to Riker's. I never received an acknowledgement or a thank you letter, a disappointment to me.

About a year after I had sent my "care package" to my favorite window washer, my widows became as dirty as they had been before we had met. By chance, we met again at the exact spot on 57th Street. He looked good however he had no bucket, no tools and no straps with him.

"How you doin' Cliff? I'm out! I need you! Please lend me some money so that I can buy the tools I need to get back into business, man!"

"Did you get the package I sent you? The one with the jeans, underwear and all of that?"

"Yeah! I got that."

"Well my friend. We're done. You took the time to write me a letter asking me to send what you needed but you never bothered to thank me! You only reach out to me when you need something. Now it's my turn again to give you something else, a lesson. Good bye and good luck."

I walked away from my window-washing "friend." One good lesson that so many people fail to learn is this:

Don't reach out for others only when you need them because if you do then the day will surely come when they will turn away from you. I washed myself of this guy even though my windows we due to a redo.

Not Every Driver is Goode

The overwhelming majority of people living in Manhattan do not own a car. What for? Anyone who goes from point A to B in Manhattan, driving their car should go to their room! One of the best things about living in this City is the benefit of not having to find and pay for parking when you arrive, because trains, cabs and buses don't eliminate that, not to mention walking or biking. The cost of parking, insurance, gas and the car itself is maddening. For those who own cars and live in Manhattan there may be some suitable reasons to justify the expense such as: a occupational related necessity, recreational homes, to visit friends or family who happen to reside outside The City. Or just a compulsion to spend some time "taking a breather" to "get out of town."

Several years ago we decided to purchase a car for Custom & Private New York Tours. I foresaw a great deal of benefits for the company to acquire a car. I investigated the notion extensively, looked at the numbers and realized that there was more then enough business to take that step.

It seemed very simple, just buy the right car to do the job, make the right deal, get the insurance, check out the best price, convenient parking options and hire the best driver and compensate him in a way that would be attractive for both of us. Voila!

My only major concern was how to property register and insure the vehicle for business use. That's where things got very complicated.

In New York City all "cars for hire" must be licensed through the TLC, The Taxi & Limousine Commission, a New York City Agency that has jurisdiction over taxis, limos, "black cars" etc. What that entails is

342

obtaining TLC license plates that entail high annual fees and frequent and useless inspections. All drivers must have a TLC driver's licenses in addition to an ordinary driver's license. The TLC license requires a drug, numerous cumbersome documents of all kinds and a signed acknowledgement that any vehicle that you drive will not be used to take clients to places known to be houses of prostitution nor pickup those who are on the street who are suspected of engaging in the trade.

In addition, such vehicles are subjected to frequent stops by TLC officers who harass and annoy drivers for all types of nonsense such as broken taillights, expired inspections and spot checks. They're generally just a bunch of childish ball busters.

I had decided that since the vehicle would not be a "car for hire" meaning its purpose was not to provide transportation only but rather to conduct private tours. In other words, if a client requested a transfer to an airport, after their tour had been completed, we cannot legally transfer them to the airport because that use is "car for hire." ·

Therefore, Custom & Private New York Tours acquired an SUV, a Suburban, because that's the largest passenger vehicle available on the planet. It's the same size as an Escalade and less costly because it doesn't have the "flash" and the "mark" of a Cadillac. We choose Silver because all the TLC vehicles are all black and I wanted to have a low profile to deflect TLC inspectors from harassing us, especially during tours.

Our first driver found me through Grieg's List, a retired judge. Would you believe that? The guy loved to drive! He quite after a few months because he lived with his 93 year old mother and he felt that the job took him away from her and due to her diminishing ability to care for herself he felt that she needed him there more frequently.

The second driver was a nut job. He was a very good driver but weird and quirky; with mood sudden and intermittent mood swings. He freaked out when I requested guests to tip him, in his presence. He was extremely chatty with the guests while I and other guides were presenting information during our tours.

The third driver was Mr. Goode. He was a very experienced driver always excellent behind the wheel. My guests always felt very safe with him at the helm. He had a terrific sense of the traffic flow and he poured on just the right amount of sane aggression, never overdoing it.

The problem with Goode was that he had issues, big time. Apparently he was a very angry guy loaded with tons of resentment and envy. Unlike the other two drivers he consistently wanted more money even though all the drivers were very well paid and they all, without exception, admitted that they were compensated better then any similar job that they had had.

Our financial benefit only accrued when we kept those wheels rolling beyond the threshold of breaking even on the investment. We made greater use of the car then I had thought when the car was purchased. Bottom line, the car was saving the company money. So, I had no intention of elevating any of our driver's compensation to the extent that the financial benefit for would cancel itself out.

While parked in front of an Upper Eastside hotel an adjacent car hit our car that was about to park. As a result the Suburban needed approximately $4,000 worth of repair. Upon investigation, the insurance company satisfied the claim and I realized that the vehicle was not properly insured. We needed to obtain the proper coverage to protect the company and our guests.

I called numerous insurance agents and the few who I had contacted, that specialized in the type of insurance we needed, wouldn't touch us with a ten foot pole. Even though I was not going to be the driver during tours, having no chauffeur experience.

I did some research and determined that since this was not a "car for hire" I just may not be under the jurisdiction of The TLC. A "car for hire" is strictly one that is used solely to transfer hires from point A to point B, etc. and not used to conduct tours.

I wrote a letter to the chief counsel of The TLC seeking written acknowledgment that our vehicular use was not under TLC jurisdiction. Having been ignored by her for about a month, I wrote another letter enclosing a copy of the original letter and sent them both together via certified mail return receipt requested. She called me and after a lot of squirming bullshit during our conversation she finally agreed that I was correct and she said that she would issue a letter, on The TLC's letterhead affirming that we vehicle did not require TLC plates to provide tours.

Then I got involved with the New York State Department of Motor Vehicles and that was such an endless run around whereby no two agents had the same answers to all my questions, provided incorrect information and gave me a run around that had me spinning in circles.

345

Then a fabulous idea hit my brain. Who was the previous Commissioner of The TLC? What was he doing now? I did an Internet search and found him, Matthew Daus, a transportation attorney practicing law on West 56th Street. I called Mr. Daus and we had a long and pleasant discussion. He totally understood exactly what we needed and he agreed to help. He was paid $3,000, his retainer. Within a few days two insurance agents who specialized in the type of insurance we needed contacted me. Due to Mr. Daus's recommendation, I was able to obtain the coveted insurance. He sent a refund check of $2,200 against the prepayment of his retainer him. Amazing what it takes to get things done in New York City, legally.

****

Let's get back to the finale of Mr. Goode the focus of this story.

One morning the two of us were on our way to pickup a family for a tour at The Trump International. While on our way to the hotel I had asked Goode if he would drop me off at a theatre on 54th Street because I needed to purchase theatre tickets for some of our clients. He dropped me off and I requested that he swing around the block to 8th Avenue so that he would be facing The Trump International to facilitate our ride to meet our guests and start their tour. He gladly agreed to do so. After I had purchased the tickets I walked over to 8th Avenue and noticed that Goode had parked the Suburban by the curb, illegally. The Suburban was sitting, empty, and that's no Goode! I was shocked as I saw him walking toward me, from across the street, holding a cup of coffee. I also noticed that a traffic officer was about to write at parking ticket for $115.

I approached the officer, pleaded with her not to issue the ticket and she grudgingly acquiesced. Goode unlocked the vehicle, seated himself behind the wheel as I took my place beside him and off we went.

"What did you do that for? You know that I would have gotten coffee for you if you had waited for me. I've done that for you so many times before! You needed your coffee so badly that you had to risk a $115 ticket? Who the hell did you think would have paid it? You didn't think, for a second, that I would have paid that one, did you? I said angrily.

"It's all about the fucking money with you." Goode shouted.

"Hey, you've gotten tickets before and I've paid them all because you had reasonable justification. Those tickets were not entirely your fault and therefore, I paid them. But this is different! You know damn well that you were risking a ticket for another cup of coffee. What planet do you live on?

He proceeded to drive up to Trump International and we both sat staring ahead in silence. I was fuming, fit to be tied. Such a·schmuck! He had a dream job that filled his needs and I even picked him up in front of his home every morning or at a coffee shop around the corner from his home. Who has a boss that picks them up? Incredible!

Here's the final coup. He turned his head, facing me while driving toward Trump Hotel and said,

"I don't have to drive today!"

That was about twenty minutes before the scheduled tour. He thought that he just took the power and had me by the balls. What a surprise I had in store for Goode.

I told him, "Pull the car over, please."

He did. Then I said,

"Put the car into 'park'" and he did. I leaned over toward Goode, turned the ignition key down, shutting off the engine and yanked it out of the ignition switch and told him,

"We're done. Take your stuff."

He removed his backpack from the car and walked away without saying a word.

Immediately I called a limo company, arranged for an SUV to arrive at Trump International within 30 minutes. I called the client and told him that I'd be about fifteen minutes late. He was pleased because they were running late too. I called Aline and told her to meet me at the parking lot behind our building. I told her the Goode incident when I arrived. She was totally in synch and agreed with the way I handled it. I can only imagine if the incident had occurred farther from our parking lot and we had less time to make the correction or that the client was ready to go at the planned tour start time what the consequences could have been. I would have waited until that tour ended to "can" Goode but I didn't want to subject myself and the guests to the certain pale of discontent that would have been ever present during the tour. Damage control would not have been a seamless experience. Goode acted so stupidly and he self-destructed. It boggles the mind.

Goode was a super schmuck, kissing his job good-bye because he had to have a cup of coffee! No, a coffee was not the reason for his actions, it was a mindset that compelled him to take power, so he thought, and test me even though he knew that my reaction, after working together for nearly six months, would possibly compel me to throw him under the bus. He took a chance. It was "brinkmanship" testing me to see how much of his shit I would allow him to chuck in my direction. What was the benefit and what were the probable consequences? His equation, flung at me was not merely stupid but rather it was evidence of a deeply troubled man.

In truth, it's sad that someone who needed the job, one he could never replace, would take such a risk, for nothing, and walk away just like a schoolboy in short pants.

I took the subway to Trump International from my home, a 10 minute subway ride from the hotel and met the chauffeured SUV and my guests. The "music played on" and Goode did not have a seat in the band.

One of the hundreds of respondents to my Grieg List Ad for another chauffeur was received from Mr. Goode with "I apologize."

I didn't respond. I have been working with Robert, my new driver, for over a year and his attitude, performance and appreciation of the opportunity to work with us has been terrific and we appreciate him ·too. Thanks Mr. Goode for being just not being good enough.

Chapter V
Thoughts & Reflections
****

Brooklyn: Once Fear, Now
I'm Never Too Near!

Perhaps the Dutch got it all wrong from the get-go! They named this outlying farming community Breukelen, after a Dutch town. It means broken land in Old Dutch. As a kid I always stayed away from Brooklyn. There was never any compelling reason for me to go there. The tabloid papers frequently featured headlines similar to these:

FALLING BRICK KILLS 6 YEAR OLD IN BROOKLYN

SUBWAY HIJACKED IN BED-STY

FOUR SLAIN IN BROOKLYN SHOOTOUT

SIX-YEAR-OLD BOY KILLS 3 SISTERS

DOG EATS BABY

Generally, I hung out in Manhattan and the safer environs of, would you believe, the north Bronx, yes, The Bronx! Brooklyn was the forbidden land or "The Promised Land" a place that promised trouble. Queens and Staten Island offered me nothing either back then. I should have strayed away from Queens, a vast plain of highways, airports and boulevards peppered with great diners, diverse neighborhoods and too few neighborhood parks. That's bit of an unfair exaggeration, no doubt, but try it for yourself, diverse yes, but a vast wasteland of boring urbanites, for the most part with a few exceptions, to be fair.

As a kid, and as a young man, I never traveled anywhere. I hated baseball, boring, didn't even go to the 1964 World's Fair, it was in Queens, and Staten Island was, to me, a suburb that was more like New Jersey then New York. The best thing about Staten Island, for me was, that it cost nothing to get the hell out of there, the ferry!

The names of some of the Brooklyn neighborhoods disturbed me too. Gravesend: Whose graves at the end of what? Crown Heights: What crown? Perhaps it was the crown my mother used to refer to after I committed a minor crime like leaving my dirty clothes laying on the floor, "I'll crown you!" As in break your head! Red Hook. Whose hook and why was it red, blood? Sheepshead Bay. What happened to that sheep's body? "Boy's High" School. Who's high? High on what? Greenpoint; what's the point? It's very silly but that's what kept me away from "Crooklyn." Ft. Greene. Do they really need a fort? Flatbush. "Flatbush." how'd that happen and whose bush got flattened?

The first time I had to go to Brooklyn was the day Robert F. Kennedy had died, ominous, to get my teaching license at 110 Livingston Street, the HQ of The Board of Education. I was looking from side to side for the inevitable ambush. I parked my car, an MGB, in a lot, no street parking for me. I located the Board of Education building and made my way up to the sixth floor to The Bureau of Licensing.

Miraculously, I successfully maneuvered my way through the maze of offices littered with red tape, filled with bureaucrats who were half asleep. Finally,

351

I emerged with the coveted license in my hands. To me, at the time, it was the most important piece of paper that had been ever handed to me. It was my lifeline, my ticket to avoid the military at a time when we, as a nation, were torn apart by the most unpopular war, or rather "conflict" excuse me, since 1860, Vietnam.

Next, on to The Bureau of Assignments where I obtained my assignment or district, post haste.

"We're going to give you HARLEM!" the clerk shouted, a large African American woman who roared with apparent contempt rocking me to my bones!

This was the Harlem of Nicky Barnes, the kingpin drug pusher, and a place that would have changed my image of Brooklyn to a place more akin to Scarsdale. But, it turned out not to be nearly as bad as I had thought it would be. So much for Brooklyn! I got what I came for and I left unscathed, ears ringing a little bit and my knees clacking.

Now, after a generation, time had brought wholesome and very positive change to most of Brooklyn.

Years ago my son David told me that he was moving to Brooklyn.

"Brooklyn? Are you nuts?"

I asked him.

"Yeah, Brooklyn. Dad, been there lately?"

"No, I haven't been to 'Crooklyn' lately."

My fears still dwelled within me even though I knew that David was far from stupid. I had decided to break down those barriers, those ghosts of years past. I had decided to check it out with an open mind. People generally don't do that. They have their notions of neighborhoods and never venture back, out of fear. Time after time, I've revisited rotten neighborhoods recently, those I had feared in the past, and I'm inspired and often say to myself, "I'd live here!" Amazing!

When I visited Brooklyn to meet my son and checked out the neighborhood, I had experienced a place that I had never been to before. Brooklyn Heights! That's about the most gorgeous neighborhood in the entire City! Coulda, woulda, shoulda bought a brownstone there when I could have afforded one about thirty years ago for about $80,000. Today, strap on another two zeros and you too could call it home! Yes, two zeros! But, at that time, in the 1980's there was a reason why the homes were so cheap.

David and I spent part of the day walking together through America's first suburb, the first New York City landmarked neighborhood, with 600 pre-Civil War homes featuring architectural styles such as: Georgian, Federal, Italianate, Greek Revival, Queen Anne, Neo-Classical, Beau Arts, Dutch, Brownstones and Churches with magnificent Gothic detailing, ornate Italianate framed entry embellishments, Renaissance structures covered in limestone, Flemish Bond brickwork, pediments, lintels and magnificent oak and mahogany doors with elaborate moldings.

This neighborhood, one of Brooklyn's best, is a clean, safe, vibrant place that boasts a rich history and a sense of tranquility. Truly, it is a marvelous neighborhood, merely one of many in Brooklyn that has sprung to life providing better, safer, serene and happier lives for residents of our most populous borough.

We walked beneath the Brooklyn Bridge. What a site! Such splendor, history and beauty and then went on to DUMBO, "Down Under the Manhattan Bridge

353

Overpass", aka, Brooklyn's Soho. It's a neighborhood filled with converted commercial loft buildings, new high-rise condos, small businesses, charming shops, several bookstores, restaurants, gourmet coffee shops, bars, bakeries, waterside parks, Jane's Carousel and X-Manhattanites who yearn for a bit more space, for a bit less money with rapid access to Manhattan. That's a place, with a soul.

Williamsburg, "Willyburg" and that gorgeous bridge, rich in history bearing a sign posted by the City for motorists leaving Brooklyn reads, "Oy Vey, I'm Leaving Brooklyn." For many Jewish people who moved across the river to Brooklyn from The Lower Eastside, crossing the Williamsburg Bridge was symbolically like crossing the Sinai Desert and entering the promise land.

Kent Street along the waterfront is now teaming with young adults who live one subway stop from Manhattan. Bedford Street, via the L train, is littered with more watering holes per block than just about anywhere else in the City with the possible exception of LES, The Lower Eastside or perhaps near the intersection of 34th and Lexington Avenue. Young movers and shakers are building a new community and replacing remnants of the old Jewish, Irish, Italian and Polish neighborhoods. It's giving way to a new and younger generation, bursting with energy, talent and optimism. Eager young folks are working and pushing ahead building their futures and Brooklyn's too, just as past generations have done before them. It's another layer of history in the making!

Brooklyn has become a vibrant center of culture, museums, libraries, music, art, Brooklyn Museum,

Brooklyn Academy of Music, "BAM" the Botanical Gardens and magnificent parks, old and new and bursting forth.

And don't forget Coney Island. The transformation of Brooklyn is exemplary of the conversion of New York City and it has gotten its "mojo" back as they say. What's a mojo? It's soul, identity, and trademark, its own mark of distinction, an abundance of enthusiasm, diversity, pride and charisma.

Take a walk through Ft. Greene, Greenpoint and check out some of those streets off Manhattan Avenue, DeKalb, Atlantic and Flatbush. Take a step back to the mid 19th century; Carroll Gardens, Cobble Hill, Boreum Hill, Park Slope, Red Hook, and on and on. It's almost endless.

Some neighborhoods might require a dose of courage, though less than in the past. Bed-Sty is better, Crown Heights is on the upside fast track, East New York is not and Bushwick is coming up nicely as well as a number of other places that we never thought would "make it." When the real estate gentrification genie makes it's way to Pitkin Avenue and brownstones start selling for a million plus bucks then just about all of Brooklyn will have "arrived."

The transformation is incredible. The power of optimism, people laying down roots, urban pioneering in Brooklyn has created dynamism and resolution has emerged, forging a future with neighbors from all over the world. Brooklyn is a case study in urban renewal from the grass roots, an example of change for the good, one that needs to be studied and duplicated in other cities.

Therefore, if you've been to Brooklyn, a long time ago, then you haven't been there at all. That's New York

City, change; it's the only constant, the only thing that stays the same is change.

On a nice day, take a walk over The Brooklyn Bridge. You'll get a view of Manhattan that's well worth the trip and you'll be one of the tens of millions who have taken this iconic stroll, a symbol of New Yorker's spirit and resolve. And when you get to Brooklyn look for the sign the City has installed on the bridge "Welcome to Brooklyn. How sweet it is!"

"Hey Brooklyn! Yus doin' good! We "loves ya" Brooklyn!"

Sorry about that Brooklyn, you guys don't talk like that anymore, right? Nah . . .

Who's Your Neighbor?

Years ago, Liza Minnelli recorded a song titled "Ring Them Bells." It's about a fictitious woman named Shirley Devore whose parents were fretful because she, at the ripe old age of thirty-two, had continued to remain single. They had decided to help her search for a man suitable for marriage by arranging a trip for her to pursue the lucky one who would become Miss Devore's loving and devoted husband.

As the lyrics unfold, while searching for her prized beau, she had been advised to visit the Dubrovnik coast. Off she went and met a man who happened to live in apartment 29F in the same building as she, who resided in apartment 28E, at 5 Riverside Drive in the Upper Westside in Manhattan.

Fact is stranger than fiction. Any New Yorker will "buy in" to this story. This fictional account of finding romance thousands of miles from home, with a next door neighbor, undoubtedly has happened time and again, especially for New Yorkers who often would not recognize their neighbor if they saw them at The Wailing Wall or The Great Wall of China!

Having lived in buildings with over 400 apartments or as many as 900, I have no doubt that this song conveys a true story.

While living in The Sheffield, a fifty-story condominium on West 57th Street consisting of eighteen apartments per floor, it was incapable for me to know the names of more than a small fraction of my neighbors even those who lived on the same floor! How could I consider them my neighbors, with 900 apartments and an average of two people per apartment yielding 1,800 residents, more or less? That's more than the population of most villages and small towns. Is an apartment building a small town? Who can get to "know" that many people, even casually?

People safeguard their anonymity in large cities. The only way for me to get to meet my neighbors is when and if we would wait simultaneously for the elevator, pick up our mail, hold a door or dispose of the trash together by happenstance. Usually neighbors say "hi" or "thanks" just for holding the elevator door. Introducing yourself and announcing your apartment number is seldom done. It's looked down upon and seems very peculiar in New York City. People go about their lives, plugged into an ipod, ipad, iphone, Blackberry, reading or writing emails on their way down to the lobby. The silence is odd, punctuated by the clicking of keystrokes on handheld devices and the faint sound of music, which at times isn't so "faint" it could make you faint.

Today, I live in a building that's about one-half the size of The Sheffield. There are ten apartments on each floor, two wings for a total of twenty. I have to admit that I know the name of five people who live on my floor and that's probably three more than Aline knows. She, I believe, is quite typical!

Most people lead hurried and hectic lives, especially in urban centers and they are too busy and just not interested in who their neighbors are, where they're from, what they do or what they think. We want peace, quiet, our space and security. Once our apartment doors are closed our neighbors might as well be half way around the world. But, if they were in need of help or assistance for just about anything, we'd all be there for each other. Why? We're New Yorkers and that's just the way we are! By the way, if you need a cup of sugar, "ring my bell" that's okay too, even though ·I don't have any. It wouldn't matter whether I knew your name or not. If you live down the hall, we're neighbors!

The sugar is unimportant, it's the spontaneous opportunity to say "Hi neighbor! What's your name? What can I do for you?" See ya in China, but I may not know who the hell you are! But, if we meet in Split, Croatia, we just might get married!

Who's Bored in New York City?

There are hundreds of thousands of people in this City who awaken daily without any idea as to how they're going to spend their day. It makes me sad. It's about them and not about the City. Whether it's depression, loneliness, paranoia, ill health, old age, boredom, anger, financial problems or any other deprivation, anyone who's bored in New York City is a most unfortunate soul. They must have lost opportunities to connect with themselves, others, enjoy all the beauty, events, socialization, energy and cultural opportunities that are available, many of which happen to be for free!

I've greeted a new day many times without a plan. For me, the best solution is to grab a book, get on the subway and consider all the choices that are available and, in no time at all, I catalogue them, make my choice and off I go. Thus far, I haven't made a regrettable decision. Even if my choice was not the best, it was my choice to do, see, and experience something new and different. It's endless. Just exit a subway station; one you've never been to before and as you emerge a new vista unfolds before you, a new place to have new experiences!

This City has more of what you want than any other, and quite a bit of it is free! There are street fairs, parks, The Staten Island Ferry, Governor's Island Ferry and that includes free bicycle "rentals" and the greenway along The Hudson River, The High Line, take a stroll over the Brooklyn Bridge, the views, people watching, window shopping, free kayak rentals with instructions upon The Hudson River, Central Park, Prospect Park, Greenwood Cemetery, America's second most popular tourist attraction in the early 19th century, City Island, pocket parks, the changing skyline, observing the water traffic, the sights and sounds of people talking, watching people doing their jobs, helping each other, shouting, amuse yourself, observe the way people dress and notice their weird facial expressions. The Metropolitan Museum of Art is "free" although most visitors pay the customary voluntary $25 "donation" not realizing that the fee is a donation. The sign displays the message, in somewhat smaller type, "recommended donation." And, the greatest bargains in New York City are on the sidewalks, yes the sidewalks, craft and flea markets too!

Strolling down the sidewalks provides the greatest "side show" on earth. Not only due to the opportunity to observe people but also take notice of the diversity, coming from everywhere, with different ideas, cultures, languages, features, dress and gestures. There is no face of an average New Yorker. Listen to their languages, check out their body language, their clothes, hair style, and shoes, listen to them speaking French, Russian, German, Italian or virtually every language on earth. Be amused how they light a cigarette, hold it, notice their walk, how they hold hands, tilt their hats, sip their drinks, it's free. Venture into stores, check out their window displays, hang out there, start a conversation, look at the way merchandise is featured and take it all in. Observe the architecture, the endless variety of styles, the art that adorns countless structures large and small and then roam through the City, find traces, artifacts and monuments of history that are all around you. Just look, it's all there; memorials, pieces of The Berlin Wall, statues, terra cotta carvings, buildings with

361

spectacular ornamentation are everywhere. It's a glorious urban landscape rich in history, substance and beauty.

Every block tells a story. Wander through centuries, look at the details, and hop on the subway, breeze through neighborhoods, sit and have a cup or a glass of whatever and have a chat with someone or just plunge into a bookstore, while they still exist. Grab a few books off the shelves and get lost in books and pass the time. It's free!

Venture to a place you've never been to before. There are 722 miles of subway tracks and 468 stations. For the cost of a ride you not only can travel through time but you can visit places you never knew existed. There are so many neighborhoods to visit in New York City and they all have their own karma. The City is a mosaic, a virtually endless palate; cultures, communities and experiences await you. Just go there. Take a ride to Williamsburg, a very interesting place, The Bronx Zoo, free on Wednesdays, City Island for lobster tails "on the water" for about twenty five bucks including a Heineken. Or enjoy a Philly cheese steak sandwich via the R train on Fifth Avenue in Bayridge, Brooklyn, and on and on. Did I forget to mention Arthur Avenue in the Bronx? Sure, don't leave that out. It just could be the best Little Italy in the City where the scent of cheese will knock you over, sausage that will make your eyeballs roll, pasta to die for and prices that can't be beat! It's endless, varied and fabulous. The world has laid down roots there. If you want to get happy, active and stimulated, this is the place to be. Where shall we go next? That's up to you and don't forget to bring a camera or

iphone. Slicing and dicing The Big Apple is my
favorite pastime, try it. Delicious!

Graffiti, Now and Then

As with just about everything else in New York City, graffiti has changed. It's constantly evolving, impressive, relevant and powerful. It has reached a high plateau and has earned the right to claim legitimacy as a true art form.

Art is expression, creativity and imagination bringing forth a message, hopefully. But, at the very least it conveys emotions, beliefs, culture, the urban experience, an outlook placed on a surface, a form of communication and speech that's real and filled with passion born from human spirit. It conforms to the passions of new and vibrant energy that is alive and well in New York City.

No one is qualified to judge a piece of art with absolute authority. Only we have the right to express how a piece of art touches us. It's all about belief and opinion, our own. Those who make a living, as art critics, are to be found on all sides of the discussion. Life is a bell shaped curve and that's what art is about, subjectivity. Beauty resides "in the eye of the beholder" and that includes graffiti.

There are those who will examine a piece of art and declare "it's junk" and by any measure they have the right to label it "junk" or virtually anything they wish. According to what law of aesthetics, what mathematical equation, what yardstick, or frame of reference gives one the right to determine the value, pleasure and measure of art to others? Junk to some is to others stimulating and delivers a message or is simply pleasing to look at, "it speaks to me." Art is, about individual choices providing opportunities for the viewer to decide.

Graffiti is a terrific art form for those who seek creative self-expression. For those who "write" as they say in graffiti vernacular, their efforts provide expression that casts aside our politics and emotions with little or no regard for the sanctity of "public property." "Writers" have the right to express themselves, although doing so on public space is a violation of the public trust. In some places, if it provides a positive and prideful message of a community, it should not be considered graffiti. Who's to say? We all have the right to take it or leave it.

Back in the 1970's and '80's graffiti was a ubiquitous plague that had befallen upon the City. It seemed to be everywhere. Why?

Look at life through the eyes of a kid from the ghetto at the time that the mighty City of New York was on its knees, pleading for help and on the verge of bankruptcy. The streets were filthy, schools were failing and police disengaged themselves from communities that they were there to serve and protect. A broken "welfare" system, renamed Public Assistance, frustrated and rebuking large numbers of its "clients" as those in need are known today, not "cases." Thousands of children were living in horrendous substandard housing; most were deeply frustrated and angry, single parents were struggling in environments that were saturated with illegal drugs, poverty, crime and filth. Gunshots were heard so often that many ignored the familiar sound of firearms. Police sirens screamed incessantly, money was scarce even for the price of a movie ticket let alone a candy bar or a soda. There were no places for children to find peace and quiet needed to complete their schoolwork. Running down to the store to buy momma Pall Mall's and vodka was a fact of daily life for thousands of subjugated ghetto children. What resources were at hand for them to express themselves? What role models were there to save them? Who understood their plight? Who provided encouragement, hope and the prospect of a future? Where were safe playgrounds, enrichment programs, and parents who were able to provide their children with what they desperately needed, wholesome food, warmth, love, nurturing and guidance?

Teachers were there sure, but far too many were unenthusiastic, providing substandard performance in an underfunded school system, one that recruited thousands of inexperienced teachers who were "green", ill equipped and poorly trained to teach in urban ghettos and incapable of coping with all the challenges facing them.

I had graduated from an excellent university with a degree in education and it took me about a year to balance my act as a novice teacher in a Junior High School in Harlem. I cared about my kids. Most teachers were not so inclined. For $106 a week, take home pay, most teachers were passing through the system, biding their time and teaching was not their primary mission.

The City had few options. There was no money, the environment was extremely hostile, and droves of children were living on life's edge. Society owed those kids much more then that. The least experienced were attracted to teaching in the urban ghettos of New York City as a means to avoid the war in Vietnam. For many, their interest and devotion to the teaching profession was AWOL, "away without leave" just passing through.

If only the best and most experienced teachers were assigned to face those challenges and the "greenies" were instead, assigned to the best schools it would have produced better results, for the unfortunates. It just doesn't work that way folks. It would have been politically incorrect.

The deck was stacked, most tragically, against teenage boys and girls, who lacked essential role models. They had no place to lay their anger. They found destructive outlets to vent themselves with dire consequences. Immersed in that environment as a teacher, I had learned to understand my students, their frustrations and anger. They didn't ask to be born or raised there or enter this world with all the deficiencies that their world had hurled at them. They struggled to survive, cope and endure as best way they could with an empty toolbox. Some did better than others and many of them created graffiti as a means of expression in ways they knew would draw attention from a society that tragically had turned its back on them. This "betrayal" was not planned, sanctioned or organized. Everyone in this City was aware of the degradation of those youngsters in the ghettos. The vast majority of people were focused on their own problems. Graffiti became a valve for those who sought a means of expression, a howl, their frustration and anger highlighted for all to see. "I'm here, I have a message and it's in your face!"

I hated graffiti back then because I just didn't understand it. New Yorkers looked at it and saw it as ugly, an expression of a City that had gone wild. It marred the City and provided an obscene backdrop exposing the underbelly of New York City in a ubiquitous, grotesque and gritty manner. It was a plague upon us. Clearly, this was not art; it was scribble, "junk art" and offensive. "Jose 167" written in big rounded letters with sprayed Day-Glo borders had invoked the notion that we were simply out of control! I felt that we had been invaded. This was my City, my home. "How dare you take license to disfigure it?"

The subway system took a huge hit. Subway cars, public property were all palettes for thousand of "writers." It revealed a City plunging downhill, raped by rabid teens who took over and ruled.

What will become of us? What will the future bring? My concern for us all was deep and real. I was persistently fatigued and troubled by it all. It was an appalling blight on the landscape, a rape of the environment and a reflection of a society plunging deeper into despair. Admittedly, I didn't get it. I just didn't understand it.

Those days are over. Sure, there's graffiti in New York City now. Most of it is found in the same neighborhoods that gave rise to it before but, it's not the same.

During those difficult days we had a different form of expression then we do now as those neighborhoods have changed. Today, talented artists express themes with enormous skill and creativity. Verve has replaced nerve and locals respect it for what it is. This new art or evolved form of graffiti has become more accepted, even welcomed. Today there are many examples of graffiti that are extraordinary all over the City. Themes depict children on their way to school laden with books, chess pieces adorn school walls, elders are illustrated as active and happy people, black and white folks are engaged in conversation, ethnic themes exist expressing pride, Yankee heroes were adorned recently at 157th Street and River Road in The Bronx, a spectacular display, clean and unmarred, a work of art, on a building wall dated 2004. Why? Apparently, locals respect and perceive these visuals as legitimate expressions of their culture and values. This is not "junk art." It's real and it touches the heart. It is validation that conveys the impression that artists are delivering a message one that is timely and important. It is part of the community, it's culture, uplifting, vibrant, prideful and positive.

It's a new day. No longer a competition of yelling, "Look at me." Rather it's "Look at you, look at us, look at our community, school and our City!" That's the difference and it's big. "The artist" is now part of something, a community that strives and expresses pride in itself. They're not destroying it. They are celebrating it. That is the new message, embracing, not rejecting, loving and not hating.

Yes, graffiti has changed and it is visual evidence of the maturation of New York City, another example of how this town has survived, endured and how people in New York City have improved and evolved. We reach and create with all the guts and passion we have. Viva graffiti. It's the true urban art, and that's only one man's opinion. What's yours? "Write" man. It's the "write" thing to do.

Going, Going, Gone!

The true litmus test for a New Yorker is the refrain, "Oh, I remember when that was there!" It is just one sentiment about this town that speaks to me. I have lived here since day one. I recall so much that has defined the images and imagination that have peppered my childhood, images that are chiseled in my brain, images that no longer exist are a distant memory evoking welcomed nostalgia dwelling deep in my heart and soul.

I too have morphed into one of those who walk the streets of New York City and silently say to myself, "I remember when that was there!"

I too have become another encapsulated walking archive, a time machine, of New York City's past and present with a curious anticipation and apprehension bent toward the future. I fear uttering phrases that reveal my melancholy, as I would risk giving myself away as an elder, one who carries a senior metro card and a social security debt card in my pocket.

Putting myself in the elder category, a long time New Yorker, one who looks back on a full and active life etched in the stone and steel of a City gone by, is a mixed blessing. Change has been dramatic through nearly seven decades and has made me who I am. There are countless images locked in my brain that most will see only in films, photographs and words "painted" by historians and fiction writers.

The wicker subway seats, ceiling fans, tungsten light bulbs, cigarette ads, "Most Doctors Smoke Chesterfields" and the "Meet Miss Subway" signs, Checker cabs, elevated trains, private payphones, subway tokens, wooden turnstiles, low hemlines, seamed stockings, ubiquitous fedoras, buses

370

bellowing black smoke in your face, no site of sidewalk scaffolds, BMT and IRT subway signs, double breasted suits, Bishop Crook Lampposts, The Camel billboard in Times Square billowing smoke rings, wing tips, double decker City buses, bow ties, one cent chewing gum vending machines installed on subway beams providing two pieces of Chiclets in little cardboard boxes, 5 cent newspapers, women wearing hats with enormously wide brims, 5 cent candy bars, dark blue 3 cent postage stamps featuring The Statue of Liberty, subway tokens, free street parking, men wearing fedoras, and no elderly ladies wear the brand, Red Cross Shoes, and on and on.

What's even more remarkable was the absence of all the electronic gadgetry way back then; ipods, ipads, Blackberrys, color flat screen television, cable TV, curved flat screen TV, WiFi, X-Box, credit cards accepted in taxis and iphones, Metrocards, the internet, Facebook, twitter, computerized street parking machines accepting credit cards, lit street crossing signs displaying that the light will change counting down the seconds, bike paths, street stations that access bicycle rentals, subway elevators and escalators, accordion double length buses, pedicabs, stainless steel newsstands and bus shelters, bike lanes, epoxied gravel sitting areas in public squares, beautiful flowered pots, and on and on.

I'm not an alien who has landed here for a visit. It's people such as I who are part of this transformative experience; the changing human experience that defines this City and flows through the veins of those who've been here long enough to reflect and take in the astounding differences in just a few short decades.

371

This rite of passage runs deep. I have earned the right along with all those who have walked these streets, experiencing all of the 1950's, 60's, 70's, 80's, 90's, 00's and I've held firm to a vision and commitment, the belief that this City is much more then the comeback City. It's a City that has morphed into a place better than ever before.

As I walk through the streets of the City, one that differs vastly from the one I knew only ten short years ago is, in fact, a futuristic activity. My daily consciousness, sense of increased well being, feeling of safety, full of optimism and pride that I carry provide a constant source of comfort and satisfaction. Such thoughts, a short time ago, were rare and fleeting.

Unlike most cities, New York City is an organic City. I look around at everything and wonder how the changing landscape of people and streetscapes has affected us all. I inhale what I see now with enormous enthusiasm and wonder. I gaze and ask myself questions, constantly. Why is this here? Who was behind it? Why is it still there? Why hasn't it been replaced yet? Who makes those decisions and why this way and not that way?

People look, gasp in wonder at One 57, the new 1008 foot glass condo designed as a waterfall, that has risen across the street from Carnegie Hall at the time of this printing, the tallest poured concrete building on earth and the tallest residential building in the Northern Hemisphere. But hold on folks because one block west the foundations are being excavated and poured for two sky busters quite similar and each over 200-300 feet higher. And then, as if that's not enough of a game changer, at 432 Park Avenue, Mr.

Harry B. Macklow has another such building due to be completed in 2016 that will stand 400 feet higher then the One 57 building. That will be higher then World Trade Center roof height, topping out at 1,398 feet. Mr. Macklow purchased the fabled Drake Hotel for $400 million and immediately demolished it. Why? His words, "Because, at $7,000 per foot for the highest floors in the new building, 432 Park Avenue. Why not?" The sky's the limit or is it the money or ego of a handful of ambitious real estate developers and the technology and market demand that justify such incredible structures?

How would I feel if the City stayed the same as it had been since 1960? Boring! What would be the thrill of venturing through a city that stands still? I'd love to experience a trip back to the New York City of 1960 and feel the difference, the look, the people and all the other subtleties that still remain in my head. Liken to a noir movie that captures the emotions of the past, gone forever, memories are indelibly etched in my head, as so many others who share similar thoughts and emotions must join it. For those who have spent their lives in cities such as Paris, Athens, Rome or London live their lives less shockingly as dramatic changes are far less a part of their urban landscape.

Stagnation, sameness and constancy are not what cities are for, in the mind of a New Yorker. We demand change, we make change happen and that's the best evidence that we continue to stay fresh by lurching ahead. It's a visual expression of our dynamism, our energy, inventiveness, imagination, drive, resources and creativity. If we don't change then we are inert and in New York City that just doesn't "cut it"! What worked yesterday doesn't work today, and what works today will not work tomorrow. That's New York City!

I remember when the glorious Pennsylvania Station stood. Undoubtedly, the most significant edifice that has been deliberately destroyed in this City, by its own people, to be replaced by a fast food mall invented by the self-serving, self-righteous real estate interests that only look at the bottom line.

The new Penn Station is the bottom, the cesspool of terminals, a disgusting symbol of a City gone mad. The rats are having a blast, feeding on piles of scraps. The shame is the quintessential essence of greed and moneyed interests gone wild in cahoots with a city politic that looked the other way or were too stupid or greedy to understand the consequences of their ways. It's a same on them and the powers that were. Surely they were "in bed" with the vultures who feasted on the spoils, worse than the innocent rats devouring fast food trash.

Imagine Caesar taking down the Coliseum in Rome and replacing it with a fast food mall! He would have been fed to the lions. I dare say that we, as a City, one that leaps toward the future, have come a long way. Grand Central Terminal is still standing thanks to Jackie Kennedy Onassis and her cohorts. The original Hearst Building still stands although as a shadow box, for a $500,000,000 Sir Norman Foster "erector set" dia-grid behemoth. We seem to have struck a balance, building the future and preserving much of the sacred past. Good lessons don't come cheap. We've paid the price, in spades.

When The Coliseum, built in 1957 at Columbus Circle, it was such a big deal that the U.S. Post Office issued a stamp, three cents, to mail a letter, commemorating the event. Abandoned, in large part, due to its inability to compete with the Javits Convention Center, it was demolished giving way for the Time Warner Complex less than forty two years after its construction. This is a story that virtually defines this City. I remember when The Met Life Building used to be The Pan Am Building and what a horrendous monster that will always be to millions of New Yorkers an overbuilt pile of cement grotesquely invading the sky. It's a perfect example of building junk. We've been very good at that in the past.

I recall working for my father on Saturdays at 1190 Sixth Avenue, between 47th and 48th Streets, as a kid in the late 1950's. Peering out of a third story window I saw brownstones, across the street, with makeshift store fronts that have since been replaced by huge structures of concrete, glass and steel; towers hovering over fifty stories high framing the entire Westside of Sixth Avenue from 42nd Street to 55th Streets. Frequently, I pass by; enter the deli that now occupies my father's former place of business where I had worked, a camera store and film-processing lab.

Occasionally, I enter, purchase a coffee, and glance across the street asking myself, "Where has it gone?" or "Why did it change?" I ask those questions, rhetorically and even though I know it is always about money. It's about seizing and creating opportunities that this City serves up on a silver platter for those who put those complex deals together and fatten their wallets. They gloat that they have mustered the power and influence to re-create this City. I do believe, for the most part it's good for us too. Brownstones simply cannot house all those who come to work in those glass and steel towers. They are a necessity providing space for a growing City that has mushroomed into vast canyons of glass and steel.

I've imagined if Abraham Lincoln were in midtown in the 1860's he would have seen those brownstones too, or something quite like them. Lincoln would have marveled at the transformation of five story buildings replacing two or three story wooden frame structures. He may have said, "Well, it's about time! Where do we go from here?"

Imagine the next series of changes. Who can conceive of the deliberate destruction of those towers, making way for the next bold leap to grab more space from four-acre lots? Is the endgame at hand? Did those of generations gone by believe that the City had reached its final maturation, as in "we're done?" Look at every block and notice the older structures that line the side streets. There's plenty of room for more. If we were able to come back in one hundred years and have a look, it would be confirmed that the City that we had thought had reached its "endgame" was a City still in process, a turn of the page. That's one of the "magical mystery tours" of New York City, the tour through time. Unlike anywhere else it moves and it flies in a most impressive way.

New York City's constant is change, a vibrant society, always lurching into the future, people who experience more change in less time than even New Yorkers could have ever imagined. In a City that is always short of time, the "New York minute", we have managed to accelerate the speed of change faster then ever before.

Reflecting on all this rapid change, living in New York City is an experience unlike any other. Surely, change occurs in other cities at lightening speed such as Dubai, San Paulo and Shanghai. These experiments are ongoing and those cities will never acquire the magnificent historic footprint nor enjoy the richness of a City that is layered and built on a foundation of an incomparable history with a soul that is imbedded deep in its soil.

The difference is that such places, planned cities, are fabricated by so called experts, urban planners, who are textbook engineers, creating environments that lack layers of historical context and importance. Foundations of the past are absent, history is non-existent, and roots of a culture will not be found. Those cities are likened to a Disney World Theme Park without a sense of "place" such as defines New York City. Here every block tells a story, has a history and its own culture is embedded deep in the soil and in our souls.

When you walk through New York City you walk in space-time, through a place with a history and a destiny. It's about concentration on the second hand of a clock and you can always watch it moving. It never stops and that journey is the expression of all the energy and imagination that has made New York City what it was, is and yet to be.

Why is New York City so Special?

If you lived to be one hundred and stayed in the same village all your life, plowed fields, thrashed grain, carried water to your home and went to sleep at the end of every uneventful day, at about 8 PM, then your long life would be short of accomplishment, change, creativity and excitement.

Imagine, a city whose age is measured in three digit numbers, four hundred for example, and you claimed that that City, in many ways, is older than any city in Europe. How could that be?

In Europe, long phases of its history had been stagnant and change just didn't happen. Change was perceived as undesirable. There was a constancy of life that was imprinted upon the mindset of the populace; nothing to reach for, no grasping toward the future, a future that had always been perceived as destined to mirror the present as well as the past. Society clung to its timeless ways and embraced the now. Life, it was believed, was doomed to dwell in a place known as stagnation. It was assumed that the steadiness of the present would serve future generations far into the distance of time. Values, beliefs, the mode and pace of life were perceived as sufficient and acceptable. Life would carry them through and enable them to occupy those places as they always had for time to come. There was no need to seek more nor change their way of life. "Don't change our lives because change is frightening and fraught with risks of the unknown."

There is no doubt that there were many who rejected those precepts but they could not alter the power of the thrones, princes of kingdoms or the tenants of The Catholic Church. Few tried and very few succeeded. Most were punished harshly for their ways. Knowledge was not power it was death. Learning was a threat to the dogma that permeated the medieval world. Only the villainous nomads and mongrels, the Huns, Visigoths, Vikings, Celts and Franks slaughtered, plundered and seized the landscapes of Europe drowning in cruel and obscene pools of blood.

Throughout mankind it had been believed that the earth was flat. How many courageous scientists, astronomers and mathematicians had proven that it was not so at risk of life and limb? Curved shadows of the earth on the moon, celestial mechanics, the disappearing horizon were evidence that was tossed aside by the multitudes of the powers that be. Fear of change was the driving force that kept villages and emerging "urban centers" indeed villages that lay in darkness for millenniums subjugated by religious dogma and black magic fanatics, dreadful fear of excommunication, torture, death or banishment from a primitive society that remained in ruins.

Those who lived in villages and rural areas, as most did, lead fearful lives dreading marauding barbarians who often invaded their simple abodes, raping, plundering, enslaving and burning their villages, torturing and killing like animals with unspeakable viciousness. The prospect that their simple way of life would be plundered into ruin and death was ever present. They were constantly defenseless and vulnerable living in constant fear, a life not worth living.

For hundreds of years many European cities had lain dormant, void of change, change that did not come for approximately fifteen centuries. The Medieval Ages, aka the Dark Ages, experienced nearly two millenniums of stagnation, obduracy, zealous religious beliefs, prodigious dogma highlighting the importance of the hereafter, superstition, blind devotion to canons of faith and the dread of so called advancements in science, reason and logic. Those who sought to break down barriers by searching for new and better ways were banished from a terribly stagnant society. Excommunicating, burning pagans at the stake and inflicting horrendous punishments such as being drawn and quartered, impaled and enduring disabled fates economically and socially amidst a reign of cruelty and terror that millions had to bear through Europe and most of the western world. People stayed stuck and lived out their lives, if you can call their existence "lives"!

Great cities had remained as they had been since the death of Christ. For centuries cities had decayed in filth and were afflicted by war, fire, disease, roaring crime rates, tyranny and despotism, starvation and life in cities laden with unbearable stench and diseases. Peasants for generations lived out their lives the same way their ancestors had and all expected that life would remain for generations to come as it had always been.

It didn't take long for Henry Hudson's sponsors, The Dutch West India Company to get down to business back in 1624. Once they became aware that New York was rich in fur, beavers roamed the hinterlands by the millions. They funded the first arrivals, French-speaking Belgium Huguenots and shortly thereafter the Dutch themselves dug in their heels. They didn't come here to preserve the past, rather they came here to put the stamp on the future and as such, they came with an open mind and most importantly making money, the driving force that resulted in a forward thinking society, was one that would be built upon shipload after shipload of beaver pelts.

If an idea, innovation, creation or way of thinking could propel and project their society, one that would push their objectives forward, then they would seize upon it enthusiastically. They grasped every opportunity to cast aside the old ways and above all, create a new place that had begun as a business deal. The purchase of the island of Manhattan or at the least, a pact, an act designed to create privy with the Indians was a seminal even, the creation of a partnership. The rise of those who came to these shores from afar and the demise of those who received the newcomers, unknowing that their futures were destined to be foreboding, and eventually lead the a great society, one that was destined to lay in ruins.

Despite no shortage of lecherous, lascivious, reckless and lawless citizens, the settlement succeeded to sow the seeds of what would become New Amsterdam and then The City of New York with a bloodless takeover by the British in 1664, a city named in honor of the King's brother, The Duke of York.

It wasn't always a smooth and seamless transition to say the least. The tragic Kieft's War and the Peach War, under Dutch rule, had spelled death and destruction, cruelty and treachery for the Indians as well as the Dutch.

The Dutch embedded cultural activism into their society and that footprint still reigns firmly and securely to this day. This City, legally named, The City of New York, was established as a business model. If it helps us to succeed and makes us money than it's good. If it promotes success and success was about money and it creates a society that would be more stable and productive then this too is good. If it impeded their objectives and created uncertainty and negative energy then steps were taken to stamp it out, as was the summoning Peter Stuyvesant, "Big Daddy" who was mustered to impose strict rules and regulations to restore and maintain law and order then so be it and it too was good.

In short order, the Dutch recognized that change was the key to success, always reaching and building a better future, discarding the ways of the past, fostering change as had been thought, for the greatest good providing more wealth and greater opportunities for the little Dutch settlement to continue to thrive and prosper.

Ideas advanced a good and wholesome environment for people who were determined to find better ways, by using their minds and their assets to build, design and carve out better lives and futures for themselves and their children while discarding many useless ways of the past. Conceptually "the past was the past" and the future was theirs if only they pushed forward, unafraid to take risks and continuing to toss off the dogma and shackles that had held "the old world" stagnant for over a millennium.

The Dutch have always been a liberal society. Throughout the ages they have fostered diversity. "If they want to work, then let them come." If they are law-abiding people they were always welcomed and if they had money to invest then they were welcomed with opened arms.

The Age of Reason and The Age of Enlightenment, the movements that cast off stagnation that had pulled down the shade over Europe for centuries had roots that are traceable to the Dutch. The Dutch established the world's first Republic and they were the first society to dump a King, William of Orange. Even today, it is perhaps the only country in the western world where prostitution and marijuana are legal in the same place, albeit guided by sensible restrictions. I am not endorsing that as a value proposition rather as an example of their "live and let live" ideals and liberal roots. They are examples of a hands off culture that permits people to live their own lives without an intrusive government. Their approach, their government was not one to be dictated by kings or queens. No government interference in the "affairs" of man, where same sex marriage has been tolerated long before it became a respectable issue of discussion in America. There is no place for government to mettle or disrupt the lives of their citizens as long as they are contributing to society as a whole and obeying laws that uphold its precepts, a precursor, if you will, of our Declaration of Independence, "Life, liberty and the pursuit of happiness" is, in fact, a Dutch phrase. How many religious and moralistic notions creep through the cracks of our constitution, violating our sacred freedoms? "Live and let live and don't impose your sacrosanct values and lifestyle standards upon others." Shouldn't that be the preamble of our Bill of Rights? And if not: then why not? Your freedom ends where mine begins and vice versa. "Don't Tread On Me."

383

What about our own country's grasp of such precepts? What ever happened to "the pursuit of happiness"? "The pursuit of happiness for whom?" What business do our states, federal and local governments have to impose legislative "values and morals" regarding abortion, same sex marriage, stem cell research, upon anyone else? The answer is; whatever pleases politicians and lobbyists from imposing their values or path to re-election, their paths to their survival and survival is their highest priority, upon us. Toss out conscience, civic duty and honesty. The politicians are in it for one thing and it isn't our betterment. Wake up America! We as a nation, certainly not as a city, have slipped back to the ideals and ideas of the Middle Ages in far too many ways. Let two women get married. Why is it anybody else's business? Back off Washington, D.C. and Albany, and get out of town! New York City doesn't need you to decide or judge our moral values and create laws for us to live by, laws that are clearly unconstitutional. Laws being written by religious zealots who espouse poisonous venom upon those who disagree with their rhetoric? Such hypocrisy abounds among righteous evangelicals who literally are caught violating their own values. Do you recall those crocodile tears streaming down Jimmy Swaggart's bawling face, caught with his pants down? Imagine, a U.S. congresswoman claiming that she and her husband have cured people who were homosexuals! It happened! Imagine, we have people in our jails for decades for smoking a joint! Incredible. The most technologically sophisticated country on earth with stone-age morality and anti-Darwinism science still taught in some of our public schools funded with taxpayer's dollars! We've seen and heard about some of that in the print and TV media. God help us all! Stop playing God as if you know better than "the people." America is not a big Sunday school for New York City and it never will be. Take your religion and your precepts and your sacred second amendment rhetoric back to where you came from and keep it there. We don't judge you but don't judge us either. Shoot your guns and we'll "shoot the breeze" with our open minded and open hearted love for all and that includes common sense laws that help keep "firearms" out of the hands of those who are mentally or criminally insane. If you want a neighbor who is mentally insane with an arsenal of weapons with 30 shot clips then stay away from us. Have fun and good luck and don't forget to sign up and become a member of the "Mass Killing of the Month Club."

America has lost its way. Your religion is good enough for you and mine is good enough for me, as long we don't trample upon each other's beliefs. Many of those who profess their allegiance to "American Values" are zealously driven to stamp their values upon us all. Those, among all the fanatics who acknowledge loyalty to the four corners of The Constitution are blindsided by their exuberance for their own values. The Constitution forbids harshly imposing religious beliefs on others. I've read about such societies and the history is not pretty.

New York City enjoys the fruits of liberty and let us hope that, the blessings of liberty will bear more fruit and go on forever. We, here in New York City, don't agree with much of the rest of America on many issues but we never loose sight of the fact that you have the right. But, we are concerned that much of the rest of America has a hateful and skeptical bend on New York City. That's a shame, such a shame.

New York City's culture is deeply rooted in Dutch traditions. Truly, they are New York City's real "founding fathers." I often imagine; what if the Dutch had pushed back the British in 1664 with some help from the French. They accepted and encouraged a pluralistic society, sort of welcomed blacks, tragically not always without limitations and Jews, with some restrictions too, Catholics and others from the world over have "paid their dues" to fit into the matrix of New York City. Anyone who came to work, live peaceably and abide by their laws was welcomed, "Let 'em stay!" Although the Dutch were not perfect, considering 17th century norms, they were quite exemplary. Can you think of a more perfect culture to have founded this City?

As soon as the Dutch hit land they fervently went about their business, building outposts and bowery's, that's old Dutch for farms. Without a moment to waste, they cleared the land and established their little village, New Amsterdam. They built a rudimentary fort, log style homes, cleared roads and, of course, dug canals. In a very short time they created a small foothold at the southern tip of Manhattan and a thriving little village took hold. By the time the British arrived in 1664, uninvited of course, the population had settled within the village as far north as Wall Street named for the wall that Gov. Peter Stuyvesant had the black folks build from river to river to protect the village from wild beasts and Indians. Men guarded the wall defending it from would be Dutch thieves who sought to remove its wooden planks to use as firewood. Only Jews were exempt from such duties however a tax was imposed on them instead. Asher Levy, a wealthy and influential Jewish merchant, petitioned the Dutch West India Company's Board of Directors to enable the Jews to participate guarding the wall in lieu of being taxed. Much to Stuyvesant's chagrin and bewilderment the directors of The Dutch West India Company agreed with Mr. Levy and the custom was changed, perhaps, in a sense, the first act of religious freedom in America. Many others had ventured further north, carving out a village up in Harlem, trading with the Indians and also clearing land "upstate" now known as midtown!

The pace of change continued relentlessly by the Brits, who built, traded, manufactured and thrived as well. Shipping and commerce soared and impressive churches rose higher then before and the center of the "new world" began to emerge and thrive.

Boston and Philadelphia, two cities founded upon principles of religious freedom, not commerce, culture or diversity, were growing much more slowly and never regained their status of primate cities in the "New World." As they dwelled in their pews, New Yorkers went about the business of building their city on fundamentals, other than religion, focusing on commerce, inventiveness, innovation and of course large doses of debauchery and lascivious behavior. New York City was destined to become America's primate City never again to be challenged again.

From the very beginning, New York City was about growth, innovation, ideas, hard work, diversity, commerce, fast paced activity and action; never sitting back waiting for others to lead the way but rather setting a breath-taking pace, forging ahead, a steadfastly forward and upward, a never ceasing spiral of growth, innovation and power.

New York City possessed the world's busiest harbor, The South Street Seaport, the world's tallest buildings, the most luxurious and largest hotels would come to be, The St. Denis, The Astor House, the first Waldorf and the street grid conceived in 1811 to be constructed upon a flattened landscape facilitating growth faster then before.

The world's first and largest department stores, A. T. Stewart's, Wanamaker's, Bloomingdale's, Lord and Taylor, Macy's and O'Neal's rivaled the best that Paris and London had to offer. We set out to build the world's largest subway system, by far, with innovations never before conceived by other cities. We constructed the world's first landscaped public park, for all the people, not merely the nobility, built and paid for with public money on a scale never before imagined. The world's first escalator, an amusement ride at Coney Island, five cents a pop, the country's first building code for tenements requiring bathrooms on every floor and windows in every room and the construction of The Brooklyn Bridge doubling the span of the longest then existing steel cable bridge, St. Patrick's Cathedral, The Cathedral of St. John the Divine, all New York City firsts were impressive groundbreaking wonders of the world.

New York City was about change, constant and forever carving out the future, never clinging to the past, breaking new ground, always growing, higher and higher with a breath that overwhelms other cities from every corner of the world.

Recently, Asian cities such as Dubai, Singapore, Beijing, Taipei and others bear names, some that have been seldom heard until recent times and have become mega metropolises, urban monsters whose populations have skyrocketed virtually overnight. All preconceived within the framework of a "well planned" infrastructure without environmental, transportation, social, health and educational infrastructures necessary to provide superior quality of life for their surging bursts in population. New York City has been there, done that and throughout centuries of change and adaptation we have blazed trails and created the mechanisms to wield the improvements that have continued to improve the quality of life for our citizens and newly minted residents.

Additionally, there are few historic roots embedded into preplanned modern expanding cities created by urban planners and multinational corporations. A mirage has erupted in those cities, built over or adjacent to tin shacks, slum neighborhoods one against the other. They are little more than endless seas of squalor, misery and despair: Rio de Janeiro, Mumbai, Shanghai and New Delhi to name a few.

How can this be compared with New York City from a historic perspective? Our city is the result of four hundred years of fast paced evolutionary growth, measured by changes driven by technology, needs that were recognized, satisfied and resolved over four centuries; cultures, vastly different have become intertwined since the dawn of our short history, a mosaic of the entire world dwells here unlike any other place on the planet.

Creating "model cities" carved out of deserts, built on artificially engineered islands or planned on a boardroom table with computer modeling, designed by a few urban planners creating inorganic and synthetic neighborhoods ill conceived, transient and rootless. It's the origins, the bedrock of New York City that can never be duplicated or transplanted, no less in a heartbeat. That is why this City is so special, so exceptional and unique.

Dubai's Palm and World Islands seem to be failures, not only economically but environmentally as well. They are paying a high price. Growth must be organic, natural and man made within the framework of providing safe and natural environments enabling practical, sustainable, efficient and expedient living, not brought about by a commissioned sales force that hawks condos through elaborate financing schemes and promotional lures but rather managed by good governance balancing all of societies needs and interests placing quality of life upper most in mind.

Jane Jacobs vs. Robert Moses, the great "builder and destroyer of New York City", is the best example of opposing urban developmental strategies. She put the kibosh on a mid-Manhattan expressway that would have torn the City in half and destroyed much of Chelsea, The Village, Soho, Tribeca and Downtown. Surely, this City has been a great experiment from the start and its roots are embedded in each man, woman and child who have left their footprint on the pavement, in every factory, wharf, alley and dark unpaved street where layers of history are imbedded beneath our feet.

"The only thing that stays the same in New York City is change!" It has been said,

"If you haven't been here for ten years then you haven't been here at all."

For those grand and glorious cities in Europe that claim to be thousands of years older than New York City, I say,

"Sure, you've won the numbers game but what have you done during all those years since way back?"

Compare that with someone who has lived ninety years and was in a coma for forty years or an octogenarian who spent most of their years incarcerated with a vibrant, talented and accomplished musician, writer, researcher or even an ordinary person who has raised a family and retires after the end of a long "career". Who's older? Sure we both know the answer. Who has accomplished more? Who has given the world more and who has had a more successful life? How long did Mozart or Lincoln, John Lennon, George Gershwin, MLK or RFK live? The answers are 35, 56, 40, 39, 39 and 42. In their tragically short lives their accomplishments were enormous. Imagine what this town will be like a short thirteen generations from now, the time forward compared with the time past when our ancestors had arrived. Oh, what it would be like to peer into that magical looking glass? No one knows what lies ahead. Imagine!

In the short period of time that New York City has existed it has experienced more periods of change, creation, novel concepts, innovative methods of manufacturing, discoveries, attempts, inventions, reinventions, successes, taught and given more, providing the world with thousands of ideas, artistic treasures, new scientific discoveries, medical breakthroughs, creative achievements, literature, and more commercial firsts than anywhere else! Most of all, we have provided the best evidence, that the world has ever known that working and playing together harmoniously in this place known as New York City is unlike and unmatched by any other city on earth.

Come see the world, come to New York City. Put on your seatbelt because this is the City that never sleeps and never stops. It's a ride without end and it's a trip you'll never regret one that will always be remembered not only in your head but deep in your heart as well.

Who Goes to Coney Island for "Nothing"?

One hundred years ago nearly everybody in New York City went to Coney Island for just about anything! With over 1,000,000 visitors on a typical summer Sunday, Coney rocked like no other place in New York City history. That "island" has been merged with Brooklyn proper, with landfill therefore, it is actually Coney Peninsula. Where did all that landfill come from? Did it come from the subways? Sure, where else? And when the subway was extended to Coney Island or peninsula you could get there for a nickel or on foot or bicycle if you were fortunate enough to live close by or you had two good legs to walk upon back in an age of infectious diseases, rampant street fights, poor medical treatment and roving gangs. Best of all, an amusement ride such as The Cyclone or The fabled Parachute Jump was the best ride in town a menagerie of fun and a place to frolic for just a hand full of nickels.

That was the age of no air-conditioning and no highways that could to take you that far to the east end of Brooklyn. Who had cars anyway? Besides, Jones Beach did not yet exist so Coney was virtually "the only game in town." Only the upper class had other options to get away from the grunts and grinds of urban life, if you can call that "life." Life was experiences at "Coney" a place that everyone loved except people like my father who would never drive to a beach in a car without air conditioning creeping through bumper to bumper traffic. For him, schlepping to a beach on the subway was a non-starter, also void of air-conditioning back then too.

With a virtually endless boardwalk, Atlantic Ocean beaches had an abundance of so many bodies in attendance that you could have walked upon them, leaving your footprints in the sand was purely a fantasy. Be careful for what you wish for; a sea of humanity basking in the sun, enjoying the ocean breezes, taking a respite from city strife and each other came with a price. It was simply one urban crowd transformed from one place to another.

Those who stayed behind had the City all to themselves, just like today. Sure, you can get a table just about anywhere on a Saturday night in June, July or August in Manhattan, just about! Yes, families by the thousands spent their nickels and for one or perhaps even two days a week, during the short New York City summer, the masses had brief vacations on the cheap and eight square feet of sand that they could call their own. I would have opted to go to an "air cooled" double feature movie in Times Square!

Mr. Nathan Handworker opened his first Nathan's there in 1916 on the southeast corner of Surf and Stillwell Avenues. You'd have found crowds cramming the "stand" salivating, waiting to chomp on those delicious 'dogs, for more than the original price of a nickel, but still a bargain. Perhaps Stillwell Avenue should be changed to "Stillthere" Avenue! Just taste one of those 'dogs and you're hooked! He "slammed" his competitor across the street. How? He gave discount coupons to doctors and nurses who worked at Coney Island Hospital and they all rushed over to savor the unique, spicy, succulent hotdogs made with his delicious incredible secret Romanian recipe. People "knew" that Nathan's 'dogs were healthier. Sure! It's just another New York City ploy, a fascinating story. "A gimmick!" That's all you need, an idea and if it's good enough then the rest will fall into place. You make it happen with an idea and with the breath of life, enthusiasm, love and sweat peppered with sweat and tears.

I peered out the front window of the first car of the B train, on my way to Coney Island not too long ago, a train that runs on the ground through most of Brooklyn. My recipe for escape, as a baby boomer, way back in my youth, had not been Coney, rather, it was Jones Beach, West end 2, parking lot 6, the Hamptons or off to more distant places or just a short hop on a plane. The amusement parks, all three of them, at the height of Coney Island, Luna Park, Dreamland and Steeplechase Park, have deteriorated and remain terribly diminished. For the most part due to abuse and disuse, a faltering neighborhood, the construction of encroaching highways and the explosion of the popularity of the automobile after World War II. The Cyclone roller coaster is a toy compared to what Six Flags has to offer today and that's what people want; the big, glitzy high-tech parks boasting more attractions, zany high-tech rides affordable only by mega corporations that offer investment opportunities for thousands of investors. The neighborhood has also become extremely blighted and overused, riddled with abundant crime, grime and slime. Therefore, why would anyone, such as I, want to go there in 2015?

For curiosity, adventure, to learn, to experience, and to take a trip back in time, a time before my time, and to grasp a sense of the "ghosts" and chomp a delicious Nathan's hotdog, crinkle cut fries and a coke, make that diet coke. As a New Yorker who yearns for the taste of the past, visiting a place that is tired, worn and historic, meeting a few of the locals, enjoying

395

some chatter about their lives and experiences, hearing them reminisce about the ol' days and catch a glimpse of the past that is gone forever, for me, is very exciting.

The past, respect it, experience it and inhale it. Look at the flaking paint, struggle to read the worn out signs that can be seen beneath the new replacements, shed a tear, swallow that lump in your throat and embrace the past because that is how we got to where we are now.

All the good that you see and experience is built upon the past. The black and white days gone by, the cheap thrills, a simpler place and time, the hardscrabble days of doing without have created a City layered with history. This is who we are. Peeling away the vestiges that conceal our past is a trip back, a time machine that enhances the connection that true New Yorkers crave. It's called nostalgia, a powerful and emotional compilation that continues to fuel us onward.

Who hungered for computers, fancy cars, let alone cars, any cars, the fistfight that you nearly had, the holes in your shoes and the two shirts you owned to cover your back. That charlotte rouge you couldn't afford to buy for your gal, those down and out days; were they really the good ol' days? They're just a few things to think about at Coney, eh!

Plans have been made, investors have come forward, and locals, community groups and politicians are lining up to re-create this wonderful place, this vital piece of New York City history. With an ocean beach connected by an air-conditioned subway that's able to connect millions of people, the right vision and opportunity will arise. It's just a matter of time. And next time it will be much better, safer, vibrant, and it will morph into the greatest playground that this City has ever known. Perhaps there are others too who go to Coney for "nothing" or maybe, most who've sweltered in those sun baked subway cars, would now love to experience the change with a deep and powerful sense of nostalgia. To be in touch with the past with a burst of longing is not for "nothing."

Take me back! I want my nostalgia. Let's just hope that a new Coney will not morph into another Disney type park. It's got to have that taste and feel of New York City, the soul of the past that will satisfy those who have experienced it or heard about it from their parents and grandparents. Let's make it a real deal, New York City, once again. Hope to see you standing in line, behind me of course, at Stillwell and Surf!

Brooklyn is "Sweet 'n' Low"

Back in the early 1950's Mr. & Mrs. Benjamin Eisenstadt operated a small family business on Cumberland Avenue in Brooklyn. Their company packaged tea into individual, tea bags.

As the story goes, one afternoon they were having coffee at The Cumberland Diner taking a well earned break from the stresses of their little business. As Mrs. Eisenstadt was about to dip her spoon into a sugar bowl she remarked to her husband.

"Ben! Look at those disgusting clumps of brown sugar from prior users. It's terrible! Why don't we put sugar instead of tea into those tea packets? Perhaps we can make a pile of money!"

That brilliant idea led to the origin of Sweet 'n' Low, the artificial sweetener! Everything starts with an idea!

An idea has no value, unless someone takes it to a place, breathes life into it and pushes it forward toward success. As a result of this incident, they began to market sugar, individually packaged, a first and it began in, where else, Brooklyn! It turned out to be a sweet success. It was a time of health consciousness, weight loss with diet concepts hitting the marketplace, Jack LaLanne, exercise, calorie counting, and TAB, the first artificially sweetened soda exploded on the health craze scene.

Saccharin, at that time was a primary ingredient, an additive in food manufacturing, and a liquid sweetener. It was unavailable for direct consumer use. A stroke of genius prompted the Eisenstaedt's to ask their son Marvin, a chemist, to reformulate saccharin into a granulated compound, a powder. He succeeded and they were granted U.S. Patent

3,625,711 and U.S. Trademark number 1,000,000, without the $ sign!

For over thirty years they had held a monopoly on the artificial sweetener market in the United States. They battled the Food and Drug Administration as laboratory tests revealed that the sweetener was carcinogenic, allegedly if you feed insanely huge quantities to rats!

Therefore, other compounds were formulated over time to reduce the hypothecated ill effects, due to the demands of the FDA, the folks who care about your health and perhaps their own pockets and, of course, avoiding risky decisions that may imperil their jobs. It's far safer to reject a new product then to approve it, right? Nah!

The mafia moved in too and demanded, "turf." Numerous competitors tried everything in the book to crush them. Sweet 'n' Low's legal fees piled up, higher and higher, and that crushing toll tore the family asunder. Wills and inheritance issues create rife and strife among them. It's a classic tragedy, one that is well known among otherwise successful family enterprises. I was personally a participant in similar experiences years ago, a family business. The only difference is that my story did not have a sweet ending.

The name Sweet 'n' Low was derived from a song written in 1863 by Joseph Barnby whose lyrics were based on William Lord Tennyson's poem called, "The Princess: Sweet and Low."

Sweet and low, sweet and low Wind of the western sea, Low, low, breathe and blow, Wind of the western sea! Over the rolling waters go, Come from the dying moon, and blow, Blow him again to me, While my little one, while my pretty one, sleeps. Sleep and rest, sleep and rest, Father will come to thee soon; Rest, rest, on mother's breast, Father will come to thee soon; Father will come to his babe in the nest, Silver sails all out of the west Under the silver moon! Sleep my little one; sleep my pretty one, sleep.

Later on, the song Sweet 'n' Low was put to music by the composer Harry Warren (1893-1981). He also wrote "September in the Rain" and "Jeepers Creepers." That, Sweet n Low" was a song that the Eisenstadt's had danced to when they were "keeping company" a term from World War II days for being engaged or "dating" or in more recent vernaculars, "hooking up" or "going steady" or "dating."

Take a look at the back of a Sweet 'n' Low pink package and if you are wearing your eyeglasses or are young enough to read the fine print, check it out, Cumberland Packaging, Brooklyn, New York. Sweet 'n' Low is the third largest producer of artificial sweeteners behind Equal and Splenda. I guess the FDA must have mutated healthier rats since the days when Sweet 'n' Low or "engineered" rats that are graft resistant or partnered with rats that failed to smell the sweetener but had keen noses for the money!

But, you can't beat the original, and for one very simple reason. Jackie Gleason, "The Great One" remarked about his beloved Brooklyn, it is posted on a street sign, on the Brooklyn side of the Brooklyn Bridge. "Welcome to Brooklyn. How Sweet it is!" and that includes Sweet 'n' Low! "Has to be!"

Beggars, Panhandlers and the Homeless

The most accessible cash for street hawkers in New York City is carried in our pockets, duh. We are walking money trees, ripe for pickin' as the gutter urchins surrounding us ply various styles of the coin grab and snatch game; aggressively politely, aloofly, tenaciously, timidly, faint-heartedly or bullying, they ply their "game" begging for "scratch."

They come in every shape, size and color all wrapped in various garb using their own style from rag-tag to blending in with the rest of us, these "zero-per centers" reside at the lowest end of the socio-economic strata. Yes folks, they're a sad scruffy bunch, the beggars, that flock, rovers occupying the City. It's part of the landscape that is New York City and it seems to be, even during hard times that they appear to be relatively under control.

We all expect to be approached by these tragic desperados now and then. New Yorkers are pretty good at spotting them but, at times, even the best of us get caught off guard and the most unsuspecting turn out to be members of the subterranean street commerce culture.

Most are very good at what they do. It's a living. There are numerous ways to perceive, thwart and disengage them, or if you like. You can give away your money for a quick fix, for you and the perp.

Your money is seldom spent on what they need, but rather, on what they want, just like the rest of us! Ever think about that? Yes, the needy have wants too and most of them are very good at satisfying them and in many instances, they're better than the employed. The big difference between them and us is that they are unbridled with financial commitments and obligations.

"I got no lock on da door, dat's the way to be." They've got no house to have a door on, right?

I do sympathize with them. How lucky we are not to be in their shoes, if they even have shoes. We just may have a few more zeros that define our own financial "problems." They live on the edge of the edge, like many of the employed middle class and the lower part of the upper class, which I consider to be those living in Manhattan who's family income is $350,000 per annum gross or less. That's just about enough to make it appear that you're "makin' it here buster!

Three hundred and fifty "K" ain't enough to live "large." That's one bedroom in Manhattan, own or lease a four year old Honda, put one kid in private school, buy a few goodies on 47th Street, take your wife out to dinner nice, once a week, see a Broadway show twice a year and fly off to some island every year and have an inkling as to what a savings account actually might be.

Did you know that most New Yorkers are living on the edge? 21% of us are actually living below the poverty line and 58% of New Yorkers have a net worth of less than $5,000! I wonder how many of those have zero net worth or even a negative one! You know who you are out there! You're the guys with the $2,500 watch and the ladies are sportin' those $1,800 LV bags, the real ones with $18 in their pockets and wallets with maxed out plastic in those French bags they're totin', eh?

We, the more fortunate, often groan that we cannot afford to decorate our homes or afford too buy the apartment we want, the best seats in the house, that watch in the jeweler's window that we pine or the leap to the larger BMW or Audi. What a shame, what a game! It's crap, pure and simple.

Up until the recent past I always admired the guys who sported impressive watches, Rolex and the like. They appeared to be the guys, who were successful, their "red badge of debt." Now, I am fascinated by the well dressed men who are wearing Pulsars costing $9.95 with ten year batteries that do more for less and most of all reveal that they're not out to impress those who are overwhelmed by the high-end time pieces that are evidence of the "look what I have mentality." Who are the winners in that match up?

It's a struggle for most of those folks who pursue their trade with their hands held out seeking a coin or two. In a sense we're all beggars, such is life, just wearing better clothing and seeming more legitimate doesn't reveal that you are "make it." We wear the uniforms of legitimacy, suits, $160 silk ties and shined shoes disguising our true mission; to make as much money as we can and toward what end? What's the reward, dud? Naturally, it's a spectrum, those who are authentic and provide real value to those who they work for and those they care about and the others who are scammers, wolfs in sheep clothing are the pretenders who are phony, vacuous creeps who lure the insecure suckers who want to be seen with those who appear to be real. Who of us is totally and completely honest? Let them "caste the first" C note. Are the fat cats those who burn the midnight oil at Goldman Sacks, or rather "Sacks of Gold Man", figuring out how to get richer off their client's losses by dreaming up multi billion dollar schemes with thousands of sucker clients who are tanking and not

403

thanking their money mis-managers who are overpaid for stealing their client's dollars. It's not begging it's called "white collar crime" another name for stealing.

Who becomes homeless? How does it happen? Is it bad luck? Is it a consequence of poor parenting, non-parenting, their own laziness, illness, mental challenges and deficiencies, divorce, lack of medical care, cultural deprivation or a combination of the above? There are reasons for everything, "there by the grace of God . . ." Providing for our homeless and downtrodden is a New York City tradition. The City helps them much more than most. I believe, that is virtually a New York City creation, caring for its own in innumerable ways. The first public hospital in The United States is Bellevue Hospital, just one example.

Shelters! Okay, they're not the Ritz, but they provide food, medical care, training and a benevolent heart for those in need. New York City pioneered public assistance and support for its poor. We raised the bar and made history and many other cities followed our model of generosity, care and support.

One evening, at nearly 1 AM I was walking across 57th Street off 8th Avenue returning to my apartment. A man approached me and told me that he was very hungry. "Please, please PLEASE give me some money so I can get something to eat. I'm so hungry!" he pleaded.

"Sure, there's a diner across the street. Let's go inside, grab a seat and order whatever you like and I'll pay for it." I told him.

"But no, I don't need no food now! I want food for breakfas' for tomorrow for my six-year-old son and me. Don't you understand me?" he begged.

It had been another crazy night and I had a bit of trouble processing it.

"So, what are you saying? You're not hungry now? You don't want food, but you want me to buy food for you to have breakfast with your son? Am I right?"

"Yeah, you right!" he said.

"Like what? I thought that you were hungry?"

"I want to have breakfas' with my son I said!"

He took a picture of his alleged son out of his wallet and showed it to me.

"He go to school and I wan' him to eat righ'." he told me.

"Sure, let's go around the corner and I'll buy you what you need. Sound like a plan?" I suggested.

"Yeah, let's do it!" he replied.

Together, we walked around the corner to a Korean Deli located at 56th Street and 8th Avenue. I bought him eggs, bread, orange juice, milk, butter and bacon. Total cost was about sixteen bucks and when the cashier gave me the change, I turned it over to him.

"Thanks a lot man. You the man!" he said.

"My pleasure! Give your son a big kiss for me and good luck to you!" I replied.

I felt good about what I had done, the preverbal good Samaritan, that was me, yeah!

The next day I entered the same deli and the cashier recognized me. She asked,

"Aren't you the man who was here late last night and bought the food for that guy?"

"Yes. Why?"

"After you turn corner he come back, return all food that you pay. He tell me to give him back money and I give him back money!"

405

That was extremely disappointing. I was duped. How sad. A life tossed in the trashcan. What a waste. ·

I used to see the same panhandlers "working" their usual locations day after day. I guess they knew the City pretty well. Apparently their spot was their "business" location, as savvy retailers too know all about pedestrian traffic, demographics, volume and times of day to make the big score. Panhandlers choose their spots, with science, in order to make the best return on their "investment", their time. Are they looking for wealthier traffic, liberals, older or less fortunate souls, tourists, the younger crowds or those who have barely escaped the same fate and had "been there done that?" I just don't know that business every well, thankfully, and hope that I never will. But, just for fun, I've imagined panhandling as a learning experience, taking a shot at it, just to see what it's like.

My business model, if I were to be a panhandler, would be to wear a Tuxedo with all the trimmings, carnation, gold studs, patent leather shoes, and all "the works." I'd do the subway thing, come up with a fabulous pitch with perfect articulation, expression, diction and syntax and let it rip.

"I am so grateful to be here with all of you, fine ladies and gentleman of this wonderful City. We all know that we are living through very tough times. As for me, my Mercedes has been repossessed. For those of you who do not know, that means, taken away from me. I've lost my condo on the beach in the Hamptons, the bank took it away from me, non-payment. The five-bedroom ski house in Vermont and even the Rolls has been repossessed. I no longer have a business. I have no money, and no honey. Please help me. I've been in your seat many times and I've given generously and never thought that this fate would fall upon me. Please, a $5 bill would be perfect. No change please! Open your hearts and please help one New Yorker get back on his feet. I will be forever grateful. I'm not going to ask for God to bless you as others do. This has nothing to do with God! It's about you. I also have a swiper scanner on my iPhone 5 that will enable you to make your donation via your credit card. That way, you can earn sky miles. Perhaps I'm the only panhandler in New York City who can provide you with that benefit. See, I'm looking out for you; it's not just about me. PLEASE!! HELP ME!!

Have you ever seen a tuxedoed man beg for money? Would you prefer to give him money than one who is clad like he walked out of a hamper? PLEASE let me know. Perhaps that will be my sixth career change opportunity!" See you on the A train or should it be the 1, 4 or 7? Pick a train that will give the most, that's a sociology study that some kid at Hunter should delve into.

I used to see an African American woman almost daily, very short hair, petite, wrapped in a torn, ragged grey wool army blanket, sitting on the sidewalk, shaking, pretending to be shivering and holding a cup, looking very desperate, crying and begging in a low muttering, mumbling voice, never saying a word, collecting lots of dollar bills, doing quite well, much better than all the rest that I've seen. She looked like she was at the bottom heap of humanity, such a pity; it made your heart go out to her. On one occasion suddenly, I saw her get up, very nicely dressed beneath the well-worn wool army blanket meeting a friend and promptly telling her in a loud strong voice.

"Come on you'll, let's get somethin' to eat, I'm outa here!"

Her voice was loud, strong, confident and crisp!

Recently, after many years, I saw her doing her sidewalk "thing" in front of Trump Tower on Fifth Avenue just beneath the Atrium sign, "Open to the Public". Some contrast! I stopped, turned around and asked her,

"Where've you been sweetheart? I haven't seen you for a long time." She looked up and gave me a wink and a smile.

"I'm doin' fine!"

Perhaps she had remembered me? "Did I make an impression?" Sure, "someday my prince will come!"

"The Donald" should have her on The Apprentice to teach others how to generate income without assets, something that few can even imagine doing in the "real world." (Her picture is stuffed in between the pages of this book)

Years ago there was a talk show, one of the first, The David Suskind Show. One evening he welcomed a guest, a panhandler who had "worked" the streets of New York City for many years. His technique was, as he put it, primed to the way he shouted "please!" He'd pronounced, "please" with a long, yawning howl, loud and strong with a hearty melodic cadence, **"PPPLLEAAASSSEE!!!!** He blurted out this refrain over and over again. Every time the rhythm and pace had a different chime, tone and pitch. It worked!

According to him, during the interview, after he had collected about $200, not a bad tax-free payday back in the late 1960's, he went to a mid-town parking lot, retrieved his Buick Electra 225, the top of the line, four-porthole beauty, at that time, and drove back to his home in Bayonne, New Jersey. Then he'd settle into his two family house and rested from the rigors of his workday. His wife had a normal good paying secure job, as I recall, a teacher. You can't get health insurance from panhandling, as far as I know but, as I recall, it was available for free if you had no assets, or your assets were in someone else's name. It really didn't matter. His wife's job had him covered, no doubt. She probably prepared him dinner and cleaned up the kitchen too while he sat back and watched "All in the Family" glued to his hero, Archie Bunker.

They're out there and although there's a law on the books against asking people for loot it's seldom enforced. Should it be? Both parties, giver and taker, are breaking the law and it violates the spirit of quality of life initiatives that began in New York City in the early 90's.

In Seattle there was a tenacious crackdown on the problem- and, as a result, panhandling virtually vanished. Isn't this a City of great innovation? Let's do the same thing and provide adequate and accessible means for the homeless and hungry to obtain nutritious and ample food, medical care, job training and adequate shelter.

The law may not be constitutional due to the first amendment that protects the right of freedom of speech but let 'em do their thing. If we all refrain from giving money to them then they would stop looking for handouts. Ever leave a bowl of milk outside your doorstep for a cat? What happens next? We all know the answer.

409

Panhandling is also illegal in the subway and it always starts the same way,

"Ladies and gentlemen, I don't mean to disturb you but I lost my job and I'm just trying to get something to eat and stay out of trouble, aka, steal, rob, mug, beat or kill!

The veiled threat, pay or die!

I'm still "keeping an eye out" for the guy who scammed me out of $20 that night at the deli but I doubt that I'd recognize him. I am sure that he's looking for me too, not knowing, of course, that I'm aware that I had been a victim of his sting.

I still feel sorry for anyone who finds himself in such desperate shape that has to resort to this type of activity to "survive." I cannot judge them, in good conscience, because we're all products of nature and nurture. I suppose that good gene pools and quality parenting, wholesome environments, mentoring, love and support make the difference. I know from my own personal experience and will confess that I consider myself to be one of the lucky ones.

I never understood why our public schools do not provide a course in parenting mandated by a new curriculum. How many times did we learn, over and over again, about Christopher Columbus? Those lessons omit the truth about that murderer, rapist, kidnaper and torturer. Check it out, I'm not kidding, not a nice man! He is just another deified "American" hero. Perhaps he too would have been a terrific panhandler. Why don't our schools teach what's really important and not continue to stuff that historic tripe down our throats generation after generation?

410

"Manifest Destiny" who really blew up the Battleship Maine in 1898? How did America acquire Arizona, New Mexico and southern California? Look that up in your Fifth grade American history textbooks published by Holt and Co. Let's teach life lessons and prepare our next generations for a life of success.

Panhandlers have had other lives, a past, and to us it's a complete unknown. It could happen to any of us. I look at them and wonder. Was she a nurse? Did her husband abuse her? Did he lose his job or become sick, divorced, bankrupt, alcoholic or clinically depressed? We're all human and that's what should reside in the front of our brains! All of us entered and will leave this world the same way we all got here and depart on equal terms as well. Although the wealthier will have 1,000 per square inch woven Egyptian cotton sheets to "shit the bed" and the rest of us will be on Wal-Mart made in some Chinese city that we've never heard of. Do you care? Nah! Why mess up a $600 sheet, right?

We're all entitled to food and shelter in a society that prides itself on morality and good conscience but, we as a society have come up a bit short on that score. The more we give on the streets the more acute the problem becomes.

I suppose the growth of panhandlers is a function of how well they perceive the job the City is doing when they show up for help at a shelter compared with how much they can "make" on their own, pursuing their trade on the streets. Let's hope their numbers dwindle for all the right reasons and not because we are not providing generously.

The City or some independent "think tank" outfit should do a survey among the homeless and ask them why they do not avail themselves of what the City has to offer them and evaluate it with the street scene so that we know how to improve the public system to feed, clothe and shelter them.

We, as a society, need to learn how to provide those folks living on the edge of the edge with opportunities to have meaningful and purposeful lives. Just try spending a day sitting on the sidewalk with a sign asking for spare change in the heat, cold or rain. That is a change we would not wish for ourselves. Hey guys, ready to give up your Rolex for a Pulsar?

There are some political zealots in New York City who ask for donations to support a constitutional amendment that would guarantee housing for all. How would that work? It's unimaginable! I do understand the moral and human right to food and shelter but the free housing idea is off the radar screen! In the meantime, I'm in favor of giving panhandlers food and not money. Don't be intimidated by these folks. Just pretend that you don't hear them or don't understand them. Talk back in a faux-foreign language and shrug your shoulders! "No speaka da Engla!" Bottom line, it's about the equation: Am I better off panhandling or going to a City facility to get what I need or, should I become a criminal? We have the power to tip the scales and clean up our act. Let's build on what we've done and do better!

There's Propulsion for us "Somewhere"

Our subway system cranks out an abundance of hefty noises. Trains are, of course, the greatest source of noise down there, but herds of kids take a very close second place and at times they rank #1. Express trains roar through stations and pound our eardrums. At times there's more than one train at a time, one for each ear. You vibrate, "shake, rattle and roll." I've witnessed many people who cringe and stick their fingers in their ears as the roar of the express trains reaches their peak. Some stations, with curved tracks, causes wheel flanges to squeal and scratch against the rails emoting sounds reminding me of scratching a blackboard with my fingernails, a sound reminiscent from childhood. Even just the threat of nails scratching a blackboard brought chills and shivers to me, in anticipation!

There are mysterious sounds frequently present, such as clunking and clopping sounds coming from beneath C trains as they accelerate and decelerate. It seems as though parts are loose down there, they probably are! I also hear the click clack of the wheels rolling down the tracks, over the joints connecting the rails, is somewhat unnerving.

A number of French subway lines have rubber-lined wheels reducing train noise enormously. Montreal has the first totally rubber wheeled subway system, bravo for them. Why not here? I guess it's about money, what else is new, not that the French are "rolling" in dough, silence yes, dough no. New York City's subway system is huge, no rubber for us, eh? Could it be due to a shortage of rubber because of the City's initiative to give away millions of condoms to help reduce the spread of AIDS and reduce teen-age

413

pregnancy? Maybe they should be recycled and our subway train's wheels should be covered with used condoms? It's long been a New York City tradition to recycle and find new uses for old stuff. Just look at The Highline, the lobby of 200 Fifth Avenue now it's Eately or The Meatpacking District is suddenly "The Pack Meeting District" or Jane's Carousel, Gantry Park and its Pepsi sign now a landmark and how about Chelsea Market, a reborn incarnation as if the food messiah finally landed. Come on folks, the more condoms we use to cover subway train wheels, the better our hearing will be. "Recycle condoms and protect our precious hearing." Now that's an issue I can support! Certainly Senator Schumer, the biggest schmuck in town would be all for it!

The sounds of people; some speak so loudly you can hear them from the opposite end of the subway car. Babies, my personal favorites, crying and school children shouting at each other are the most annoying and unpleasant part of a subway ride.

For years I've walked up to crying babies and put my face in theirs and I tell them in a deep, direct voice with a frown:

"There's no crying here. I'm the crying police. There's absolutely no crying allowed."

And they stop, about 95% of the time and the parents appreciate the gesture. Amazing stuff! True!

The most intriguing sound that I've ever heard in the subway is a three-note melody that is exactly on pitch with the first three notes of the song "Somewhere" from Westside Story. The lyrics that correspond to those notes are "There's a place" (for us). I knew I wasn't imagining it. It wasn't random or erratic, because I had heard it many times and only on certain subway lines when those trains pull out of the station. I do have a pretty good ear for music and I was confident of the consistency of the melody and I was confident that I wasn't loosing my mind.

I had asked some people who use the subway about my observation. No one knew what the hell I was talking about! They thought I was nuts! I did ask a number of riders seated or standing next to me, on several occasions, immediately after the three notes trumpeted the melody and no one had paid any attention so there was no confirmation of what I was hearing. It's very typical in New York City. People see but don't look, people hear but don't listen. People are too busy texting, listening to their music, reading or sleeping. They've all escaped into their own encapsulated worlds.

Sometime in early 2009, I picked up my copy of The New York Times, outside my apartment door as always and I glanced at the first page before I set it down on the table. I was very amused reading an article about a propulsion system on some of the new models of subway cars that the MTA had purchased recently! A newly designed propulsion system "excited" the third rail, the one that provides 700 volts powering the trains. That propulsion system emits the three notes that I had been hearing, the frequency of the first three notes of the song "Somewhere"! Amazing!

According to the New York Times article of February 21, 2009:

"The newer transmission, alternative current that is chopped into frequencies that excite the steel and produce the sounds, in this case, the beginning of 'Somewhere', said

415

Jeff Hakner, a professor of electrical engineering at Cooper Union. Other trains running at different frequencies fail to produce similar recognizable sounds."

So now, if you are fortunate, next time you're in the subway and you're unplugged from your ipad you just may be treated to a piece of a Broadway show! Tickets please, take your seat!

Horn Honking and Other Needless Noises

Driving in New York City, particularly Manhattan, traversing its bridges and tunnels, during rush hours, in wet weather or on Friday afternoons, most of all, tries the souls, patience and ears of us all! While horn honking is at times a necessity, the vast majority is willful and needless. Excessive horn honking is "road rage" a certifiable mental disorder, a form of adolescent behavior, misplaced anger and is thoroughly childish, stupid and unnecessary.

I've never forgotten an incident that I had encountered many years ago while I was waiting in a long line of traffic impatiently about to enter the Lincoln Tunnel. I tooted a short honk to the guy in front of me, a tap. He immediately emerged from his car, with much effort, about 280 pounds and lumbered over to me, grabbed my side view mirror and wrapped his enormous hands around it, securing a tight grip on my side view mirror and threatened to twist it off if I violated his ears again. I "made with a short neck" shrugged my shoulders, and with my palms facing up began to babble in faux German like, "Danka, mein heir! Danka, danka!"

There are times when horn honking is justifiable, of course, but rarely. Most often, horn honking is a display of anger and impatience derived from those monsters that dwell in the heads of childish assholes. Far too many motorists, cabbies and truck drivers put pedestrians and other drivers in their "line of fire." The most common examples are; honking at pedestrians who cross the street while the traffic light changes in favor of the traffic or, honking at a driver in front of you because they have not decided to "run" a yellow light and stopped instead. Stopping at yellow lights in New York City can be dangerous stuff, perhaps even more then passing through a yellow light because most drivers anticipate that motorists will "run" a yellow light and the motorist behind you may just accelerate into your rear end! Crunch! Add to the list; honking at the vehicle directly in front, one that is traveling slower than the honker's desired velocity. Honking at motorists who are attempting to make a turn while pausing for people who are crossing the street, a duh, and honking for no reason at all. It happens constantly!

"I'm here and I have a horn. So, why not just use it? See if it works!"

The stupidest are those honkers who blast their horns at "grid lockers" those who enter intersections knowing that it's unlikely, or even impossible, that they will be able to pass through the intersection when the traffic light changes. These folks are not accomplishing a thing by exposing their childish emotional crapola, selfishness and stupidity. "Shut uppah!!!"

If traffic enforcers would issue tickets to those schmucks in a similar fashion such as the approach taken to get a hold on the rising crime rate starting back in the early 1990's, I believe that this town would be a lot quieter and richer. Isn't that a quality of life issue? I'd love horns to be loudest inside the vehicle because that way we'd put the raps on it. Ouch! Truly, the horn honkers are stupider than the "grid lockers." I'd love to see cops with Day-Glo spray cans armed with the authority to spray grid locker's cars using a stencil that reads,

"I'm a grid locking schmuck."

That's the way to go! Sure, screw up the paint jobs on a few cars! They'll get the message. Go after the out of towners in mass; teach them a lesson for being so stupid to drive into Manhattan.

While living on West 60th Street, about eight years ago, I was awakened suddenly by a "ka-lunk" sound. It kept reoccurring every few seconds. Ka-lunk, ka-lunk, ka-lunk, ka-lunk!!" "What the hell is that? I got out of bed attempting to find the source. I opened the window, KA-LUNK, KA-LUNK, KA-LUNK!! What the HELL is that? I wondered as I looked at my watch. It was about 3:30 in the morning. I identified the origin of the noise. Two large steel plates, about eight by eight, placed in the middle the street on 9th Avenue between 58th and 59th Street directly in front of St. Luke's Roosevelt Hospital. A hospital! Repair or construction work was apparently ongoing and presumably at day's end the construction crew placed the steel plates back over an open hole in the street. But the street was either not level or the plates were warped and without wedges inserted between the macadam. Those plates were rockin' an rollin' and that created the noise every time a vehicle rode over them. Can you imagine how many people this affected? Apparently, incompetent and uncaring or careless workers placed them directly in front of one of the largest hospitals in Manhattan without giving a shit about the consequences. Could it be that it was a conscious prank? Sure, why not?

"Joe, put the freekin' plates on crooked like last night, eh? We'll keep them sickos awake another night!"

The next morning I sprung into action. Mr. Concerned Citizen or fed up New Yorker, I called 311 to report the problem to the City.

"Well, that's probably Con Ed doing some repair work, we really can't help you sir!"

That was the 311 operator's reply.

"Thanks for nothing, and have a nice day!"

I called Con Ed and they provided no relief, "Nada buster!" They "kicked the can down the road" and told me to call the City's noise complaint line, 311.

I returned to my plan so I called 311. After about TWO WEEKS the problem was resolved. Wasn't there a police officer that was aware of this? Not a doctor, nurse or relative or friend who was visiting or caring for a patient had heard this? Was there at least one patient in the hospital who had been bothered by this? No one attempted to correct it by bringing it to the attention of a member of the hospital staff! I'll never know but just like the out of synch walk sign down the block. It amazed me that thousands of people never bothered to take action, in New York City!

It's known as "bystander effect" a term that arose from the tragic death of Kitty Genovese who was murdered in the street in Kew Gardens, Queens on the night of March 13, 1964. Numerous neighbors watched in horror. Not one of them called the police! Not ONE! Someone, who me, called about the steel plates though, because that may have disrupted the sleep of those recovering in the hospital too, eh? I'm so sorry that I wasn't in Kew Gardens on that fateful night back in 1964. It's incredible!

Have you ever walked passed a City bus stop while passengers are getting on and off the bus? Have you ever heard the burst of noise emitted from a City bus? It's an air propulsion sound, hydraulic, whatever, very loud, that signals passengers that the bus is in kneeling mode? It's loud enough to awaken people from great distances. Why does it have to be that loud? Subways have a nice ding-dong warning sound signaling that the doors are about to close. Why not try that instead of the annoying, grinding bus blast? There's got to be thousands of people who live in apartments that are in earshot of bus stops throughout the City who must suffer terribly on a continuous basis. Perhaps it's unavoidable, let's wait and see. "Mike, help!" How about flashing lights instead? Imagine living in a ground floor apartment with a bus stop in front of your window? That will do wonders for the value of your abode and quality of your life.

I have no doubt that fire engines and I hate to pick on the firefighters, but sirens are over used. Why blast them, incessantly, especially late at night or in early morning hours when there are practically no cars around? Streets are clearly visible. The horns and sirens are constantly pounding pointlessly. It's overkill! Childish first responders get over it and grow up! OH yes, and be safe.

Firefighters are truly the bravest and most precious people we know but I'd love just a little effort here guys.

Recently, the NYFD announced an experiment to diminish the use of sirens in Queens when fire engines are not on their way to an emergency! Well, it's about time we attempted to put an end to needless noise. How long will this take? Perhaps the FDA can approve a new drug before the "jury" is back. So far, about a year later, nothing has come of it!

Has anyone thought of how to make a quieter garbage truck yet? What about motorcycles without mufflers or with mufflers that are designed to produce the loudest sounds heard in the City? Aren't there laws on the books to prevent that? Yes there are but no one gives rat's ass.

I live on West 97th Street supposedly a much quieter neighborhood than West 60th. My first six months there were quiet and then the noise arrived! Construction began next to my building, big time. A mega residential and shopping complex with 700 apartments covering a three-block stretch on both sides of Columbus Avenue, a humongous residential shopping center was under construction. There were approximately three construction contraptions with ultra hardened bits chomping away at the bedrock, Manhattan schist, to excavate the foundations. I was wishing for the good ol' days of the steel plates back on 60th Street!

Several weeks after this incessant noise had started, a Monday through Friday occurrence, from 7 AM to 4 PM, I saw a guy on the corner of Columbus Avenue and 97th Street unlock a medal box, installed on a telephone pole, that read, "EPA Noise Abatement Unit." I asked him what he was doing and he explained to me that he was there to remove a statistical circular graph document, a mechanically plotted graph etched upon it that electronically recorded the level of noise in that area over time. I inquired,

"What do you do with that information?"

He told me that he hands it to his superior for analysis.

"Then what does he or she do with it?"

"Beats me!" he replied.

Well, I'm so glad that the City is hard at work doing, well, something that apparently provides no benefit. At least there are a few people out there who have jobs, on the City payroll, no less. Noise, from this construction project, continued for well over two years, just before I had decided that it was too late to have my ears removed!

By far, the most annoying and frequently disturbing noise, the one that not only violates our ears but makes us go insane are the automated auto alarms that "go off" at the slightest sound or vibration often triggered by an insect or a drop rain that touching 1988 Honda Civic, resale value approximately $275.00 minus transportation costs.

Have you ever noticed that only cars that even the most desperate criminals would not even think of stealing are alarmed? It reminds me of George Carlin's comment that the only women who are opposed to abortion are the ones that you wouldn't want to sleep with!

The alarm that I love, just kidding, the best are the car alarms that cascades a variety of electronic sounds from: hee haw, hee haw then, awee, awee, awee, and then, yang yang yang yang and finally zeeeep, zeeeep, zeeeep and then repeat, repeat, repeat. The sheer joy when it stops makes you feel as though you got your finger released from a slammed door!

Okay Bill, here's my solution: Tow cars away whose alarms go off without good reason, that is, if the vehicle has, a blue book value, of less than $5,000. If it's value is more than $500 then fine the owner $500 or exchange their wheels for the '78 Sentra.

It's unbelievable that just the other morning, starting at about 5 AM a loud and crazy alarm went off in the

423

rear parking lot of the complex where I live. It must have disturbed no less than 18,000 people, probably much more. The police were called, never came, my building doorman didn't have access to the records as to who rented that parking spot because the "management" office was closed therefore he could not identify the owner of that vehicle or whether or not the vehicle was parked there illegally. Thus, every fifteen minutes or so until about 8:30 AM the alarm blasted. I do hope that rocket scientist got to work on time.

I love my weekends more than ever and appreciate my peace and quiet beyond belief. Perhaps I should have moved up to 130th Street or beyond? Who knows? It's probably noisier up there and at least it has lyric, melody and rhythm bursting forth with a familiar and distinctive Latino and Hip-hop musical flair. Despite this, I will never leave Manhattan. Perhaps they'll have to carry me out. Quietly, on a Harley three-wheeler!

Hallowed Ground . . . Zero

In the early 19th century New York City was protected from foreign invaders by three forts that were strategically located at the entrance to our harbor. Any form of attack would have been easily disabled from any foe that dared to invade New York City by sea. Known as Ft. Wood, Ft. Gibson and Ft. Clinton they defended us well. I remember the names of these three forts: "President Clinton had a Gibson and got a Woody!"

A navel attack could have been executed simply by landing troops in New Jersey or the eastern edge of what was to become part of New York City such as Brooklyn or Queens. An attack waged via Long Island Sound or from the continent via The Bronx certainly would have been problematic for us because Manhattan has big borders, all shoreline. There were numerous forts built in Manhattan and the outer boroughs providing further protection from a would be attack as well, However, Manhattan, an island, was impenetrable from the Upper Bay at the southern tip. No enemy ships had ever attempted an invasion upon the heart of New York City by ship since The Revolutionary War. A Normandy type invasion, with numerous small landing craft could have been successful only if the enemy's small ships danced between the cannon balls. Never did a flotilla of small ships make that attempt.

Fort Totten on Willets Point near Bayside in Queens, Fort Jay on Governors Island, Castle Clinton in Battery Park, and Fort Wadsworth on Staten Island protected the Narrows keeping us safe. Fort Wood on Liberty Island and Fort Gibson, the former name of Ellis Island all together put any ship in range of cannon

425

balls, together with other two harbor forts, our batteries defended New York harbor quite well from invasions.

As a result, no enemy ship ever entered our harbor however; the British did blockade New York City successfully during the War of 1812 and they had the good sense never to venture into our firing range.

It seemed that we were safer then and more secure with brick and mortar forts, armed with ancient guns that would have laid waste to frigates commandeered by those who would have dared to attack us.

Fast-forward to September 11, 2001 and by any measure we were attacked by terrorist monsters from caves in Afghanistan that plotted the most horrific loss of life, destruction and carnage this country has ever known from outside invaders. Our forts have fallen into disuse ages ago. Remnants from a time long past, a time when life was simpler but far more difficult to endure was unbelievably safer. Nowadays, we are equipped with laser guided weapons, "smart" bombs, supersonic fighters, GPS, satellite imagery, night goggles, global intelligence, ordinance laden pilot-less drones, surveillance apparatus, and stealth technology, to name a few, all at our disposal at a cost of hundreds of billions of dollars. All of that billion dollar hardware fail to protect us adequately.

These high tech weapons did not prevent the heinous attacks on that fateful September morning; attacks launched on from our own skies using U.S. commercial aircraft as weapons of death and mass destruction. Certainly, we are less safe now than we were in the 19th century.

The idea of building The World Trade Center originated with David Rockefeller, the former CEO of Chase. He pined for a way to revitalize the financial district and halt the continued loss of its luster to the midtown business district after World War II. Rockefeller Center and Grand Central Terminal were the driving catalysts for developers and, as a result, the midtown district enjoyed unprecedented growth of commercial, residential and retail development throughout the second half of the 20th century. Downtown or The Financial District lost its gleam and glitter. Mr. Rockefeller built a new corporate headquarters for Chase in 1960, a sixty story international modern structure with courtyards, magnificent amenities and sculptures that he had hoped would seed a new construction boom in the financial district re-creating the lost glory of Wall Street as the center of finance and commerce as it has once been. His vision, hoping that the new Chase Headquarters would jump-start the process simply did not take hold.

In the late 1960's David Rockefeller together with Nelson, the governor of New York State, put together a new vision. The Port Authority of New York and New Jersey issued revenue bonds purchasing the "Radio District" a sixteen-acre site in lower Manhattan through passage of eminent domain legislation and built The World Trade Center consisting of seven buildings included the signature Twin Towers as the centerpiece to become the heart of a new downtown upon its completion in 1973.

New Yorkers took enormous pride in "The Twin Towers" a crowning symbol, a colossus of our commercial strength and global supremacy as the

"Capital of capital of the World." After forty-three years the Empire State Building was surpassed as the world's tallest building by those gleaming twin temples, a technological achievement of unprecedented innovation and imagination and hubris.

As New York City has always done, after 911, we embarked on the path of renewal and replacement creating a spectacular new World Trade Center, a vision that came to life replete with an impressive memorial park featuring two memorial pools, "Reflecting Absence" serving as the centerpieces of it all.

We are beholden to our first responders; mourn all those who perished, and all the first responders, heroes, each and every one who are enveloped in an eternal vale of sorrow after the attack of our glorious City and its people. The towers were symbols of our greatness and of the victims, families and friends who lost loved ones on that most horrific of days. It is an eternally enormous burden, one that is unbearably difficult to accept and or comprehend.

And to our fallen brothers and sisters whose lives were taken in innocence, their courage to summon the best that dwelled within their hearts struggling against the odds helping their fellow co-workers and strangers who happen to be beside them desperately seeking to find a way out saving so many lives in the worst circumstances imaginable. We will never forget, never.

Our firefighters, 343 men whose precious lives were taken, who raced to the site, many not called to duty, rather by their instinct, dashed to their final fire. Their memory will always burn in our hearts. How gallantly they sped undeterred into the face of danger and stared down death to save people who they had never met, people who will never know their names, people who surely will, in eternity, be grateful for their unbelievable courage and ultimate sacrifices. Not one of them turned back knowing that they were entering the most horrific building fires, unprecedented in history. That's the stuff of New Yorkers, gallant, fearless and devoted to their fellow citizens at the risk or even certainty of losing their lives to save strangers, people they had never met and not one, not one turned back. They walked upstairs to die while others walked downstairs to live.

We, as a city, are rebuilding and nothing will ever stop that. Again and again, we have, in a short four hundred years, demonstrated to the world that New York City is unstoppable. When our new World Trade Center site is completed we will rejoice, somewhat painfully, that those whose lives were lost will forever dwell in our minds and hearts. How tragic that the rebuilding process has been mired in politics, legalities, incompetence, financial entanglements and overwhelming emotional conflicts; that is unfortunately all part of the process. Ultimately, that will fade into the past and we will endure, our temples and memorials as well.

The effects of 911 dwell deep within the hearts and minds of all New Yorkers. Images of ordinary people, "the general public", looking after their fellow citizens, risking their lives out of concern; far beyond kindness are indelibly engraved within us all. How many of us would have imagined that even in New York City, on a day unlike any other, strangers, the

429

people you ride to work with and never exchange a word, people who cut in line ahead of you to grab their coffee, people whose lives are a mystery to you, people whose skin is not the same color as yours and faces that reveal that their origin is from places unheard of by you. They were all New Yorkers entwined in a run for their lives as if tied together in a web, a unified dash for survival, like a herd of zebras fleeing a pack of lions. Many stayed behind, setting aside their own precious lives, and their love of their families to rescue total strangers. We as New Yorkers are family. We were then and we are now. More than ever 911 has proven that New Yorkers truly have deep love and compassion for their neighbors and fellow citizens. Who among us had known, the connection that had been there before 911? Perhaps we just didn't know it at the time, but we certainly know now.

There is no shortage of heroism in New York City. It pours forth into the streets, people reversing course, providing life saving aid to those who were gasping for air, offering their last drops of precious bottled water, giving their last ounce of strength to enable a stranger to take their next few steps forward to safety. That is the essence of New York City.

Put your CSI, Law and Order, Special Victims Unit and all those TV crime dramas in the closet. This is the real New York City, unrehearsed, one take, final shoot, not the reality program we ever wanted to provide to the world. It's the indelible and un-sponsored truth. There are no better people on earth then the brothers and sisters who live here in New York City.

We are beyond deeply saddened by the events of 911 and although we cannot turn the clock back, we can look ahead with grateful pride that New York City responded in the most heroic and generous way the world has ever known. God bless New York City, all the people who love this town and all the wonderful people who did not live here who came selflessly and heroically to our rescue. Come to the 911memorial and to the spectacular museum and pay your respects to all those who are tragically no longer with us.

Tonight Giz, a Love Story

New Yorkers are prolific animal lovers. The dog population is over 230,000 in Manhattan alone. You'll see them everywhere, except restaurants, coffee shops and pharmacies. They have good lives here in the City even though, if given the choice, many would rather live in the country with those wide-open spaces. But for those who have been born and raised here they relish the pleasures of our abundant park system. We've got dog parks, dog runs and they are allowed to run freely in Central Park before 9 AM and after 9 PM. For the vast majority, they know of no other life. Typically, New York City it the only home they know.

Dogs come in all breeds, shapes and sizes. They mingle, sniff, bark and gather. Did you ever see a dog walker with six or eight leashed dogs walking together as a pack? They seem to know each other, get along well and move along as if they're the ones who are getting paid to walk. Unlike dogs that reside in the country they too, like the rest of us here, have more socialization. Hey, they're city dwellers.

Yorkshire Terriers are the most popular breed in the City. Space is at a premium, the greatest luxury in New York City and Yorkies, one of the smallest breeds and undoubtedly the most adorable, is our number one choice.

My current Yorkie, Moe son of Gizmo, occupied our little apartment on West 60th Street until 2006 when we moved to West 97th Street a somewhat larger apartment with a smaller bedroom. The West 60th Street apartment's bedroom was large enough for us to have a king size bed and that suited Moe just fine.

He slept with us quite comfortably, a five pound hound.

Now that we have been reduced to queen sized bed, due to our new smaller sized bedroom, as a result, Moe has opted not to sleep with us choosing to relocate into the living room and sleep alone on the couch. Poor Moe! That little five-pounder has become a victim of our shortage of space in the City.

The night Moe lost his father back in 2004 I sat down and wrote the following sentiments. It was a mind-expanding experience for us both. So many feelings, otherworldly visions and emotions burst forth from with us both. The last night for Gizmo was in Florida. Please share this sad but amazing story of how man and dog can communicate love and sentiments to each other.

*****

Tonight Moe and I were walking along the Intracoastal Waterway. It was early in the evening after a rainy summer day of unsettled weather in south Florida. The sky was painted a deep, yawning blue. It was the kind of blue that evokes emptiness. It was a shade of blue that gives rise to the meaning for "blue" as a synonym for sadness. The sketches of clouds in the sky spelled a foreboding message. It told a tale of wetness of the rain that had just ended synchronized with tears that had fallen from eyes that doused the cheeks of mourners. Aline, my wife, and I had wept over the loss of Moe's little father, "Giz" or Gizmo, our loyal, loving and devoted five-pound Yorkshire terrier who had to be "put down" earlier that day. We lost Giz suddenly and knew that we could not accept that we would see him no more.

It had been only the two of us outside that night. As Moe and I walked together we were lonely as three was always the right number.

I sensed that Moe knew that Giz was not there and then I was convinced of it. Sure, it was naïve to even consider that Moe was unsure that his only close canine friend was not with us. He occasionally twisted his little neck askew after lifting his leg to relieve himself, a gesture, searching for his little companion as he had done so often in the past. He was hoping against hope that somehow Giz would suddenly appear. We shared a similar sadness and frustration, me not being able to explain it to him and he not able to comprehend it.

His little dark eyes were fixed, fast and hard, glued upon me in earnest. They pierced mine with unwavering intensity as if asking or demanding, "Where is he?" and "Where did he go?" Or, much less favorably "Where did you take him?" Or, "Why did you remove him from us?" I never thought that he would have questioned me as removing him from "me", but rather of course from "us." Dogs are unselfish beings. They are clannish, pack animals, and sense losses. I do believe that they feel their family members experience loss too. I cannot explain why I believe that but that very notion, in some way, helps support my opinion that it is so. I only had wished that I could explain to Moe where Giz had gone in order to put order or closure in his little head and heart. I knew that his pal was gone and to him he was MIA, missing in action.

I find it amusing to ponder that Moe may have been thinking that Giz may be somewhere else. Did Moe think that when Aline and went out and left him home, that he, resting with his eyes shut was imagining where we were and what we were doing? So it might be that he could very well imagine where Giz may have been or what he was doing at that very moment. Why not? The love and concern is there and the ability to carry such thoughts exists in canine heads. After all, their greatest concern is the safe and swift return of their family members to their abode or lair.

The limitation of language without words that separates man from canine is intriguing especially when there is a loss. How often I had wanted to express my thoughts to Giz about how much he meant to me, most of all when I needed him at my side. I, unlike him, had all the words I needed to convey the thoughts that I had wanted to express to him. Could it be that it was my limitation not perceiving he knew exactly what I wanted to tell him? Or, that I had no clue that he was one step ahead of me knowing that languages made of words are not necessarily the best, perhaps as every smart dog well knows. Only those who use language without words would know better. I do hope that is true. I also hope that he understood the words that I conveyed to him as well as the actions, gestures and physical contact that we shared as I stroked, held and kissed him tenderly as any one would embrace a child with their love and affection. I am sure he understood that very well.

Words are inventions of man and if the behavior of our little canine friends is any indication of love and loyalty then they are not suffering a loss without knowing how to express words.

I know of no one who has ever had a dog who felt that their dog failed to communicate their love and affection fully and completely without the need to utter a word conveying those sentiments fully and completely. We learn from our little lovable pets those "hounds" convey so much to us without words. Their eyes tell us much, their tails and even their facial expression and body language conveys what they are thinking.

Language, the type that uses words is not the only means we have to express our emotions or everyday sentiments. We rarely rely on words as the best conveyance of thought when intense emotional moments occur.

Isn't it tears, smiles, laughter, screams, crying, body language, whimpers and barks and gestures of all kinds that convey the true message that is in our minds and hearts? So it is with dogs, expressing their emotions void of words, only their gestures, body language and eyes are their means to tell us how they feel at every moment. And Moe, that five-pound Yorkie inspired me that sorrowful night to put these thoughts on paper without a word passing between his "lips" is evidence, to me, of that.

We two "a man and his dog" the remaining dog, produced by a dog just lost were beginning to learn how to bond with each other in an entirely new, deeper and more important way then ever before. We looked at each other as we transmitted the same messages without a word. We communicated with our eyes and the waves of emotion passing through the air between us. Suddenly, we were equal, our abilities to convey our thoughts were comperable. My education, language and life experiences were of

436

absolutely no use to me. Moe's language limitations evaporated before me as I gazed into his eyes wide with moisture beaming unflinchingly at me. We both felt in our hearts the very same loss and we knew that we were each experiencing the same loss. Our eyes and silence told the tale. And as we stared into each other's eyes I knew exactly what he was thinking and he knew that I did. Of that I have not the slightest doubt.

Later on we expressed our thoughts through tenderness, he being close and resting upon me and me holding him fast, petting him and supporting his little head next to my cheek, shushing him as if I were singing him a lullaby. I would kiss his little neck and stroke his head caressing it in my palm with tenderness while repeating to him, "It's okay Moe, it's okay." Those moments were sweet, innocent, pure and very sad. We moved on together through this difficult time focusing on our mutual loss and building a stronger bond between us.

In the past, I had shared my love with each of them in different ways. They knew they were a pair, each having a part of me. They were never competing with each other for my attention or affection. They were happy to be a part of the threesome and moreover a foursome as Aline, my wife, embraced them with her love and affection as well. Now the communication was binary, direct and necessary this night outside, as we had walked along the intercoastal waterway. We were sharing our loss, a loss that was for each of us our own private loss. We were drawn together as a loss draws people together. The difference was that it was completely authentic and sincere.

At such times most human families are thrown into turmoil and tossed asunder for generations over feuds and conflicts that produce endless bitterness, hatred, financial disputes filled with rife over the loss of a family member and their own share of the assets of the departed. Moe, a dog, was drawn closer to his "mother and father" without any other consideration. It was his way of filling the gap. There are no hidden motives. There is no agenda. There are no wills, inheritances, insurance or property rights. There are no remainder men, contract rights, life estates or jewelry. It is a loss, pure and simple. That puts them, our little lovable friends, on much higher ground then us. Theirs is an agenda of a love and mourning, pure and simple.

Moe is Giz's son, formally named Gizmo. He, Gizmo, was the dog that had entered my life at a time when I was alone in between marriages. For quite some time there had been the four of us, Giz, Moe, Aline and me. Aline was reluctant to accept this little seven week old Yorkie a mere two pounder when I came home from the breeder three years prior to that fateful night, a surprise for her. I knew ultimately that she would welcome him into our home and she learned to love him enthusiastically. Giz, on the other hand, didn't "send" for him and had no interest in sharing his home with this little pup, his son. This tiny innocent "baby" slept on Aline's neck every night and needed a lot of love and physical contact. She called him "crazy glue" because he was always stuck to her, Giz or me. Having come from a litter of five he, the runt, was accustomed to being next to at least one warm and cozy living thing. He quickly became his father's appendage always finding a spot to lie next to

Giz gathering warmth and security in the safety of his father's furry curl. Giz learned to accept him and in time they became a pair always sleeping, resting and lying together.

A life so little in size was claimed, suddenly by cancer, and put to sleep or as they now say "put down" with only an hour of prior warning for us. For me, no life was ever larger in love and effect. His was a life with a history. It was a history of love, patience, loyalty and obedience. Aline had always said, "Giz was the easiest dog you can find."

The opportunity that was given to him, by living with me, a sociable outgoing resident in midtown Manhattan, gave Giz enormous exposure enabling him to touch so many and give love and happiness on a day to day basis to so thousands of pedestrians on the sidewalks of New York City. We rode the subway countless times. We walked through Central Park, and I tucked him inside my coat and I walked down Fifth Avenue amidst the Christmas shoppers watching them point and smile at his little face peeking out of my coat nested warmly within. Countless thousands of people had been handed a photo of him (see photo featured inside this book) with his little head tilted and his tongue sticking way out reaching for the bacon that his nose could scent. So often people hurled questions at me. "What's his name?" "What kind of dog is that?" How much does he weigh?" "Is he a male?" "How old is he?" I had thousands of copies of that picture printed with all of the answers to those questions on the back of his picture. People took such interest in him. It was his tiny size and the breed, the cutest on earth, that has such universal appeal. Ultimately, many people stopped us and asked for another copy of the ubiquitous photo for a friend or an office mate.

"Oh, I look at that picture every day. It's on my refrigerator! Could I please have one for my friend?"

"Oh, I love that picture, he's so cute!"

That picture appeared in a magazine! Apparently someone wanted to share it with others. That was quite a surprise for me, to say the least. Gizmo took it in stride.

There were three rainbows that night while Moe and I were walking along the Intracoastal Waterway! Aline was watching us from our second floor apartment balcony. I yelled, with this little five-pound Yorkie connected to me clasping him tighter than ever before.

"Aline, there are three rainbows out there! There are three!" I shouted gleefully.

As she tilted her head up smiling at the sight and I believed the symbolism was a message from Giz. My well of emotion was unknown to her nevertheless she shouted in astonishment.

I wondered why there were three rainbows. One or even two would have been more than enough to evoke the sensitivity that gave rise to the thoughts that had come over me. The color and glamour gave substance to the descending light enabling the night to take over the day as death takes over a life giving meaning and breathe to the departed one.

I'd never seen three rainbows in the same place at the same time before. Only then, at this moment had I seen them when my heart was so heavy with loss. I was yearning to find answers to simple questions, a solution that perhaps the sky could provide. Was Giz looking down at us and sending a message? I cannot

440

believe that such things can happen for people who have departed let alone dogs, less important mortals we are told. We who have the opportunity to share the love of animals cling and tend to hold tight to irrational and endearing symbols of our departed pets. We search for all we can to add meaning and clarity to their lives especially after they have left us. That helps us to heal. They are gone in physical presence; their spiritual essence, their true meaning and purpose live on.

They live on through us. We are the means upon which they exist beyond their natural years. We are the connection that they have with the present. Our love and passion for these little lovable creatures extends their lives. Who has the right to say that they are less important mortals then we? Dogs do not hire lawyers or cheat. No dog ever lied or deceived another. Only abused or genetically deprived canines need to be hunted, caged or rehabilitated. They, as a species, are forever kind, caring, and loyal and as a result, they dwell in our hearts and minds forever.

Perhaps there was a reason for those rainbows and perhaps the reason was Giz. And if Giz did not make it happen, and that must be true, then surely the messages the rainbows evoked defined his presence not in body but more importantly in spirit.

I cannot claim credit for inventing questions about three rainbows without the connection that Moe and I had together that night. I did not expect him to make such an egotistical or self-serving claim even if he could have spoken. For me, it was a crutch; one that I had created to provide comfort and closure. I know that if he had been given the ability to express his thoughts then assuredly he would not have omitted the role that I had played in shaping his thoughts, feelings and ideas, how sweet and endearing they surely had been.

I asked Aline that night if we were better off having Moe after Gizs' departure. Was it a plus? Did it help us emotionally or was it a burden?

I knew that Moe enabled me to continue to have the pleasure of a dog in our lives and this loss pushed this little dog and us forward to explore and deepen our love for each other. I was painfully aware of the suffering that Moe was experiencing and how much that loss was locked deep inside him not having the opportunity to express his bereavement to his satisfaction. To me, it was complete and right as rainbows. He alone filled the gap and I hope that Aline and I filled the gap that dwelled in his little heart too.

Good night Giz. Good night.

Moe too was laid to rest on April 26th 2014
Good night Moe. Good night.

Not Every New Yorker is so Smart!

Recently, I was walking down 44th Street approaching Sixth Avenue in midtown when I had reached Sixth Avenue I came upon a great deal of commotion; fire engines, police cars, sirens, crowds of people, stopped traffic, yellow police tape all over the place and a taxicab with a shattered rear windshield.

It was quite a scene, scary! What was going on? Hey, this is New York City and events of this nature, whatever the cause, were not uncommon. Sirens are heard constantly, dozens of police cars with flashing lights during practice exercises with ambulances, fire trucks are often seen and heard, the uncommon is common. It's all part of the urban landscape, nothing new, business as usual.

I approached a gentleman, well suited, briefcase in hand, standing with his head tilted straight up, staring intently. His fixated glare was glued to The Bank of America Tower, then under construction. Many others were all motionless, standing like stone all with their heads tilted up. I too looked up and still had no clue as to what was going on. What were they looking at? Apparently, all I could conclude was that they were looking directly at the Bank of America Tower, and something must have gone terribly wrong. My thought was that this post-modern "green" beauty's frame was completed and a few remaining windows were being installed. This was to be the second tallest building in Manhattan, tied with the Chrysler Building, after The Empire State Building, again the tallest, tragically reclaiming the title after 911.

"Hey! What's going on up there, sir?" I had asked the nearest observer. His answer was shocking! It absolutely floored me!

"There's glass falling from the building!"

He shouted, never looking at me, not taking his eyes off whatever was happening or about to happen from above. Like mimes, they were all frozen in time, fascinated, still, eyes up, incredible!

That hard to believe clarification, "glass falling" explained the smashed taxi windshield and building janitors who were busy sweeping up huge jagged shards of broken glass off the sidewalk. The yellow police tape had been placed to prevent pedestrians from venturing into the danger zone, compliments of our bravest and finest. That however, could not save New Yorkers from their own lack of good judgment, aka stupidity.

Despite the efforts of our public safety professionals with the "best of intentions" together with "the smartest people on the planet" sometimes we just can't save ourselves. Who knows? Perhaps the yellow police tape was placed to corral morons from entering the danger zone, those who craved best views!

There are limits as to how much protection can be provided to those who insist on remaining on the wrong side of stupidity. Stupidity is not a crime, but it can be deadly. If only they could have radioed above to ensure that the glass would fall only within the yellow taped boundaries!

One of the two cables supporting the cement buckets, designed to prevent them from swaying into the building as they descended, had become disengaged. That caused one of the buckets to swing into the side of the building and smash numerous windows as it was being lowered. As soon as a construction crew member figured that out they halted the bucket's decent and secured the loose cable.

I left the scene immediately, exceedingly perplexed by the hundreds of New Yorkers who had stood there gazing, face upward, literally exposing themselves to enormous danger. Could it be that they did not know they were targets of another possible barrage of glass guided by wind and gravity? How could that be?

New Yorkers are amazing people. Smart, innovative, hard working and strangely at times capable of incredibly stupid behavior defying the imagination. Certainly, there was not one among them who didn't realize the threat that they were imposing upon themselves. So then, what was it?

New Yorkers are very curious and will cast off "common sense" to witness unusual events. How often we see people running toward danger? Shouldn't they be running away from danger? Weren't people rushing toward the Twin Towers on that most tragic day to bear witness, taking pictures or just there to be able to tell others, if they survived, "I was there!"

Not all of them were looking to become heroes.

There's got to be something in human nature, a dark side that compels many to go into denial and witness the macabre and bizarre, despite risking their lives. And as it is with most events that life provides, New Yorkers will be there in great numbers, even if it's far from the smartest thing to do.

Hey, perhaps most were lawyers ready to pass out a few cards, ambitious New Yorkers seeking to capture another opportunity! As I left the scene, I stooped down and pickup up a card, from a law firm, it read:

Dewey, Rob, Steele, Chetham and Howe, LLC

Chapter VI
Other Experiences
★★★★★★★★★★★★★★★★★★★★★★★★★

"Fraud Alert!"

Career change! Now, those two words strike fear in us all especially when laid at your doorstep without an invitation. If career change crashes upon you involuntarily, especially later in life, like 60ish, and add to that, your industry has vanished. It's an extremely devastating, disheartening and frightening life-changing event. Toss in a mountain of unpaid back taxes, unresolved divorce obligations, ruined credit and last but not least, there's no jingle in your pockets. You're in deep shit unless or until a new opportunity kicks one that will provide a means to re-invent yourself.

There are times when you are handed lemons and the sweetness of life turns against you. It's easy to feel sorry for yourself and believe that you are the victim of bad luck and circumstances that you have had no control over. You believe that you have reached an irreversible dilemma and you'll never get out of the morass and life just sucks.

"It's hopeless. How can I ever rebuild? What am I going to do? Shit, SHIT!"

That's how it feels. I know. That's where I was back in 2005 and I never expected that I would ever climb out of that bottomless pit. K Mart security guard, here I come.

I had recalled my father's advice from way back in the late 1970's when his business had crashed and I had been working for him for approximately ten years, helping him manage and build his business, one that had evolved into a large film processing plant employing over 200 employees. We grew the family business, purchased the newest and best equipment, computerized the operation and reckless rapid growth resulted in a dangerously undercapitalized and "un-bankable" business with "cat shit" filling the business's financial statements. Ultimately the business failed and I went adrift left penniless, without a job and no business. Eastman Kodak sued my first wife and me for nearly one-half a million dollars and I was tied up with a non-compete covenant that restricted me from selling film processing for nine years within a 75-mile radius of New York City. Tuff beans, eh? Toss in two little kids, wife and a mortgage and that situation was quite a mess.

My father's advice was,

"You have the ability to make a living. Put one foot in front of the other."

"Great dad! Thanks a lot. That's like telling me, 'Life is just a bowl of cherries!' Got the Dali Lama's phone number?"

But, he turned out to be right. I know now what he meant. That was, just get on with it. Tap into your own resources and stop feeling sorry for yourself. Break your ass and point yourself in the right direction. Look for opportunities and you will find them. How right he was.

Fast forward to 2005 when Aline and I were looking to buy a business, one that had similarities with the retail one-hour photo business, a retail service business, which had been our primary source of income since we've been married. It had been a very lucrative business until digital photography replaced

448

film in the consumer marketplace. Photography had become a computer driven business as the overwhelming majority of amateurs and consumers started to print their own pictures at home or simply stored them on discs, floppies or hard drives. One-hour photo stores were dropping like flies and in 2012 Eastman Kodak, "the great yellow father", as they had been known, in the industry, filed for bankruptcy, something that had been unthinkable even a few years back.

Aline and I looked for independent fast food establishments, gourmet coffee shops featuring minimal food preparation and no cooking in New York City. They were all service businesses and that, in many ways, was similar to the one-hour photo business; purchase the raw materials, prepare, market and sell the hell out of it. Provide excellent customer service, staff the business with motivated people and create a brand and build loyalty. We knew how to do such things, profitably. A well satisfied customer base could be built in a short period of time by providing excellent service, quality and value. That would yield substantial income without the cost and hassle of "carrying" huge inventories and purchasing expensive equipment. The markups are very high in retail food service and low cost unskilled labor could run such a business with good supervision, training and controls.

We spent quite a bit of effort searching for such a business. Every business that had seemed to be ideal wound up having fatal flaws. The lease was too short, the business was too expensive, the seller wanted to be paid entirely in cash or there were restrictive covenants in the lease that were deal breakers for us.

Other businesses had location problems; too many competitors or they were simply on the wrong side of the street. The most frequent deal breaker was that the seller was just plain full of shit.

One opportunity that we got close to forging was owned and operated by a woman who was a vicious liar and cheat. I spent several days watching her ring up sales at the cash register, with her approval, of course. I tallied the sales on a pad in front of her nose for an entire day. When she gave the cash to me to verify the amount that she had rung up she provided exactly $1,000 more then she had actually taken in! I had seen her plop the money into the cash register during the day when she thought I was distracted.

Another potential seller offered what seemed to be a sweet deal until I had discovered that a major construction project was about to begin directly across the street from his establishment, a subway and PATH train hub on Fulton Street.

Then, at last we found exactly what we had been looking for. The location was perfect. The seller was honest and very accommodating. The help was hard working and the food venue was highly profitable and required quick and easy preparation. The store was doing a brisk business and the hours were not overbearing, closing at 6 PM. The terms were very attractive requiring a small down payment with low interest notes to satisfy the balance. I spent four weeks there from opening to closing and learned a great deal about the business from top to bottom.

Aline and I had agreed that it would be a great start and a bright future lay ahead for us. We were very excited about this opportunity, we took the next step and scheduled a meeting with the co-op board.

The building was a co-op, meaning a board of managers or directors had the right and obligation to review all applications for the sale of all the residences above the street level, as well as sales of retail businesses "on the street." We were confident that together we were well qualified, on every level, to purchase the business. We appeared before the board with every expectation that this would be a "done deal." We were counting on it.

The board assembled in an apartment six floors above the store. Wow! It was huge. The rooms were oversized and complimented with high ceilings, maple floors, large windows and elegant furnishings. We were very impressed but not intimidated.

The board members introduced themselves. They seemed pleasant and welcoming except for one member who was dour and distant. Aline and I looked at each other and transmitted the same message; this guy whoever he was, was going to be troublesome.

This kingpin was very tall, well into his seventies, wearing pajamas and slippers; to us that signified arrogance and power. He appeared to us to be a Meyer Lansky type, the old and physically fragile man who welded all the authority in the room. He projected an aura that was extremely grim and disconnected as though we were interrupting him like he had much more important things to do. We were just a couple of slouches who were seeking to buy a coffee shop. We learned that he was the board president, owner of multiple multi-million dollar units in the building. He was the decision maker, the deal breaker or maker.

451

We had provided all the documents they had required from us; financial statements, documents of citizenship, identifications, references, biographical essays and Aline's credit report as well as bank statements. This transaction was hers alone. I was there as a participant and advisor.

The "jolly old giant" took control of the meeting with brio. He avoided eye contact with us and spoke as though he was the master of the house and did all he could to make us as uncomfortable as possible as his underlings looked on and kept their mouths shut, for the most part. We knew we were facing a very adversarial situation, duh!

He launched each question, as a lawyer, which he was, or had been. We felt that we were on trial rather than attending a gathering that was to cement benefits, an engagement a *quid pro quo*, not a trial or indictment. He plodded on and created an atmosphere of suspicion and mistrust, projecting a sense of conflicting purposes between the parties.

"I see on your credit report a notice marked 'fraud alert.'" he mused.

He pointed a finger directly at Aline as if she had committed fraud. This was not a Charles Dickens novel but it seemed that we were about to be toasted.

He, as an attorney, knew that that notation on a credit report was a warning, a flag that someone had stolen or had attempted to steal her identity. There was no representation that Aline's credit report earmarked her as a fraudulent party, but rather a potential target of a fraud being perpetrated by an outsider against her reputation and credit worthiness.

This scumbag was on the attack because he had a gripe with the seller of the store, as we had learned after that fateful meeting. We were squarely in his line of fire.

I had told him during the meeting that Aline's credit score was sky high, as was evident, and that she never even received a traffic ticket in her life. Further, I continued that he knew exactly what "fraud alert" meant.

He rebuked me by vehemently denying that was what it meant. He was a low life and a liar. The other board members sat void of expression, in absolute silence like a flock of blind sheep.

It was apparent that we were not going to get their approval to purchase the business. Then I let him have it.

"You know sir, it's people like you who sit on a high horse and live life taking pleasure thwarting others, while knowing that it is antithetical to your best interests and those of your colleagues and neighbors. As an attorney you have found a mechanism upon which to hang your hat and prevent my wife and I from pursuing what we are well qualified to do. We are hardworking people and can add much to the value of this building by providing a service for the community. But, because you are driven by your twisted agenda we're outa here empty handed except for the next opportunity that will surely come."

We got up and left, saying nothing more, not to him or the flock. It seemed as though the world was against us. We were back where had started except our bank account was further diminished. We needed to find something soon as our options were dwindling. We were frightened and deeply discouraged.

Looking back at the entire incident, the board president did us a big favor. Running that coffee shop operation, even with the ideas and imagination that we were going to pour into it would have been an exhausting burdensome operation with long hours and plenty of headaches. We would have taken on debt and been at the mercy of the board once again if we ever wanted to sell that business. Life is funny because something that we had wanted so desperately slipped through our fingers and it opened the door to our next big thing. Interesting how nearly every situation that, at the time, seemed to be a major setback or disappointment ultimately turns out to be a benefit.

Within the following year Custom & Private New York Tours was born.

"Darling, I'm about to be Arrested!"

While taking thirty of our guests down to the Wall Street Heliport in a minibus my cell phone rang as we were passing Trump Tower on Fifth Avenue.

"Darling, I'm about to be arrested!" Aline shrieked.

"What!"

"A police officer wants to take me to the police station for tossing a cigarette out of the van!"

This made absolutely no sense to me.

At the time, Aline was in a van with a driver about to leave and transfer our guest's luggage to Newark Airport who were bound for, Paris. To ensure that there would be no tampering with the contents of their luggage, by the driver, she was going with him to the airport, keeping her eye on the luggage.

Apparently, while sitting in the van with the driver, a shoddy and disheveled looking guy, and she a fair skinned well presented looking woman, a peculiar looking pair, were parked directly in front of a "high value target" The Plaza Hotel. This unlikely couple in an old rickety van loaded with luggage, weighting the van down, raised the suspicions of a vigilant police officer.

This occurred approximately two weeks after the thwarted attempt to set off a bomb in an SUV on West 45th Street in Times Square.

The officer had reasonable or "probable cause" after Aline had failed to produce ID as requested. He asked her where she was going and when she replied "Newark Airport" he retorted, "You're going to the airport and you don't have any ID?"

"I'm here to ensure that the luggage arrives safely and securely at the airport. I am not flying anywhere. My husband is taking the people who own this luggage to the heliport to be transferred to Newark airport. We are in the private tour business. Let me call my husband. I'm sure that he has ID."

"Where do you live? What's your zip code? What's your phone number?" he asked her.

When I received Aline's phone call I was about three blocks down Fifth Avenue. I left the bus, told my guests that I would meet them at the heliport and that I had to take care of something of urgent importance . By the time I reached the van the officer had left, after Aline's answers to his questions had satisfied him that she was "legit."

We all live in demanding and frightening times. Certainly, New Yorkers need to be alert and smart. The police officer, in my opinion, did the right thing. We live in a world where we need to carry photo ID and not toss cigarettes onto the street. Vigilance is the order of the day. I give kudos to the NYPD officer and to all those who protect us.

New York City in a Blizzard

Blizzards are uncommon here. So are earthquakes, hurricanes, avalanches, tsunamis and tornadoes. But, we do have plenty of horrible weather. But, it's very rare for our weather to threaten our lives and property, at least until Sandy, one of the worst storms in American history that somehow our government officials refused to label, a hurricane. It has been referred to as "a super store." This disaster has gone down as the second most costly and damaging weather event in our history, second only to Katrina.

Predicting weather in New York City is, at best, difficult and very iffy. Typically, weather here is very changeable and bizarre! I have never cultivated a love of meteorology growing up in an age before satellites and the onset of sophisticated weather forecasting technology, which is still an inexact science. It's been a long time since I've heard weather forecasts from Carol Reed, the CBS TV weather reporter from way back in the late '50's. In a town where you can dip into a subway station, normally not too far a distance, purchase an umbrella on the street for as little as three bucks, why bother to track the weather. Hurricane Sandy was a game changer, big time. We have to get serious about storm surge technology and solutions. It will be interesting to see how our governments and businesses handle that tomato!

New York City was blessed, not everyone would agree, with a huge blizzard in January of 1996. According to the official weather bureau records, 20.2 inches of snow fell on Central Park and over 30 inches were reported in some of the outer boroughs. At the time, I was living on West 57th Street, between 8th and 9th Avenue. This was the first time I had the opportunity to experience such an astonishing event. In New York City, blizzards pose more inconveniences for those who live in the hinterlands and the outer boroughs because the major mode of transportation in Manhattan is underground. Building owners and managers clear sidewalks in front of buildings that they are responsible for. City snow removal services are most often quite good and the emphasis is always in Manhattan first.

It had been predicted, the weather reports were coming in that a possible record breaker, the largest snowstorm, or at least nearly the largest in New York City history, was about to fall upon us. It turned out to be number four; March 12-14 in 1888 was the second, December 26-27 in 1947 was the third largest and The Blizzard of '06 (2006) kicked in as the largest at 26.9 inches according to statistics maintained since 1869.

It was late afternoon when the first evidence began to descend. Snowstorms of this magnitude have blanketed the City during my lifetime. I recall my parents talking about the blizzard of 1947 for years. In those days we were not equipped to remove snow as efficiently as we are now. It was always the granddaddy of all blizzards. This time we were ready. I do recall that there were elders talking about hearing their predecessors, when they were children, talking about "the blizzard of '88", 1888! That's the blizzard that resulted in the installation of our electric and telephone lines below ground! From bad there's always some good!

After the snow, thick, fluffy and very dense, had stopped falling, the '06 blizzard and had laid claim to the City. I dressed up for the occasion with long johns, gloves, earmuffs, boots, scarfs and a hat, "the works" and ventured out around midnight.

I had entered a time warp, a surreal landscape of white glaze, silent and still. Not a car, taxi, truck or bus was in sight. The noise of the City had completely vanished and there were only a few people out there. A few horses were visible with mounted police officers eying the City, a completely new and different vista in front of them unlike anything they had ever seen before. Two men were cross-country skiing down the center of 57th Street, dogs roamed unleashed and people were knee high in snow taking photographs. The city had fallen into a weird quiet that may not have occurred before. It was the quietest, purest, beautiful and pristine backdrop that occurred in Manhattan since the Lenape Indians ruled this island.

It took me back to a time, a time I could only have imagined, read about or seen in old black and white noir movies, or photographs. No image, no photograph, could have captured the silence I had experienced. The quiet amplified the sites, as is said of those who have a sensory loss, blindness, etc. providing their other senses with enhanced acuity.

Gazing at fifty story buildings towering above with no one in sight, void of vehicles, the lack of the incessant blasts of horns and sirens was dreamlike and had provided me with an incongruent experience as if I had landed on another planet. Without the odor of fumes emoted from countless exhaust pipes, no disruption from blearing sirens, a City standing still as though it was 1888 but without the recurrent sound of the clip clop of horses hooves, the cadence of

459

people's hasty gaits always complimented a frenzy and commotion not seen or heard in our lifetimes.

This urban landscape was a kaleidoscope of 20th century steel frame buildings rising into the haze of the old world, a world gone by. It was mesmerizing. How fortunate I was to experience this wonderment, knowing that the switch would flip by morning light and the City would inevitably trudge back to normal. I was glad about that too.

This snapshot of a slow paced, quiet and peaceful New York City was a treat for those who were fortunate enough to step outside, into the past, if only for one brief moment. The experience was truly well worth the effort. I do hope to slip back in time again some day. Until then, I will enjoy the City that I love, just the way it is.

Hopefully, some day, I'll be talking about the blizzard of '19 with a wide-eyed little child who will hear me, another old man, recalling the blizzard of '06!

"I remember that, yes I was there. Were you here too little one? Surely, you're too young to remember. You would have loved that one."

Back to the Future with a Metro Card

We all have "uneventful" days now and then, even in New York City. Recently, I had an amusing idea, a whacky out of the ordinary thought on an uneventful day in Manhattan.

I had "launched" two tours that day, a Chinese and a Spanish language tour one at The Gramercy Park Hotel and the other at Le Parker Meridien in midtown. Starting out, by subway, from West 97th Street I emerged from the subway at the Flatiron Building on 23rd Street where Broadway and Fifth Avenue intersect. From a quiet Upper Westside neighborhood I surfaced from the subway realizing I had entered a vastly different environment compared to were I had started, one adorned with historic late 19th century and early 20th century buildings, The Flatiron (1902), The Metropolitan Life Tower (1906), The Fifth Avenue Hotel (1909) and a park that once was Manhattan's town square, Madison Square Park where a cottage belonging to President James Madison once stood.

There the pace of life was highly energized and urban characterized with throngs of pedestrians hurrying along the sidewalks, briskly crossing streets, car horns blearing and people going about their day. The streets were filled with traffic, much more congested then The Upper Westside and void of the slower sluggish gait typical of uptown neighborhoods pedestrians, seemingly with too much time on their hands.

It was my first transformative experience of the day. I had entered a different time, space and place, a vast contrast from what I had experienced when I had left my home in the morning.

461

A short walk to The Gramercy Park Hotel took me past the church where Eleanor Roosevelt had been baptized, whoopee, and a few blocks from where cousin Teddy was born and raised. I walked past the home of Dr. Valentine Mott MD, founder of The New York University School of Medicine, who died suddenly on the evening of April 15, 1865, Good Friday, upon learning of the assassination of Abraham Lincoln. It is an elegant townhouse located on Gramercy Park West. A beautiful collection of middle 19th century townhomes can be found there including one owned and occupied by James Harper, publisher and mayor of New York City, elected in 1844. I peered through the iron fence at Gramercy Park, the only park in Manhattan requiring a key, bearing a statue of John Wilkes Booth's brother, Edwin, New York City's most popular Shakespearian actor in the mid 19th century. Samuel Tilden's home, the unsuccessful Presidential candidate in 1876, stands on the south side of the park and New York City's first cooperative residential building stands on the eastside of the park guarded by two knights in armor.

I turned the corner at Lexington Avenue and recalled that I was gazing upon the home of Cyrus Field, the genius behind the laying of the first successful Trans-Atlantic cable over a century ago. Technology has come a long way since then.

I had entered another contrasting neighborhood, older then the one I had witnessed emerging from the subway at the Flatiron Building. I entered the middle 19th century while at Gramercy Park. The evidence was abundant, rich in history, beauty and wealth. I took a short walk down Irving Place and spotted the home of Washington Irving and Pete's Tavern where

O'Henry wrote "The Gift of the Magi" a classic short story with a well known ending with a classic twist.

After I left The Gramercy Park area I dipped back into the subway and stepped out at 57th Street and Seventh Avenue. As I exited, Carnegie Hall came into view, City Spire, Carnegie Tower and Metropolitan Tower, a span of architecture that covered an entire century and the excavation of a building currently under construction and marketed as One 57, due to be the tallest residential building north of the equator, but only for a short time. Why? Because there are four others under construction within a stone's throw of One 57 (located at 157 West 57th Street) that will each be taller. Check back in a few years' folks and see for yourself.

Within the span of a fifteen minute subway ride I was transformed from the mid-19th century to the next turn of two centuries and literally seeing the future in the making.

The changing palette is extraordinary and the contrast is incredible. To the immediate east of Carnegie Hall are three huge late 20th century structures, Metropolitan Tower (716' tall 1987) and Carnegie Hall Tower (778' tall, 1991) and City Spire (814' tall, 1987) and they appear to be touching each other. Three huge siblings casting shadows on the music hall but never diminishing its glory; setting a backdrop that illustrates the incredible process of change that has always defined New York City.

After I completed my mission, I got back on the subway and was off to The West Village to capture a photograph I needed of 66 Perry Street, the fictitious home of Carrie Bradshaw of "Sex and the City." Incidentally, the home is on the market as of this writing for $9.9 million. I suppose it would be worth a lot more if it were not a favorite stopping place for sightseers, ya think? This time, the clock wound back to the early 19th century. The streetscape appeared as it had back then, over 200 years ago. Various architectural styles such as Federal townhouses, traditional brownstones, neo-classics, Italianate adorned townhouses with tall second floor windows, a la "*piano noble*" meaning noble floor, cats sitting on windowsills gazing indolently, the bark of an agitated dog and others engaged in quiet conversation between several passers by.

In New York City change has transformed the urban landscape, layer upon layer providing evidence that the past keeps a sacred place here always peeking at us. All it takes is just a small dose of imagination to transform you back in time. You can see it, feel it and experience it if only you try.

It's just one of the magical benefits of Manhattan and most of the City as well.

Our neighborhoods, rich in personality, depth and character possess impressive personas and histories that are visible, vibrant and beautiful.

Moving through the streets, one neighborhood suddenly drops off and another greets you. It's a walking historical slide show, one that's rich in architecture, culture and nostalgia. Your eyes and sensibilities provide the switch if you just think it. It's like traveling to many cities, one after the other, through time, all co-existing in one tightly knit space, a quilt, a mosaic blended together forming a vast composite in space and time.

I was immersed in a world where everything happened a million times before. But it was the conscious desire to experience the City more passionately with reverence and reflection that had made a usual day so exceptional.

Perhaps tomorrow will be filled with a new and different type of excitement. If not I'll just grin and love it as a *flaneur* or *promeneur* in Paris, gazing at it all and inhaling the City's endless wonders with joy, deep admiration and awe. Ah, New York City!

Chapter VII
So Now You Know
****

Mannahatta, My O' My. Have You Changed!

Peering into the distance from behind a clump of rocks I saw the future. No, it couldn't be true. My people, my ancestors, have lived here for over four hundred generations and I have been told that this has been written in a white man's book.

We have never disturbed the beauty and abundance The Great Spirit has provided us. We have maintained our land, rivers and forests, our wealth and we have given back to the land, never abusing but always sustaining it with the resources and the tools we could muster. We have always protected and respected the great gifts we have received. We have lived off this rich gorgeous land, the great river and our rich hunting grounds. We have always had all that we needed and do much more; more than we had ever needed and could ever have wished for. The waters have provided an abundance of food and the land has sheltered and delivered sustenance for us.

We have dwelled here peaceably, as a family, a great nation, free from the diseases and weapons brought here by the white man. We have always grown our own food, hunted, fished, clothed ourselves and provided shelter for our families on this "island of many hills" and believed that we would be able to do so forever.

Who could or would ever change this island? We have never imagined that that could happen. Why would anyone ever want to change a perfect place like Manna-hatta?

466

Our years are measured by generations, not by events or inventions. We lived in a world that remained unchanged and for us that was good. As Lenapes we had always been content, self-sufficient and pleased to find a way of life that was inspiring and built upon strong kinships. We have always been closely connected with the land. We were entwined in a symbiotic relationship with the land and waters. We always believed that that relationship would go on forever.

Our dear departed have been interned in the land and they "live" on through our relationship with the soil. No one owned land. It was ours to enjoy, live and work upon as a great people, a glorious nation. We were all attached to it in spirit and it was deeded to us forever in life and the afterlife; bound by kindred spirits, inseparable and everlasting.

We took good care of each other. We sought no material gain, only the gifts of the land and waters all derived from our labors and our faith in our creator, "The Great Spirit." We had no need to change a thing, just to carry on, endure and nurture the land replenishing and restoring the soil. Truly, it was our support system and that was pure and good. We have always loved this island and it had been our home; a safe and secure place to raise our children and teach them the ways of their ancestors building their futures as our forbearers had helped us to built ours.

We are a simple people with strong and proper values together with environmentally responsible customs and values. We know of no other way. Love, truth, justice and peace are our eternal guidelines. We are a caring people embracing love and concern for our families and neighbors. With pride in our communities together with those sacred principles we have always defined our way of life and our great nation.

****

The island of Manna-hatta, the Lenape Indian word for Manhattan, means "island of many hills." Now, not yet 400 years after the first European settlements were established here, thirteen short generations ago, it is the most geologically transformed urban environment on earth, created in such a relatively short time; a heartbeat in the history of mankind.

How would those Lenapes feel if they came back today? "Culture shock!" That's an understatement. How interesting it is to imagine, after the Pilgrims landed on Plymouth Rock in 1620, that this transformation had not yet started. In less than 400 years, look at what time has wrought? How incredible it is to consider that this little island, only 23 square miles, seventeen percent of which is landfill, has become "The Island at the Center of the World" truly, the fulcrum of civilization.

"If you want to see the world, come to New York City." Come and visit Manhattan and become a part of the greatest place on the planet. Celebrate the world, "the melting pot." We thank you, the Lenapes, for providing us, though certainly, not voluntarily, with a treasure that is truly beyond belief. And if there are any Lenapes out there, please return and become a part of our great diversity. We certainly owe you a huge debt of gratitude. Join us and continue to build this great place with us. May love reign in your lives and families for generations to come.

Neighborhood Names, More than You Know!

Is there a troll of neighborhood names? Could it be a secret that someone is paid by the City to sit in a closeted office, in City Hall, appearing promptly at 9 AM, takes their place behind an old oak roll top desk, wearing a translucent green head shade beneath an old copper lamp made of gold plated BX cable and cranking out names of New York City neighborhoods for $65,000 per year plus about $50,000 in annual benefits, sick days, personal days, paid vacations and a free flu and shot annually?

Certainly! With all the new neighborhood names cropping up these days, this official is grossly underpaid for all the good work that is done. The list never stops growing. How do we measure the value of the work that this commissioner does? The benefits to the City are enormous.

"The Commissioner of Neighborhood Identifying Classification" Division or The NIC, works for the Division of Streets within the Department of Transportation under the authority of The City Council, managed by the Manhattan Borough president who is in the pocket of The Mayor. What does all this effort add to the significance of our town?

How boring it was when just a small handful of neighborhood names dotted the City supplementing the names of the five boroughs. Space became scarce, we were confined and living closer together to our neighbors as our population grew the space between us shrunk. These enclaves, or neighborhoods acquired unique character and they have been anointed with names that help define them.

469

What's in a name? Neighborhood names can serve merely as a label or a destination creating a sense of belonging, an identity, and a test for a cabbie, who may barely speak English, which by the way has become less and less important. Or can a name be a destination name created by astute real estate developers who breathe "value" in neighborhoods to create a more cherished sense of place. "Take me to DUMBO!" These names serve as a sense of pride for people, who proclaim, "Now I live in BoCoCa, a new amalgamated name for three neighborhoods, Cobble Hill, Borum Hill and Carol Gardens!"

Isn't it a little insane, or just a little New Yorkish? We, as New Yorkers, have always sought to find new ways to define ourselves, as our City constantly changes, adapting and revising itself; necessitating redefined locales with odd and unusual place names.

Place names of the past won't do. Old names, in many cases, no longer reflect the current venue. "Hell's Kitchen" is now known as Clinton, nothing to do with Hillary or Bill, but rather De Witt Clinton, the inspiration behind the street grid and the Erie Canal. Some have labeled that neighborhood Midtown West in recent times. The Financial District is "FiDi" to the hipsters, trendy and up to date. Not everyone would agree with that new name, most New Yorker's, no doubt, never heard of FiDi! The Flower District, what's left of it, was "Floma", meaning flower market located on 6th Avenue in the high 20's. There's a place known as Viaduct Valley, where the terrain takes a dip between 116th and 134th Streets from Broadway to Amsterdam Avenue or you can get away with "ViVa" the more Latino mode of expression. The Photo District or the Flatiron District is also known as

"The Fashion District" a change due to technology. Perhaps, it should be the Digital District, or "DiDi." South Harlem has anointed itself; "SoHa" and you guessed it, North Harlem, "NoHa" and "SoCa" is a new label for Inwood in northern Manhattan, translation; south of Canada. The dreaded South Bronx or Mott Haven has a new label too, "SoBro" for south Bronx, not bad, eh?

And now West Chelsea, you can call "Wechee" if you like. Interesting, we have an Upper Eastside and a the Lower Eastside but no "Middle East." Instead, we have Murray Hill thanks to the Murray family who were owners of huge tracts of land, back in the 19th century. They were residential developers who built neighborhoods adjacent to Turtle Bay. The British perceived that the bay on the East River, which is not a river but a tidal straight, was shaped like a turtle, along "Blood Alley" another neighborhood, where slaughterhouses reigned where the United Nations complex stands. Interesting that the world's principle peace keeping institution stands on what was once known as "blood alley" ominous, eh?

Neighborhoods have been given names of prominent former New Yorkers such as Carnegie Hill, Hamilton Heights, Washington Heights, Stuyvesant Heights, Bed-Sty, a shortened Bedford-Stuyvesant, Ft. Greene, a Revolutionary War General, Nathaniel Greene, who coordinated Washington's retreat after the disastrous Battle of Brooklyn. Williamsburg is named after the surveyor of Williamsburg. Other less known neighborhoods such as Clinton Hill, Farragut, the Admiral, Morris Heights, Bedford Park, Astoria (Astor), Douglaston and on and on. Jerome Avenue in The Bronx is named after Winston Churchill's grandfather, Leonard Jerome! Oye, let's not get started with street names, we'll never get finished!

It's too bad that many New Yorkers simply cite the name of their borough as their home eliminating the pride or shame of their space place, their neighborhood. I am never satisfied with the borough as an answer of a person's home place because boroughs are quite large and have numerous distinct neighborhoods. Saying you live in Queens or Brooklyn or any other borough tells very little about precisely where someone lives. Why say you are from Queens when you could be a resident of the more desirable Forest Hills Gardens or historic and diverse Jackson Heights? Why not say Jamaica Estates, or North Shore Towers?

Residents of Queens had better be careful because Queens is the only borough not recognized by the U.S. Postal Service as a proper mailing address. Your postal address must have your neighborhood name if you expect to receive mail in Queens. No one addresses a letter or package to Manhattan, New York, because the name of the borough is New York. Our friends in The Bronx, Brooklyn and Staten Island can do so too, use their borough name for mail purposes, so why not Queens? Do you feel sorry for Queens? They had better know where they live; their neighborhood name or their tax bills may go undelivered as well as their refund checks, if they should be so lucky. Queens is the largest borough, 110 square miles, and certainly, Manhattan and Brooklyn have more residents and businesses receiving mail addressed to the name of their respective borough, so why not Queens?

There are three Greenwich Villages now, once called The Ninth Ward then changed to Greenwich Village. Now we refer to that neighborhood as: The West Village, Greenwich Village and The East Village. Alphabet City claims to be part of The East Village but we'd better check with our imagined commissioner. It may become The East East Village down the road. I've always wondered why the Avenues were named with letters instead of names similar to Lexington, Madison or Park. It had occurred to me, Ave ABCD, actually means Assault, Battery, Coma, Death! Not anymore! That neighborhood has come a long way and is one of Manhattan's most vibrant, exciting and amusing places. It's pretty safe now too!

If I were the naming commissioner, I'd choose names that reflect what's going on now, not what went on in the past. For example, Midtown would be Midcity, uptown and downtown signs would be changed to Downcity and Upcity, because we are no longer a town. We're a city! But, nostalgia kicks in and people want to cling to the past, even in a City that constantly lurches to the future. Greenwich Village is not a village so it should be known as Greenwich, period! The Lower East Side aka LES should be Chinatown; the Chinese have virtually taken over the entire neighborhood. Little Italy needs to be renamed Teeny Tiny Italy, Tintaly, with three blocks of restaurants and souvenir shops, many now owned by Chinese shopkeepers. Italians own "Happy Family" and "Lucky Gift" or are they owned by Chinese? Guess! One very cleaver Chinese storeowner named his store in Little Italy, Tony's Gift Shop. It's a dead giveaway because all the employees are Chinese!

473

Battery Park City is another example. The only batteries you'll find there are Duracell and Eveready because the batteries of cannons are long gone except recollections of a distant past where people were assaulted and "batteried" aka assault and battery. How about Times Square? That used to be Longacre Square before Adolf Ochs convinced his pal August Belmont, the man who built and owned our first subway back in 1904, to name the 42nd Street station, Times Square. Hey, Herald Square, aka Bowtie Square, was named after a newspaper too, a competitor of The New York Times, fair and "square" but Times Square ain't square!

Williamsburg, I'd change to Barburg for obvious reasons, on second thought, maybe Condoburg or Condomburg would be even better. Coney Island would become Coney Peninsula because that's what it is now, a peninsula. Turtle Bay should be changed to No Turtle Bay, Spanish Harlem to East Harlem, Greenpoint to Warsawpoint and finally Kips Bay should be renamed The Middle East because that's actually where it is, in between The Upper Eastside and The Lower Eastside.

No one knows exactly how many neighborhoods exist in New York City as boundaries are constantly changing. Ethnically there's a constant ebb and flow and borders are, in many cases, ill defined. But, we do know that wherever New Yorkers call home, it's their neighborhood and they all contribute to make our City a diverse and fascinating place.

Got any names you'd like to offer? Call 311 and ask for the Commissioner of NIC. Stay on the line because you're bound to get a busy signal or "Please hold while I serve another caller" or you'll hear the ubiquitous, "I'm either on the phone or away from my desk."

For those born after 1995, a busy signal is a repeating beep sound that indicates that the phone number that you have "dialed" is in use and the person you have called does not have an automated answering device, a digital retrieval system, call waiting, call forwarding, voice mail or an alternative party to accept your call. But keep trying. In truth they're either helping a client or discussing last night's Yankee game. Perhaps their phones should be placed in the bathrooms along with their desks. That way a lot more work would get done. Ya think? Eh, who knows? You just can't take this stuff too seriously.

Wait! Even tho' the Sign Says "WALK"!

While living on West 60th Street, just off of 9th Avenue, I had walked through the intersection of 59th and 9th hundreds of times.

This intersection is not typical because Ninth Avenue traffic flows one way, southbound or motorists can turn right at 59th Street. There is no street east of 9th Avenue at 59th Street because a co-op complex occupies the ground where 59th Street east of 9th Ave would have been.

I had noticed a disturbing problem regarding the synchronization of the traffic lights and the walk and don't walk signs at 59th Street and 9th Avenue.

Essentially, if a pedestrian crosses 59th Street and the traffic light is green permitting vehicles on Ninth Avenue to proceed, those vehicles who choose to turn right 59th Street are hazards to pedestrians crossing 59th Street. At such times the walk/don't walk sign should be in the "Don't Walk" mode. But, it wasn't synched and the "Don't Walk" mode was set when it should have been in "Walk" mode, when all traffic was halted at a red light. Obviously, this was a very dangerous situation.

A major hospital is located on 59th Street one block west of 9th Ave and The John Jay College of Criminal Justice and numerous elementary, middle and high schools too. As a result, there are lots of young children, college students, doctors and nureses, professors as well as elderly people who visit people who are being hospitalized or trekking to their doctor's offices. There are many who slowly lumber to the hospital for treatment, less able street crossers, as we all know. And, of course, there were hoards of others many with young children in strollers, and last but not least, dog walkers such as I. What to do? Hum?

I called 311, the phone number established by Mayor Bloomberg to report complaints regarding graffiti, items of interest or importance such as the out of synch walk and don't walk signs on 59th and 9th.

I was referred to the DOT, Department of Transportation and began a seven month journey punctuated with tenacity, patience, frustration and a diehard commitment to provide a necessary benefit for my fellow citizens and dogs too. After numerous letters, written confirmations, case numbers, reference numbers and phone calls to and from the DOT I received a letter stating, "The problem had been resolved." That was pure fiction! Nothing had changed. Another dose of tenacity was needed. It really pissed me off and I was more determined then ever to see this through.

How could they have sent me a letter that the problem was resolved if it wasn't? Why seven months? How many people had crossed that intersection, in harm's way, before the DOT finally took care of it? How many people were "near hits" due to the inexcusable inaction of the DOT? Do you want to kill a person? Call the DOT and tell them to change an incorrectly synchronized traffic light and in about seven months, they might, if you stay on their ass take care of it. Unbelievable! Eventually, it was fixed and every time I pass by I smirk and take pride that in that little corner of the world, I made a difference.

Running a City like this must be a nightmare. The point is this: because some citizens do something, say something and are pro-active we have a better chance of making New York City better and safer.

Look both ways, and when the sign reads "WALK" because you never know who, if anyone, including the City is looking out for you! People often cross streets without looking because they rely on the accuracy of mechanical devices that may just provide information that could kill them. Why? People install them, people who "work" for the DOT. I must admit however there are nearly 12,000 traffic signals in New York City and the overwhelming number of them work just fine but don't be the one who crosses the street without looking, you never know!

One mistake . . . and you're "road pizza", and that's not the kind of pizza New York City is famous for!!

Shop Smart!

You can purchase just about anything in New York City. Those who sell merchandise or provide services such as retailers, wholesalers, street hawkers, newsstand clerks, artisans, crafters, scammers, food vendors and all the rest provide limitless choices. "Caveat Emptor" buyer beware! In New York City you are, to some, prey, with open season here, where the unscrupulous ply their trade, side by side with the righteous.

You can get "screwed" "rooked" "ripped off" "taken" "snagged" "tagged" "flipped" "gipped" or "beaten down" in a heartbeat. How would you know? How can you find out?

As Syms, a defunct retail clothing chain, chanted its mantra, "An educated consumer is our best customer." You have got to do your homework or you'll find out the hard way. "The Big Apple" can be rotten to the core and not sweet at all. Here's how to ensure that you're getting your money's worth and avoid being cheated.

Some vendors of electronics such as video, audio and photo equipment, binoculars, ipads and similar items perceive people as targets for "highway robbery schemes." So, "you better shop around!" Independent stores located in tourist areas such as Times Square have a reputation for being "tourist traps." Many of my clients have purchased cameras sold at approximately 40% less at B & H Photo located at 34th Street and 9th Avenue, which is closed on Saturdays. P. T. Barnum, a New Yorker of circus fame, built his emporium and circus business on the mantra, "There is a sucker born every minute." There are exceptions, be one! Sometimes, there are two or even three born every minute! In Times Square they swarm like flies!

Be aware of the old "bait and switch" scam. That's the oldest "trick in the book" used by unscrupulous retailers who display cameras, computers and the like in well lit store windows at incredibly low prices to lure you in. Once you express your interest in a specific item with an unbelievably low price that you saw in their window, they tend to "push" a "similar" item extolling its superior benefits and espouse the flaws or defects of the item featured in their window.

I have spoken to many visitors who have lamented their disappointment by purchasing the right item at the wrong price or vice versa. Don't be impressed by the "Licensed by the New York City Department of Consumer Affairs" sign, displayed in their windows. This has no more value than the Parent's Magazine Seal of Approval, or the Better Business Bureau sticker either! It's worthless and provides no protection whatsoever. Don't even go there, the DCA is asleep except on payday! Try Consumer Reports, friend's recommendations and your brain. Tripadvisor is a good source too; it's all about what customers have written. That should work and follow your instincts.

The Department of Consumer Affairs is mandated to regulate sightseeing guides too. I have never seen or heard of an unlicensed guide getting snagged by a City official nor have I ever been asked to whip out my license. I've written letters to the Mayor that we, licensed City of New York guides, have demonstrated our competency as far as knowing a minimal amount of information needed to get a passing grade giving us the privilege of paying the fee for the license. They allow out of town guides and unlicensed locals to take work away from licensed guides in front of their noses. Those who are supposed to enforce the laws do not and who might that be? Hum? The cops don't know this, I've even asked a few, huh?

Let's allow cops from elsewhere, who are not licensed in New York City to make "collars" here too. Why not hire out of town cops, who are not licensed to work here? The City allows unlicensed out of town guides to work here so why not Firemen, Police and others too? Sure, when hair grows on my palm!

Rise Up! The City employees couldn't care less if you are "hustled" or scammed. Who's paying them to not protect licensed New York City sightseeing guides? Good question! If you have a problem, sure, run down to 42 Broadway, fifth floor, and complain to a DCA employee! Whether they're awake, have a pulse or their eyes are open.

Fill out some forms and get on the plane, train, bus or car back home, minus the $750 that you paid for a $250 camera or a tour with an unlicensed guide who doesn't know The Chrysler Building from The Empire State. Adios amigos! Your fault! It's too bad but you should have known better! Honestly, there are exceptions at the DCA but don't waste your time. As George W. Bush said, "Fool me once shame on me! Fool me twice, ah ah shame on a a a duh me?!#%){:-}. He should be our next commissioner! "Scammers Wanted Dead or Alive" Vote for Dubbyah! "Bring 'it on! Eehaa!" Wanted Dead of Alive!

Souvenirs! That's another story that requires a little common sense before you plunge. Canal Street is the best place to buy "I Love NY" T Shirts, hats, knock off bags and watches, all made in, you guessed it, downtown Ka-Ching, as in the sound of their cash registers, or in the back hills of a country that you never heard of!

Be careful about buying those high-end knock-offs because it's illegal and they're made by young children who work long hours for pennies. You could get arrested for buying Louis Vuitton, Hermes, Channel bags or Rolex watches. I've seen it happen! The NYPD have their hands in the pockets of some of these luxury brand companies who are determined to "protect" their brands. I've heard from a very reliable source. Very! Currently, The City Council is considering passage of a law that would impose up to one year in prison and a one thousand dollar fine for buying such "swag." The prison sentence doesn't bother me but the $1,000 fine has me shakin'! Shakin'!

If you are suckered into a basement or a sequestered room behind a store or even a van, with blackened windows parked on a side street, by rouge vendors, most often Asian, to buy "knock-offs" then you are taking a big risk!

I know of an experience when police arrested several tourists, women from Belgium. They spent the night in jail, got into a whole bunch of trouble, not to mention a ruined vacation. Canal Street, sure, go for the bargains, but be careful, you're taking a big chance on the knockoffs! Besides, if you love that stuff so much, buy the real deal! You only have to pay for it once.

Recently I walked into a Coach store in Columbus Circle and saw a gorgeous leather attaché case for my computer. It was priced at $368. I told the saleswoman that if they knocked off 25%, I'd buy it.

She knocked off $100, 27%! Just ask, what have you got to loose?

Another example: I provided a tour for fourteen teenage girls from Greenville, SC and during our tour we were walking around Times Square when one of them asked where they could buy a real New York hotdog on the street. I took them over to the nearest vendor and asked him,

"How much is it going to cost all these young ladies for a 'dog?'"

"Three dollars." he replied.

"Look buster, I'm a New Yorker, got it? We ain't payin' three bucks. Try again."

"Okay, two fifty."

"Your getting close my friend."

"Okay two"

"Okay ladies line up."

The point is this . . . ask!

Barter with vendors on Canal Street. You usually can save money. Besides, what's the harm of trying? Do everything you can to appear and speak like a New "Yawka". If they perceive that you are a tourist, then your chance of cutting deals gets a lot slimmer. "They see you coming!" I've seen this in action and my intervention has resulted in big savings for many of my guests. Vendors know when you're a New Yorker. They get it right, most of the time. Practice saying "cauffee" and "becauuze"! Tawk, the tawk and wawk the wawk. They're the biggest scam artists on the planet in the opinion of some green eyed newbies.

Macy's is an excellent place to make a purchase. The quality is good, the selection is huge and the world's largest store has built its reputation by offering their customers very good value. If you get screwed there

483

you're deaf, dumb and or blind. Go to your room! Try to "catch" Saks, between 49th and 50th Streets on 5th Avenue, when they are running a major sale. The staff is very predatory because "they work on commission" period.

If you have tons of money, don't like money or just love to get rid of it than Madison Avenue, New York City's Rodeo Drive, Fifth Avenue, Soho, The West Village and The Meatpacking District is the place for you! Was Rodeo Drive, named to drive money from your wallets as if you were at a rodeo, eeh haa! All the prestige brands have set up shop there, the quality is "high-end" and so are the prices, insane. So, if paying top prices is not a factor for you then bring a fat wallet to Madison Avenue loaded with plenty of plastic and you'll go home feeling a lot lighter. Talk to your money, and say "Bye bye!"

Buying books on the street can be a great bargain. The best streets to buy books are Broadway, on the Westside of the street, from 72nd Street up to and passed Fairway toward 80th Street and on Sixth Avenue just south of where a Barnes & Noble once stood, south of 8th Street in "The Village." Street vendors sell hard cover best sellers for much less than Barnes & Noble and there's no tax either! Street vendors will tell you it's included in the price. Sure it is, they're knocking off 8.875% and mailing their checks to Albany, sure! Do we care, nah!

Watches: Take 57th Street, where Tourneau is located, and subtract 10 and that equals 47th Street and the discounts are huge. But, if you buy used merchandise, be very careful. Get the factory and warranty documents if you're purchasing a watch that is nearly new. Compare the serial number on the watch with the serial number on the guarantee certificate. You could save 50% or more on a slightly used watch compared with the retail price for a new one. Watches are like used cars, they depreciate like a stone. "Just be smart!" Pretend that you're a New Yorker! Shop around; put together some comparative prices. Don't flaunt your love for any item. Play the game, "I have another one that's very similar to this." "It seems just a little too big." "It's a bit over my price range."

Diamond Jewelry: The Gemological Institute has created a classification system that grades diamonds as to weight, color, flaws, clarity, table (depth), etc. If you are seeking a specific size and type of diamond then go to 47th Street between 5th and 6th Avenue and visit a number of vendors. Bargain with them because the first price is not the "last price" as in "give me your last price first." There's a big difference between the two, your money! It's the culture. Let them know that you're shopping around. If you return, let them know that you are ready to buy but you're still somewhat apart in price. You like "the goods" but the price is a bit too high.

Ask, "Do you want to do business right now?" That's a question diamond vendors will generally ask you! Try to take control of the conversation; it's the way to go. They'll come down, be patient. If you come back they will assume that you've shopped around and coming back is a sure sign that you haven't found anything better at a comparable price. Try to inject the element of competition meaning, there are other "goods" out there that you are considering. Don't seem anxious, play poker! Use your wife or significant other and apply the "good cop bad cop scenario." She's anxious and you're not. Say things like, "What do you need it for?" "We'll call Harry (the jeweler) when we get home. He's been good to us."

Never accept the first price offered in an establishment that can cut the price. Never make your buying decision in the first store you enter if you are buying an expensive item, especially a "blind" item like diamonds. Watch out for shills. That's someone who works for the vendor, stands on your side of the counter, pretends to be a customer who praises the merchant as an honest and fair trader. Follow your instincts. "If it walks like a duck . . ." then get the hell out of there. Most often, if a buyer gets screwed it's just as much their fault as the vendor's. "It takes two to tango." Do your homework before you buy and remember, these merchants are more anxious to make the sale then you are to buy. You can walk around all day and buy nothing. Your life doesn't depend on spending your money.

The point is, find the bottom price or a price that you are willing to pay. Respect their need to make a profit. Generally, you can sense when their price has hit bottom and if your homework reveals that the comparisons you've made have convinced you that you've got a good deal then make the right decision. After your due diligence you should be able to sense the right deal.

If you are seeking an expensive diamond then ask for the gemological certificate and get some comparison prices. If they're honest, why shouldn't they accommodate your request? If not, "bye-buy"! Then, use that information as a tool to make comparisons up and down the street. Remember, you're not buying insulin. You can always live without a piece of jewelry especially if you're unsure about the article or price. Remember, if you don't buy, you're stuck with your money and then you've lost nothing.

Crime, Way Down and "How"!

Any city, large or small, thrives, shrivels or dies, based on its rate of crime. All other things being equal, even a city with a well-educated populace, good affordable housing, an effective education scheme, adequate and available medical care, a competent government, clean streets, nearly void of street trash, will be doomed if the crime rate is off the charts. Its tax base flees in large numbers and public and private investment dives into an abyss. That results in further reductions of vital services and a continued hastening of a downward spiral that creates a city that goes straight to hell in a hand basket.

In fact, crime was so high in New York City a generation ago that The Statue of Liberty had both hands up! "Get 'em up!"

The chasm for New York City occurred between the 1950's to the early 1990's. There was no foreseeable way out. The City was on the verge of bankruptcy in 1975 and was forced to turn to Washington, D.C. for help; loan guarantees, not hard cash. Albany, the seat of our state government, didn't love us either, even though New York City is a cash cow for the State. Taxpaying citizens fled New York City in droves seeking refuge in the suburbs where schools were generally much better, streets were safer, taxes were lower and the quality of life was far superior albeit much less exciting. This mass exodus exceeded over 700,000 people, the largest migration out of New York City in history except, by percentage, when the Brits entered New York City in 1776.

"The Bronx is Burning," "Fort Apache," The Taking of Pelham 123," are movies that depicted this City in ruins. The Con Ed Riots, The Son of Sam, murderer of innocent young couples randomly, terrorized the City, putting a grip on New York City that was already going "south". Failing schools, illegal drugs ruled, street crime soared and the City's coffers ran dry. These and other horrors of daily "life" left people trapped in an urban environment that was living on the edge, a cesspool of squalor, crime, corruption, madness and mayhem.

The Con Ed Riots, the night of the most arrests in the history of New York City exemplified a City gone wild as thousands of marauding desperados seized the "opportunity" as an invitation to loot, plunder, burn neighborhoods, destroy businesses and unleash their frustrations built up over many years. Pent up anger and resentment spilled over into a ferocious frenzy especially in The Bronx, Brooklyn and Harlem. New designer drugs, made "on the cheap" were given away to twelve and thirteen year old kids. That snagged them into a downward spiral compelling them to do anything necessary to finance their daily "fix."

Then, part two, the inevitable conversion to paid drugs, pushing the crime rate up, through the roof! Street gangs roamed, street gangs ruled. They used the subway to transport themselves to the best neighborhoods to pillage and plunder wealthy citizens who were not found upon the streets in their own neighborhoods.

Places that had previously attracted the wealthiest, the most beneficial taxpaying solid citizens on the planet could not have been lured back, even if their apartments were free for the taking.

Streets were strewn with massive piles of trash. Abandoned cars remained on the streets for months providing housing for rats and vermin. Most of these "car-cases" were shells, without wheels, or seats, missing fenders and various parts that thieves removed and sold to buy "junk" the lexicon for heroin.

It was a vicious cycle, a daily bill of fare, defining an urban landscape that would not be tolerated today. Nowadays, we have mustered the tools to prevent this. We were, a City out of control without any prospects for the future.

Discipline was a "joke" in the public schools. Kids did just about whatever they wanted. Teachers and administrators had their hands tied by mandates restricting the means to impose discipline resulting in diminished expectations, plunging results and morale to the lowest levels never seen before. Most children, in ghetto neighborhoods, learned little or nothing. Only a precious few had the good fortune to receive a decent education in the dwindling number of good neighborhoods ones with balanced, stable homes, where good parenting was the norm.

Massive layoffs, by the City administration, were across the board without exception. Services diminished to appalling levels, firehouses were shut, education, sanitation, police, health and hospital, public assistance, referred to as "welfare" back then were terribly underfunded, mismanaged and understaffed. Our Transportation infrastructure maintenance was a disaster. Potholes were ignored, graffiti was everywhere, public trashcans were overflowing, and parks were unsafe, not maintained at all and in deplorable condition. Much of the City was a no man's land. Sanitation Department agents ticketed storeowners for littered storefronts and sidewalks, harassing business owners. The agents were under pressure to raise needed cash. Perhaps a quota was imposed to ticket the City to death to get it back to fiscal health. It was clearly a scam of desperation created by Mayor Abe Beame who urgently needed to raise revenue in a City starved for cash. I had experienced this personally as a tax paying, storeowner on West 23rd Street who was providing employment for some hard working New Yorkers. I went nuts time and again when I was issued summonses by a Department of Sanitation agent many times who saw a piece of paper on the sidewalk in front of my store after I had just swept the sidewalk! It truly was a City on the verge of complete collapse, pure and simple.

The establishment of "Big MAC" was the significant breakthrough that created the solution. The Municipal Assistance Corporation, under the guidance of Felix Royhaton, with Federal guarantees in place, sold billions of dollars in bonds funding the City, improving its credit rating and enabling the process of rebuilding the future of New York City. President Ford, who refused to support the federal loan guarantees, as expressed by the Daily News headline, FORD TO CITY, DROP DEAD, finally "got it". New York City was the best investment the Feds could make because if this City went "belly up" then other municipalities throughout the country would have tanked too. The United States without a solvent New York City! That's just not possible.

The 1980's were a major disaster. Crack and crank were both big hits on the illegal drug-shopping hit parade. In the late 80's and early 90's Mayor "Do Something Dave" Dinkins finally did something about

491

crime but it was too little too late. His administration was beyond rescue. Although he hired 5,000 additional cops, due to his stalling and indecisive nature, he laid the red carpet for Rudy to take the reins. It was not possible to get all those cops trained and on the streets before his run for a second term as mayor. Deservingly so, he has the singular distinction of being the first African American mayor of New York City and the only mayor of a major American city to loose his bid for re-election. "Good job, Dave!"

The Crown Heights Riots exploded and became a violent and horrid stain on the City. As Dinkins stood by idling and turning the other way we experienced a leadership void. No decisive action was taken. The situation was out of control and a city that's not in control is a recipe for disaster. What the hell was he thinking about?

The riots were triggered by the accidental and tragic death of a young black child who was killed by a young Hasidic Jewish man, Yankel Rosenbaum when his car collided into the child during a parade memorializing Menachem Mendel Schneerson, the Lubvaitcher Rebbe. A black man, Limerick Nelson, stabbed Mr. Rosenbaun to death at the scene and that ignited a riot that lasted for three days. This was the final straw for Mr. Dinkins and it propelled Rudy Giuliani into City Hall. Surprisingly though, without Staten Island, having the largest Italian-American population of any county in The United States, percentage wise, whose overwhelming number of votes was cast for Giuliani then he would not have succeeded to defeat Dinkins. Amazing! With all that was going on it took Staten Island to save New York City from an administration that was hopelessly incompetent. I can't imagine what life would have been like here under another four years of the Dinkins administration. Smile Dave, your neighborhood is safe now! The man could play a darn good game of tennis and was quite the nifty dresser but a little too many double-breasted threads, eh Dave, couldn't save you? Be well! He did the best he could. Imagine, without Staten Island, "the forgotten borough" Giuliani would have lost and perhaps never run for mayor again. This renaissance, the one that New York City has been experiencing began in 1993 and without Giuliani it never would have happened. New Yorkers owe Staten Island a huge debt of gratitude and New Yorkers don't even know it. I Love Staten Island!

On January 1st 1993 Rudy took over the reins at City Hall. He began his administration by focusing on crime reduction. By taking the City back from criminal elements, the street punks and the mafia who controlled unions, sanitation, construction, trucking and much more, he launched this City into a new era, a renaissance that continues to this day!

William Bratton, the former Chief of Police in Boston, a vigorous advocate of an innovative new policing concept featured in The Atlantic Monthly, on March 1982, "Broken Windows: Restoring Order and Reducing Crime in Our Communities" by Catherine M. Coles and George Kelling provided the framework for a new anti-crime strategy.

The key elements of the crime initiative were these:

"Community policing" a more direct approach, closer and more effective communication, applied concern that compelled the police to change their habitual routine of cruising in cars. More police were assigned

493

to foot patrol, projecting themselves as caring citizens, connectors and protectors in their respective communities. They learned what was going on from the locals, where the trouble was and who the culprits were. They got to know the residents and they experienced the communities "up close and personal." Over time, they had earned the trust and respect of their respective communities and used all the valuable information they could muster to target crime in a way that had never been done before. It was brilliant, efficient and effective. Their assets were applied in the most effective way, making the difference and uplifting the City.

The police focused on "quality of life" crimes such as; public urinating, smoking and selling marijuana in the streets; alcohol consumption in public, jumping over the subway turnstiles, 170,000 incidences per day, aggressive panhandling, loitering, "squeegee boys" hostile men and boys who wiped car windshields for money, street prostitution, etc.

Police Commissioner Bratton converted numerous buses into portable police stations and streamlined the paper work process for arrests as well. Approximately one-third of those who were arrested, for quality of life crimes were either carrying illegal weapons, illegal drugs or were wanted for "priors." They were removed from the streets and they paid the price. Truly, the City initiated "The Tipping Point" as expressed in Malcolm Gladwell's book that bears that title.

Governor Pataki signed legislation that stiffened sentencing laws for convicted criminals and all but eliminated the "suspended sentence first offense" refrain that resulted in the incarceration of thousands of criminals the got them off the streets providing further dramatic reductions in crime. Those criminals, removed from the streets, sent a message to their ilk that they too would be next. We had suddenly become a City that just wasn't going to take it anymore. The chant, "You do the crime, you do the time" replaced the mantra "first offense, suspended sentence."

Another factor that complimented these efforts was the legalization of abortion in The United States in 1973 (Roe v. Wade) although in no way was that the intent of the court's decision. By the early 1990's many children, who would have been born, many from impoverished and incompetent mothers in blighted urban ghettos never "hit" the streets. Certainly, Roe v. Wade was not decided on the basis of reducing crime however, there are statistics that confirm that this ancillary effect of the Supreme Court's decision was a sidecar and remains an incessantly controversial issue.

Another leg of the stool was the improvement of the streetscapes, vitally important for an aggressive and effective anti-crime initiative.

If you enter a city riddled with graffiti, marred by broken beer, malt liquor, vodka and rum bottles, and littered with trash, had an abundance of vacant stores and abandoned cars, large dogs that are unleashed roaming the streets, hookers plying their trade conveying the impression that no one cares and no one was watching is a recipe for failure. It's guaranteed that you would get the hell of there, in a New York minute!

However, on the other hand, if you find yourself in a city that is clean, has no graffiti, no "broken windows" an absence of unbundled piles of trash and a well maintained environment with freshly planted flowers, trees and potted plants, tables and chairs placed in numerous streets intended to reduce vehicular traffic and increase space for foot traffic then the right message is received. The message is this: Someone cares and is watching and this city is in control and you're not! All of that provides a major deterrence to criminal activity according to Keller and Coles and to all us here in New York City.

Take a look at the images of New York City in the 1960's '70's and '80's and have a look today. The difference is huge. The level of voluntary compliance and civic pride in the City has soared and the crime rate has plunged to the City's lowest levels in history.

It is unfortunate that more cities throughout the world have not adopted these policing strategies. With the reduction in crime in New York City by over 75% due to the efforts of Mayor Giuliani, Mayor Bloomberg, Police Commissioners Bratton and Kelly, the NYPD as well as the body politic, New York City has enjoyed a spectacular renaissance, one that hopefully will continue for many years to come.

One hopes that when New York City falls on difficult economic times, such as we had experienced in 2009, our leaders will not permit a backslide by attempting to balance state and city budgets by slashing funding for those strategies that have gotten us out of that mess a generation ago. Investing in crime reduction is simply a self-liquidating investment. "An ounce of prevention is worth a pound of cure." Crime robs us all and that includes the coffers of our vital government agencies.

Sure, you can save money today by slashing budgets. However, when the tax base flees, businesses close, unemployment rises, some people become desperate and do stupid things that will, in the long run, cost us much more blood and treasure. The lessons of the past are clear.

Investing in the City is the path to prosperity and the failure to "fix broken windows" leads to the inevitable failure of urban life. Let's hope that history doesn't repeat itself and that our governments, our courage and will to invest has provided the means to propel New York City to continue moving forward reaching greater heights that will raise our living standards, productivity and love for each other and our great City.

Food Shopping, Manhattan-style

Many times people who do not live here have asked me a peculiar question: "How do you go food shopping in New York City?"

It never occurred to me that would evoke so much curiosity. What's so strange or unusual about buying food for your pantry in New York City? After some reflection, I realized that we do not buy our groceries like most people who live elsewhere.

Typically, people from other locales drive their cars to big box supermarkets and purchase enough food and household needs to last a week or so. That's just not possible in Manhattan unless you have a car and a place to put all your provisions. When you leave the supermarket you'll need to have four pairs of arms to load and unload your bounty. Modern day food carts are frequently equipped with brakes with locking wheels when the cast is beyond close proximity of the supermarket. Even if you drove to your local supermarket you would not be able to wheel your goods to your car.

The risk of putting your vehicle in front of your home in New York City, typically a building that is some distance from your parking lot, if you have one, may cost you a parking ticket and the combined cost of your food bill together with that parking ticket will make you wish you had eaten out more often, as many New Yorkers do. You would have wished you had eaten most of your bounty on your way home saving you the trouble of figuring out how to carry it all! Hey, with 24,000 restaurants in this town many folks apparently still can afford to eat out!

New Yorkers limit what they buy to all that they can carry. Therefore, New Yorkers shop for food almost on a daily basis. Buying necessities weekly is out of the question. Rather, most New Yorkers often bring home what is needed until tomorrow plus staples such as milk, coffee, salad, bread, ketchup, eggs and OJ, etc. It's about "fill-ins" on a day-to-day basis. As a result of logistics, I see young people using granny wagons; those foldable steel cages wheelies to move their food from the market to their door. I have one but I refuse to use it. I feel that it's an assault on my effort to guise my age. Honestly, it's time for me to just get over it.

At times, New Yorkers take several daily trips, on foot, to buy food because they cannot carry all they need in one trip. Also, often one food store doesn't "carry" everything needed or one store or another has better pricing or selections then the store that sells a favorite brand of whatever.

My neighborhood, 97th Street off Columbus Avenue provides many choices. For example, if I choose to buy my daily needs and go south to 96th Street I pay more, a lot more. For example, a one-liter bottle of Canada Dry Club Soda is priced at $1.69 on 96th Street whereas; at 100th Street a two-liter bottle costs $1.25. That's a 63% difference in price!

Prices vary quite a bit from neighborhood to neighborhood. These disparities are based on retail rent rates, competitive pressures, the willingness of shoppers to compare prices, the distance from their homes and the motivation to walk a few blocks out of their way to save money. Retailers perceive what they can "get for each item" and charge the highest price people are willing to pay without suffering significant loss in trade. As with running any business isn't that what they are supposed to do? Most New

499

Yorkers will not run around their neighborhood buying watermelon in one store and club soda in another. That strategy has increased since the great recession of 2009, which, as I understand is still with us, for many, in 2014.

I have become much more conscious of food prices since 2000 and have saved a bundle. Don't believe the statistics that flow out of Washington regarding inflation. All you have to do is do your own price check and gasp at the prices that you're paying now compared with what you were paying a few years ago. Washington tosses out more bullshit then a Texas rodeo.

Whole Foods, terrific food merchandisers, with new stores opening throughout the City, has a huge following. Their prepared foods are pretty good, the quality and selection of their products is unbeatable. But, their organic buzzword eliminates such items as Oriole cookies, Heinz Ketchup and Hellman's Mayonnaise. Whole Foods is organic and they're purveyors of "green" minded food. Their wares are displayed very impressively and are thoroughly organized. They have the longest lines and the fastest check out system I've ever seen. It's truly amazing how fast they get people out of there. Express lines flow in lightening speed, most often; aided by staffers who direct shoppers to the next available register together with a spectacularly high tech system that generates order and efficiency. Medium size boiled and peeled shrimp are about $17.99 a pound whereas on Canal Street they're $5.99 a pound, but once frozen. I generally buy shrimp, if I have the urge, only when I happen to be in the Canal Street area. You can also get three live lobsters there for about $21.00.

Lobsters hate Canal Street. They think they're worth more than that!

Recently, while at Whole Foods, I had gathered seven items, went straight to the "10 items or less" sign, first in line. A woman entered behind me and challenged me to get behind her because I had entered from the front and not from the proper entrance at the rear but I did position myself at the end of the line anyway. "The Enforcer" had arrived! You know the type!

"Lady, you have about 16 items!" I told her. She was indignant and complained to numerous other customers about me! I gave her a New York City retort,

"Who are you, my principal? Just keep your lid on, get a grip, and get on the right line lady."

Truly, she was an exceptional woman!

Big Box stores have just started invading Manhattan. What took so long? Perhaps it's zoning laws, the high cost of space and the recognition that there's not enough parking to enable the high volume of customers they need to make it to park. Without a car, how much can a Manhattanite carry out of a store and take home? Perhaps that is what has prevented the building of big box stores in Manhattan in the past.

The average purchase per shopper, per trip, is unlikely to meet that type of retailer's business model, therefore, big box stores do exist in the outer boroughs where real estate is far less costly, with ample sized parking lots that take up vast amounts of space. Costco has a few stores, in Brooklyn and Queens, not too far from Manhattan. They opened one in East Harlem a few years ago, east of Pleasant Ave.

501

It's about four long blocks from the Lexington subway line. Word is that their sales are reaching surprising proportions and I'm a bit shocked! I thought, who's going to shop there? People from out of Manhattan will not drive here because they've got the same stuff in the outer boroughs and Manhattanites are nearly 80% carless, on a per family basis, the lowest percentage of car ownership of any county in The United States. Costco is far from stupid and they must have done their homework. Apparently, there are enough folks who live in Manhattan with cars that are attracted to what they have to offer.

The prices at the big box stores are terrific, the quality is up there and the selection is quite good. However, unless you need to buy huge bulk quantities of spaghetti or corn chips, etc. then this is not the place for you. Besides, where is the average Manhattan resident going to put all this stuff? The bathtub or terrace, if you have either one it may work. Those are the only places I know of to stash all your stuff unless you park your bootie all over your apartment.

Fifth Avenue, Tribeca, Park Avenue, West End Avenue, older uptown prewar buildings, Central Park West and Sutton Place residents have extra space, but they also have lots of money therefore, Costco is not their likely shopping choice. Next time I'm seated next to an odorous person on a bus or subway I'll just suspect that they have food and cleaning products stored in their tub. I'll be kind and keep my mouth shut, change my seat, or stand near a woman who's over dosed with cheap perfume that was probably purchased at a big box store, right here in Manhattan.

In most cases those folks who live in cavernous apartments don't do their own food shopping anyway. They hire help to do that for them. Chances are they don't have food at home. That's what restaurants are for! No doubt, restaurant owners send their employers to Costco to stock up their shelves, eh!

I have taken the subway, two trains, then got on a bus, walked about five blocks, a one-hour trip to get to Costco in Queens. Getting back is a different story. When I exit the store, with my wagon filled to the brim, I look around for an old TLC (taxi and limousine commission) "black car" for hire, taxi or van and get a ride back to Manhattan for about $20. The cost of the ride, factored into the savings is well worthwhile and the Latino music in the car is a big plus. Red tassels swing and sway around the perimeter of the front and rear windshields. I also love the little toy dog with its head swinging and swaying as we move along dodging and dipping into the potholes. I love doing this. It's so New York City!

Fresh Direct, an on-line grocery purveyor provides a terrific service. Set up your account online, enter your order on their website and it's delivered directly to your apartment in a refrigerated truck within your two-hour requested time frame and delivered in sealed corrugated boxes. Their slogan is "Only Our Customers Are Spoiled." This service is perfect for hungry New Yorkers who love delivery and the convenience. That's how we live, "delivery"! You can get anything delivered in New York City, anything, anytime!

For me one of the best "games in town" is Associated Supermarket on West 100th Street. If you spend over thirty bucks you can have your order delivered with you as you leave the store, in a wheeled cart pushed directly to your front door at no charge by a happy young lad who appreciates your $5 tip more than you can image. The prices are terrific because at 100th Street, the only way to survive, for many of the nearby residents is to grab "ghetto pricing." When it comes to money nobody is stupid and the poorest among us are no exception.

Many small food stores, particularly in lower income neighborhoods, provide excellent service. Korean delis are consistently the best, offering excellent service, wide selections in clean and well-kept establishments. They use their limited space efficiently and with science. Their stores are spotlessly clean, well stocked and they are open for long hours. Some are open 24/7. There is always fresh hot coffee, excellent "salad bars" both hot and cold. Thousands upon thousands of New Yorkers take home a pound of food ready to eat daily. The best one in the City, that I've seen, is located at 5th Avenue between 18th and 19th Streets in Manhattan. Take a look. It's an amazing place, textbook perfect and a great attraction for visitors too.

Who needs a kitchen? What's a kitchen? I think my aunt has one. Kitchens exist for people to talk to each other, right; they're the new living room. Someday kitchens will disappear in New York City, it's inevitable. Eventually, they'll become sub-rentals for those who can't afford to live here; in the kitchen they'll go. Or perhaps closet space, which makes a lot of sense too. The day will surely come, in Manhattan when we'll be sleeping like horses, standing up!

Gourmet food stores such as Zabar's on the Upper Westside, Citarella and Dean & Deluca, provide phenomenal selections, great food and more than 100 varieties of cheese. That's more than in France! Prepared foods and exotics are abundant too, however; you'll pay a hefty price for all the choices and terrific quality. They're worth the price if you're a real gourmet, have lively taste buds and abundant cash. Check out the Food Market at Grand Central Terminal at the Lexington Avenue entrance at 43rd Street. That's the place for those with thick wallets.

And then there's Fairway, that's another story. It's the leader in big New York style grocery stores with price, quality and value all up there. It's excellent! There are two on the Upper Westside, one beneath the Westside Highway at 128th Street with ample parking boasting a huge selection. The deli department is first rate and they have a "cold room" with varsity jackets hanging outside the door to keep customers warm as they roam for fresh fish, juices, milk, meats, etc. Now there's a Fairway in Red Hook, Brooklyn too and it enjoys a huge volume of business. The original is on Broadway at 75th Street, you can't miss it. Walk in and experience a place that's unique, "Like no other."

Chelsea Market, a major draw has marshaled the fuel that changed the Meatpacking District, is not only a place to eat but also to hang out, shop, drink, people watch and kill half a day. Check out the fish, sushi and lobster, but don't inhale in that store if you hate the smell of fresh fish. Grab a few shrimp and try eating with your eyes open, after you've paid for them buster! Ahhhh! This district, The Meatpacking District is now a hangout for the "rich and famous" and others who seek to find mates, matches, fast lane friendship and love. The clubs, bars, rooftop scenes and restaurants have grown like weeds. Perhaps the name of the 'hood should be changed to the Pack Meeting District! We do things differently in New York City and no matter how you slice it; we have choices that are unbeatable. You, unlike your wallet, may fatten up a bit too! Bon Appetite but one bus or subway seat per customer! Consider, New York City consumes the equivalent of a fifteen-mile long freight train filled with food, daily. *Mangia, fres,* munch, dine, chew and swallow New York! Burp!

Take a Hike and Watch for the Bike!

"Look both ways" and "Don't cross the street in the middle, in the middle, in the middle in the middle in the middle of the block"! That was an infocommercial jingle that blanketed the airwaves for many years way back in the 1960's. Those infocommercials heightened our awareness of the danger of cars while crossing streets. That's nothing compared with the danger brought to you by many of those bicycle messengers who plague the streets of New York City! "Walk" and "Don't Walk" signs won't help you, looking before you cross, in the direction of the oncoming traffic won't help you, praying won't help you and body armor won't help you either. What will? Your only defense from bicycles, especially bike messengers, is to look both ways and get back on the sidewalk, where there are fewer bikes. Messengers are extremely aggressive because they are compensated based on the number and distance of "runs" they complete. Therefore, they are always in a hurry. They routinely disobey the traffic laws, run red lights; and pedal in any direction they please. Many of these bike maniacs use "road" bikes that have no brakes! "Road" bikes stop by not peddling and putting pressure on the back pedal, which slowly brings their bikes to a gradual stop, we hope! Stopping slowly is an iffy proposition if you happen to be in their way. It puts you in grave danger as in danger of winding up in a grave.

They weave in between people crossing the street anticipating where pedestrians will be when they arrive in approximately a half a second and they provide no warning. Some, who are more considerate, yuck, shout or whistle a warning that is seldom heard above the street noise and barely missing numerous people who glare or shout at them in the process.

You don't know whom you are dealing with so it's best to keep your mouth shut and avoid a confrontation. Many 'cycle messengers are very angry people and when you're in their line of fire, you could lose, big time. Don't let it happen. Many of them are nuts! Occasionally, they'll turn around and confront you angrily in the most intimidating and threatening way. They are pissed off at you because you have slowed them down. Never mind your injury, they couldn't care less. It's about their time, and in that business time is money, and nothing else matters, nothing.

Being hit, head on, by a bicycle carrying a man weighing over two hundred pounds, together with the weight of the bike moving at high speed, is potentially life threatening. There's plenty of evidence of that. On average over 500 people are hospitalized annually due to bike collisions. Many more are hit because not all go to the hospital for necessary treatment, schmucks. Far too many of the injuries are extremely serious; kneecaps removed by bicycle pedals, fractures, concussions, broken bones, ligaments, heart attacks and organ damage. A doctor that treated me for a broken finger, a specialist, told me that he was putting his kids through college from income derived from pedestrian related bicycle injury patients. There is no doubt that walking is now the most dangerous means of conveyance in New York City.

Bicycle messengers run their own marathons whereby they map out itineraries of various routes competing for prestige amongst them, racing through the streets challenging their competitors, demonstrating who among them was the fastest messenger therefore, the most reckless and dangerous. Brilliant!

Where are the police? Who's enforcing the traffic laws? Why are bike messengers allowed to do whatever they please? Round up a few hundred bikes, take them away from violators, return the bikes when their fines are paid and if a biker piles up more than three fines then lock 'em up! Licensing with photo ID's should be mandatory and a point system must be instituted, as with motor vehicles. Throw in mandatory insurance coverage too and enforce it!

There's too much inconsistency when it comes to safety in New York City. I've seen people get hit. I've seen painted white bicycle memorials all around the City, and I know where to find them. They each signify the death of a cyclist.

Truthfully, bike messengers are the most ubiquitous danger in the City, for those who are "out and about." Please keep this in mind when you take a hike, look out for the bike, both ways and always! You could be wheeled into a hospital or morgue with Schwinn imprinted on what's left of your forehead! "Different spokes in different folks!"

The new bicycle-sharing program began on May 27th 2013, after delays due to software problems and hurricane Sandy, damaging bikes and equipment. It'll be a while before we can determine whether the bike share plan will succeed. My concern is safety above all and I hop the program is doomed.

If the City doesn't get serious about traffic enforcement including bicycles, a lot of people are going to get hurt and killed. There's barely enough

509

space for cars, taxis, buses and trucks in midtown. The streets are clogged and many drivers who are nuts. They drive carelessly, aggressively with road rage, a certifiable mental illness and too may are just plain stupid. We're got thousands of motorists who drive into Manhattan from distant places and they don't know what the hell they're doing. I see it all the time; cars with out of state plates are a dead giveaway. Steer clear of them buster! They're clueless!

Bicyclists, especially those who will be participating with the new program will be more likely to be inexperienced bike riders on the streets of New York City. If the purpose of the program is to provide alternative transportation producing no carbon in the atmosphere, I believe the program will not succeed.

People, who would otherwise have walked or taken the subway or a taxi, would be the most likely bicycle riders. With or with passengers, taxi still are cruising the streets going about their business. So, what's the benefit? Take a safety course that could be an hour program on a computer, carry an ID card that certifies that they've taken the course and have insurance. I'm waiting to hear about the next fatality while I hold my breath. It'll happen.

I believe a major overriding reason, no pun intended, is that Mike is cozy with banks and Citibank's corporate logo is all over the bikes and share stations. They paid for the whole thing. It could make them a lot of money and we all know that the world runs on three things: money, money and money!

Subway Music and Art

If you enjoy live music and would love to hear the most varied assortment of music; jazz, classical, Mexican, Rap, African drums, bongo drums, banjos, steel drums, Chinese "pling, plang" (Oye), Mo-town, Do-Wop, Gospel, Ecuadorian, barbershop quartets, etc. etc. then buy a metro card and take yourself on a musical tour of the New York City subway system. "Music Under New York" (MUNY), is an organization that promotes public music and provides over 150 free weekly performances at twenty-five locations throughout the subway. They sponsor auditions for musicians who compete for the most desirable locations, by selecting stations for musicians to perform. They compete for the highest volume of music friendly and generous straphanger stations. You're more likely to find violinists at the 1 train station at 66th Street and Broadway at Lincoln Center. Jazz flourishes at the southern end of the Columbus Circle Station on the platform serving the blue and orange lines. One of the best jazz trios in the city is frequently heard there in late afternoons. Check it out!

Listen to a country music guitarist at the Museum of Natural History station, 81st Street at Central Park West and enjoy the show at the Eighth Avenue and 34th Street station featuring either Ecuadorian ensembles or African-American song and dance presentations and country music style banjo, guitar and blues singers howling out country and blues. Give them a buck if you like what you hear. They make a big contribution to our lives in New York City and they work hard to win your appreciation and earn some needed "coin."

511

Okay, so it's not the Paris or Moscow subway system, both adorned with magnificent stations. Some have claimed that they'd marry their daughters off there because they are so gorgeous, the stations not the daughters, that is. Many would be happy to marry off their wife's in our subway stations even if they're dirty and tacky; you figure that one out!

Squire J. Vickers, the chief subway architect and designer for over thirty years, designed over 300 stations giving us the "arts and crafts" motif. That design celebrates the subways' function, traditional craftsmanship, simple forms of decoration, glorifying the industrial age when they were built and shedding off the clutter of the Victorian era and the exaggerated ornamentation of the Beau Arts period. His colors, geometrics and mosaic station name panels, terra-cotta embellishments and playful designs are classic in New York City. It's something worth noticing while waiting for the welcomed roar of your oncoming train. Who gives this a thought? Nearly no one! They're there, always have been and will always be a kind of "sub" conscious visual display unnoticed by the masses.

Check out these impressive examples of subway art:

Edith Kramer's glass and mosaic panel at the C Spring Street station on the north side of Spring Street, just before you descend the stairs from the street this outstanding piece of art can be seen before paying your fare. It depicts the 14th Street station. Bring your camera. It's simply gorgeous.

Eric Fischl's mosaic "Garden of Circus Delights" at 34th Street at Penn Station; depicts the circus; animals, acrobats and fire eaters in action! Awesome!

512

Faith Ringgold's "Flying Home Harlem Heroes" is a major piece; a collage of musicians, writers, artists, civil rights and religious leaders that seem to be flying home though the air joyously at the 125th Street Station.

My favorites are Tom Otterness's "Life Underground" pieces at the 14th Street and 8th Avenue station, the most creative and whimsical art form in the entire system. His work is spectacular. It features numerous bronze sculptures placed everywhere, the ceilings, benches, steel beams, and floors too, portraying, for example, an alligator emerging from beneath a manhole cover whose jaws are clenching a crawling toddler's diaper from behind. It's based on the folklore of many New Yorkers who have returned from Florida with their children toting a newly minded alligator. Their new little adorable pet grows over time and rather than subjecting their children to becoming alligator snack food, their parents opt to dispose of the new family member in the canyons of the subway to take up life among the endless supply of rats! Every now and then a 'gator gets snagged by an MTA employee.

Otterness provides us with characters that are short and stout, vested, with top hats carrying huge subways tokens, coins, personified animals, elephants with hats, dollar signs ($) giraffes and mounted melted "pay phones" on steel beams.

Otterness had considerable hurdles to climb to overcome the objections of MTA bureaucrats. He considered that to be a part of the creative process and fortunately, for us all, his shear genius and resolve prevailed.

513

The outer boroughs boost a spectacular array of art too. Visit the Nereid, Myrtle and Wyckoff Avenues in Brooklyn; Burnside Avenue in The Bronx, Woodhaven Blvd and Jamaica Centre Station in Queens or check out New York Subway art on the internet. There's a lot more and for the cost of a metro card it's another New York City bargain. It's the largest museum in the City, with wheels to take you from one exhibit to another. Not bad for $2.50, or less. To view all the best subway art go to mta.info/art/app

Income disparity is a part of our diversity. The super rich are nested in cavernous buildings with all the right touches. Generally, you know where they are and how they look. They're dotted all over Fifth Avenue, Madison, Park, Sutton Place, East End Avenue, The Village, Soho, Tribeca, The Upper Westside particularly located on Central Park West, Columbus Circle, Riverside Drive and numerous enclaves around the City.

The shrinking middle class, by some measure, is less than 10% of the entire City living scattered in all five boroughs dwelling in rent controlled and stabilized apartments, city housing, homes grandfathered by their ancestors and purchases made by working couples a generation ago that have paid off their mortgages. Many are living on pensions and small inheritances and other struggling couples "get by" with meager jobs that barely provide enough after a lifetime of employment. In fact, if all the people who live on the Upper Westside had to purchase or rent their apartments at today's prices all but 10% of them would have to flee. The environs of upper Manhattan are home to the least financially able Manhattan residents, generally Harlem, Washington Heights, Inwood, Hudson Heights and Hamilton Heights. You can also throw in The East Village, Lower Eastside, for now, and East Harlem. This island is littered with City housing units, and Mitchell Lama subsidized housing projects from top to bottom but void in midtown, the Upper Eastside, most of the Upper Westside, Gramercy, and Murray Hill and numerous other wealthy neighborhoods throughout Manhattan. The least affluent neighborhoods in this City are generally located in the "South Bronx", central Brooklyn east of Prospect Park and scattered areas in eastern Queens.

Wealth accumulation is ordinarily attained through inheritance, excellent well paying jobs, good business sense, connections, luck, and professions built on a long education food chain, years of sweat, the lottery, smart investments, and crime both white collar and blue. Marriage or money, foul play, schemes, kickbacks, cash streams, backend residuals, black market goods, drugs, burglary, robbery, good old American Greed, medicare and mediaid tax fraud, sale of cigarettes imported from other states or Indian reservations and the mother of them all, Ponzi schemes a la Bernie Madoff or rather "Made-Off". Countless others, politicians, bankers, retailers, labor unions, construction contractors, purchasing agents, and others have plied their trade engaging in every conceivable legal and illegal activity known to man to acquire their fortunes.

In this town fancy real estate footwork creates mega opportunities for very few, those who have the connections, credit, government cronies, friends with powerful connections, "the best judges that money can buy", mafia types, city council buddies and other denizens of the deep. Most New Yorkers, overwhelmingly, grind through their lives as employees, working at jobs that are monotonous, un-challenging and tedious. Their jobs do not provide enough to put shoes on the baby, a roof over their heads and the joy of a six-pack at day's (daze) end. There seems to be no way out of that "trap" never to find a way to aspire to 740 Park Avenue, 15 Central Park West, River House or 1 West 72nd Street known as The Dakota or a classic 3½ room apartment in a doorman building that millions just dream about. Like other curious New Yorkers, I attempt to peer through windows on Fifth Avenue, Park Avenue and Central Park West apartments for a glimpse of how the "chosen ones" live. The Metropolitan Club's first floor windows are deliberately raised high enough for insiders to peer out at pedestrian traffic but not low enough for outsiders, like us, to peek inside. I wouldn't peek in, would you? Nah! Eh, well? Here are few illuminating numbers for crunching: The top 1% of households in the City has soared to claim 44% of the city's wealth up from 17% a short twenty-five years ago! The income share of the bottom 90% of households is 34% of the City's wealth. In zip code 10021 located on the Upper Eastside wealth, on average, is forty times higher than the bottom 20% of striving New Yorkers with over $100,000 annual income per capita and that includes children. According to the Forbes 400, citing the wealthiest people in the world, 72 live in New York City, each with a net worth exceeding $1 Billion. There are more billionaires here than in any other city on earth. Many of those billionaires who live in New York City are smart enough not to use New York City as their primary residence for tax avoidance purposes. David A. Koch, for example, purchased Jackie Kennedy's apartment but lists his primary residence in Kansas where his business headquarters is located. Way to go Dave! It's so obvious why people do that and no one shakes 'em down! That's amazing! Huh! Just a Pied-à-terre, right Dave!

It never ceases to amaze me that people with a stratospheric net worth cannot escape the opportunity to screw the country, but hey, it's legal!

How did that happen? It wasn't the middle class, right folks? That's democracy, fairness and "the games people play."

You can't take it with you Dave, as you will find out in due time, like when you inhale your last precious breath. I suppose when you're gone you won't have to be concerned about what's good for the country, just like now, right Dave? You can't take it with you big boy!

Isn't it fascinating how the super rich love America but not Americans? "Let 'em eat cake and let's grab that Bush tax cut saving them, about 80 billion bucks per year and reduce medical aid for the working poor and deny good nutrition for children via more tax revenue from the rich and eliminate food stamps!" Let's not forget to trash Planned Parenthood and toss out the free ovarian and breast screening benefits too. "No billionaire left behind!" Destroying the middle class so that they can leave big bucks to their descendants is a great idea but when the country collapses the "fat cat's" money will become worthless.

I suppose since the Republicans maneuvered to include pizza in federally subsidized school lunch menus, as a vegetable because it contains tomato sauce should adopt the refrain, "Let 'em eat pizza." Sleep well fat cats because one day, due to the deficits in large part due to your 13% tax rates, and two stupid wars that filled the pockets of the Halliburton cronies translates into war is a great business. There'll be blood in the streets and large fat cat co-ops, yours, which you just may have to barricade.

Don't fret, your doorman, with grey hair or no hair and a 44" waist will protect you from the 99% that will roam the streets of desperation!

Don't you know that the larger and stronger the middle class is then the more stable and enduring democracy becomes? Seems like a pretty good investment to me. What scares you more? Cutting your net worth or the 99% storming the Bastille?

Here's one last statistic to consider. The Federal poverty level for a family of four is an income below approximately $23,500 per year, gross right, after taxes. Forty six percent of all families of four in New York City are making less than 150% of that, which is to say, $35,250! To consider that 46% of our families with two children survive on $35,250 or less, and that's not net "take home" pay is an abomination! About the only person who is in that 1% category that came out and said something about that is Warren Buffett. He couldn't justify why his secretary's tax rate was higher then his. Can you? I can't.

Fracking, that new ubiquitous technology to extract gas is going to rear its ugly head some day, as in let the water pour and burn. What's in your water, Mr. Cheney?

Recently, I toured with five couples from Texas who were in the oil and gas business and they were about to get into the fracking business. I told them that they should name the new company, "Mother Frackers!" We roared! They may be the frackers and we'll be the frackees. Incidentally, Mr. Henry Clay Frick, the coke and steel baron who was Mr. Andrew Carnegie's partner a bit over one hundred years ago would have been a fracker today. Surely, he'd have called his business Frick Fracking!

Staten Island is the wealthiest borough in New York City, per capita, with average income of over $81,000 per household. It's also the only borough with single digit poverty level of 9.8%. The Bronx is the poorest borough with an average family income of $46,298 with 27.1% of its residents are living at or below the poverty level.

When I graduated from college in 1968 my income goal was to earn $1,000 per year times my age. Today that goal would be more realistic closer to the 10,000 times age equation. Money, huh, I look at a $100 bill now and it looks like a "20" and has the same purchasing power as a "20" did back in 1968, not that long ago. We're moving closer to the precipice so you'd better spend your money because it's going south under the stewardship of all the cities, towns, counties, states and the Federal deficits. Add up all that debt and then write your Senator and Congressman to continue the Bush tax cuts. Better buy a wheelbarrow now, much cheaper than tomorrow. Haul those greenbacks for some "bread" man, it's comin'! Just the other day I walked into my neighborhood Duane Reade to buy a candy bar. The price was $1.49! I walked out empty handed and checked out the Rite Aid across the street; two packs of M & M's, $1! Gotta shop around. I stopped at a newsstand last week to buy a copy of The New Yorker and two packs of gum, price, $6.99 for the magazine, and $1.75 for a pack of gum; total cost, $8.74. I halted and just didn't do it. I do recall that once upon a time my favorite magazine, MAD, "What me worry" was 35 cents plus ten cents for two packs of gum, total 45 cents. The subway was 15 cents in my lifetime, now it's $2.50. We got problems . . . oy! How about a slice of pizza and a coke, both for a quarter when I was a kid, now we're creeping back. I got two slices and a coke for $2.75 recently! 75 cents a slice is back in New York City and it's a moneymaker, there's a Times Square price war. Eat up Republicans and toss aside the broccoli, asparagus and peas. Ok, there are plenty of Democrats that live extremely well too. So, I'm sorry for picking on the Republicans.

They only thing that I can't understand is why anyone would be against providing health insurance benefits to a child who has a previous existing condition. If anyone, out there, who is reading this and knows the answer then please contact me immediately. Maybe I'm crazy!

It used to be that someone whose net worth was one million dollars was rich. Today it means they can own a co-op apartment in Manhattan, basically, if they pass the muster of the dreaded board. Rich today means earning one million dollars a year, not having a million. Back in 2001 only 1.3 million families in The United States had a net worth over one million dollars. There are now about 27,000 families with wealth exceeding $30 million, and a lot of them are living in and around New York City, as many as 10% of them.

As for treats, trinkets and staples that these folks are accustomed to, let's have a look or take a peek at a shopping list: Bed linens, $6,000, a full set of linens with Fuseli lace, from Italy, and to think that we suffer slumbering on Wamsuta, a mere 400 threads per inch! No wonder I can't sleep at night, I need my Egyptian cotton pillowcases! And now many are considered members of the underclass; that's short for former middle class, largely gone. Forget about a mausoleum site at Greenwood Cemetery, that's $180,000 without goodies, you know, landscaping, a few trees to cool you off during the summer months. It's just the site, an empty place. Not bad for a few blades of grass for the final "rest." That's too much money for the "underclass" you think? We'll all be part of the "underclass" when we're dead, unless you burn. The upper class will be above ground so I fear that they'll be renamed the upper upper class after life and most will be the lower lower class!

How about a 36 minute commute from the Hamptons to Manhattan via Associated Aircraft Group aboard the latest Sikorsky 'chopper for $6,000. That's equivalent to 2,400 swipes on your metro card, unless you have an unlimited card which you can swipe at eighteen minute intervals which would take you 148 days and a quart of elbow grease unless you can afford to hire a swiper at minimum wage, no benefits, of course. And for closers, perhaps you'd like a place to put your Mini Cooper; at a cost of about $250,000, or so, in your own parking spot at Dietz Lantern, a condo, in Tribeca, with a remote-control door, video cameras and concierges tossed in. Or, check out the new building on West 24th Street and 11th Avenue. You too, like Nicole Kidman and Keith Urban and Dolce & Gabbana that have that too for a cool $10 million, a bargain because the asking price was $12.5 million with the "*en suite garage*" kicked in. "En suite garage" is a luxury that enables the owner to drive their car into an elevator entrance and drive their car out of the elevator and park in front of their condo or coop.

I guess I can discard my Zipcar card now, and just take the bus. Any takers? Oh yes, there's a catch.

there's a waiting list for those parking spots and waiting on lines is just not my thing so I'll just have to pass even if I did own, or lease a car! No friend of the house there!

Many lucky "silver spooners" have purchased their apartments over forty years ago. As I recall, an apartment in The Dakota was running for less than $100,000 a room about thirty years ago. Now they're about twenty times that price.

I also recall when townhouses on Striver's Row in Harlem were on the market for $30,000 a piece. Add two zeros to get a key now, a price that's hundred times higher then forty years ago. It was a nice buy then but the catch was you wouldn't have wanted to live there at that time. There are those who still feel that way today even though Harlem is far better but I guess it's not for everybody. It is interesting that the closing costs alone, the legal fees, title search, title insurance, escrow payment, bank fees and the mortgage tax, aka "The New York Handshake", if you financed only 70% of that purchase, would cost you today about twice the price that you would have paid to purchase the townhouse back in the '70's. Hi Sheldon Silver, our state legislator majority leader, Hi Albany, the classic case of the tail wagging the dog, Oy!

Oh yes, one more thing, there's a very large brownstone townhouse, that looks suitable for at least eight apartments, on the south west corner of Central Park West and 84th Street that just went on the market. Take a guess. It's featured for $32 million and currently is the only building for sale on Central Park West.

Let's boil all this down, in perspective. Twenty one percent of New Yorkers have nothing or less, are in deep crushing debt and therefore all of them have a negative net worth. They're living below the poverty line, "under water." Mr. David Koch's net worth of $20 billion plus is equivalent to the poorest 1.5 million New Yorkers. Add the former Mayor, Mike Bloomberg, and together their net worth equals perhaps the bottom 35% of all New Yorker's income, give or take a few percentage points. Hey brother, can you spare me a million, annually? Thank you! Sure, I can spare about 100 million to become mayor for the third time and hey if I gave you a million a day I wouldn't miss a meal or a cent of my principle. Hey, Mike's a smart guy, nobody handed to over to him. He made it happen. Good job. No, great job!

There's another gent named David, David Martinez, a Mexican Hedge Fund mover and shaker who paid $54 million for his duplex condo at The Time-Warner complex at Columbus Circle, aka 10 Columbus Circle. That would pay some rents for a number of others I would imagine! But poor Mr. Martinez didn't get a toilet, refrigerator or finished floors for that place. It's called "raw space." No wonder! I saw a guy with a full-length mink and diamond stuttered tiepin wandering around Home Depot recently! Could be him, who knows? What was he shopping for?

But Mr. Martinez's record-breaking purchase, which is now about one half of the new current record price for a home in New York City was broken in November 2011 due to the sale of Mr. and Mrs. Sanford Weill's 15 Central Park West 6,700 square foot triplex with a multi-terraced condo facing the park for $88 million and that record has already been crushed a number of times. He paid $43.7 million for it in 2007! He, and his wife, gifted the profit to charity. They'll never miss a meal or tax write-off either. Nice!

In June of this year an unidentified buyer went into contract to purchase a 10,923-square-foot penthouse on the 89th and 90th floor of One57. The actual figure will become public information when the purchase is "closed" and the deed is conveyed. Due to a non-disclosure clause in the contract that information is private. There is still a unit in the building to be sold that is 13,500-square-feet and has a solarium. It's on a higher floor therefore it is likely that that unit will break the holy grail, the $100 million price tag, never reached for a price paid for a home in The United States. I wouldn't be surprised if the sale price exceeds $125 million and if not then our friend, Mr. Harry B. Mackow, see first "slice" in this book, will probably get over $135 million for a top floor at 432 Park Avenue.

Estimates vary as to the former Mayor's net worth. However, you slice and dice it and it's way up there in the stratosphere. Estimates have ranged in the $30-$35 billion stratosphere according to Forbes. Most of it is stock in Bloomberg, LLC, so I've heard. Therefore, the possibility of liquidating it all in one shot is not an option. What a shame. How many suits can you buy in a day Mike? I think we're about the same size, 40 short? I wonder if he buys them at Jos. A. Bank when they have their buy one, get two free promos, like I do. I must make a note to "drop him a line" so he can take advantage of their sales. I'll take Mike with me on a shopping spree and he'll help himself to buying the company. Perhaps I can give him one of my freebees for his retirement. Just a little thank you for the terrific job he's done, in general.

Make no mistake he didn't make that working for The City of New York. For that, he got a buck a year, his choice. But, I suppose he's worth every penny. "Mike for Mayor" "Mike for Mayor" "Mike for Mayor" that's 1, 2 and 3 terms! Nice job, glad you were the mayor.

Why Did New York City Get so Big?

Philadelphia, Boston, Baltimore and other major east coast cities have not achieved the size and impressive statue athatNew York City has by any measure.

Why have they and all other east coast cities had far less impressive growth compared to New York City? Most New Yorkers seldom ask themselves that question and that's a big mystery to me. Those whom I have asked have some notion why; such as: "great harbors", "the immigrants", The Hudson River "We're the best" rah rah rah, etc. etc. It's amusing to hear people struggle to offer their perception as to why this City has grown so large and so fast, faster than any other city on earth except perhaps artificially made cities such as Dubai. New York City's population of 60,000 in 1800 grew to 3.3 million in 1900. That has never happened before anywhere, ever!

Why did New York City become so indispensible, globally important, unique and significant? It became exceedingly productive, diverse, innovative, powerful and dominating. Why? Generally, it all boils down to three key reasons:

First, the geography, nature made and revised by man. Second, the roots of our culture built and established primarily by the Dutch, the first settlers who came here. Third, the plethora of immigrants, each with their own cultures, skills, ideas and capabilities contributed creating fusion, a "melting pot" for a young growing city. The combination of these factors resulted in gathering many of the best and brightest, not just the poor and downtrodden to create a new life for themselves, families and descendants but, in addition, to build a City that is far greater than the sum of its parts.

527

Sure it was the harbor, deep rivers on both sides of Manhattan with a protected harbor surrounded by Staten Island, Brooklyn, Governor's Island and New Jersey forming the Upper and Lower Bays, Buttermilk Channel and The Narrows, an inlet providing additional shelter from harsh ocean currents were all major factors.

At first, most trade was conducted on the East River because The Hudson River, formally The North River, was subjected to much stronger winds from the west posing grave threats to small sailing ships.

The South Street Seaport became the busiest seaport on earth prior to the arrival of larger and heavier steam powered ships. Sailing ships were lined up in the upper bay and waited, at times, for an entire day for the opportunity to drop their anchors and unload their cargo, reload and sail away. Fortunately, The East River's depth was sufficient to accommodate the shallow draft of sailing ships and the relative safety of the gentler west winds, due to the ideal placement of Manhattan. Heavier steam powered vessels favored The Hudson River, due to their deeper drafts and the ability to weather more powerful west winds, buffered by Manhattan's land mass. Those ships were made of iron or steel powered by engines that were capable of withstanding powerful currents than the "Tall Ships."

The harbors alone could not ensure this City's spectacular growth. It was The Hudson River that provided New York City with the only "super highway" a wide navigable river that provided access to the interior of the continent. In many ways, that sealed the deal because New York City is the only city on the east coast that has that incredible advantage.

That made it economically attractive for New York City entrepreneurs to gather and transport the treasures, found in the hinterlands far from our harbor much more quickly, safely and cheaply then any other city on the east coast.

By saving enormous time and money transporting huge amounts of goods over The Hudson versus on land, especially prior to the age of railroads, was huge! No other city on or near the east coast could have competed with New York City. As a result, goods from the interior were shipped to New York City via The Hudson River enabling us to become the port of export of beaver pelts, agricultural products, cotton, coal, timber and much more. The cost to transport goods over land was approximately $30 per ton versus $5 a ton shipped via the river and the time required to move goods on land was up to thirty times longer.

The completion of the 362-mile long Erie Canal completed in 1825, at a cost of over $7 million, handed New York City still further far reaching access to what was then known as "The West."

Thomas Jefferson thought the scheme was sheer madness. Having purchased the Louisiana Territory from France in 1803 at about twice the price of the Erie Canal was the greatest real estate deal in American history. Jefferson had failed to recognize the significance of this "big ditch" as the enormous asset and catalyst for growth. It gave us reach as far as the nation had spread at the time, an incredible, daring engineering and commercial achievement. Poor Tom just didn't get it!

You name it; beef from Chicago, fresh water fish from the Great Lakes, coal, wheat and all goods, manufactured, captured, fished, logged, trapped, mined or harvested came directly to New York City and that gave rise to the need for financial, insurance, legal, brokerage and transport experts and infrastructures with a wide variety of skills and labor needed to make it work. Hence, the immigrants poured onto our shores to build, fix, fashion, create and feed a growing city. This was a boom like never before. Conversely, this export business colossus, The Erie Canal, anointed New York City, the logical place for imports too. We had become the busiest commercial port in the nation and the rest is history.

This City didn't blossom; it burst at the seams, exploded, providing new wealth, opportunities, and enormous new challenges that other urban centers never dreamed possible on such a huge scale. Compounding the glorious confirmation of this City came spectacular growth. The confluence of numerous languages and cultures were thrown together; living and working in a never before pluralistic city, was another first for "Gotham" and indeed the world.

The Dutch culture injected the human factor that gave rise to New York City's growth as the primate city on the Atlantic. They came, not for religious freedom as the Pilgrims and Puritans of Boston or the Quakers of Philadelphia, two cities whose primary objective was not commercial but rather the establishment of peaceful monolithic societies where freedom of religion was their vital linchpin. The Dutch, came here establishing New Amsterdam, as they had named it, arriving under the sponsorship of the mighty Dutch West India Company. Their goal was to make money, and money they made, enough to provide an annual return of 10% for their investors year after year. This was no Ponzi scheme. It was capitalism at its best at the time, imperfect yes but plowing forward as never before dreamed of.

Henry Hudson ventured up the river that bears his name, on September 12, 1609, in search of "The Northwest Passage" to India and China and he knew well that he had found something far better then he had been hired to achieve.

"A thousand ships could find safe harbor here," he had penned in his diary. He, an English explorer, hired by Dutch entrepreneurs laid claim that his discovery of the harbor and the river was the best example of being off the beaten path but on the right track.

As he continued to sail up the river that bears his name, he noticed that the water continued to remain salty, ocean water, and that the depth of the river continued to maintain its depth as well. He was certain that at every next left turn, around a bluff or beyond the next mountain, the Pacific Ocean would reveal itself. .

The Dutch have always been a liberal and diverse culture, imperfect, at times, but nevertheless they were a driving force never loosing site of their mission. They welcomed those seeking refuge, a home, and an escape from oppression, despotism and tyranny. The Dutch were an inspiring source of action and resolve playing a major role driving Europe out of the Dark Ages and into the Age of Enlightenment and the Age of Reason. They contributed to the annihilation of many dogmatic religious beliefs, staid and superstitious ideas that they had discarded as antithetical to their values and beliefs, imbedded in

531

their psyche. They fervently tossed out the driving forces thwarting scientific advancement, research and discoveries for over 1,500 years. They were not impassioned attendees of churches, as many other European cultures, most notably those from the southern regions of Europe supporting church beliefs and dogma as the centerpieces of their lives and existence.

It took the Dutch thirty years to build their first church in New Amsterdam! The concepts of liberalism, diversity, reason, innovation, pluralism, entrepreneurial drive and spirit together with their pioneering spirit, crafty, entrepreneurial and inventive ways still remain the cornerstone of New York City's culture.

The Dutch loved to make money, but that was not all. They loved to play hard too. They were liberal, we still are, diverse, we still are, entrepreneurial, we still are and we, as a culture, do not run to church on Sundays in droves either, although in a city as diverse as this there are large sectors of our society that cling to a path of devout observance of their religious beliefs. The encouragement of diversity, entrepreneurial spirit and liberalism is certainly not at cross-purposes with religious belief nowadays and, as a New Yorker, I fully accept that and would never conceive of discouraging those from abandoning the pursuit their religious beliefs and observances.

We have continued to maintain our focus on this world, "the now" and not in pursuit of other worlds or hereafters as the fulcrum of our lives. The Dutch, emphasized, the here and now, not akin to other societies who sought to dominate life's purpose, preparation for the afterlife.

The capital of culture and finance in this country is where the East River and The Hudson River wrap around Manhattan and that will never change. It just keeps getting better, bigger and more spectacular all the time!

Want to see the world, come to New York City!!

From Zigzag to Straight and Flat!

Manhattan is very easy to navigate on foot, north of 14th Street. If you do not agree then go to your room! For the most part, the majority of streets, north of 14th Street, are numbered in consecutive order, parallel and perpendicular, surprisingly flat and straight. How did that happen, on this "island of many hills", Manahatta, as named by the Lenape Indians?

The streets that lie below 14th Street are, for the most part, not numbered nor are they parallel or perpendicular due to their construction prior to the Grid Plan, or Commissioner's Plan, enacted in 1811. Below 14th Street one needs to know the street layout and that takes knowhow. In order to get to where you are going you may wind up walking in endless circles if you're a novice or even the average New Yorker!

The West Village and The Lower Eastside are, by far, the most confusing terrains to navigate in Manhattan. For example, you'll find Little West 12th Street and West 12th Street separated by Gansevoort, Horatio and Jane Streets a labyrinth that would divert a mouse scenting cheese. You may walk on West 10th Street and find that you're south of West 8th and 9th Streets. These twists, turns and meandering streets were created by 17th and 18th century road builders and city ordinances that had allowed paths to become wider roads around boulders and rocks, depressions of earth and mounds or hills that would have been too costly to remove in an age void of modern mechanical road building equipment. Thus, due to the limitations of road construction technologies, layout and design were quite daunting back then. Therefore, the Dutch and English did not create streets following a pattern or plan. It would have entailed too much trouble and toil.

As if life was not difficult enough back in the 17th, 18th and 19th centuries with all the grime, crime, grit, overcrowding and stench of New York City, it was a nightmare trying to navigate. With so many immigrants, vast numbers of new arrivals, speaking so many languages, huge challenges communicating directions to each other, became a terrifying and nearly impossible task!

Imagine, an Irishman telling an Italian woman how to get to Laight, Desbrosses, Lispenard or Frankfort Street while standing on the corner of Mulberry and Grand. With people from so many countries, speaking languages that were so divergent, it must have created havoc. Imagine, stopping a fellow New Yorker and asking them how to get to Desbrosses Street when your pronunciation would have been totally misunderstood. This was not an age when people pulled out a map, GPS or googlemap.

Enter The Grid Law of 1811. The mandate called for surveying and planning the streets of the future. It defined their widths, routes and provided for a few exceptions from 14th Street north to 155th Street. Imagine what a political hot potato that it was. A law was going to carve up properties, plan streets through owner's estates, without reasonable compensation. It was such a hot button that the City insisted that the Albany legislature take the authority to write the law and remove it from the hands of locals.

Essentially, the plan was the brainstorm of DeWitt Clinton mayor and future governor of New York State. He laid out short blocks, narrow side streets, wide north-south avenues, and intermittently wide two way traffic east-west streets to facilitate cross town traffic such as 96th 86th 79th 72nd 59th, 42nd 34th 23th 14th and so on.

Blocks were intentionally planned to be short thereby creating more corners because corner properties are worth more money, providing more light, superior ventilation and two views all very beneficial features especially in an age when air-conditioning and electric lighting did not exist.

Streets were numbered sequentially to facilitate communication among the masses. People's queries were answered with the dab of a pencil, a number written on a piece of paper, the street in question was provided and those who had been lost found their way. That's all it took, less language barriers or frustrations. It was a connective mechanism for the immigrants and it facilitated communication making it less frustrating and consequently much more effective.

The law mandated roads to be flattened, rocks and mounds of earth had to be removed before streets were paved; that's why most of the hills that were on this island are gone. For the most part, they're all gone and that made Manhattan the most geologically transformed City (at that time Manhattan was New York City) on the planet. You can still find plenty of hills laden with huge clumps of Manhattan schist located in parks especially in Northern Manhattan. In certain parks such as northern Central Park, with a most notable example that can be seen along Central Park West between 103rd and 106th Street, Morningside, Riverside, Highbridge, Inwood and Ft. Tryon Park, Marcus Garvey Park are all in northern

Manhattan. There are huge clusters of rocks protruding through the soil known as "outcroppings." In fact, Central Park was planned to end at 106th Street however the rocks were so huge that it had been decided to extend the park to 110th Street instead.

Next time you take a walk around town, try to imagine what New York City had been like four hundred years ago and the great transformation that was conceived and achieved enabling it to work so well today. It would have been better if the side streets were somewhat wider to facilitate cross town traffic however, you can't fault the designers since vehicles of today did not exist back then. How nice it would have been if alleyways had been created with entrances on the avenues for trash collection at the rear of our homes, rather than enduring the inconvenience of trash pickups in front of our homes as it still is, cluttering sidewalks with piles of trash, unsightly messes and foul smells!

As you travel the world compare our street grid with other major cities. Despite a few glitches, our Grid Law is perhaps the most forward thinking and innovative geographically favorable urban roadway plan on earth.

Way to go New York City! Just try to be a little patient when venturing into those narrow cross-town streets. Hey buddy, lay off the horn too! No doubt many pregnancies ended, or nearly ended on side streets behind garbage trucks! My daughter was nearly on her way into the world on 77th Street between 2nd and 3rd Avenue back on February 22, 1973. It was a close "caul."

537

Parking Signs are Rocket Science

Recently I encountered a couple of tourists standing on the sidewalk in midtown Manhattan who seemed a bit confused. That's nothing new. They stopped me as I walked by and asked me,

"Are we allowed to stand here?"

"Why do you ask?"

Their reply,

"There's a sign there."

Pointing directly to it, one of them continued,

"That sign reads, 'No Standing'!"

I nearly collapsed and hit the sidewalk hysterically! After all, there wasn't a sign that read no sitting, slouching, leaning or laying down.

If you have a PhD, are a fortune teller, dice roller, win at three card Monte, yeah right, bingo and the lottery then you have a shot at parking for free in New York City. Throw in a brother-in-law who's a judge in traffic court, a cop who was the best man at your wedding and for closers, toss in your first born child, which some may actually want to do in order to avoid paying a parking ticket and you may, just may, park free. With your fingers crossed, a dream and a prayer, you'll walk away from a fine for not understanding the signs posted down the block where your car was grievously parked and summarily removed. There's no doubt that the cost of so-called public street parking in New York City has soared over time. The cost of a parking spot, per square foot, exceeds the cost of an apartment rental, even in The Bronx! Currently, metered parking is 50 cents for ten minutes on Columbus Avenue off of 97th Street. That calculates to $2,110 by the month for a space that's six by twelve feet.

Ever wonder what glove compartments are for? Not for gloves but rather a place to stash all those parking tickets that you have ignored. We all know that parking tickets just don't go away. It's sort of like herpes, except with parking tickets the City can't help you and with herpes. Perhaps that's why the cost of parking tickets is so huge in New York City; to provide funds to treat herpes? There's a new designer disease, borne from birds, that has hit the streets recently allegedly borne in the Pack Meeting District. It's called Twerpies. No worries though, it's tweetable!

It takes a lot of effort to make them go away that is, parking tickets, unless you pay. You could be snagged by the police and thrown in jail overnight. That may spell tickets and bedbugs, a nice "sidecar" for your car ticket trouble.

A son of a friend of mine suffered that fate, was put in the "clink", and met a variety of very interesting people who do and say things that you never knew. A friggin' parking ticket! Lock 'em up without bedbugs and herpes! Let's figure out a way for the bedbugs to get herpes! That would take care of both problems, right?

Let's say, you're in the City, looking for a place to park, in midtown, and need to run into a tuxedo store or pickup a package, a cup of Joe, whatever, and after twenty minutes of circling the block you decide to take a shot. You call the retailer, tell the clerk that you're about to run in, that you'll be double parked, and want to grab your tuxedo, post haste. You have their full cooperation. After all, you're their customer. You find a spot alongside a truck parked directly in front of the establishment. You check your rearview mirror, side view too, look ahead and behind, check for meter maids and you're in the clear, or are you? You've read the sign. That took only about four minutes to read, and you don't see any No Double Parking signs but there are No Standing, No Idling and Snow Emergency Street signs. There's no snow so that's not an issue, No Commercial Traffic, and there are Do Not Park, Driveway signs and not a hint of Don't Even Think of Parking Here signs. There are no Don't Honk $300 fine signs.

You dash out, running, trip on the curb, weave through the foot traffic on the sidewalk, enter the store, present your receipt, are greeted with a smile, and the clerk retrieves your package in record time. You provide your fastest scribbled signature, say your good-bye as you dash out like you're running thirty yards in the Super Bowl and as you see your car a Traffic Cop appears who has already written a ticket, this time with the benefit of a computerized handheld device. You know, the kind that's got the data bank that just happens to have your vitals. Total elapsed time from exiting and returning to your car, fifty nifty seconds! Not bad, but not quite good enough! Where's OJ when you need him; where he belongs, in the slammer for of all crimes, stupidity, hubris and "if I can get away with double murder then I can get away with anything." He can't help you now! How's that for mixed emotions?

You confront the officer and she cites the violation as number 46 of the violations code without taking her eyes off the citation as she enters your license plate number, digitally, the time of day, location, date and other unknown evidentiary data into her hand held device. Worst of all, judges' love these devices, they're never wrong!

'What's 46?" you exclaim at a roar just slightly below a shout!

Well, she was not about to provide an answer, it's one of those, "see you in court" moments. I'll tell you what it is, here and now, right off the NYC.gov website:

"Standing or parking on the roadway side of a vehicle stopped, standing or parked at the curb; in other words, (*that's my favorite part, in other words*) "double parking". A person may; however, stand a Commercial Vehicle alongside a vehicle parked at the curb at such locations and during such hours that stopping, standing and parking is not prohibited when expeditiously (*and who's the judge of what is expeditiously?*) making pickups, deliveries or service calls, (*What's a service call? Servicing what, who and how, hum?*) provided that there is no unoccupied parking space or designated loading zone on either side of the street within 100 feet. "Double parking" any type of vehicle is not; however, permitted in Midtown Manhattan (the area from 14th Street to 60th Street, between First Avenue and Eighth Avenue inclusive). Except where otherwise restricted, midtown double parking is prohibited between 7 am and 7 pm daily except Sundays. (See Code 47.) (*Where's that? I guess directly* after *46 and before 48. How many codes are there?*)

Now that clears it up, right! And to think that I've been driving in New York City all my life and I never knew that! Who writes this stuff and how are we supposed to know it?

As has been said,

"Ignorance is no defense for breaking the law!" Fine: $145, next case. Oh yes, and don't forget about the other ticket for using a handheld phone while circling the tuxedo shop, "bing", another $115!

Who stops to measure 100 feet? Who decides if a delivery or service call is "expeditious" and what if the curbside space suddenly becomes vacant while you're doing your thing, like an urge to go to the bathroom? Every motorist, even from "Jersey" is supposed to know the geographic boundaries of midtown, "inclusive" right? You want to be a smart parker? Put you car in a lot and chances are that statistically you'll save a fortune.

I just love when people from the hinterlands, you know, Jersey, Connecticut, Long Islanders are just passing through in a new Mercedes, BMW or Lexus and circling the block twelve times looking for a parking spot in a City where the parking signs might as well be written in Mandarin, the third most widely spoken language in the City by the way, just to save a few lousy bucks!

How about the possibility that your $105,000 car gets hit by an adjacent motorist who is attempting to park and you didn't have a De-Fender, that rubber drape that protects your precious rolling stock and your over valued "wheels" get crunched?

"Oh Shit!! I should have put it in a lot. Honey!"

"You're damn right you cheap bastard! It serves you right!"

"Yes, Honey, and where were you when I was circling the block for half an hour searching for a spot?"

"Don't blame that on me dearie. You made your choice. It wasn't my fault!"

"Since when did you crawl under a rock? You have a mind and a mouth! The one time I would have appreciated your advice you clam up!"

"Don't talk to me like that, it's your fault. Pay the ticket and next time, try a parking lot, you penny pinching cheap creep!"

"I'm outa here! I'm not spending this evening with you! I'm going home."

It was just another enjoyable night on the town for a pair of losers. That's the fun of it all!

Put the "wheels" in a lot, save time and spend it on fun! Eat, drink and be merry. Get a life, not a spot, you cheap millionaire, accountant, dentist, pharmacist or doctor. Why are some people so well . . . You fill in the blanks?

I don't even want to go there because well, I found a great spot. I live in Manhattan, and am totally carless, not clueless! Wana avoid a parking ticket, don't park and don't drive!

Numbers? Go Figure

There are several hundred Duane Reade drug stores throughout the City established back in the 1960's by Eli Cohn and family, locals. Their first store was located on lower Broadway, between Duane and Reade streets. I've been shopping at those stores for years and was reasonably pleased with the service except that the stores were always understaffed; there are seldom enough cashiers, consequently lines are too long and New Yorkers, most of all, being in a hurry just hate to be kept waiting. I can't understand why large retail operators in New York City, who stock their stores with thousands of items and pay extremely high rents fail to recognize the wisdom of staffing their stores better than their competitors. If they did then the increased payroll of these low paid employees would be a great investment driving customers to their stores and away from Rite-Aid and CVS.

Several years ago Walgreen's, a huge national drug store operation, acquired the Duane Reade Drug chain and what happened seemed to me to be some retail engineering that is so not New York City, a disaster.

For starters: I immediately got the sense that the New Duane Reade management just didn't know how to do business in New York City.

For example, on the first of many occasions, I was handed my receipt, about 18 inches long with all kinds of "deals" values and specials had created an annoyance for me. Stuffing all that paper in my pocket and together with my change transformed me into a messenger! Then and there, the cashier told me,
"Have a nice day and be well."

The next time I made a purchase, upon my departure the cashier said, "Be happy and have a nice day!"

It was painfully obvious that a high level manager had instructed the cashiers to say two nice things to each customer, or "guest" as they refer to shoppers these days upon the customer's departure. We're not customers any more, we're "guests."

Don't you love if you happen to be standing on line at McDonald's, in need of an iced tea or diet coke when hear the cashier say,

"Next guest please!" Since when are we now "guests" at McDonald's? When did that shit kick in?

So, I asked the cashier at Duane Reade if their manager required that they wish each "guest" after making their purchase two nice salutations, not just one. She told me yes, with a smirk.

After that encounter, I noticed that all the cashiers in all of the Duane Reade stores were doing the same thing. Why are the "managers" of Duane Reade, now imported from the mid-west by Walgreen's, so off the mark when it comes to New Yorkers? To us, it's such obvious bullshit.

Another piece of news brought to you by Walgreen's, is that they raised their prices, sky-high. Just who do they're not kidding? What a sham or shame, both! The cost of my purchases at Duane Read is far most costly then at CVS directly across the street.

Now here's the kicker! On one recent evening I went to the Duane Reade behind my building to buy a few items. I approached the cashier, she seemed pleasant and eager to help me, her next "guest." She rang up the sale, $25.41, the "games" were about to begin.

I gave her two $20 bills, $40 bucks. Then, noticing that I had a $5 and a single I told her that I was replacing one twenty with the $5 and the single dollar bill. But, she had already entered in to the register that I tendered two twenties. Therefore, the cashier was not able to have the cash register to calculate the amount of change due me!

She was noticeably miffed and very confused. She froze, stared into the cash drawer and absolutely could not calculate my change!

"You can't provide me with the change without the register?" I asked, amazing!

Then she blurted out, "69 cent right?"

"No!" I said in a huffy tone.

So, she called for help. The other cashier had just completed her sale and was hastily summoned to assist.

"This guy is giving me trouble! He's a real problem!"

The other cashier came to our rescue, or so I thought. I recited the transaction, the amount of the sale and the transfer of one of the $20 bills to a $5 and a single, $26 in total.

She reached into the register and withdrew a $10, a $5 and a $1 dollar bill and handed the bills to me. I believe she was totally lost, didn't use a calculator, one was on the counter, apparently provided for such purposes.

Why did this happen? First, it is apparent that a Fortune 500 company that either has a deficient hiring process hired these young ladies or they have to settle for such candidates who are sorely deficient in basic mathematics. The cause lies squarely on the shoulders of our public school system.

Whether it's the curriculum, the teachers themselves, or the inability to teach effectively due to disciplinary problems or parents who are not keeping their eyes on their children's scholastic lack of achievement, I just don't know.

The real question is how will this City and this nation compete in a world where we have slipped down to a very disturbing rank of scholastic achievement. How will those jobs that require much better educated people be filled? Perhaps the gap between needed skills resides at the bottom of the ladder and the ability to fill highly skilled jobs is much easier.

How sad it is that finding cashiers in this day and age apparently is a major problem and with a budget of $19,200,000,000 is just not enough for New York City's Board of Education to prepare our children well. I believe that another ten billion or so wouldn't make a bit of difference except it would create more waste and could under educate about another 500,000 kids.

Therefore, the next time you become a "guest" standing in front of a retail cash register, make sure that you get the correct amount of change. It's very sad because everyone with the ability to learn is entitled to learn. We, as a nation, deserve a failing grade and are "screwing" our children and disabling their futures and the future of our country. Something must be done.

And now, the answer you've been waiting for: Did I return the excess money given to me? Yes, and the only reason was, because it was not my money. Never mind the rationale that the money should have come out of the cashier's pocket because she deserves to learn a lesson, how to calculate change without any external device. That's not my responsibility. Perhaps I should have kept the $16 to "teach her a lesson" but she's not my charge and I would have violated my own principle, "it was not my money."

A Few Parting Thoughts

Hopefully you have enjoyed this tour as much as I have putting it together. No doubt, you have learned a lot about New York City; trivia, how we live, our cultural mores, how things get done here, how we have evolved and much more.

Perhaps you have a new sense of New York City and a better understanding of us, a multi-cultural City that breaths life into everything we do. We are not the arrogant, rude and crude society that we have been known for in the past. Time has created a more lovable, admirable and productive society.

New York City has evolved into a place where kindness abounds and innovation can be found everywhere. Creativity thrives; artists of all types, researchers, teachers, musicians and doctors cure, fireman save, tour guides guide and together we all give perhaps the greatest abundance of gifts that the world has ever known.

We are movers and shakers; we are prideful, connective, demonstrative and inquisitive. This is the place to come, to play, work, love, think and expand our lives in endless new and different ways. It's a place to try new things, devise new ideas, open minds and hearts and become a part of the greatest City the word has ever known.

Visit us for the first time or come back again and if you do then you will take back something big, very big, love for a place that you will always yearn to return to again and again. Join 52,000,000 visitors, who came here in 2013, a astonishing record breaking number. Feast yourself and breath in the world's largest and most spectacular playground for young and old that the world has ever known.

Custom & Private New York Tours Provides Memorable Experiences!!

Best Private Tours Nomination
2011 New York City Association
of Hotel Concierges

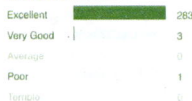

99% 👍   Save

Ranked #6 of 802 Activities in New York City

📍 Certificate of Excellence 2014

⬤⬤⬤⬤⬤ 287 Reviews

Type: Sightseeing Tours

More attraction details

●●●○○ Verizon 🛜   1:34 PM   🔋 ■ ›

🌐 customandprivate.com

Together with our sister tour company, Best
Guides in New York, our unique approach
to private...

Reviews

#6 of 1,955 in New York City
⬤⬤⬤⬤⬤ 287 reviews

Excellent		283
Very Good		3
Average		0
Poor		1
Terrible		0